The First Jewish Revolt

The First Jewish Revolt

Archaeology, history, and ideology

Edited by Andrea M. Berlin
and J. Andrew Overman

London and New York

First published 2002
by Routledge
11 New Fetter Lane, London EC4P 4EE

Simultaneously published in the USA and Canada
by Routledge
29 West 35th Street, New York, NY 10001

Routledge is an imprint of the Taylor & Francis Group

Typeset in Garamond by Exe Valley Dataset, Exeter
Printed and bound in Great Britain by TJ International Ltd, Padstow, Cornwall

British Library Cataloguing in Publication Data
A catalogue record for this book is available from the British Library

Library of Congress Cataloging in Publication Data
The First Jewish Revolt: archaeology, history, and ideology / edited by Andrea M. Berlin
and J. Andrew Overman.
      p. cm.
   Includes bibliographical references (p.) and index.
   1. Jews–History–Rebellion, 66–73–Causes. 2. Jews–History–168 B.C.–135 A.D.
   3. Jews–Politics and government–To 70 A.D. 4. Excavations (Archaeology)–Israel.
   5. Galilee (Israel)–Antiquities. I. Berlin, Andrea. II. Overman, J. Andrew, 1955–

DS122.8 .F57 2002
933—dc21   2001058879

ISBN 0–415–25706–9

In honor and memory of Anthony J. Saldarini

Contents

Figures

Tables

Contributors

Mordechai Aviam is the district archaeologist for eastern Galilee in the 'Akko office of the Israel Antiquities Authority.

Dina Avshalom-Gorni is a staff archaeologist in the 'Akko office of the Israel Antiquities Authority.

Andrea M. Berlin is an Associate Professor of Classical and Near Eastern Archaeology at the University of Minnesota, Minneapolis.

Hanan Eshel is Senior Lecturer in the Department of Land of Israel Studies at Bar Ilan University, Ramat Gan, Israel.

Sean Freyne is Professor of Hebrew, Biblical, and Theological Studies at Trinity College, Dublin, Ireland.

Nimrod Getzov is a staff archaeologist in the 'Akko office of the Israel Antiquities Authority.

Martin Goodman is Professor of Jewish Studies at Wolfson College, Oxford University, Oxford, England.

Erich S. Gruen is the Gladys Rehard Wood Professor of History and Classics at the University of California at Berkeley.

Richard A. Horsley is Distinguished Professor of Liberal Arts and the Study of Religion at the University of Massachusetts, Boston.

Jodi Magness is an Associate Professor in the Departments of Classics and Art History at Tufts University, Medford, Massachusetts.

Eric M. Meyers is the Bernice and Morton Lerner Professor of Judaic Studies in the Department of Religion at Duke University, Durham, North Carolina.

J. Andrew Overman is the chair of the Classics Department at Macalester College, St. Paul, Minnesota.

Tessa Rajak is a Reader in Ancient History in the Department of Classics at the University of Reading, Whiteknights, Reading, England.

Anthony J. Saldarini was Professor in the Department of Theology, Boston College, Boston, Massachusetts.

Neil Asher Silberman is Director for Historical Interpretation for the Ename Center for Public Archaeology and Heritage Presentation in Ename, Belgium and a contributing editor for Archaeology Magazine.

Danny Syon is a staff archaeologist in the 'Akko office of the Israel Antiquities Authority.

Acknowledgments

This book includes all of the papers presented at a conference organized jointly by Andrea Berlin, of the Department of Classical and Near Eastern Studies at the University of Minnesota, Minneapolis, and Andrew Overman, of the Department of Classics at Macalester College, St. Paul. The conference took place April 21–23, 1999, with sessions held at both institutions. Anthony Saldarini could not attend, though he had already written his paper for consideration by the other participants, and it is included here. The editors subsequently invited Dina Avshalom-Gorni and Nimrod Getzov to contribute a paper, as their research is specifically pertinent to the topic. The conference benefited from active and engaged discussions between all participants and the large audiences that attended every session. In retrospect, we are sorry that we did not record these exchanges, for they provided wonderful opportunities for productive conversation across generally untraveled scholarly divides. We hope that this volume will allow and encourage similar cross-disciplinary conversations.

A successful conference depends utterly on much hard behind-the-scenes work. Even two years later, we can easily recall the wonderful support provided by Judy Scullin and Kathy Walsh (Doyle) of the University of Minnesota, and Jackie Bennett of Macalester College. We thank them for their tireless care of our seemingly everchanging and often far-flung needs. In the preparation of this manuscript, Barbara Lehnhoff provided substantial assistance by scanning all of the images and creating the accompanying map. The conference received generous financial support from Steven Rosenstone, Dean of the University of Minnesota's College of Liberal Arts, Classical and Near Eastern Studies Chair William Malandra, the Macalester College Department of Classics, and the Office of the Provost of Macalester College. We received additional support for the preparation of this manuscript from the Dworsky Fund of the University of Minnesota's Jewish Studies Program. We thank these many contributors, whose work and generosity have made this publication possible.

Andrea M. Berlin and J. Andrew Overman
Minneapolis and St. Paul, Minnesota
May, 2001

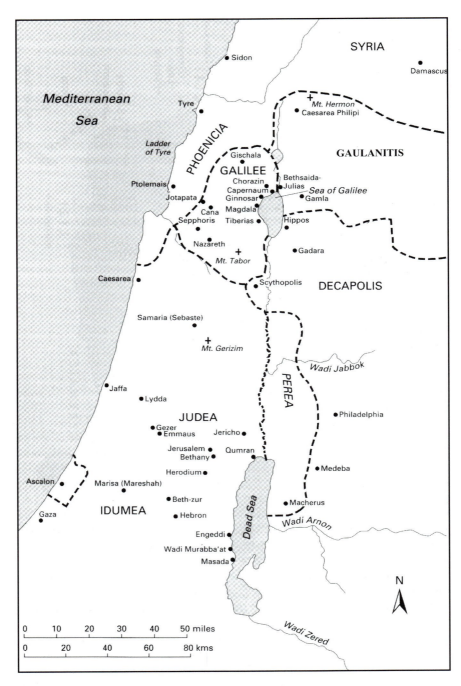

Frontispiece Palestine with administrative divisions in effect from 6 to 44 C.E.

Introduction

Andrea M. Berlin and J. Andrew Overman

> Titus, on entering [Jerusalem], was amazed at its strength, but chiefly at the towers, which the tyrants, in their infatuation, had abandoned ... "God indeed," he exclaimed, "had been with us in the war. God it was who brought down the Jews from these strongholds; for what power have human hands or engines against these towers?"
>
> (*War* 6.409–12)

With these words placed in the mouth of the General Titus, the first century historian Josephus (37–97 C.E.) offered an apology and an explanation for the destruction of Jerusalem and the First Revolt against Rome, which occurred from 66–70 C.E. In this passage, Josephus asserts that God had sided with the Romans during this time and epoch. And the rebels of Judea and Galilee, the so-called "tyrants," had opposed God and the Romans, through whom God exercised rule. Social conflict, theology, personal hubris—these are only three of the possible causes for what was, for Josephus and his Jewish contemporaries, a momentous event. This famous and provocative first-century historian is the single most vital source of information and interpretation about the Revolt. Josephus produced his corpus between ten to twenty-five years after the Revolt and the destruction of Jerusalem. His first major work was *The Jewish War,* followed by the exhaustive *The Antiquities of the Jews.* The former was most likely finished during the short reign of the Emperor Titus (79–81 C.E.), and the latter was written during the longer reign of Titus' brother and successor, Domitian (81–96 C.E.). Under Domitian Josephus also produced two shorter works, his *Life,* an autobiography, and a defense and explanation of Judaism called *Contra Apionem.*

Josephus pursues a number of questions and agendas as writer and historian. He is a defender of Jewish traditions and the Jewish people to a predominantly Roman audience. He often depicts the people of Judea and Galilee as noble, virtuous, fervent in their commitment to their God, and on the whole good citizens of the empire. He was an eyewitness to many of the developments and events surrounding the Revolt and therefore constitutes an invaluable though, as has often been noted, tendentious historical source.

Josephus lived to write about these events, he tells us in *War* 3, by ultimately capitulating and working with the Roman forces in their efforts to quell the unrest in Judea and Galilee and to capture Jerusalem for Rome. His very name, Flavius, denotes his loyalty and service to the imperial family and line, the Flavians. Yet in important respects Josephus attempted to remain true to his role as a leader among his people (in *Life* 12 he tells us he was both a priest and a general in the Revolt prior to his capture) though he was ostensibly in the employ of the Emperor Vespasian and his sons. Most notably Josephus believed that his small nation could and should work with Rome and that various popular and rebel leaders should not foment rebellion. This only spelled grief and destruction for the Jewish people. While providing us with the story Josephus also has time to defend himself, explain his own background and qualifications, provide an impressive recital of Jewish history, and exhibit his knowledge of Greek culture, philosophy, and language. His work provides a wealth of information, not just for the Revolt, but for the history of Judaism as well as all of the various forms practiced during the Second Temple period. The Josephan corpus also provides important information and insight into the geography and topography of the ancient Middle East, Roman imperial actions in the Greek east, and the social and political environment that helped shape post-70 C.E. Judaism and Christianity.

Neither Judea nor trouble in Judea were new to Rome by 66 C.E. As early as the mid-second century B.C.E. the Hasmonean rulers in Judea had established official and cordial relations with Rome. I Maccabees 8 details an alliance that the Hasmoneans struck with Rome with the aim of sparing Judea from Seleucid hegemony. Rome could and did effectively scare off the Seleucids. The author of I Maccabees attempts to recite the very treaty agreed upon by mighty Rome and the fledgling eastern Mediterranean client state. By the middle of the second century B.C.E. the Hasmonean kingdom of Judea had obtained the official and advantageous status of "ally and friend of Rome," a friendship largely comprised of Roman expectations for the client state and king. Henceforth Judea was officially part of Rome's orbit, concern, and propriety. That relationship proved frail less than a century later, in 63 B.C.E., when Pompey the Great invaded Jerusalem on the pretense of resolving the civil war between two Hasmonean brothers. That event is remembered, albeit from different perspectives, by the Psalms of Solomon and by Josephus (*War* 1.141–58). Judea and Galilee were absorbed into a larger Roman administrative reorganization of the Greek east, conceived by Pompey and engineered by his general Gabinius.

By the middle part of the first century B.C.E. Rome was enthralled in a civil war that shook its foundations. Competing leaders divided the realm and drew various regions into their race for rule. Judea was no exception. Most of Egypt, Judea, and the larger region supported Mark Antony in his struggle with Octavian. Herod served as governor of Galilee in the midst of this struggle, set up initially through the offices and influence of his father

Antipater, and established himself as a firm, if not capricious ruler. Herod became governor of Judea following the murder of Antipater (43 B.C.E.). He was forced to flee to Rome in 40 B.C.E. when a rival leader, Antigonus, was enthroned in Judea as a Parthian client lord.

In 37 B.C.E., however, Herod was back. With Antony's support he secured Jerusalem, thus reasserting Roman interests and cutting off Parthian access and influence. When the Roman civil war concluded after the battle of Actium in 31 B.C.E., and Octavian emerged victorious, prospects paled for Herod and all other eastern clients who had backed Mark Antony. Herod hurried to Rhodes to meet with Octavian (soon to be Augustus). Josephus recounts the episode (*War* 1.388–90), in which Herod presented himself as, fundamentally, a fierce supporter of the throne, as well as someone who excelled at keeping the peace. He was persuasive enough to save his life and keep his job, and he returned to Judea reaffirmed as king and as the new and best friend of the Emperor. Thus began one of the most storied and significant political periods and relationships in Judean history.

Herod's reign was characterized in antiquity as riddled with popular discord. Both Josephus and the Gospel of Matthew present Herod as cunning and ruthless (*Ant.* 15; Matthew 2). Resentment of Herod's aggressive courting of Roman favor coupled with heavy taxation and selective use or manipulation of the local Judean elite exacerbated tension in Judea and Galilee during his reign. As governor of Galilee, Herod had distinguished himself as someone unwilling to tolerate resistance or rebellion. As client king, Herod ruled with an iron fist (e.g., his slaughter of the brigands hiding out in the cliffs near Arbela, *War* 1.305), which was simply expected from the Roman imperial point of view. While Herod's reign represented order and productivity to Rome, however, it spelled oppression and hardship for many in Judea and Galilee. Upon his death there was widespread revolt. Some portions of Herod's kingdom sought refuge from his capricious rule with Rome herself. People from Gadara and portions of Iturea asked if they could fall under the rule of the Province of greater Coele–Syria and not Herod's kingdom. The citizens who made this embassy to Augustus to seek his help were rejected by the Emperor and ended up committing suicide rather than return to Herod's kingdom and rule.

Upon Herod's death his kingdom was divided among his three sons. The sons' successes and careers varied. The eldest, Archelaus, ruled Judea for a few short years (he is mentioned briefly in the birth story in Matthew). His rule in Judea is understood by that author as unstable and reckless. In a dream Joseph is told to take Mary and Jesus to Galilee and to settle there, steering clear of Archelaus. Archelaus was recalled by Rome in 6 C.E., probably because he was viewed as a destabilizing presence in the region. The youngest son, Herod Phillip, is depicted by Josephus as noted for his equanimity and the careful manner in which he held court and mediated justice. He would travel his kingdom in northern Galilee and Gaulanitis with a chair from which he could hear court cases, entertain requests, and allow people to seek relief from misfortune. Phillip and his brother Antipas, Herod's middle son, enjoyed quite successful reigns. Both initiated building projects, though nothing on the order of their father Herod. Neither were characterized in antiquity as either particularly brutal or prone to suppression, again as opposed to Herod.

Nevertheless, tension in Judea and Galilee appears as a consistent feature of life in the first century C.E. The Roman definition of peace was maintained, but at considerable cost to the local population and their traditions. Resistance to Roman rule and presence grew in some quarters. There is little mistaking the good fortune Roman presence spelled for certain local elites. It is a pronounced view of later Talmudic authors that the wealthy in Judea were largely responsible for the Revolt (see Saldarini, Chapter 14 in this volume). Similarly, in his 1987 work, *The Ruling Class of Judaea,* Martin Goodman suggested the failure of the ruling class to execute its responsibilities played a crucial role in the cause of the Revolt. Examination of possible contributing causes should not, however, be limited to issues and developments within Judea or Galilee.

In the years immediately preceding the Revolt in Judea we should recall that Rome was herself poised on a similar precipice. The historian Tacitus describes this period at the outset of his *Histories* as one "rich in disasters, terrible with battles, torn by civil struggles, horrible even in peace" (1.2), and later adds that it was Vespasian who "purged the whole world of evil" (4.3). The instability and disorder of the final days of the Julio–Claudian line are well documented. To many it looked as if Rome would descend once again into the mire of empire-wide civil war, as had happened a century earlier when the Republic gave way to the Empire under Octavian's single control. Enough Roman writers mention the troubles in Judea that we can be confident that the Jewish revolt was far more than the literary creation and manipulation of one author. The Roman elite were aware of the troubles in Judea and the threat that they posed to Rome's entire eastern front. Revolts also occurred in Batavia, along the Dutch–German *limes*, and in Spain, where the dissident governor Vindex and his rebellion garnered considerable attention from several Roman writers (cf. Suetonius, *Nero* 40). The greatest fear may well have been that the communities and cities on the Euphrates River—the border with Parthia—would catch this rebellious spirit and try to break away from Rome. At one point in the *War* (3.108–9), after a long and detailed description of the Roman army's operations and organization in the field, Josephus unapologetically explains that the digression is intended "to deter others who may be tempted to revolt." In the *War's* opening paragraphs, he makes a point of announcing that he has already written a similar account "in my vernacular tongue ... [for the] Parthians and Babylonians" (1.3, 6). Thus, whether we can say with Tacitus that "the entire world was convulsed with revolt" at Nero's death in 66 C.E., we may certainly conclude that Roman control was shaky in several quarters of the empire, including but not only Judea. The instabilities in Judea and Galilee reflect both local issues and broader Roman political problems.

Revolt actually broke out in Judea during the reign of Nero in 66 C.E., and Nero sent his general Vespasian to put it down. Vespasian, who had had experience in Syria and was familiar with the Roman east, arrived in 67 C.E. with his son, the eventual emperor Titus. After marching east from the port of Akko–Ptolemias, he first engaged—and defeated—the Jewish rebels at Jotapata (Yodefat) in Galilee. Jotapata's fall brought Josephus himself into the hands of Vespasian, who siezed the opportunity to express his belief that Vespasian would soon become emperor (*War* 3.401, though some Roman writers believed that Vespasian was first hailed as Emperor in Egypt; cf. Tacitus *Histories* 2.79, Suetonius *Vespasian* 2). Whatever the historical particulars may have been, the general Vespasian decided to make his grab for power and the throne while out east with his troops. Vespasian was only one aspirant to the throne, however; the year 69 C.E. is known as "the year of the four emperors," highlighting Roman imperial instability. In fact the preceding few years *were* politically unstable, and it may well have appeared as though the vaunted and expansive Roman Empire might actually fall apart. The instability and tension that Josephus detailed in Judea and Galilee then should be seen as part of widespread instability and uncertainty.

Nonetheless, subsequent history and traditions recall little of the Batavian revolt, unrest in Roman Spain, or even the fortunes and misfortunes of Vindex. It is instead the revolt on the eastern edge of the Roman world, in a province few Romans outside of the political and literary elite would have even known of, that has outlived all others. In part, this is due to the fact that the history of the Jewish revolt was intertwined with the history of the eventual new emperor. When Vespasian emerged as emperor in 69 C.E. he set about the business of restoring order to the empire and encouraging confidence among the people. He wanted to send a message that *pax*, order, honor, and grandeur had returned to Rome. Vespasian and Titus' victory over the Jews in the east could, and did, serve as a vital, central piece of that message (see Overman pp. 213ff.). The Flavians allowed, actually encouraged, the memorialization of their Judean victory by supporting Josephus in his writing, by constructing a series of monuments in Rome, and by minting coins that proclaimed the event (the *Judea Capta* series). The Jewish revolt soon became one of the most significant victories and events of the imperial period.

The Revolt had a profound and enduring impact on the development and shape of Judaism and Christianity (see Silberman in this volume). It is safe to say that had there not been a Jewish revolt in Judea in 66–70 C.E., Christianity and Judaism, as we know them today, would not exist. The forms, structure, and theologies that are part of both of these great religious traditions owe much to the crisis provoked by the Revolt and the destruction of the temple in Jerusalem. Many have argued that the destruction of the temple in Jerusalem in 70 C.E. constitutes the seminal event in the formation of both early Christianity and Rabbinic Judaism. By the late second century Christian writers like Melito of Sardis interpreted the destruction of the temple as God's judgement on Israel and proof that the Christian Church constituted the new Israel, while the tannaitic rabbis made of the destruction of the temple a borderline between earlier and current Jewish practices: "How could sacrifice be made now that the temple is in ruins?" asked the post-Mishnaic document *Avot Rabbi Nathan*. Out of the dust of 70 C.E., Christianity and Judaism as we know them today emerged.

The Revolt's importance and impact has ensured scholarly attention since antiquity. Broad and steady study notwithstanding, a surprising number of fundamental questions remain. Was it an accident of circumstance or a planned, communal enterprise? How relevant is the Revolt's "prehistory," the two generations or so in which Palestine's residents lived under the political jurisdiction of Rome and the religious oversight of Jerusalem? Was the Revolt in fact a single event, or an eventually linked series of regional actions and reactions? And finally (though these questions by no means constitute an exhaustive list), was it in fact an event of contemporary empire-wide importance or simply one so susceptible to ideological interpretation that both ancient and modern historians and commentators have found it an irresistable exemplum? Contributors to this book consider these questions from several angles.

One clear point of consensus that emerges is that the Revolt was never a single event, neither from the point of Jewish organization nor Roman response. Goodman points out that the connected, cause-and-effect account of Josephus notwithstanding, the "ideology of the rebels" can be seen as considerably diverse and diffuse. It is true that Josephus himself provides the first written evidence for this very proposition, with his famous division of the Jews into four revolutionary groups (*Ant.* 18.23–4; *War* 2.119–66). In this book, both Freyne and Horsley provide considered analyses of the historical circumstances in Idumea, Judea, and Galilee that reveal long standing differences in social and political organization among the country's Jewish population. Freyne documents episodes of armed conflict between Jew and non-Jew (the latter most often a Roman administrative or military official), as well as strong economic disparities and divisions within Jewish society irrespective of Roman rule. He makes the acute point that there were as many revolts as regions, and he documents some of the specifics of each. In Idumea, opposition to Herodian rule had crystallized during the reign of Herod the Great, making the imposition of Roman control in 6 C.E. much "the lesser of two evils." Galilee had a very different trajectory. When direct Roman control began there in 44 C.E., upon the death of Agrippa I, many Galileans were hostile from the start; and subsequent Roman reactions, such as the establishment of nearby Ptolemais as a colonia, only increased the sense of "the Roman noose tightening." These differing backgrounds help explain each region's different treatment by Vespasian during the course of the Revolt.

Galilee's specific history, society, and archaeology is the subject of six contributors to this book (Berlin, Avshalom-Gorni and Getzov, Horsley, Meyers, Aviam, and Syon). Archaeological evidence from pre-Revolt Galilee, presented by Berlin and Avshalom-Gorni and Getzov, illuminates seemingly deliberate "social apartheid" between Jews and Gentiles. Avshalom-Gorni and Getzov describe the types and distribution of ceramic storage containers made by Phoenicians and Galilean Jews in the first centuries B.C.E. and C.E. Their specific, separate distribution patterns show that the two groups began using different market systems in the time of Herod the Great. Berlin also identifies this particular period as crucial in the archaeological record of Galilee. She demonstrates that prior to Herod's reign, Jewish and Gentile sites contained a very similar array of household goods. From the time of Herod to the time of the Revolt, on the other hand, Jews in Galilee apparently no longer purchased one particular type of ceramic: red-slipped plates and bowls, known commonly as Eastern Sigillata A (ESA). Berlin argues that these brightly colored, fancy table vessels "performed a convenient communicative role ... as a manifestation of foreign, and ... specifically Roman control," and that Galilean Jews deliberately rejected them in "a political statement of solidarity and affiliation with a traditional, simple, unadorned Jewish lifestyle."

This "archaeological pre-history" reveals some of the real-world background to Freyne's regional reconstruction, and also supports Horsley's careful and nuanced consideration of Galilean unity and/or disunity. Horsley focuses primarily on the trajectory of events in Galilee leading up to and during the crucial year of 66–7 C.E. He works to see through the scrim of Roman administrative structures and reactions as well as through the tilted lens of Josephus's account to examine how life was organized in the years leading up to the Revolt. Horsley dissects the goals and strategies of the self-appointed provisional government in Jerusalem, focusing on their actions in Galilee as well as multiple Galilean reactions. Older "conflicting power-relations" between the Galileans and Romans, which had concentrated Galilean opposition to outside rule, melded with "hostility to their immediate [Jewish] rulers" in Sepphoris and Tiberias. The (probably inevitable) result was a riven and weakened Galilee. This may have been the view of Vespasian as well, which would help explain his confidence in its rapid conquest.

The Revolt, taken to mean a period of four (or seven) years that saw a continuous series of Jewish uprisings against Roman rule, technically began in the month of Artemisios (May) 66 C.E., when the Roman procurator Florus sent troops to plunder a portion of Jerusalem. The Revolt, taken to mean the series of sieges, battles, and military victories that ensued between the Roman army and the local Jewish population, actually commenced exactly one year later, when Vespasian led the Roman army into Galilee in May 67 C.E. It is at this point in his narrative that Josephus gives his memorable and detailed description of the marching order of the three legions, 23 auxiliary cohorts, six cavalry wings, and various allied troops that comprised Vespasian's force (*War* 3.115–26). The point of his description, he says, is to impress his reader not only of the size and fighting capacity of the Romans but also of the folly of any group that would oppose them in battle. In this book, Meyers, Aviam, and Syon describe the archaeological remains from three important Galilean sites: Sepphoris, Yodefat/Jotapata, and Gamla, all of which illuminate and amplify Josephus's none-too-subtle point as well as the resultant reality.

Meyers presents a clear summary of the remains found on the citadel at Sepphoris. Excavators encountered a strange situation there, in which an enormous fort dating from the second and first centuries B.C.E. was found filled in, apparently on purpose, sometime between 53 and 70 C.E. Careful excavation and recording of the nature of the fill and the few finds within it convinces Meyers that the tremendous operation that it represents "was undertaken by the citizens of Sepphoris as an outward demonstration of their policy of cooperation with Rome." The resultant appellation of Sepphoris as a "City of Peace," acquired prior to the death of Nero in 69 C.E., remained integral to the city's persona, and may have played a part in its future prominence in the calmer days of Roman imperial rule during the second and third centuries C.E. In this crucial first year of operations in Galilee, however, the filled-in fort provides vivid material testimony that supports Horsley's thesis of Galilean power struggles.

The excavations at Yodefat and Gamla provide a view wholly opposite to Sepphoris, and in so doing reveal the very real tenacity, organization, and unity of their Jewish defenders. Yodefat's position at the northwestern corner of Galilee put it in line to be the first large fortified site that the Romans encountered, and Aviam describes plentiful evidence of the Roman siege and attack. Almost all of the archaeological details confirm the vivid description given by Josephus, though Aviam believes that the historian heightened the story's emotional intensity in part to justify the city's fall and in part because he experienced the trauma first-hand. The excavations provided some intensity of their own, in any event: one of the most stunning, and unexpected, finds at Yodefat was a cistern containing the skeletal remains of about twenty individuals, including women and children; this is the single largest group of human remains from any Revolt battle site. As Yodefat, so Gamla—in terms of the level of detail and pathos in the narrative of Josephus, in terms of both Roman and Jewish military investment, and in terms of the outcome. Syon describes Gamla's archaeological remains, which reveal a town turned into a refugee camp. Located at the opposite end of the Roman route of march through Galilee, Gamla became the last secure place for northern Jews still determined to defy Rome. The excavations uncovered cooking ovens and storage jars crowding both a stone-paved public square and even the inside of the synagogue, the town's only public building. The most striking finds from Gamla are six crudely struck bronze coins that depict a chalice and carry an inscription reading "For the redemption of Jerusalem the Holy" (a seventh coin was found in a small excavation at

Gamla during March 2000). Syon sees these coins as a powerful challenge to the view that the Jews of Galilee were fragmented and "preoccupied with internal strife." They reveal that "even under the most difficult conditions, the people of Gamla still remembered the original aims of the revolt." The remains from Yodefat and Gamla are revelatory, for they provide vivid demonstration that many Galilean Jews made a strong and prolonged stand against the Romans despite their recorded deep disinterest in co-operating with Jerusalem.[1]

Taken together, the historical and archaeological records of the background to and the first year in Galilee mesh perfectly to reveal the fundamental fissures of the region's Jewish population. The historical and archaeological record in Judea, though not as richly documented as that in Galilee, presents a similarly riven view, and several contributors here provide evidence pertinent to that situation. Horsley shows that inter-Jewish conflict was much greater in Judea than in Galilee, because the temple and its Jerusalem-based priestly aristocracy required goods and services in disproportionate quantities. In the course of the first century, reliance by temple personnel on supplies from the countryside, coupled with the connected dependence by farmers on the temple market, had led to overt imbalance and resentment. By the second year of the Revolt, that resentment exploded in Jerusalem, with Judean farmers taking over the Temple Mount itself. Horsley describes this as "class warfare in the city," and points out that Josephus's own account gives the lie to his claim that Judea's ruling class was in charge in Jerusalem.

Divisions among Jews in the south and their differing modes of demonstrating opposition are also discussed by Freyne, Eshel, and Rajak. Freyne points out that in the later stages of the Revolt some Idumean Jews moved to Egypt while others joined the fight on the Temple Mount, evidence that reflects the region's divided allegiances and less than wholehearted support for Jerusalem's priestly aristocracy. Eshel presents four new papyri found in the caves of Wadi Murabba'at in the Judean desert that are private economic documents dating before and during the Revolt, together with three similar documents of the same era already known: two more from the Wadi Murabba'at (one of which had been written at Masada) and a third said to come from Qumran Cave 4 (though Eshel doubts this origin). Two fascinating points emerge from these simple records of private commerce. The first is that Jews did not all use the same dating formulas. The Qumran papyrus seems to have been written in Jerusalem in the 40s C.E., and is dated according to the years of the High Priest. One of the Wadi Murabba'at papyri, on the other hand, written in the Judean village of Sobah in the 50s C.E., was dated according to the year of the Roman emperor. This acceptance of Roman rule in the countryside is striking when set against the deliberate snub of the Jerusalem writer. A second point concerns language. Though the active spoken language of Judean Jews was Aramaic, four of the documents—including the one written in the 40s and dated according to the High Priest's rule—were written in Hebrew. During the second, Bar

Kokhba revolt, leaders mandated the use of Hebrew as a reflection and expression of "nationalistic feeling." No such linguistic command occurred during the First Revolt, however. In fact that period's documents, in which Hebrew and Aramaic are both used, reflect an opposite point, which is that not everyone may have seen the uprising as a "nationalistic" act.

Rajak examines the literary record in search of evidence that the Revolt's prime movers in Jerusalem were "fired for their struggle by the certainty that the End was at hand." She demonstrates that while some Jews were certainly primed to view the Revolt as a sign of the End of Days (the Qumran sectarians, for example), there were others who saw the situation as another stage in a long cycle: "You will hear of wars and rumors of wars. See that you are not alarmed, for this must take place but the end is not yet" (Matthew 24.8, Mark 13.8). Rajak explores the continuity of the theme of "messianic drama" in the Jewish written record beginning with the biblical prophets. She acknowledges that while the Second Temple period is particularly marked by "charges of false prophecy and of spurious messiahship ... not every look forward to cataclysmic events is necessarily involved with a sense of the approach of final things." After detailed scrutiny, Rajak finds no connection between the Revolt's organized Jewish resistance and public or personal anticipation of the End of Days.

What of the Romans? Several contributors examine a variety of issues from their point of view, beginning even before the Revolt. Goodman points out that it is crucial to isolate and examine remarks made by Roman writers about Jews in the years just before and just after the Revolt, and suggests that it is *prima facie* reasonable to expect an increase in hostility in response to failed rebellion." Here Gruen does exactly what Goodman asks, and comes to the opposite conclusion: "inspection of the texts on both sides of that chronological divide" do *not* differ significantly. Gruen makes a strong case for reading Roman attitudes as casually ill-informed and essentially un-threatened even after the Revolt's resolution. This, of course, is the stance of Romans in Rome, where Jews exercised neither political influence, economic power, nor social clout.

Magness looks at Roman legionary life in Judea, as represented by archaeological evidence from Masada and post-conquest Jerusalem. She succeeds in explaining the very different ceramic remains from these two sites as resulting from two distinct modes, one representing "an army on campaign" and the other "an army of occupation." Most pertinent is how disengaged the Romans remained from local styles and habits of dining. At Masada soldiers must have depended on their own metal mess kits. In Jerusalem, it appears that one of their first actions was to establish a pottery production site (located now next to the modern Jerusalem convention center of Binyanei Ha'uma) that could supply fine table vessels of Italian shape, size, and decoration. Magness compares the Jerusalem legionary workshop to other military establishments in Europe, and finds the strongest similarities of range and style of output with fortresses established in Britain. From the

Roman point of view, these were regions that could be characterized as "remote, hostile territory where the native potters were not trained in the Roman ceramic tradition."

The Binyanei Ha'uma finds reveal some aspects of the point of view of the Roman army. Other archaeological finds from post-70 C.E. Jerusalem show that the production site was in fact one of the few new establishments in the city; and that Jerusalem was a small and quiet place during the remainder of the first century (Geva 1984, 1997). This is a picture that squares poorly with the barrage of late first century literary and material imagery by which the Flavians explained, excused, and justified their involvement in a small region's singular conflict. At this point, where the raw data of archaeological remains and demonstrable events meets the literary record, history and ideology collide.

The extent to which ideology has, and must, permeate discussion of the Revolt—its causes, specific progression, aftermath, and meaning—cannot be overstated. To begin with the most obvious: our only connected narrative is that of Josephus, a Jerusalem aristocrat and rebel turned Flavian apologist whose account was necessarily permeated by personal needs and biases. Goodman and Freyne both point out (*pace* McLaren 1998) that "all histories of Judea in the first century C.E. are trapped into adopting Josephus's historical perspective." There is thus an integral collusion between any explanation of events, their causes, and their meaning. Interpretation has always been an individual event, of course, as Saldarini reminds us: "Historical ... facts do not exist in nature, waiting for recognition. Rather, we shape phenomena into facts ... that make sense out of human actions."

In this book, contributors offer various "takes" on specific actions and subsequent reactions, and are not always in agreement. On Titus and his destruction of the Temple, Gruen reads the words of the Roman commander as reported by Josephus at face value; their outrage and incredulity at Jewish ingratitude "still rings true" and provides reason enough for the decision to destroy the temple. Goodman, on the other hand, sees the destruction as an accident of war, an understandable byproduct of a huge Roman force run amok, and thus presents Titus as purposefully refashioning events as having been ordered and deliberate. In this view, the words of Josephus himself would be seen as part of the Flavian program, a point that Overman makes explicitly.

Overman traces the development of Flavian attitudes. At first the Revolt was one piece of a much larger picture. The new emperor initially cast himself as the bringer of an empire-wide peace, a characterization that made sense only if rebellion threatened equally in Gaul and Germany as in Judea. This is the construction of Tacitus, who credited Vespasian with calming "a world that was in upheaval." This great achievment notwithstanding, the insidious problem of legitimacy confronted Vespasian; and to counter it he devised a significant propaganda program in which his eldest son's sole military achievement was cast as an epic accomplishment. First came the

Judea Capta coins, which were struck in various mints and distributed across the empire for over a decade—a phenomenal material celebration unique in the annals of Roman military victories. Second came the dedication of the *Templum Pacis* in Rome, in which were displayed the treasures from the temple in Jerusalem. Set within the context of Rome's dazzling and revitalized ancient city center, this particular Flavian victory was transformed into "an event owned ... by the entire Roman world."

From the point of view of ideological reconstruction, the few generations immediately following the Revolt were the busiest. Several contributors address this era, from both Roman and Jewish stances. Overman discusses the final stage of Flavian amplification and the unintended distortion that ensued. Domitian, who had even less in the way of personal military success than had Titus, oversaw the construction of the single most vivid surviving material document of the Revolt: the victory arch dedicated to Titus, with its monumental relief depicting the spoils carried in the triumphal procession. Overman emphasizes the importance of the inscription, which bombastically (and incorrectly) celebrates the achievment of Titus in destroying the city of Jerusalem "which all generals, kings, and peoples before him had either attacked without success or left entirely unassailed." Domitian's need to align himself with his father's and brother's achievment led to continued and even increased "imperial anti-Judaism," which in turn encouraged similar attitudes in the private sphere. Overman concludes by connecting this latest phase of the Flavian propaganda campaign with its most enduring and unhappy result: the generalizing and negative characterization of Jews by contemporary early Christian authors, especially the author of the Gospel of John. During the second and third centuries C.E., these Flavian-period portrayals "blossomed into more expansive and explosive early Christian anti-Judaism."

Jews in Palestine also searched for appropriate lessons and a larger meaning to be gleaned from the disaster that had befallen them. Here, the rabbis were responsible for creating a story and crafting a moral that could both teach and convince. Saldarini summarizes recent scholarship on the rabbinic response in general, and then investigates in detail the rabbis' teachings on the specific subject of wealth, particularly as it affected the behavior of some prominent Jerusalemites before and during the Revolt. For the rabbis, history provided a series of object lessons, and the Revolt's importance lay in the fact that its catastrophic events made for an especially clear view of cause and effect. An ultimate good was necessarily sought, and found, in the living consequence of the Temple's destruction, which clarified the duty and role of every individual vis-à-vis their community and Torah. The rabbis' stories taught that good came from evil, for the disaster forced Jews to substitute their own study, prayer, and good deeds for the second-hand piety of the Temple's priests. This must have been a resonant moral for people living under imperial rule, Roman or Sassanian, in the second, third, and fourth centuries C.E.

Silberman carries the story up to our own day, tracking both Jewish and Christian agendas. As time put distance between the event and the living, and turned the Revolt from memory to history, Jewish writers followed the rabbinic tradition by using the Revolt as a lesson with a moral. In medieval mystical literature, that message was "the existential confrontation of the Jews with the triumph of evil." For medieval Christians, on the other hand, a different lesson shone forth, elicited via continued transmission and translations of Josephus. The riven Jewish community, scheming priests, and "bloodthirsty rabble" on view in the *War* could only reveal one message: "the Destruction of Jerusalem was God's way of announcing that the Age of Christianity had arrived." Silberman concludes that the Revolt's modern "afterlife" may be seen essentially as a recast foundation story, an ideological chameleon now valuable as a tale that values heart over head and emotion as an agent.

The most powerful ideology underlying consideration of the Revolt is the most basic: that it was and remains an event so epochal that it deserves, and even requires, careful, probing, and repeated historical analysis. In effect, this book adds to that case. In his opening essay, Goodman provides an historiography of recent scholarship and notes that it has concentrated on four areas, without reaching consensus in any. These four are: (1) the value of Josephus as a source; (2) the status of Jewish leaders of the rebellion; (3) the ideology of the rebels; and (4) the war's aftermath in Judea. As an entry in the ongoing scholarship of the Revolt, we would conclude by summarizing the most important points of consensus demonstrated in this book:

- *Detailed study of the political and social background of each region reveals that there were as many revolts as regions and Jewish groups.* In Idumea there was tolerance and even acceptance (Freyne); in Judea there was a steady rise in inter-Jewish tension (Rajak, Horsley, Eshel); in Galilee there was a long-lived and increasingly overt hostility against any outside authority (Berlin, Avshalom-Gorni and Getzov, Horsley) joined by a determined and fierce—though not wholly united—Jewish resistance (Meyers, Aviam, Syon). The Revolt was a sequenced series of contingent events, of actions that collided.

- *Though the Romans thought little and infrequently of the Jews, and must therefore have been taken by surprise when the Revolt began, their subsequent packaging of it is as much a part of the story as the Jewish resistance.* The fact that Romans living and writing in Rome shortly after the Revolt ended were as uninformed and unconcerned as earlier writers (Gruen) makes the eventual deployment of the Flavian propaganda machine that much more noteable (Overman).

- *Ideology of one stripe or another has been intertwined with the events from the beginning, and cannot be separated from them.* All treatments of the Revolt have had an underlying purpose (Saldarini), and an associated irony is that, beginning with Josephus himself, many of the retellings have been by and for Jews who have turned this great defeat into an uplifting saga (Silberman). History may belong to the victors, but its lessons are made only by those who choose to tell the tale.

In this book, we seek to show that the Revolt was not a single event but an era, and as much a set of conflicting expectations as a series of episodes. The Revolt is better understood within the intersecting arcs of Jewish and Roman history than as a singular explosion. The Revolt has collected attention and bibliography, and it has provided example and inspiration and warning. It has been, in other words, singled out. We hope, with these papers, to reinsert it into its historical place, for only by such reintegration can we view it properly and learn from it fully.

Note

1   A third Galilean site whose remains reveal a picture very similar to that of Yodefat and Gamla is Khirbet el-Hamam, probably ancient Narbata (Zertal 1995). Excavations there have uncovered three small army camps, a circumvallation wall, and a siege ramp (apparently never finished). Zertal dates the system to the year 66 C.E., and interprets the remains as evidence of a precautionary maneuver by the Roman commander Gallus.

Bibliography

Geva, H. (1984) "The Camp of the Tenth Legion in Jerusalem: An Archaeological Reconsideration," *Israel Exploration Journal* 34: 239–54.
—— (1997) "Searching for Roman Jerusalem," *Biblical Archaeology Review* 23.6: 34–45, 72–3.
Goodman, M. (1987) *The Ruling Class of Judaea: The Origins of the Jewish Revolt Against Rome, A.D. 66–70*, Cambridge: Cambridge University Press.
McLaren, J. S. (1998) *Turbulent Times? Josephus and Scholarship on Judaea in the First Century C.E.*, Sheffield: Sheffield Academic Press.
Zertal, A. (1995) "The Roman Siege System at Khirbet al-Hamam (Narbata)," *The Roman and Byzantine Near East. Recent Archaeological Research, Journal of Roman Archaeology* supplementary series 14.

1 Current scholarship on the First Revolt

Martin Goodman

The last ten years has seen the publication of only one monograph specifically dedicated to the First Revolt, the detailed study by Jonathan Price of the history of the groups which struggled for control within Jerusalem during the war (Price 1992), but there has also been a plethora of smaller-scale studies on particular aspects of the Revolt. The main focus of these investigations has been in four areas: the value of Josephus's narrative as a historical source; the status in Jewish society of the leaders of the rebellion; the ideology of the rebels; and the aftermath of the war (on the ideology of the rebels, see Chapter 3 by Freyne on Galilee and Idumea and Chapter 4 by Berlin on Galilee, in this volume). It seems fair to state that, despite considerable progress in each of these areas, no consensus has been reached, so that it is not yet really time for a new synthesis to be attempted. Nor, despite the light shed on many interesting side issues by excavations, have recent archaeological investigations and the welcome publication of the final reports from sites such as Masada up to now had a major impact on the direction of research, in contrast to the role played by archaeology in the recent study of the Bar Kokhba Revolt. What is offered here is an indication of the direction in which current scholarship seems to be heading and some suggestions for the future.

The debate about the value of Josephus's history as a source is in some respects quite obviously fundamental. So much of our knowledge depends on his narrative that each attack on his veracity threatens to undermine study of the subject altogether. It is worthwhile speculating on how deep our ignorance would be if only the rabbinic and classical pagan sources about the Revolt survived. We would know there had been a great uprising, that the rebels were divided into factions, that Titus destroyed the Temple, and that Yohanan ben Zakkai fled from Jerusalem, but for any more complex explanation of these events there would be no real clue. The veracity of Josephus is most obviously called into question by the discrepancies between the *Life* and the *War*; attempts by Tessa Rajak to downplay the significance of such discrepancies by attributing them to different perspectives on the same events (Rajak 1984) have not been universally accepted. More generally, there has been a huge upsurge in the study of Josephus's historical method

(Parente and Sievers 1994; Mason 1998), in which perhaps the most significant development in evaluating his accounts of the Revolt has been an increased awareness of the pressures under which he came during the thirty or so years he lived and wrote in Rome (Schwartz 1990; Goodman 1994b). In some ways Josephus emerges as a hero from this examination, since his 'apologetic history' of the Jews, as the *Antiquities* has recently and justifiably been dubbed (Sterling 1992), was written and published from within an imperial court replete with the anti-Jewish propaganda on which the Flavian dynasty based its claim to power. However, at the same time new and widespread scholarly interest in his last work, *Contra Apionem*, has effectively pointed up the extent to which he was willing to manipulate half-truths to serve the rhetoric of his polemical and defensive arguments (Feldman and Levison 1996; Barclay 1996; Goodman 1999b).

In some ways the most important observation in recent years on the difficulties in using Josephus for the history of the Revolt has been the demonstration by James McLaren of the extent to which all histories of Judea in the first century C.E. are trapped into adopting Josephus's historical perspective (McLaren 1998). Josephus was, for purely personal reasons, intent on explaining the most crucial events in his life, all of which had occurred between 66 and 70 C.E., and so he searched the annals of his society in the years before 66 C.E. to find the causes of the disaster. This was natural enough; but we now, with the benefit of distance and a chance to be comparatively dispassionate, must question whether Josephus's perspective is helpful. Josephus was keen to stress each episode of unrest he could uncover from the sixty years before the Revolt broke out since for him there had to be an explanation and someone to blame. We, in contrast, can entertain the possibility that there was nothing inevitable about what took place and that it was all a tragic accident.

The issue of the status of the rebel leaders has to some extent arisen specifically in reaction to my book on the ruling class of Judea (Goodman 1987). The argument of that book was essentially that the deep involvement in the revolt of the rich, mostly priestly, Judean elite was an important factor both in encouraging Rome to treat the uprising as full-scale rebellion and in provoking the splits which plagued the short-lived independent Judean state. I also argued that the Judean ruling class was driven into revolt by its inability to control pressures from the rest of Judean society which in turn had primarily economic causes, and that this incapacity to control was a result of the lack of prestige enjoyed by the ruling class because its position had originated from the patronage of Herodian and Roman rulers who were themselves despised by much of the Judean populace.

Some of this analysis seems to have been generally accepted. Thus, for instance, the picture of the Judean rulers as a heterogeneous group defined more by Roman preference for rich provincial allies for local government than by local criteria was in essence reached independently and by different routes by James McLaren and by Ed Sanders (McLaren 1991; Sanders 1992).

On the other hand, other elements have been hotly disputed, although this has been partly because I have appeared to some readers to have thrown the whole blame for the Revolt onto the Judean magnates, which was certainly not intended; on the contrary, I stated specifically that the causes of the war clearly lay in a combination of factors.

What do I now see as in need of change in the light of all this later discussion? The answer is: a considerable amount on the edges of the argument, but not its core. So, for instance, with regard to the composition of the ruling class, I somewhat underestimated the continuing importance throughout the first century C.E. of the influence of the descendants of Herod, in particular Berenice and Agrippa II; Josephus was doubtless influenced in his presentation of them because of his relationship to Agrippa in Rome while he was writing, but much evidence from other sources confirms their sometimes pivotal role (Kokkinos 1998). I also under-estimated the extent to which the office of the High Priest in time conferred prestige on its holder and his family regardless of any dubious origins: just as the new Roman aristocracy created by Augustus gained gravitas within a generation and Roman patronage enabled new oligarchies to establish themselves securely in other provinces in the early imperial period (Syme 1986; Brunt 1990: 521), so too the family of Ananus, who was "extremely fortunate, for he had five sons, all of whom, after he himself had previously enjoyed the office for a very long time, became high priests of God—a thing that had never happened to any other of our high priests (*Ant.* 20.198)," will have come to be regarded by their fellow Judeans with awe (Sanders 1992: 327; cf. Goodman 1994a). According to Acts 23: 2–5, Paul, who had once gone on a mission to Damascus on behalf of an earlier High Priest (Acts 22: 5) did not recognize the current incumbent Ananias. When his objection to being struck on Ananias's command in front of the council was condemned by those around him on the grounds that he should not revile the high priest, he accepted the rebuke, saying, "You shall not speak evil of the ruler of your people."

There has also been much debate about the mechanisms of social control used by the members of the Judean ruling class. Rather than stressing what this group found it difficult to do and why, more recently some scholars have concentrated on the modes of exercise of such power as they did have, emphasizing their role as rural patrons (Schwartz 1994) or mafioso-like tyrants (Shaw 1993). Concentration on the highly peculiar role in Galilee of John of Gischala as portrayed by Josephus has proved fruitful in this regard, since here was a man whose apparent lack of institutional authority was more than compensated for by the influence of his friends in high places and his capacity to draw in supporters from the surrounding countryside (Rappaport 1982).

More direct, but I think less tenable, objections have been raised to the central claim that the ruling class was "responsible for" the Revolt. The claim was described as perverse in a thorough critique of the whole thesis by

Peter Brunt (Brunt 1990: 517) in which he restated but also modified his earlier view that the Revolt was essentially a popular movement, admitting in the new version that although the main enthusiasts for rebellion were naturally all from the lower classes, their resentment was less against Judean aristocrats than against Rome. Now, it is universally acknowledged that there is much evidence of social unrest as an underlying cause of the war (cf. also Goodman 1987: 51–75; see also Chapter 4 by Berlin and Chapter 5 by Avshalom-Gorni and Getzov in this volume), so the issue is essentially whether the evidence for the participation also of members of the elite as recognized by Rome before the war demonstrates their general participation or (as Brunt claims) the actions of a small number of class traitors. I am not sure that this question can ever be finally resolved: it is of course correct to state that Josephus always portrayed the natural position of the Judean elite as lying on the side of Rome, but the assertion of this was one of his motives for writing history in the first place, so his veracity is always in doubt. Thus I see no reason to reject wholesale my original claim, but it is worth noting that if, for instance, the objections raised by some to my suggestion that the eventual Jewish commander-in-chief, Simon son of Gioras, was also a member of this elite are correct (so Fuks 1987), it would become more likely that the involvement of most members of the ruling class was indeed, as Josephus of course claimed, only a temporary phenomenon at the start of the Revolt (cf. Rajak 1984).

For Brunt, the difficult question of why class conflict of a type not markedly different from that found elsewhere in the Roman empire in this case evolved into full-scale war is resolved by alleging that it must have been caused by the single factor which distinguished Jews from all other peoples—that is, their religion (Brunt 1990: 528–30). Since Jews believed that divine providence was bound to aid them in their bid to recover the independence they had enjoyed under Maccabean rule, they were willing to set aside their differences in the search for freedom. Such a view is of course possible, but other peoples in the ancient world, including many of the Greeks, could similarly look back to a glorious past of political independence and the gracious protection afforded them by their gods, and the Jews may appear so different only because the writings in which they expressed their aspirations happen to survive. It was certainly not the case that nationalist emotions seized the whole Jewish people in 66 C.E.: after the war, Rome blamed all Jews for the Revolt, but in fact diaspora Jews remained strikingly quiescent from 66–70 C.E. despite, in some cases, much local provocation.

Brunt's perspective is essentially that of an expert in the administration of the Roman empire, as is that of Doron Mendels, who attributes the Revolt to a rather ill-defined sense of nationalism (Mendels 1992), but some other scholars who approach the same issue from a deep knowledge of the Jewish material have come to similar conclusions. Most notably Martin Hengel has reasserted in a new foreword to the English translation of his classic *Die Zeloten*, originally published in 1961, his long-held view that Jewish society before the war was riven with unrest promoted by religious fanatics (Hengel 1989; cf. Stern 1989); Hengel sweeps away the objections of those who have insisted on distinguishing between the different groups mentioned by Josephus by asserting simply that they must have misunderstood his original claims: now that they can read his views in English, rather than German, they will see the force of his arguments (Hengel 1989: xvi), which depend to a considerable degree on the assumption that the term "Zealot," which was certainly sometimes a name of a specific party or group (cf. *War* 4.161), could also be a more general description (cf. *War* 2.651).

More recently John Collins and William Horbury have separately attempted to re-establish the role of messianic expectation as a force in Jewish history in this period (Collins 1995; Horbury 1998; cf. Oegema 1998; Zimmermann 1998; and now Chapter 11 by Rajak in this volume). Both began their studies with analyses of the literary remains, pointing out correctly that although messianic beliefs may have been extremely varied in content, they were pervasive: an appreciable proportion of the more recently published Dead Sea Scrolls contains messianic elements of one sort or another, confirming the importance of messianic ideas at least within the sect (cf. Eisenman 1996). More difficult to show is the link between such ideas and the various uprisings of the Jews both before and during the Revolt. Messianism, however pervasive, may have little effect on behavior when it is only a long-term dream; conversely, even a small group imbued with eschatological fervor in the belief that the end is in the present may have a dramatic impact. Josephus, the only source of a narrative about the behavior of the Jews in this period, puts down very few of the specific instances of unrest he mentions to messianic or eschatological expectations, and the common argument that Josephus suppressed or distorted mention of the messianic hope of the Jews because it was politically dangerous (Hengel 1989: 291, n. 339) is directly contradicted by his explicit statement at *War* 6.312 when discussing the oracles which preceded the war: "What more than all else incited them to the war was an ambiguous oracle, likewise found in their sacred scriptures, to the effect that at that time one from their country would become ruler of the world."

The counter-trend, to emphasize the variety of attitudes attributed by Josephus to the different groups involved in the war, championed originally by Morton Smith (Smith 1971), still has many followers. For the period before the Revolt, a series of studies by Richard Horsley has emphasized the heterogeneity of the movements described by Josephus (Horsley and Hanson 1985; Horsley 1987; 1995), and the same task is done in great detail by Jonathan Price in his discussion of the politics of Jerusalem during the war itself (Cotton and Price 1990; Price 1992). In general it may be said that this approach takes the distinctions in the detailed narrative in Josephus very seriously, a procedure justified on the face of it by the difficulty of ascertaining what apologetic aim Josephus could have fulfilled by inventing such distinctions if they did not correspond to reality.

My own preference continues to be to accept the complex picture to be found in the pages of Josephus. He admits quite openly that some Jews found religious reasons for revolt, but he demonstrated through his own career that it was possible to be a deeply committed Jew and yet loyal to Rome just as Jews had been loyal to other gentile empires in the past. Jews too could be patriotic Roman citizens (Goodman 1996). It has become evident since the discovery of the Dead Sea Scrolls that beyond a small common core of beliefs, the types of Judaism to be found in first century Judea were even more varied than can be gauged from the writings of Josephus (cf. Goodman forthcoming). To assert that their religion necessarily impelled Jews to rebel against Rome is to ignore the clear evidence not just of Josephus but of Philo and others that this was not the case.

The view from the other side—the Roman view of Jews—has also been much discussed in recent years, although (rather oddly) not often directly in connection with the Revolt. Opinion remains divided on the extent to which Jews were already marginalized in the Roman world by the early imperial period (Feldman 1993; Schäfer 1997; Yavetz 1997; and see now Chapter 2 by Gruen in this volume). The argument on both sides has been based to a surprising extent on attitudes expressed in extant literary evidence rather than behavior described. It seems worthwhile to urge the necessity of distinguishing at least in the Latin sources between those remarks about Jews made before and those made after the Revolt: it is *prima facie* reasonable to expect an increase in hostility in response to failed rebellion, especially when the suppression of the Jews was so vociferously trumpeted by the state.

In some ways the clearest evidence that Rome in the years before 66 C.E. did not believe Judea to be a province so intrinsically hostile to Rome as to be constantly on the brink of revolt lies in the arrangements made for the governing of the province. It was clear that Rome could not afford Judea, which lay on the route from Egypt to Syria, to fall into hostile hands, but the state took little defensive action. A few auxiliary cohorts, mostly stationed in Caesarea, were expected to keep under control the whole population. The fact that Jews were permitted to congregate in vast numbers in Jerusalem at the pilgrimage festivals (Goodman 1999a), despite the general Roman tendency to deep suspicion of mass gatherings of all kinds, argues strongly that nothing worse was expected in Judea than the level of urban violence and rural banditry endemic elsewhere in the Roman world. With increased hostility expected from the Jews after defeat, there was a greatly increased military presence, with a legion permanently stationed in Jerusalem.

It seems to me that what was exceptional about the Jewish Revolt was not any religiously inspired ideological objection by Jews to Rome nor any general Roman anti-Semitism but the extraordinary amount of evidence to survive about the war. On the one hand this was a product of the preservation of Jewish writings from antiquity to the present through two continuous literary traditions, one Jewish, one Christian; on the other hand it was a product of the intense Flavian anti-Jewish propaganda after the

Revolt, which served to justify Vespasian's seizure of power in Rome (on which see Overman in this volume pp. 213–20). That is to say, it is quite possible that many other provincials felt as oppressed as did the Jews, but their objections do not survive in extant literature except through chance finds, such as papyrus copies of the so-called *Acts of the Pagan Martyrs* (Musurillo 1954).

It is also quite possible that Rome suppressed many other revolts but without leaving to posterity any account of the wars in question because they were inglorious; more than ninety separate provincial uprisings, including some not simply extensions of the original war of conquest, are recorded in passing from the early imperial period down to Commodus, but of these only a small fraction are discussed in detail in the extant sources, at least forty-five are said to have occurred but nothing more at all is known about them, and some revolts considered worthy of full description by one author are passed over in silence by others (Goodman 1991). It is clear that despite our best efforts historians are still at the mercy of imperial propaganda, although epigraphic discovery can always alter our notions of which revolts were trumpeted and which buried in official silence: the general reticence of the Roman state about the Bar Kokhba war, which has led some to doubt whether the war was really significant at all (Bowersock 1980), has been reappraised in recent years in the light of the inscriptions erected by the commanders involved (Eck 1999). Nonetheless information about most rebellions may well have been suppressed or ignored, and it is worth recognizing to what extent the Roman state was held in control through terror so that failure to rebel did not necessarily indicate acceptance of the status quo (Goodman 1997: 159–64).

In sum, the general picture that revolt was not all inevitable in 66 C.E., and that it broke out through an unfortunate concatenation of mischances, still seems to me to be plausible. The initial Roman reaction by Cestius Gallus was not excessive—in retrospect, of course, it appeared positively lackadaisical. It has been suggested plausibly that Jews were more difficult to conquer because their allegiance to a single sanctuary encouraged them to unite in defence of the city of Jerusalem, unlike other nations whose religious allegiances were more diffuse (Bohak 1999). But I would still argue that no one could have predicted the awful consequences of the outbreak of rebellion. Rome often turned a blind eye to disaffection in other far off places, like Armenia: Judea had been left under independent Jewish rule both under Herod and Archelaus, and, more recently, under Agrippa I in 41–4 C.E. Since Rome went to war in protest at the cessation of the loyal sacrifices, it was reasonable to expect the Romans to be content with the installation of a new high priest more friendly to Roman rule.

Josephus claimed that the destruction of the Temple, which ensured that in fact loyal sacrifices would never be offered again, was a mistake not intended by Titus (*War* 6.241). Whether or not he was correct, much of the anti-Jewish propaganda which followed after 70 C.E. was a product of that destruction. Once the disaster had occurred, Vespasian and Titus had little choice how to react. To express regret at their sacrilege would hardly benefit a new regime seeking legitimacy both human and divine. The alternative was the route they took: they revelled in the demise of a temple cult now deemed unworthy to survive in the Roman world under its new leaders.

Bibliography

Anat, T. (1996) "Remarks on Josephus Flavius and the Destruction of the Second Temple," *Zion* 61: 141–57 (Heb.).

Applebaum, S. (1989) "Josephus and the Economic Causes of the Jewish War," in L. H. Feldman and G. Hata (eds.) *Josephus, the Bible and History*, Detroit: Wayne State University Press.

Bammel, E. (1989) Review of Goodman, *Ruling Class*, *Journal of Theological Studies* 40: 213–17.

Barclay, J. M. G. (1996) *Jews in the Mediterranean Diaspora*, Edinburgh: T & T Clark.

Bilde, P. (1988) *Flavius Josephus between Jerusalem and Rome: His Life, His Works, and their Importance*, Sheffield: JSOT.

Bohak, G. (1999) "Theopolis: a Single-Temple Policy and its Singular Ramifications," *Journal of Jewish Studies* 50: 3–16.

Bohrmann, M. (1994) *Flavius Josephus, the Zealots and Yavneh: Towards a Re-reading of the War of the Jews*, New York: Peter Lang.

Bowersock, G. W. (1980) "A Roman Perspective on the Bar Kokhba War," in W. S. Green (ed.) *Approaches to Ancient Judaism* 2: 131–41. Brown Judaic Studies, Atlanta: Scholars Press.

Brunt, P. A. (1990) *Roman Imperial Themes*, Oxford: Clarendon Press.

Casey, M. (1990) Review of Goodman, *Ruling Class*, in *Palestine Exploration Quarterly* 1990: 75.

Collins, J. J. (1995) *The Scepter and the Star: the Messiahs of the Dead Sea Scrolls and Other Ancient Literature*, New York: Doubleday.

Cotton, H. M. and Price, J. J. (1990) "Who Captured Masada in 66 C.E. and Who Lived There Until the Fortress Fell?" *Zion* 55: 449–54 (Heb.).

Donaldson, T. (1990) "Rural Bandits, City Mobs and the Zealots," *Journal of Jewish Studies* 31: 18–36.

Eck, W. (1999) "The Bar Kokhba Revolt: The Roman Point of View," *Journal of Roman Studies* 89: 76–89.

Eisenman, R. (1996) *The Dead Sea Scrolls and the First Christians: Essays and Translations*, Shaftesbury: Element.

Feldman, L. H. (1993) *Jew and Gentile in the Ancient World*, Princeton: Princeton University Press.

Feldman, L. H. and Hata, G. (1989) *Josephus, the Bible and History*, Detroit: Wayne State University Press.

Feldman, L. H. and Levison, J. (1996) *Josephus' Contra Apionem: Studies in its Character and Context*, Leiden: E. J. Brill.

Fiensy, D. (1991) *The Social History of Palestine in the Herodian Period*, Lewiston: E. Mellen Press.

Fuks, G. (1987) "Simon bar Giora, GERASENOS," *Zion* 52: 41–52 (Heb.).

Geiger, J. (1989) Review of Goodman, *Ruling Class*, *Journal of Roman Archaeology* 2: 291–3.

Goodman, M. (1987) *The Ruling Class of Judaea: The Origins of the Jewish Revolt Against Rome, A.D. 66–70*, Cambridge: Cambridge University Press.

—— (1991) "Opponents of Rome: Jews and Others," in L. Alexander (ed.), *Images of Empire*, Sheffield: JSOT.

—— (1994a) Review of Sanders, *Judaism: Practice and Belief*, *Scottish Journal of Theology* 47: 89–95.

—— (1994b) "Josephus as a Roman Citizen," in F. Parente and J. Sievers (eds.) *Josephus and the History of the Graeco-Roman Period*, Leiden: E. J. Brill.

—— (1996) "The Roman Identity of Roman Jews," in I. M. Gafni, A. Oppenheimer and D. R. Schwartz (eds.) *The Jews in the Hellenistic–Roman World: Studies in Memory of Menahem Stern*, Jerusalem: Merkaz Zalmon Shazar.

—— (1997) *The Roman World, 44 B.C.–A.D. 180*, London: Routledge.

—— (1999a) "The Pilgrimage Economy of Jerusalem in the Second Temple Period," in L. I. Levine (ed.) *Jerusalem: its Sanctity and Centrality to Judaism, Christianity, and Islam*, New York: Continuum.

—— (1999b) "Josephus' Treatise Against Apion," in M. Edwards, M. Goodman, and S. Price (eds.) *Apologetics in the Roman Empire: Jews, Pagans, and Christians*, Oxford: Clarendon Press.

—— (forthcoming) "Josephus and the Limits of Variety in First-Century Judaism," *Proceedings of the Israel Academy*.

Hadas-Lebel, M. (1993) *Flavius Josephus: Eyewitness to Rome's First Century Conquest of Judaea* (trans. R. Miller), New York: MacMillan.

Hengel, M. (1989) *The Zealots: Investigations into the Jewish Freedom Movement in the Period from Herod I until 70 A.D.* (trans. D. Smith), Edinburgh: T & T Clark.

Horbury, W. (1998) *Jewish Messianism and the Cult of Christ*, London: SCM Press.

Horsley, R. A. (1987) *Jesus and the Spiral of Violence*, San Francisco: Harper and Row.

—— (1995) *Galilee: History, Politics, People*, Valley Forge, PA: Trinity Press International.

Horsley, R. A. and Hanson, J. S. (1985) *Bandits, Prophets and Messiahs: Popular Movements at the Time of Jesus*, Minneapolis: Fortress Press.

Huntsman, E. (1996–7) "The Reliability of Josephus: Can He be Trusted?" *Brigham Young University Studies* 36, no.3: 392–402.

Ilan, T. and Price, Jonathan, J. (1993–4) "Seven Onomastic Problems in Josephus' Bellum Judaicum," *Jewish Quarterly Review* 84, nos. 2–3: 189–208.

Jackson, K. (1996–7) "Revolutionaries in the First Century," *Brigham Young University Studies* 36, no. 3: 129–40.

Kokkinos, N. (1998) *The Herodian Dynasty: Origins, Role in Society and Eclipse*, Sheffield: Sheffield Academic Press.

Longenecker, B. (1998) "The Wilderness and Revolutionary Ferment in First Century Palestine: A Response to D. R. Schwartz and J. Marcus," *Journal for the Study of Judaism* 29.3: 322–36.

McLaren, J. S. (1991) *Power and Politics in Palestine: The Jews and the Governing of their Land 100 B.C.–A.D. 70*, Sheffield: JSOT.

—— (1998) *Turbulent Times? Josephus and Scholarship on Judaea in the First Century C.E.*, Sheffield: Sheffield Academic Press.

Mason, S. N. (ed.) (1998) *Understanding Josephus: Seven Perspectives*, Sheffield: Sheffield Academic Press.

Mendels, D. (1992) *The Rise and Fall of Jewish Nationalism*, New York: Doubleday.

Mitchell, S. (1986) Review of Goodman *Ruling Class*, *Journal of Jewish Studies* 39: 108–12.

Musurillo, H. A. (1954) *The Acts of the Pagan Martyrs: Acta Alexandrinorum*, Oxford: Clarendon Press.

Oegema, G. S. (1998) *The Anointed and His People*, Sheffield: Sheffield Academic Press.

Paltiel, E. (1991) *Vassals and Rebels in the Roman Empire*, Brussels: Latomus.

Parente, F. and Sievers, J. (eds.) (1994) *Josephus and the History of the Graeco-Roman Period*, Leiden: E. J. Brill.

Paul, G. M. (1993) "The Presentation of Titus in the *Jewish War* of Josephus: Two Aspects," *Phoenix* 47: 56–66.

Price, J. J. (1992) *Jerusalem under Siege: The Collapse of the Jewish State 66–70 C.E.*, Leiden: E. J. Brill.

Rajak, T. (1984) *Josephus: The Historian and His Society*, Philadelphia: Fortress Press.

Rappaport, U. (1982) "John of Gischala: From Galilee to Jerusalem," *Journal of Jewish Studies* 33: 479–93.

Sanders, E. P. (1992) *Judaism: Practice and Belief 63 B.C.E.–66 C.E.*, London: SCM Press.

Saulnier, C. (1989) "Flavius Josephe et la propagande flavienne," *Revue Biblique* 96: 545–62.

Schäfer, P. (1997) *Judeophobia: Attitudes towards Jews in the Ancient World*, Cambridge, MA: Harvard University Press.

Schwartz, S. (1990) *Josephus and Judaean Politics*, Leiden: E. J. Brill.

—— (1994) "Josephus in Galilee: Rural Patronage and Social Breakdown," in F. Parente and J. Sievers (eds.) *Josephus and the History of the Graeco-Roman Period*, Leiden: E. J. Brill.

Shaw, B. D. (1989) Review of Goodman, *Ruling Class*, *Journal of Roman Studies* 79: 246–7.

—— (1993) "Tyrants, Bandits and Kings: Personal Power in Josephus," *Journal of Jewish Studies* 44: 173–203.

Smith, M. (1971) "Zealots and Sicarii: their origins and relations," *Harvard Theological Review* 64: 1–19.

Sterling, G. E. (1992) *Historiography and Self-definition: Josephus, Luke-Acts and Apologetic Historiography*, Leiden: E. J. Brill.

Stern, M. (1989) Review of Goodman, *Ruling Class*, *Zion* 54: 125–9 (Heb.).

Syme, R. (1986) *The Augustan Aristocracy*, Oxford: Clarendon Press.

Van Praag, H. M. (1991) "Against Josephus Flavius? The Struggle of a Jew with Multiple Loyalties," *Journal for Psychology and Judaism* 15: 213–30.

Windsor, R. R. (1994) *Judea Trembles under Rome: The Untold Details of the Greek and Roman Military Domination of Palestine During the Time of Jesus of Galilee*, Atlanta, GA: Windsor Golden Series.

Yavetz, Z. (1997) *Judenfeindschaft in der Antike: die Münchener Vorträge*, Munich: C. H. Beck.

Zimmermann, J. (1998) *Messianische Texte aus Qumran*, Tübingen: Mohr.

Part I

Historical and archaeological background

Roman perspectives on the
Jews in the age of the Great
Revolt

Erich S. Gruen

The "Great War" of the Jews against the Romans struck Josephus as a
contest of monumental significance. He spared no rhetoric in the preface to
his *War* (1.1): this war was not only the greatest of any in his own time
but nearly the greatest of any conflict between cities or nations throughout
history. This, of course, is wild hyperbole, a patent attempt to imitate
Herodotus and Thucydides who made similar claims for the wars about
which they wrote—with rather more justification. For the Jews, to be sure,
this conflict did have momentous implications. To confront in all-out war
the predominant imperial power of the world could only have been viewed as
a clash of colossal proportions. Such, at least, would be a Jewish perspective.

But how was it perceived in Rome? Who were these strange, mad
creatures, the Jews? Many a Roman must have asked himself that question
when word arrived of the outbreak of rebellion—and, more particularly,
when the rebellion persisted and the rebels persevered. How could this puny
nation venture to challenge the awesome might of the Roman empire? For
many Romans, the uprising must have appeared bizarre, inexplicable, even
unthinkable. Certainly it provoked a harsh and brutal retaliation that left an
enduring mark on all subsequent Jewish history.

Not that the Jews were unknown or unfamiliar to Romans. Roman governors, procurators, tax-farmers, various public officials, military officers, rank
and file soldiers, visitors and tourists had spent time in Judea over the past
two generations. And even Romans who had never been abroad knew about
the Jews. A large Jewish community existed in the city of Rome, indeed had
existed there for a long time. Philo reports that they occupied a substantial
proportion of Trastevere, most of them freedmen or descendants of freedmen
(*Embassy to Gaius*, 155). Moreover, the Romans knew full well that close
ethnic, political, and cultural ties bound together the Jews resident in Rome
and those in the homeland or elsewhere in the diaspora. They had occasion
to appreciate that fact as long ago as the age of Cicero. When the Roman
governor of Asia, L. Valerius Flaccus, prohibited the exportation of gold
from his province, he struck, whether intentionally or inadvertently, at the
Jews resident in his jurisdiction who were accustomed to sending their
annual tithe to Jerusalem. The matter had a direct impact in Rome. The

Jewish inhabitants of the city sent up a howl, organized demonstrations at public gatherings, and, when Flaccus himself came to trial (on other charges) in 59 B.C.E. drove Cicero, his defense counsel, to some nasty vitriol about Jewish crowds in the streets.[1] A half century later, after the death of Herod in 4 B.C.E., a delegation of envoys, fifty in number, arrived in Rome from Judea to make a case to Augustus for terminating the rule of the Herods. Their cause was immediately endorsed by eight thousand Roman Jews who lobbied Augustus vigorously on their behalf (*Ant.* 17: 300–1). The Romans had thus had first hand experience with the manifestations of Jewish solidarity, the interests that linked members of the tribe across the Mediterranean.

A number of questions spring to mind. What image did Jews possess in Roman eyes? When word came of the rebellion, what impressions were likely to be triggered among Romans, and what effect might those impressions have in determining the vehemence of the Roman response? Did the uprising bring to the surface latent "anti-Semitism" or what some now prefer to characterize as "Judeophobia"?[2] Did Roman leaders and populace find their anxieties confirmed by this troublesome and vexatious people, atheists who scorned the proper gods, misanthropes who held aloof from normal society, dangerous proselytizers who contaminated decent Romans, and perpetrators of alarming practices like refusing to perform duties on the Sabbath, refraining from eating pork, and mutilating their genitals?

Not easy questions to answer. We have no direct testimony on the immediate repercussions among Romans when the rebellion exploded—or when it persisted. But we do possess a fair number of remarks by various Roman writers about Jews that offer some entrance into the Roman mentality and permit the construction of at least a tentative picture. This investigation confines itself to a circumscribed range of texts: those composed by Romans living in the years shortly before the Great Revolt and in the generation after its conclusion—essentially from Seneca to Juvenal. That is not to suggest that their attitudes—or, more precisely, the expressions of their attitudes that have survived for us—are necessarily representative. Nor can one claim that those expressions give us the full story of how Romans regarded Jews, what they expected of them, or why they retaliated as they did to Jewish resistance and insurrection. But they do provide valuable insight into the intellectual atmosphere at Rome insofar as it pertains to Jews. And they afford a glimpse into the understanding—or lack thereof—that the Romans exhibited on questions of Jewish character, principles, and practices. Roman discourse on the Jews from approximately the mid-first through the early second century C.E. supplies a window on the conceptual prism through which Jews were perceived in the age that preceded the Revolt—and that of its aftermath.

Inspection of the texts on both sides of that chronological divide elicits a most surprising result. The Revolt itself does not appear to signal a watershed in the discourse on the Jews. Official policy toward Judea changed, to be sure, quite drastically so. The destruction of the Temple, the installation of a major garrison, the decimation of the ruling class, and the imposition of a Roman tax to be delivered annually for support of the cult of Jupiter Capitolinus altered the relationship of the empire to the province of Judea in the most profound ways (Goodman 1987: 231–51). But no comparable shift can be discerned in the perception of Jews, or rather the characterization of Jews, in our Roman sources. An unexpected conclusion— but a significant one.

Did the Romans reckon Jewish practices or beliefs as cause for concern? It is not easy to imagine that the great imperial power felt anxiety about a peculiar, but largely powerless, people off in Judea, or indeed those of them in their midst. What would they have to worry about? Jewish monotheism perhaps? Eminent scholars hold that the single-minded Jewish devotion to Yahweh represented some form of challenge to the religious beliefs of the pagan world, that it defied the pantheon of Roman gods, that it was un-patriotic and blasphemous, an expression of disrespect for the divinities who guaranteed the security of the Roman empire (cf. Feldman 1993: 149–53; Feldman 1997: 44, 51–2; Schafer 1997: 183–92). A reasonable enough surmise, it might be thought. Yet no trace of this idea appears in the ancient texts. Greeks and Romans did not even have a word for "mono-theism." And its opposite, which we cavalierly ascribe to the pagan world, "polytheism," would hardly be comprehensible as a religion—any more than "paganism" was a religion.[3] The ancients worshipped different gods in different places and in different numbers. Why not? Of course, the Romans knew that the Jews had but a single deity. So much the worse for them. That seemed obtuse, but hardly threatening. Even Tacitus, no friend of the Jews (to put it mildly), did not reckon monotheism as such to be an abhorrent practice that needed to be stamped out. In fact, his reference to the Jews as conceiving just a single divinity (*unum numen*) contrasts them not with Romans but with the despised Egyptians who worship multitudes of animals and multiformed images.[4] Now *that* was abhorrent! Nothing in the texts implies that adherence to Yahweh constituted a menace to the religious—let alone to the social and political—order of the realm.

To be sure, Jewish faith did not strike the Romans as especially wise or admirable. Greek and Latin writers regularly labeled the creed of the Jews as *deisidaimonia* or *superstitio*. The calumny goes back at least as far as Cicero who branded Jewish practice as *barbara superstitio* (*In Defense of Flaccus* 67). The phrase surfaces subsequently in writers as different as Seneca, Plutarch, Quintilian, and Tacitus.[5] Their comments are snide and contemptuous, an expression of Roman disdain for practices that seemed meaningless or unintelligible. They disclose conventional Roman scorn for alien cults and benighted beliefs.[6] But nothing suggests that Jewish devotion to Yahweh gave the slightest reason for anxiety.

Indeed, Roman policy prior to the Revolt suggests the reverse. At least so far as official pronouncements went, the Romans frequently reiterated their protection of Jewish religious rites and practices, accorded the Jews various privileges, and granted them a number of exemptions to allow observance of Sabbath requirements, dietary laws, and the obligation to send moneys to the Temple in Jerusalem. Testimony to these decrees, edicts, and letters resides in Josephus's *Antiquities*, ostensible transcriptions of official documents (Josephus, *Ant.* 14.185–267, 14.306–23, 16.160–78, 19.280–91. Cf. Philo, *Embassy to Gaius* 158, 314–15). And, although his version contains numerous flaws, inaccuracies, chronological confusion, and even mindless duplication, the authenticity of the documents—or some such documents—remains unshaken.[7] The blunders themselves in Josephus's account constitute a good argument against fabrication. The circumstances that called forth the decrees varied, and the motives differed. But Roman policy in general stands out as clear and consistent. Far from nervousness at the practices of Judaism, the Romans repeatedly endorsed and defended those practices. If the Jews insisted on their foolishness, leave them to it.

Tacitus, of course, did not much like the ways of the Jews. In his perception, they stood at the opposite pole from his own: "they hold all things profane that we regard as sacred, and everything they consider permissible, we consider anathema."[8] "Perhaps some of their rites," he observed, "have the justification of antiquity; but all the rest are wicked, foul, and abound in depravity."[9] Not exactly a sterling recommendation. But Tacitus reserves his fiercest tirade less for the Jews than for those who have "crossed over" to Judaism: they abandoned their ancestral religions, scorned their native gods, deserted their nation, and even hold cheap their own parents, children, and siblings (*Histories* 5.5.2). Tacitus here excoriates apostates, but suggests no Jewish conspiracy.

Was there perhaps a more concrete reason for Romans to be wary of the Jews? Did they regard them as a rebellious folk, prone to turbulence, chafing under Roman rule, a threat to the stability of the empire? Seneca, in a rare outburst, described the Jews as a most pernicious people (*sceleratissima gens*) (*apud* Augustine, *City of God* 6.11). The phrase is often cited as emblematic of Roman hostility, an index that Jews were perceived as a nation prone to criminal activities. Just what Seneca himself meant remains obscure (cf. Yavetz 1998: 87). But it is worth observing that he was not exactly obsesssed with anxiety over Jewish wickedness. In the vast extant corpus of Seneca, one that contains an astonishing array of diverse writings, the Jews nowhere else receive explicit mention—although there are one or two places where he appears to make indirect allusion to them (*Letters on Morality* 95.47, 108.22). Furthermore, the notorious passage at issue does not, in fact, come directly from Seneca. It derives second-hand from Augustine's *City of God*. Both the context and the intentions of the writer elude our grasp. If ever a case for caution is justified, this one surely is. The statement hardly qualifies as evidence for any general Roman apprehension about the fearsomeness of Jews.

Tacitus remarks that Jews set up no images to divinity: no statues stand in their cities and none in their temples. They refrain from such adulation toward their own kings and withhold such honor from Roman emperors (*Histories* 5.5.4). How to take this? The assertion might appear to signify a branding of Jews as recalcitrant subjects who reject the authority of the Roman government (so, e.g., Wardy 1979: 629–31; Rosen 1996: 115–17). In fact, it was nothing of the kind. Roman emperors had long acknowledged Jewish avoidance of ruler worship as legitimate, and accepted readily the substitute practice of Jews sacrificing to Yahweh on the emperor's behalf, simply another mode of expressing loyalty (cf. Philo, *Embassy to Gaius* 157, 232, 356; Josephus, *War* 2.197, 2.409; *Ap.* 2.77). Indeed the Jews of the diaspora made dedications to the emperor in their synagogues (Philo, *Embassy to Gaius* 133; *Against Flaccus* 49). Only Caligula broke the mold—as he did in so many other ways. But his insistence on direct worship was anomalous, aberrant, and abortive. And even he pulled back from the brink, rescinding his order, reluctantly but inevitably.[10] As for Tacitus, his comment about Jewish unwillingness to worship the emperor did not constitute a reproach. Tacitus was no fan of emperor worship himself (cf. Tacitus, *Annals* 15.74). Elsewhere he reports the Jews' resistance to Caligula's order of a statue in the Temple and readiness to take up arms in a tone that suggests grudging admiration.[11]

Tacitus, in fact, delivers an unexpectedly positive verdict on the Jewish engagement in the Great Revolt itself. He acknowledges that Jews showed restraint under cruel Roman governors until their patience ran out in the procuratorship of Florus—thus placing blame on Roman misgovernance rather then Jewish rebelliousness.[12] Even more strikingly he notes that those who were besieged in Jerusalem amounted to no fewer than six hundred thousand, that men and women alike and of every age engaged in armed resistance, everyone who could pick up a weapon did, that a larger proportion showed courage than could have been anticipated from their total numbers, and that both sexes showed equal determination, preferring death to a life that involved expulsion from their country.[13] Tacitus, to be sure, ascribes this more to foolhardiness than to wisdom. But he plainly does not regard it as a treacherous undermining of the Roman order.

The satirist Juvenal, like Tacitus writing after the Revolt, does appear to take a hard line on the matter. He maintains that Jews are wont to despise Roman enactments, preferring instead to learn, obey, and fear Jewish law which Moses handed down in some secret tome.[14] On the face of it, that looks like a reference to Jewish rejection of the Roman system and embrace of an alternative authority (so Schafer 1997: 185). But it is hazardous to place too serious an interpretation upon Juvenal's sardonic wit. The comments come in the context of Juvenal's broader mockery of Jewish adherence to the Sabbath, dietary laws, circumcision, and rigorous exclusiveness, all, in Juvenal's eyes, more laughable than dangerous. His contrast between Roman *leges* and Jewish *ius* does not present a clash of competing legal and constitutional systems, but a satirist's mode of expressing the absurdity of the Jews' idiosyncratic customs.

In short, Roman anxiety is nowhere in evidence. The Romans did not imagine that the empire was in any way menaced or compromised by the laws of Moses.[15] Jewish peculiarities, of course, did make an impression. From the Roman vantage-point, Jews behaved in baffling ways. They held themselves aloof, kept to their own kind, were not great social mixers, indeed preferred to avoid the company of others lest they undermine the constancy of their own customs. The conduct could be construed as anti-social, indeed as misanthropy: Jews would have no truck with the goyim. A number of Greeks had complained about them on that score in an earlier era.[16]

But this insularity did not much bother the Romans. Tacitus, true enough, included it in his long list of reasons for displeasure with the Jews. They maintain a rock-steady loyalty among themselves but hate everybody else. They don't eat with other people; they don't sleep with them. There is nothing they won't do with one another—but they won't have intercourse with Gentiles (*Histories* 5.5.1–2). Such is the Tacitean description, certainly not a generous one. It should, however, be noted that the historian finds the roots of this exclusivity perfectly explicable in light of Jewish experience in antiquity. As Tacitus has it, when the Hebrews were expelled from Egypt, Moses advised them not to expect help from men or gods, having been abandoned by both. They have to rely on themselves (*Histories* 5.3.1). So Jewish isolationism, if not admirable, is at least intelligible. Juvenal noticed it too—and, characteristically, made a joke of it. The satirist declared that Jews will not even give directions in the street to non-Jews (14.103–4). That might be irritating, but hardly menacing. The Jews, after all, never made a secret of their preference for one another's company. The Bible abounds in references to the importance of endogamy and the maintenance of traditions free of alien contamination, themes that reappear in Jewish–Hellenistic literature like *The Letter of Aristeas, Tobit*, and *Joseph and Aseneth*.[17] Romans did not lose sleep over it.

A more serious matter, if indeed it occurred at all, would be Jewish proselytizing. Did it occur? The matter has stirred high controversy in recent years, unresolved and indecisive. No need to reargue the positions here.[18] But one point should be made with emphasis: no unambiguous testimony exists to show that Jews went about accosting Gentiles and endeavoring to turn them into good Jews (see the cogent arguments of Goodman 1994: 60–90). Of course, people did convert, male and female, persons who found Judaism or some form of it appealing, those who adopted Jewish practices or beliefs. And Jews doubtless welcomed them into the fold, taking pride in the swelling ranks of their numbers. Why not? That, however, is a very different matter from organized and determined missionary activity. And nothing in the evidence warrants belief in such activity.

A related issue, nevertheless, needs to be addressed. Leaving aside the question of whether Jews went about proselytizing, did the Romans have reason for alarm in the prospect of growing numbers of Jews and increasing authority exercised by them (e.g., Daniel 1979: 62–4; Gager 1985: 59–61; Rosen 1996: 116, 121; Schäfer 1997: 183–92; Yavetz 1998: 96–8)? A remark of Seneca might imply it. He observes that the Jewish way of life prevails so widely that it permeates all the lands of the world—so much so that the vanquished impose their laws upon the victors.[19] How significant is that statement? And how representative? First of all, be it noted, the remarks form part of that same text that reaches us only second-hand through the medium of St. Augustine. We may not have Seneca's *ipsissima verba*, and we certainly do not have the larger context in which they occurred. Further, the statement follows upon other remarks in which Seneca mocks the institution of the Sabbath, berates the Jews for wasting every seventh day in idleness, and notes that they frequently suffer damage at times of crisis because of their *inactivity*.[20] Obviously Seneca is not sounding an alarm to check zealous missionaries.

Tacitus, as we have seen, is angrier at the converts than at the Jews. They have deserted their native gods, ancestral traditions, homeland, and families (*Histories* 5.5.1–2). But he makes no claim that Jews are beating the bushes for converts or infiltrating Gentile communities everywhere. Quite the contrary. These remarks are imbedded in Tacitus' discussion of the Jews as keeping themselves entirely separate from other peoples and even shunning their company. It would not be easy to proselytize among the Gentiles if one were shunning their company! Tacitus does make mention of increasing numbers of Jews. But he refers to a stepped-up birth rate, not to missionary activity. The Jews, so he affirms, since they believe in the immortality of souls, have a passion for reproduction and a contempt for death.[21] Tacitus plainly has no fears of being overrun by them.

Juvenal's snide remark about people embracing Mosaic law and scrapping Roman *leges* also applies essentially to converts (14.100–2). But he drops no hint that their numbers are large or menacing. As is notorious, Juvenal complained bitterly about an influx of foreigners into the city: the Orontes river dumping its refuse into the Tiber (3.60–6). But no mention of Jews here. Juvenal simply despised easterners generally. Indeed, he saves his most savage vitriol for the Egyptians, that demented folk devoted to monstrous animal deities, who pay reverence to crocodiles, ibises, monkeys, river fish, cats, and dogs—and not a soul to venerate Diana; they won't touch animals but they dine on human flesh (15.1–13). Nothing that Juvenal has to say about the Jews even approaches that level of vehemence. In sum, conversion, missionary activity, or proselytizing of any kind do not appear to have filled the Romans with dread.

Was there perhaps apprehension about Jewish economic power? The notion stirs recollection of more recent slurs: the image of the Jew as money-grubber, greedy usurer, unscrupulous capitalist, the financial predator who preys upon innocent Gentiles. That stereotype, however, is sheer anachronism. Tacitus does observe, quite rightly, that converts to Judaism, like other Jews, sent tribute to Jerusalem, thus augmenting the resources of the Jews. The

Temple became the repository of great wealth (*Histories* 5.5.1, 5.8.1). But the notion that this inspired envy and hostility, that it prompted concern lest Jewish financiers threaten to control the economy of the empire, is quite incredible. Roman satirists, in fact, far from representing the Jews as plutocrats, tended to bracket them with beggars. Martial presents a typical Jew as one taught by his mother to panhandle (12.57.13). Juvenal, on three separate occasions, refers to mendicant Jews in Rome: to a regular gatheringplace for them at the Porta Capena, to a beggars' stand associated with a synagogue, and to an impoverished Jewess, stricken with palsey, who plies her begging trade by claiming to tell fortunes and interpret dreams—if you cross her palm with a few pennies (3.10–16, 3.296, 6.542–7). Disdainful remarks of this sort on Jewish indigence and beggary stand at the furthest possible remove from any image of Jews as fat cats.[22]

Any inquiry into the subject of external perceptions of Jews runs a hazard. A natural, even if unconscious, tendency inclines toward the assumption that Romans spent a lot of time thinking about Jews. In fact, Roman writers had far more interesting (to them) subjects to ponder. In general, they show indifference to Jews (Feldman 1997: 39–42). The preserved remarks are far more often dismissive than probing. The vast majority of Roman references to Judaism fall into a single category: allusions to quaint and curious Jewish traits, practices, and customs that attracted attention precisely because they seemed so outlandish. Romans showed familiarity with religious and cultural activities that stemmed from a wide spectrum of ethnic groups. But Jewish traits do seem to have provoked an unusual number of comments.

The institution of the Sabbath, of course, provides an obvious example. A widespread notion had it that the Sabbath was observed as a day of fasting. The emperor Augustus himself labored under that apprehension, evidently already a commonplace one in his day. Suetonius reports him saying to Tiberius that he had been fasting all day, more diligently even than a Jew on the Sabbath (Suetonius, *Life of Augustus* 76.2). Writers in the age of Augustus, like Strabo and Pompeius Trogus, simply took for granted the proposition that Jews fasted every Sabbath (Strabo 16.2.40; Trogus *apud* Justin 36.2.14). Subsequent satirists naturally picked up the idea with pleasure. The Neronian wit Petronius has Jews tremble with trepidation at the prospect of Sabbath fasts imposed by law (fr. 37, Ernout). And Martial, still more caustically, refers to the fasts of women on the Sabbath which give them bad breath (4.4.7). Whence this misconception derives eludes our grasp (for some conjectures, see Goldenberg 1979: 439–41; Feldman 1993: 161–3). But it nicely illustrates the point that most Romans contented themselves with a half-baked idea frequently repeated but never examined.

Others discerned a logical connection and reached an illogical conclusion. They identified the Sabbath with the day of Saturn, evidently making some association with the planetary system that reckoned Saturn as highest of the seven planets (cf. Tacitus, *Histories* 5.4.4). That interesting tidbit of misinformation can be found in writers as diverse as the elegiac poet Tibullus, the military strategist Frontinus, and the ever-fertile Tacitus—although it should be noted that Tacitus does not go on record as endorsing the idea (Tibullus, 1.13.8; Frontinus *Stratagems* 2.1.17; Tacitus *Histories* 5.4.4). This delusion provides yet another instance in which Romans preferred to repeat and transmit conjecture rather than to investigate its truth. The latter would be too much trouble.

The biographer and collector of arcane information, Plutarch, took an altogether different line. In his treatise on banquets, one of the interlocutors offers the intriguing suggestion that the Jewish Sabbath is a form of Dionysiac festival. The grounds for that hypothesis hardly generate confidence: the term Sabi served as a designation for Bacchants, the Jews invite one another to enjoy wine on the Sabbath, and (the clincher) the High Priest wears finery once a week that parallels the garb in which Bacchic celebrants clad themselves. Hence, it seemed reasonable to infer that the Jewish Sabbath provided occasion for drink and revelry (*Banquet Debates* 4.6.2). So much for Plutarch's research on the subject. Tacitus knew of this Dionysiac interpretation and rejected it out of hand. Not that he had studied the matter with any care either. He gives a comparably fatuous reason for his own conclusion: Bacchic gatherings were joyous and festive, Jewish customs were silly and sordid.[23] Roman impressions of the Sabbath thus ran the gamut from fast day to feast day. As is plain, confusions and distortions were rampant. Romans showed little inclination to conduct serious inquiry into the subject.

When they did bother to pass judgment on Jewish observance of the Sabbath, they reckoned it as monumental folly. It became almost a commonplace among pagan writers to ridicule Jews for refusing to fight on the Sabbath. Various caustic comments derided a senseless observance that caused Jerusalem to fall three times. The parade of critics began as early as the second century B.C.E. when the Greek historian Agatharchides of Knidos berated the practice that had delivered Jerusalem into the hands of Ptolemy I. The refrain was picked up by Strabo for whom the decision not to take up arms on the Sabbath allowed Pompey to take the city. And a century or so later Frontinus gave the same explanation for Vespasian's seizure of Jerusalem—even though Vespasian was no longer in Judea at the time![24] Most, or all, of this rests on inaccurate data or misconception.

As the Romans perceived it, even if the silly custom did not precipitate disaster, it represented a colossal waste of time. Seneca supposedly made the crack that, by observing the Sabbath, Jews use up nearly one seventh of their lives in idleness.[25] That sentiment was echoed by Juvenal: adoption of Jewish ways entails consigning every seventh day to sloth (14.105–6). Tacitus takes the matter a step further. For him, the seductive delights of indolence not only induced Jews to do nothing every seventh day but even prompted them to create the sabbatical year, thus idling away every seventh year (*Histories* 5.4.3).

Pagan writers plainly had a field day in lampooning this institution. The satirist Persius, writing in the age of Nero, alludes to the habit of lighting lamps on the Sabbath which spew forth smoke on greasy window sills (5.179–82). Seneca too has a laugh at the lighting of lamps, wondering why anyone bothers with it. After all, the gods don't need the light to see, and men just get themselves soiled by soot.[26] And one final twist on the custom of taking one day a week off: the assiduous researcher Pliny the Elder claimed to know of a river in Judea that dries up every Sabbath.[27] So, even the rivers rest one day a week.

Comparable lampooning directed itself against another Jewish practice: the abstention from eating pork. This too was well known among Romans and drew frequent comments, a conspicuous characteristic regularly associated with the Jews. Even the emperors noticed this peculiar habit. A famous joke line attributed to Augustus illustrates it. In speaking of Herod, ruler of Judea, who enjoyed wide notoriety for the intrigues and murders that occurred with regularity within his own household, Augustus quipped "It's better to be Herod's pig than his son."[28] And the emperor Caligula also exhibited familiarity with the dietary restriction. When a delegation of Alexandrian Jews gained an audience with him in order to argue a case for their rights in Alexandria, the satanic *princeps* led them a merry chase around the gardens and then asked them mockingly, "Why don't you eat pork?"—a question that made auditors double up with laughter (Philo *Embassy to Gaius* 361).

Roman satirists had a good deal of fun with the Jewish diet. It inspired some memorable sardonic wit. Petronius, author of the *Satyricon*, concluded that, if Jews don't touch pork, they must worship a pig-god.[29] And Juvenal characterizes Judea as the place where a long-standing indulgence permits pigs to reach a ripe old age.[30] Greek and Roman writers puzzled over this weird Jewish revulsion from a culinary delicacy that they held in high esteem. Tacitus postulated a motive for abstention from swine's flesh: the Jews had suffered a disease of epidemic proportions through contact with that animal (*Histories* 5.4.2). His contemporary, the philosopher Epictetus, expressed some irritation over the fact that Jews, Syrians, Egyptians, and Romans quarrel not over whether holiness ought to be preferred to all else but whether eating pork is holy or unholy (*apud* Arrian *Dissertations* 1.22.4 [Souilé]). Plutarch indeed invented a wholesale dialogue in which the interlocutors debated whether Jews shrank from pork out of reverence for the hog or out of abhorrence of that creature. But it is not easy to take the arguments on either side as altogether serious. The spokesman who maintained that Jews honor the pig offered as reason the fact that pigs first dug up the soil with their protruding snout, thereby giving Jews the idea for invention of the plowshare—the basis for all Jewish agriculture (*Banquet Debates* 4.5.2). And the interlocutor on the other side proposed that, among other explanations, Jewish revulsion derived from porcine anatomy: pigs' eyes are so twisted that they point downward and cannot see anything above them unless they are carried upside down![31] Not exactly a compelling reason for refraining from swine's flesh. Plutarch, one might suggest, was having his own little joke in this after-dinner debate. Gentiles evidently could not understand a decision to forbear from the consumption of pork, which they reckoned as one of the pleasures of life. In general, then, the Jews' exclusion of pork from their diet provoked perplexity, much misinformation, and a lot of amused disdain.

Another Jewish custom drew a similar reaction. This one was, to the Roman way of thinking, the most distinctive, even if not the most visible, feature that marked out a Jew, namely circumcision (cf. Feldman 1993: 153–8). Tacitus even supposed that the Jews adopted this peculiar practice precisely in order to make themselves distinct from all other peoples.[32] As Philo noted, circumcision regularly drew ridicule from non-Jews (*On Special Laws* 1.1–2). The satirists, as one would expect, jibed at it with abandon. Petronius remarked about a talented Jewish slave who possesses all manner of intellectual and practical skills that he has but two faults: he is circumcised and he snores (never mind that he is cross-eyed; 68.4–8; cf. 102.14; fr. 37, Ernout). Juvenal alleged that Jews are so exclusive in keeping their own company that they won't direct anyone to a water fountain unless he is circumcised (the satirist does not indicate how they could tell; 14.103–4). Martial has a few obscene poems that make reference to circumcision. One is dedicated to the notorious nymphomaniac Caelia who gives her favors to persons of every imaginable ethnic origin, even to the genitals of circumcised Jews (7.30.5). Another refers to a circumcised poet who engages in both plagiarism and pederasty (11.94). And still another speaks of a friend whom he often accompanied to the baths, one who always wore an enormous sheath over his organ, claiming that it allowed him to spare his voice. But when exercising one day, in full view of various spectators (doubtless curious of what lay underneath), the sheath fell off, disclosing that what might have been thought notable for its size was, in fact, notable only for its circumcision (7.82). As is clear, the practice of circumcision gave rise to mockery and parody, a valuable source of material for jokesters.

What does all this amount to? To analyze Roman attitudes from this assembled testimony as falling into the categories of anti-Semitism or philo-Semitism is far off the mark. The long-standing game of locating Roman writers (and Greek ones too for that matter) on one side or another of that divide has run its course and lost its usefulness (e.g., Daniel 1979: 45–65; Gager 1985: 35–88; Feldman 1986: 29–36; Feldman 1993: 123–287, *passim*; Feldman 1997: 39–52). Nor will it do to locate them along a spectrum that stretches from admiration to animosity. Romans showed little understanding of Judaism, but were hardly inveterate bigots. The texts reveal neither intolerance nor racism. And nothing in them suggests that Romans were bent on persecution. Jews simply had too little importance to justify harassment or repression. In fact, they had too little importance even for Roman intellectuals to undertake any serious research or inquiry about them. The latter seem satisfied with superficial appearances and impressions. Hence they retailed shallow, half-baked, and misinformed opinions. Why bother to do more? Romans were either indifferent to the Jews or regarded them with scorn and disdain. The Revolt itself made hardly a dent in those attitudes. Sneers and caricatures occur as readily in Persius or Petronius before the war as they do in Martial or Juvenal after. And Seneca can mock the Sabbath observance in the same terms as Tacitus. How could one take seriously a people who adhered to silly superstitions, who would have no social or sexual intercourse with Gentiles, who begged alms and told fortunes, who wasted every seventh day in idleness, who stained their windows with smoke and soot from lighting lamps, who would not give you directions in the street, who would not eat ham or pork chops, and who mangled their genitals?

When word came of upheaval in Judea, of false prophets and magicians, of brigands and bandits, of rural turmoil and urban terrorism, and of outright rebellion against Roman authority, the reaction in Rome can only have been one of disbelief and indignation. Romans were certainly not alarmed by Jewish economic power, population growth, proselytism or the infiltration of Mosaic law. But they must have felt outrage at the idea that this puny and insignificant *ethnos*, given to bizarre and contemptible practices, with a host of foolish and fatuous beliefs, would venture to challenge the power of Rome.

That was not all. A related feature surely intensified the wrath of the Romans. This receives clear expression in a speech placed by Josephus in the mouth of the victorious conqueror of Jerusalem, Titus, after the burning of the Temple. It indicates quite pointedly that Rome was not simply indignant at Jewish audacity in the face of superior might. Romans had, after all, not only tolerated the superstitious and irrational habits of the Jews. They had protected them from hostile neighbors, affirmed their rights and privileges, guaranteed the safety of their contributions to the Temple, and accorded them the security of the empire. And what did they receive in return? The worst of all offenses from a Roman vantage-point: ingratitude. Titus' speech in the *War* puts it unequivocally:

> We authorized you to dwell in this land and we set up kings from your own people. We endorsed your ancestral laws and we allowed you to live among yourselves and to conduct dealings with others as you wished. Most important, we permitted you to exact tribute and gather offerings for your god, and we neither warned nor stood in the way of those bearing them—so that you could grow richer and use our money to prepare yourselves against us! You have enjoyed the prosperity that we made possible and the privileges that we granted only to mount an assault upon those who granted them. Like unruly reptiles you spat your venom on the very ones who catered to you.
>
> (*War* 6.333–6)

So said Titus, according to Josephus. And it rings true. Gentile historians of the Great Revolt, unnamed and unknown, also disparaged the Jews as unworthy and insignificant opponents (*War* 1.7–8). This reflects no anti-Semitism, racism, or bigotry. Instead, it resonates with shock at the gall of this ignominious and laughable people. And it conveys fury at the ingratitude of these lowly clients toward the magnanimity of their generous patrons.[33] Roman reaction to the news of rebellion in Judea did not build upon a long-simmering hostility, but sprang from a stunned disbelief, followed by a self-righteous rage at these uppity dependents who did not appreciate the benefits of the Roman empire.

Notes

1 Cicero, *In Defense of Flaccus* 66–8. For a thorough analysis of Cicero's speech and the Jews, see Levi 1942: 109–34 (Heb.); cf. Marshall 1975: 139–54; Wardy 1979: 596–613.

2 This is not the place to rehash the innumerable arguments on the propriety of labeling pagans as "anti-Semitic," a phrase unknown before the late nineteenth century. Among many other works, see Heinemann 1931: 3–43; Goldstein 1939: 346–64; Marcus 1946: 61–78; Simon 1986: 202–33; Ruether 1974: 23–63; Sevenster 1975; Daniel 1979: 45–65; Gager 1985: 13–88; de Lange 1991: 21–37; Yavetz 1993: 1–22; Feldman 1993: 123–287; Rokeah 1995: 281–94; Yavetz 1997: 17–43, 46–53, 95–114; Schäfer 1997: 34–118, 163–211.

3 Neither "monotheism" nor "polytheism" constitutes a single phenomenon, definable and identifiable. And "paganism," of course, only came into existence as a Christian concept. Cf. Beard, North, and Price 1998 I: 212, 286–7, 312. Jewish monotheism is itself problematical; cf. Hayman 1991: 1–15.

4 Tacitus, *Histories* 5.5.4: *Aegyptii pleraque animalia effigiesque compositas venerantur. Iudaei mente sola unumque numen intellegunt.* Schäfer 1997: 39–41 rightly stresses that Tacitus' comment on the Jewish god is a favorable one.

5 Seneca, *apud* Augustine, *City of God* 6.11; Plutarch, *On Stoic Selfcontradictions* 38; *On Superstition.* 69C; Quintilian, 3.7.21; Tacitus, *Histories* 2.4, 5.8.2–3, 5.13.1; *Annals* 2.85.

6 On *superstitio*, see Beard, North, and Price 1998 II, 214–27.

7 The authenticity was unsuccessfully challenged by Moehring 1975: 124–58. See Saulnier 1981: 161–95; Rajak 1984: 107–23; Pucci Ben Zeev 1994: 46–59. All the material is thoroughly treated now by Pucci Ben Zeev 1998.

8 Tacitus, *Histories* 5.4.1: *profana illic omnia quae apud nos sacra. Rursum concessa apud illos quae nobis incesta.*

9 Tacitus, *Histories* 5.5.1: *cetera instituta. sinistra foeda. pravitate valuere.*

10 Philo, *Embassy to Gaius* 330–3; *Ant.* 18.299–301. Philo's story that Caligula changed his mind once again and ordered the construction of a new statue in Jerusalem, *Embassy to Gaius* 337–8, is a dubious concoction. Nothing, in any case, came of the matter.

11 Tacitus, *Histories* 5.9.2: *iussi a C. Caesare effigiem eius in templo locare arma potius sumpsere.*

12 Tacitus, *Histories* 5.9.3–5.10.1: *duravit tamen patientia Iudaeis usque ad Gessium Florinum procuratorem.*

13 Tacitus, *Histories* 5.13.3: *Multitudinem obsessorum omnis aetatis. virile ac muliebre secus. sexcenta milia fuisse accepimus: arma cunctis. qui ferre possent. et plures guam pro*

numero audebant. Obstinatio viris feminisque par ac si transferre sedes coaerentur. maior vitae metus guam molts.

14 Juvenal, 14.100–2: *Romanas autem soliti contemnere leges/ Iudaicum ediscunt et servant ac metuunt ius./ tradidit arcano guodcumque volumine Moyses.*

15 The argument of Rosen 1996: 107–26, that Tacitus feared a resumption of Jewish hostilities on the basis of anti-Roman prophecies, is highly improbable.

16 See, e.g., Hecataeus of Abdera, apud Diodorus 40.3.4; Manetho, apud Josephus *Ap.* 1.239; Posidonius, apud Diodorus 34/5.1–3; Apollonius Molon, apud Josephus *Ap.* 2.148.

17 On Jewish isolationism, see Sevenster 1975: 89–119. On its perception as misanthropy and Jewish responses, see Feldman 1993: 125–53.

18 The strongest advocate for Jewish missionary activity is Feldman, who has made the case repeatedly and with powerful argumentation. See, e.g., Feldman 1992a: 24–37; Feldman 1992b: 372–408; Feldman 1993: 288–341, with valuable earlier bibliography at 553–4. But an increasing number of scholars have taken up the cudgels on the other side: e.g. McKnight 1991: 11–77; Will and Orrieux 1992: *passim*; Cohen 1992: 14–23; Goodman 1992: 53–78; Goodman 1994: 60–90; Rutgers 1995: 363–70. The position of Schäfer (1997: 106–18, 183–92) seems curiously inconsistent.

19 Seneca, apud Augustine *City of God* 6.11: *cum interim usgue eo sceleratissimae gentis consuetudo convaluit. ut per omnes iam terras recepta sit: victi victoribus leges dederunt*

20 Seneca apud Augustine City of God 6.11: *multa in tempore urgentia non agendo laedantur.*

21 Tacitus, *Histories* 5.5.3: *hinc generandi amor et moriendi contemptus.*

22 On the economic situation of Jews in the Hellenistic and Roman periods, see the useful collection of material and discussion by Sevenster 1975: 57–88; Applebaum 1987: 701–27. The argument of Feldman (1993: 107–13) that references to Jewish beggary are ironic, signifying that Jews were actually envied for their wealth, is hard to credit.

23 Tacitus, *Histories* 5.5.5: *quippe Liber festos laetosque ritus posuit. Iudaeorum mos absurdus sordidusque.*

24 Agatharchides apud Josephus *Ap.* 1.209–10 and *Ant.* 12.5–6; Dio 37.16.1–4; Strabo 16.2.40; Frontinus *Stratagems* 2.1.17; cf. Plutarch *On Superstition* 8.169C. On the vexed question of whether Jews would fight on the Sabbath, see Goldenberg 1979: 430–3; Bar-Kochva 1989: 474–93.

25 Seneca apud Augustine City of God 6.11: *septimam fere partem aetatis suae perdant vacando.*

26 Seneca *Letters on Morality* 95.47: *nec lumine dii egent et ne homines quidem delectantur fulgine.*

27 Pliny *Natural History* 31.24: *In Judaea rivus sabbatis omnibus siccatur.*

28 Macrobius *Saturnalia* 2.4.11: *melius est Herodis porcum esse guam filium.* In all likelihood, Augustus made the gag in Greek, where he could pun on the words *huios* (son) and *hus* (pig).

29 Petronius, fr. 37 (Ernout): *numen porcinum.*

30 Juvenal 6.159–60: *et vetus indulget senibus dementia porcis.* Cf. 14.98–99; Schafer 1997: 77–8 1, correctly observes the absence of polemic in the satirists' comments.

31 *Banquet Debates* 4.5.3. The arguments are taken perhaps too seriously by Schäfer 1997: 72–4, 77.

32 Tacitus *Histories* 5.5.2: *circumcidere genitalia instituerunt. ut diversitate noscantur.*

33 Tacitus *Histories* 10.2: *Pace per Italiam parta et externae curae rediere: augebat iras. uuod soli Iudaei non cessissent.*

Bibliography

Applebaum, S. (1987) "The Social and Economic Status of the Jews in the Diaspora," in S. Safrai and M. Stern (eds.) *The Jewish People in the First Century*, vol. II, Philadelphia: Fortress.

Bar-Kochva, B. (1989) *Judas Maecabaeus*, Cambridge: Cambridge University Press.

Beard, M., North, J. and Price, S. (1998) *Religions of Rome*, 2 vols., Cambridge: Cambridge University Press.

Cohen, S. J. D. (1992) 'Was Judaism in Antiquity a Missionary Religion?', in M. Mor (ed.) *Jewish Assimilation. Acculturation. and Accommodation*, Lanham, MD: University Press of America.

Daniel, J. L. (1979) "Anti-Semitism in the Hellenistic-Roman Period," *Journal of Biblical Literature* 98: 45–65.

Feldman, L. H. (1986) 'Anti-Semitism in the Ancient World', in D. Berger (ed.) *History and Hate: The Dimensions of Anti-Semitism*, Philadelphia: Jewish Publication Society.

—— (1992a) "Was Judaism a Missionary Religion in Ancient Times?" in M. Mor (ed.) *Jewish Assimilation. Acculturation, and Accommodation*, Lanham, MD: University Press of America.

—— (1992b) "Jewish Proselytism," in H. W. Attridge and O. Hata (eds.) *Eusebius. Christianity. and Judaism*, Detroit: Wayne State University Press.

—— (1993) *Jew and Gentile in the Ancient World*, Princeton: Princeton University Press.

—— (1997) "Reflections on Jews in Greco-Roman Literature," *Journal for the Study of the Pseudepigrapha* 16: 39–52.

Gager, J. G. (1985) *The Origins of Anti-Semitism*, Oxford: Oxford University Press.

Goldenberg, R. (1979) "The Jewish Sabbath in the Roman World," *Aufstieg und Niedergang derrömischen Welt* 11.19.1: 414–47.

Goldstein, N. W. (1939) "Cultivated Pagans and Ancient Anti-Semitism," *Journal of Religion* 19: 346–64.

Goodman, M. (1987) *The Ruling Class of Judaea*, Cambridge: Cambridge University Press.

—— (1992) "Jewish Proselytizing in the First Century," in J. Lieu, J. North, and T. Rajak (eds.) *Jews among Pagans and Christians in the Roman Empire*. London: Routledge.

—— (1994) *Mission and Conversion: Proselytizing in the Religious History of the Roman Empire*, Oxford: Oxford University Press.

Hayman, P. (1991) "Monotheism—Misused Word in Jewish Studies?" *Journal of Jewish Studies* 42: 1–15.

Heinemann, I. (1931) "Antisemitismus," *Real Encyclopadie der klassischen Altertums-wissenschaft* Supplementband V: 3–43

Lange, N. de (1991) "The Origins of Anti-Semitism: Ancient Evidence and Modern Interpretations," in S.L. Oilman and S.T. Katz (eds.) *Anti-Semitism in Times of Crisis*, New York: New York University Press.

Levi, Y. (1942) "Cicero on the Jews," *Zion* 7: 109–34 (Heb.).

Marcus, R. (1946) "Anti-Semitism in the Hellenistic-Roman World," in K. S. Pinson (ed.) *Essays on Anti-Semitism*, New York: Conference on Jewish Relations.

Marshall, A. J. (1975) "Flaccus and the Jews of Asia (Cicero, *Pro Flacco* 28.67–9)," *Phoenix* 29: 139–54.

McKnight, S. (1991) *A Light Among the Gentiles: Jewish Missionary Activity in the Second Temple Period*. Minneapolis: Fortress Press.

Moehring, H. R. (1975) "The *Acta Pro Judaeis* in the *Antiquitates* of Flavius Josephus," in J. Neusner (ed.) *Christianity, Judaism, and Other Greco-Roman Cults*, Leiden: E. J. Brill.

Pucci Ben Zeev, M. (1994) "Greek and Roman Documents from Republican Times in the *Antiquities*," *Scripta Classica Israelica* 13: 46–59.

—— (1998) *Jewish Rights in the Roman World: The Greek and Roman Documents Quoted by Flavius Josephus*, Tubingen: Mohr.

Rajak, T. (1984) "Was there a Roman Charter for the Jews?" *Journal of Roman Studies* 74: 107–23.

Rokeah, D. (1995) "Tacitus and Ancient Anti-Semitism," *Revue des Etudes Juives* 154: 281–94.

Rosen, K. (1996) "Der Historiker als Prophet: Tacitus und die Juden," *Gymnasium* 103: 107–26.

Ruether, R. (1974) *Faith and Fratricide: The Theological Roots of Anti-Semitism*, New York: Seabury Press.

Rutgers, L. V. (1995) "Attitudes to Judaism in the Greco-Roman Period: Reflections on Feldman's *Jew and Gentile in the Ancient World*," *Jewish Quarterly Review* 85: 361–95.

Saulnier, C. (1981) "Lois romaines sur les juifs selon Flavius Josèphe," *Revue Biblique* 88: 161–95.

Schäfer, P. (1997) *Judeophobia: Attitudes toward the Jews in the Ancient World*, Cambridge, MA: Harvard University Press.

Sevenster, J. (1975) *The Roots of Pagan Anti-Semitism in the Ancient World*, Leiden: E. J. Brill.

Simon, M. (1986, first published 1964) *Verus Israel*, Oxford: Oxford University Press.

Wardy, B. (1979) "Jewish Religion in Pagan Literature during the Late Republic and Early Empire," *Aufstieg und Niedergang der römischen Welt* 11.19.1: 592–644.

Will, E. and Orrieux, C. (1992) "Proselytisme juif?" Paris: Les Belles Lettres.

Yavetz, Z. (1993) "Judeophobia in Classical Antiquity," *Journal of Jewish Studies* 44: 1–22.

—— (1997) *Judenfeindschaft in der Antike*, Munich: C. H. Beck.

—— (1998) "Latin Authors on Jews and Dacians," *Historia* 47: 77–107.

3 The Revolt from a regional perspective

Sean Freyne

In a recent study of Josephus, James McLaren, writing about the Jewish Revolt, makes the following statement: "Scholars have constructed their accounts entirely within the boundaries set by Josephus in *War* 2 and *Ant.* 18–20. As such they reinforce the extent to which scholarship, allegedly critical of Josephus and conceptually independent, parallels the description of affairs provided by him" (McLaren 1998: 207). In this chapter I would like to respond to the implicit challenge that McLaren poses, namely, to examine the events that occurred in Judea in the first century C.E. within a framework different to that provided by Josephus, thereby hopefully also providing a different perspective. The horizon I wish to explore, namely that of regionalism, asks whether it might be possible to understand the events of 66–70 and the disturbances leading up to them as being regional in character, having more to do with local factors than as part of a single plot, dating back to Antiochus Epiphanes, the point where Josephus, in the *War*, begins his narrative.

In the preface to *Jewish War* Josephus introduces his topic as follows: "The war of the Jews against the Romans—the greatest not only of the wars of our own time, but, so far as accounts have reached us, well nigh of all that ever broke out between cities and nations." While one can readily detect the rhetorical flourish here in the interests of nationalistic propaganda, it also points clearly to Josephus's own overall perspective on the events he is about to describe. For him it is a war of the *Jews/Ioudaioi*, which in this context at least cannot be reduced to "Judean" in the narrow geographical sense (Horsley 1995). Since the controlling perspective is that of the destruction of the Jerusalem temple, the term "the war of the Jews" includes all those who were prepared to fight on behalf of the distinctive Jewish way of life, expressed in the laws, customs and practices of those who worshiped at the Jerusalem temple, irrespective of where they actually lived (Freyne 1999). Galilee, Idumea, and Perea, as well as Judea in the narrower sense, all participate in the events narrated. Thus, the geographic spread is coextensive with the traditional Jewish territory as recognized in Pompey's division of the Hasmonean state over 100 years earlier. Josephus's account of the action taken by the provisional government after the defeat of Cestius Gallus in appointing generals, including himself, to take charge of the revolt in different regions is a clear indication of this regional horizon. As well as his own appointment to Galilee, others were appointed to Idumea, Jericho, Perea, and various districts of Judea itself, he claims (*War* 2: 566–8). Elsewhere in *War* as well as in his later work *Antiquities* he again makes it clear that the inhabitants of these regions—Galileans, Idumeans, and Pereans—could all be designated *Ioudaioi* insofar as they were found at Jerusalem defending the distinctive Jewish way of life in the face of Roman provocation on the occasion of a Jewish festival (*War* 2: 232; *Ant.* 17: 254–68).

At the same time Josephus does continue to use regional designations such as Galileans and Idumeans in his descriptions of the course of events, thereby at least suggesting certain elements of local concern and coloring as factors in the unfolding events. While social, cultural, and religious factors have been put forward by various scholars as part of a complex set of causes that modern scholarship has proposed to explain the Revolt, very little attention has been paid to the ways in which these might have played themselves out rather differently in the various regions. This is a curious omission in the treatment of the Revolt in view of the fact that regional variations are increasingly prominent in the more general construals of Second Temple history, as the extraordinary interest in Hellenistic and Roman Galilee over the past twenty years demonstrates. In what follows I propose to look briefly at the ways in which these variations might have manifested themselves in two outlying regions, namely Galilee and Idumea, partly because we are better informed about these regions than about Perea, for example, but partly also because of the suspicion that other more centripetal forces may have been at work in each, even though some Idumeans and Galileans are to be found in Jerusalem for the final showdown with Rome (*War* 4: 274–558). In the interests of conciseness, I will deal comparatively with both regions under certain headings relating to the main causes for the Revolt, suggested by various scholars. These topics are: Roman administration and Jewish dissatisfaction; hostile relations with the Greco–Roman cities and Jewish religious sensitivities; and social conditions, banditry and the presence of local strongmen.

Idumea and Galilee: some regional contrasts

The fact that both regions had featured prominently in the Hasmonean expansions makes a comparison between them in the Roman period all the more interesting. According to Josephus both the Idumeans in the south and the Itureans in the north were given the option of accepting circumcision, thereby joining the emerging Jewish nation, or departing their respective territories. While Kasher (1988) in particular has attempted to build a conciliatory picture of Jewish–Arab relations in both regions, his case may be weakened by the fact that, whereas the Idumeans retained their ethnic name, the inhabitants of Galilee are never subsequently called Itureans. Despite the reality that Galileans and Idumeans are both to be found in Jerusalem at the climax of the Revolt, I will argue that the evidence, when viewed through a regional lens, would seem to present rather different profiles with regard to the so-called causes of the war.

Roman administration and Jewish dissatisfaction

Martin Goodman (1987) has conveniently summarized the evidence under this heading: lack of sensitivity in terms of Jewish religious observances; low status of the appointed governors, evidenced by the right of the legate of Syria to interfere in Jewish affairs; Roman brutality in dealing with Jewish disturbances, possibly fuelled by anti-Jewish attitudes generally; and a long-lasting sense of the oppressive nature of Roman rule felt in certain Jewish circles, dating back to Pompey's intervention (though now on Roman attitudes see Chapter 2 by Gruen, in this volume; editor's note). How long did these factors apply in the different regions, were they likely to have been experienced similarly in both, and how might local circumstances have mediated their worst features?

As far as Galilee was concerned direct Roman rule was imposed only after the death of Agrippa I in 44 C.E. Yet over the next twenty years it would appear that Rome felt the need to take special measures to deal with the region, even though Josephus's accounts in both *War* and *Life* betray little direct evidence of that presence. Tacitus suggests that a special envoy, Cumanus, was charged with control of Galilee, whereas Felix was appointed over Samaria after the Galilean/Samaritan disturbances in the reign of Claudius *(Ann.* 12.24). This measure was followed up in 54 C.E. by the establishment of Ptolemais as a *colonia* on the borders of Galilee, a decision often associated with the pacification and control of some troublesome region. While there is no evidence of colonists being settled in the interior of Galilee, as had happened in the Lebanon, when Berytus was established in the reign of Augustus (Millar 1987: 267–85), the change of status for Ptolemais certainly meant that it would play an important role in Rome's policing of Galilee, as in fact happened more than once subsequently (*War* 2.503 under Cestius Gallus; *Life* 213f. under Placidus; *War* 3.29–34 under Vespasian). This perception was further strengthened by Nero's decision to bequeath Tiberias and Tarichaeae with their territories on the western shore of the lake to Agrippa II, a circumstance that did not please Justus or other members of the Tiberian aristocracy *(Life* 38). In short, any independent-minded Galilean must surely have had a much greater sense of the Roman noose tightening considerably in the 60s, a circumstance that undoubtedly is reflected both in the pacific stance of Sepphoris and the harsh Roman treatment of those places that did hold out against them.

Idumea on the other hand had been under direct Roman rule since the deposition of Archelaus in 6 C.E. (*War* 2.96, 3.55). Given the fact that Herod and his family were Idumeans, the direct transfer of power to Rome might be deemed to have been a distinct disadvantage to the region. However, the evidence suggests otherwise. Both during Herod's reign and on his death, opposition to his rule emerged within Idumea, opposition that appears to have had quite diverse components, ranging from support for the Hasmoneans, to an appeal to ancestral Idumean values, to social discontent by his veterans due to the high tax demands that had been made on them (*Ant.* 14.273–93, 15.294; *War* 2.55–78). On this evidence the situation in Idumea in terms of ethnic mix and cultural affiliation was by no means uniform, and Roman provincial rule may well have been seen as the lesser of two evils by at least some of the population. Varus' treatment of the disturbances that occurred on the death of Herod would appear to have been much more even-handed than what was meted out to other places. Sepphoris, for example, was razed and its inhabitants sold into slavery, but in Idumea he accepted the surrender of the majority and sent the leaders to Rome, where all were freed except for a few of the ringleaders who were themselves Herodians (*War* 2.66–79). Josephus's account of Vespasian's handling of Idumea as he rounded on Jerusalem is presented as part of a general strategy in dealing with the various districts to which the provisional government had sent commanders, and is therefore a highly schematic account, intended to match his earlier version of the appointment of the generals (*War* 2.566–8, 4.447–8). While two villages were destroyed and garrisons installed, there is little circumstantial detail, in contrast to the narrative of the Galilean campaign.

When all due allowances are made for Josephus's motive for glorifying the earlier situation when he himself was in charge, it would seem that there were considerable differences with regard to the two regions' experience of the Roman presence, both prior to and during the Revolt. Galilee's northerly location meant that any advance of the legions from Syria reached its borders first, and it had to bear the brunt of the Roman offensive, stung by the reverses suffered by Cestius Gallus. The special administrative arrangements that Rome had put in place in the north prior to the Revolt need to be judged in the light of their use of client kings, colonies, and direct administration in dealing with the whole troublesome region of southern Syria in the previous half century. Galilee was not immune from these suspicions. We should also take into account the change in strategy on the part of Vespasian, alluded to by Josephus from the beginning of 68 C.E. This may explain why the southern countryside seems to have fared rather better at the hands of the Romans, with the obvious exception of such strongholds as Masada and Machaerus. Perhaps the fact that the Judean rather than the Galilean countryside was the theatre of the Second Revolt in 132–5 C.E. is the best indication that this suggested contrast in Rome's treatment of the respective regions during the First Revolt is the correct one. The significance of this for our original hypothesis must await final evaluation in the light of the other "causes."

Hostile relations with Greco-Roman cities

The situation of hostility that existed between the Jewish population of Palestine and the surrounding "Greek" cities has been highlighted in particular by Uriel Rappaport, who sees this as the single issue that made the Revolt inevitable, given Rome's inability or unwillingness to deal with it (Rappaport 1981). Goodman on the other hand deals with these events in the more general context of the "bickerings of Jews and gentiles" leading to "occasional urban violence." The fact that prior to the Revolt Jews chose to dwell in these cities suggests to him that the atmosphere was not one of deep hostility, but that rather "the inter-communal violence of 66 may have been the consequence rather than the cause of the revolt" (Goodman 1987: 6–7). The immediate task here is not to adjudicate finally between these different readings of the situation but to see whether the particular outbursts of 66 may have played themselves out differently in the two regions.

A comparison of Josephus's list of the places where attacks by the Jews took place and those where Gentile reprisals occurred is quite revealing (*War* 2.457–60 and 477–80). The Jewish attacks were sparked off by the slaughter of their coreligionists in Caesarea Maritima, with the active assistance of the procurator, Florus, and they replied by reprisals on the territories of the surrounding cities. The list of the places attacked follows a definite geographic plan, beginning in Perea and the Decapolis, then moving north to encircle Galilee, before coming south again to follow the coast as far as Gaza. It is difficult to avoid the suspicion that this list is a literary figment, possibly on the basis on the Maccabean–Hasmonean attacks on "the nations round about," as described in 1 Macc. (Schwartz, 1991). In the subsequent account of the Gentile attacks on the Jews, the theatre of action shifts primarily to Syria, with Ashkelon the only southern city mentioned, while in Perea the kindness of Jerash to its Jewish inhabitants is surely contrived if, as Josephus had earlier reported, they themselves had been previously attacked by Jews.

Rappaport seeks to relate these mutual animosities to the Hasmonean treatment of the Greek cities, and, as we have suggested, the account may well have been based on the geography of the Maccabean "reclaiming of the land," as portrayed in 1 Macc. But the evidence can scarcely carry the weight he wants to place on it in terms of this being the sole cause for the inevitability of the Revolt. Scythopolis was one of the places that had suffered most at the hands of the Hasmoneans yet, as Goodman has noted, Jews had freely settled there and apparently participated in the life of the city. The problems should instead be seen in relation to the events of the Roman period. It is noteworthy that Caesarea, as the official residence of the procurator and boasting a temple to Roma and Augustus, was indirectly associated with Roman intolerance of Jewish religious attitudes during the procuratorship of Pilate (*War* 2.169–77). As reported by Josephus, there was a decidedly religious element to other disturbances that happened in Caesarea, also under

Florus, when Jews gathering to their synagogue for prayer were insulted by a Gentile citizen, offering a bird sacrifice outside the building (*War* 2.289–92). This episode was the culmination of feuding between Jews and Greeks over control of Caesarea, the former claiming that it was a Jewish city since it had been founded by their king, and the latter pointing to the pagan statues and temples that he had erected there, plainly indicating that he had intended the city for them (*War* 2.266). Significantly for the discussion of anti-Jewish sentiment in the region generally, Josephus in this context mentions that the Syrian mercenaries in the army of the procurator supported the Greeks, "always ready to support their compatriots" *(suggeneis: War* 2.268). Clearly "Greek" for him means non-Jew, and the Syrian mercenaries fall into that category also.

Philo as well as Josephus informs us of similar anti-Jewish attitudes in Alexandria, and these merely reflected the situation in Rome itself in the early imperial period, expressed by such writers as Cicero, Tacitus and Juvenal (Schäfer 1997; see also Chapter 2 by Gruen in this volume). This Roman anti-Jewish attitude was therefore a new element in the explosive ethnic mix in Palestine in the first century, with the arrival of the procurators and direct Roman rule. Herod's attitudes had been less abrasive in that regard it would seem, despite his patronage in the non-Jewish cities. As is clear from the episode in Caesarea, it is virtually impossible to decide the precise ethnicity of those whom Josephus calls Syrians, just as he cannot have meant native Macedonians in speaking of the Greeks in that city. Nevertheless, the mention of Syria as the place from which these anti-Jewish attacks originated rings true, and in that regard Galilee more than Idumea may have been particularly vulnerable. It was contiguous with the Roman province of Syria and therefore constantly open to attacks, particularly on the northern boundary, as the hostilities involving Tyrian Kedesh and Gischala illustrate (*War* 4.105; *Life* 44–5). The demarcation line between Jewish and non-Jewish settlements has been clearly identified on archaeological grounds in this region (Aviam 1993), and there, if anywhere, one would have expected to encounter the kind of animosities that Josephus refers to, especially in view of the history of such disputes, dating back to the young Herod's dealing with Ezechias the *archilestes* (to the relief of the inhabitants of Syria), and later the incursions into Galilee of Marion, the tyrant of Tyre (*Ant.* 14.159, 297–9; see also Chapter 4 by Berlin in this volume for discussion of these events).

We should not therefore uncritically accept Josephus's picture of general anti-Jewish attitudes, but attempt to assess these in the light of other evidence as well as acknowledging Josephan motifs and biases in his portrayal of events. Here McLaren's comments on the selectively critical usage of Josephus by many scholars are apposite. Even in the most desperate situations boundaries are porous and always changing, as a moment's reflection of every troublespot in our own world will testify. Thus, we find Jews in Caesarea Philippi troubled about kosher oil, admittedly within an Herodian setting, even if the city itself was strongly Roman in its allegiance, as Titus' visit there on his triumphant return from Jerusalem suggests. Trade with Tyre must also be postulated—John was using Tyrian coinage in his dealings with the Jews of Syria at the height of the troubles—but clearly there were limits to the tolerance to be shown at any given time and motives were often mixed, "the action of each (Syrian city) being governed by their feelings of hatred or fear of their Jewish neighbors" (*War* 2.478; on Tyrian–Galilean trade, see now Avshalom-Gorni and Getzov in this volume). In this regard it is interesting that he notes the tolerance of those Syrian cities more removed from the scene of the conflict—Antioch, Sidon and Apamea—who refused to imprison or kill a single Jew. Tyre also chose to imprison rather than kill many of its Jewish inhabitants.

What of Idumean Jewish involvement in these hostilities? Marisa's influence as a center of Greco–Sidonian influences for the early Hellenistic period had suffered at the hands of the Hasmoneans, and it was not restored after its destruction by the Parthians in 40 B.C.E. (*Ant.* 14.364). It is difficult to believe that all Greek influence was thereby removed, especially in view of the strong Ptolemaic administrative presence in the region as a whole earlier, to which the Zenon papyri testify. However, the efforts of Costobar to revive the worship of the Idumean god *Qos* (*Koze*) in his opposition to Herod (*Ant.* 15.253) must have been based on the hope that traditional, non-Jewish beliefs could still win support, presumably with the rural population. In addition it may point to a Nabatean connection, since a dedicatory inscription in Nabatean from their shrine at Khirbet Tannur honors this god, and an altar at the site of ancient Mamre in Idumea itself is inscribed with the name *Qos* also. Other hints of the survival into Roman times of older, pre-Jewish Idumeans may be found in the repeated name Baba, as in sons of Baba in *Antiquities*, whom Costobar protected against Herod, and Babatha/Babata on inscriptions from Marisa and in the Judean papyri cache (Ronen in Kasher 1988: 215). While this evidence, scattered and partial though it is, opens up interesting vistas of separate ethnicity having been retained by some Idumeans, at least until Herodian times, it must be said that Costobar's revolt does not appear to have had any after-life in the region, nor is there any evidence of anti-Jewish attitudes among the Nabateans, certainly not on religious grounds.

It is in the coastal cities of Gaza and Ashkelon that the pattern we have seen for Galilee recurs. While Gaza may have been added by Josephus to his list of Greek cities in Palestine attacked by Jews, for the sake of completion of the full circle, there would appear to be more substance to the animosities between the Idumean Jews and Ashkelon, since Josephus has a separate account, independent of his list of named places, of an Idumean attack on this city following the retreat of Cestius Gallus (*War* 3.13–28). The report is quite circumstantial, particularly in terms of its leaders, consisting of Niger, the Perean, whom we hear of elsewhere as the governor of Idumea (*War* 2.520, 566), Silas, a Babylonian Jew who had deserted from the army of Agrippa II to join the Jewish rebels, and John the Essene. The same three had previously been mentioned for their deeds of bravery in repulsing Cestius Gallus from Jerusalem and now they are to be found in the account of the attack on Ashkelon. Niger's role is particularly significant in this regard, since, though governor of Idumea, he appears to have operated in Jerusalem, anticipating his fellow Idumeans later, yet he was bypassed by the provisional government when they appointed two Jerusalem priestly aristo-crats to the control of that region (*War* 2.566). In explaining why Ashkelon was a special target for the Jews, elated by their success at the retreat of Cestius, Josephus mentions the Jewish hatred for this ancient city, but does not give any specific reason for this. It may be explained, partially at least by the strong Herodian attachment to the city, as has been recently argued in great detail from literary, epigraphic and numismatic evidence (Kokkinos 1998: 112–39). Even earlier still, Ashkelon was one of the Phoenician cities where the decrees of Caesar in favour of the Jews were to be posted, indicating that perhaps their rights had been significantly infringed there (*Ant.* 14.197).

The links of the Idumean Herodians with Ashkelon coupled with Josephus's account of the attack lead by Niger can throw helpful light on the nature of the Idumean Jews who were to make Jerusalem the center of their operations during the later stages of the Revolt. Clearly, there were several different strands even among the Jewish population there. It would not be uncharacteristic for those who, for whatever reason, had made an option for Judaism to have become ardent supporters of the very Jerusalem priestly aristocracy that had given them that option in the first place. Not all accepted the offer, we know, since many Idumeans appear in Egypt at precisely that time, presumably choosing the other option of leaving rather than undergoing circumcision (Rappaport 1969). The Herodians on the other hand must have originated in the Hellenised Idumean aristocracy that was associated with Marisa, and later with Ashkelon on the coast, and they were stoutly opposed by the country Idumean Jews, who were happy to see Marisa destroyed by the Parthians in their support of the last of the Hasmoneans. Such a scenario is certainly not implausible, but it would throw a very different light on the Idumean Jewish experience of hostility from the "Greek" cities than was the case in Galilee. In the one instance the hostility had ethnic roots in Syrian opposition to the Jews of Galilee, whereas on the other the animosity had more to do with social and cultural factors that were local to Idumea and its population of mixed background.

Social conditions, banditry, and the presence of local strongmen

In many recent studies of Judean society of the Second Temple period the emphasis has been on economic and social factors rather than political and religious ones. Inevitably these have been suggested as the real cause of the Revolt, most notably in the study of Heinz Kreissig from the Marxist perspective of a class struggle within Jewish society (1970). Certainly,

Josephus's account would support the view that social factors played an important part in various disturbances in Palestine throughout the Roman period. In a possibly later reflection on the Revolt Josephus, summing up the roles different actors played in the tragic drama writes: "Those in power oppressed the masses, and the masses were eager to destroy the powerful" (*War* 7.260). The burning of the debt registers in Jerusalem by the *sicarii* is usually taken as indicative of the importance of socio-economic factors in the Revolt, especially in view of the fact that on the same occasion they also burned the houses of the high priests and the Herodian palace in the city (*War* 2.427). Archaeological evidence from Jerusalem confirms the opulence of the priestly ruling class, and we also hear of the destitute class in Tiberias, aided by some Galileans, destroying the Herodian palace in Tiberias also with its luxurious fittings *(Life* 66).

The causes for these deep divisions in Jewish society were manifold, and certainly cannot be laid at the door of the Romans alone. Some Jews had benefited greatly from the increased opportunities of the Hellenistic age, thus creating a wider social gap than had existed at any other period previously. The Roman period, especially the reign of Herod the Great, must have exacerbated the situation further between rich and poor, despite Herod's occasional acts of munificence on behalf of the populace. In a previous study relating to Galilee, I have suggested that it is possible to posit the conditions for rapid economic change within first-century Palestine, namely a convergence of changes in the market, the modes of exchange, and the underlying values within the society (Freyne 1995). These changes did not benefit all equally, as the process of moving from a subsistence to a market economy created opportunities for some and penury for others, depending on one's situation within the various networks of power and privilege. Many of the factors that brought about these changes were politically controlled, and therefore designed to benefit the aristocratic and ruling elites. Land remained the primary resource, but it was in increasingly short supply, partly because of the increase in population as well as enforced appropriation because of debt, war, or other demands. Other factors were unpredictable, such as drought or plague, and for those within the subsistence bracket, failure of one season's crops led to debt and eventual loss of family holdings. Brigandage, begging, or day-labour then became the only options (*Ant.* 18.224, 20. 219–20).

These conclusions are not dissimilar to the description of Galilean social conditions put forward by Seth Schwartz (Schwartz 1994). He believes that a breakdown in the patronage system, so characteristic of the Mediterranean rural world generally, began to occur in Galilee with the rise of the cities of Sepphoris and Tiberias, modest though these places were in comparison with Herod the Great's achievements in Jerusalem, Caesarea, and elsewhere. A new elite of absentee landlords emerged who had little interest in maintaining a balance between the rulers and the ruled, and this showed itself in the hatred of the Galilean village population for places like Sepphoris, reflected in Josephus's *Life* account. There were some notable exceptions such as John of Gischala, for example, who was able to act in the patron role for peasants in his native area, and *hoi en telei* and *hoi dynatoi* among the Galileans who exhibited a patronal relationship in their dealings with the peasants. The cities were an intrusion on this social landscape, leading to breakdown of social networks and the slide into brigandage. Thus, according to Schwarz, first-century Galilee presented "the conditions that were *in part* favorable for revolt."

What of Idumea? Schwartz maintains that conditions in Galilee were not as dire as elsewhere in the country, since the Galilean social system was still functioning and the number of Galileans finally devoted to the Revolt was not very large. On these criteria, especially involvement in the final defence of Jerusalem, Idumea would have been in a much greater state of turmoil. However, the situation does not appear to have been so clear-cut. Undoubtedly, the Revolt against Rome became closely entwined in the social revolution within Judean society, and it may well be in Josephus's interest to paint such a picture. In reality, however, there are two separate issues here, one dealing with the socio-economic conditions obtaining in Roman Palestine and the factors that brought those about, and the other to do with Jewish aspirations to be free of the Roman yoke. Certainly they are related issues, especially insofar as those social conditions were themselves the result of Roman fiscal policy and the demands made by the Herodians on the populace, in order to be able to flatter their Roman patrons. Yet they are separable issues and should be seen separately, as Schwartz himself observes at the outset of his article, declaring that the changes in the socio-economic system do not explain the outbreak of the Revolt, but rather, form an essential background for it.

There seems to be no good reason for thinking that the social system of Idumea was in any greater disarray than that in Galilee. Schwartz thinks that perhaps the fact that Roman rule had come earlier to Judea meant that their was a greater drainage of wealth from the province than was the case in Galilee (Schwartz 1994: 300). Yet this surely minimizes the demands that Herodian activities made on the people generally, especially the building costs. The revolt of Herod's veterans in Idumea on his death should presumably be seen in the light of the more general protests about the taxes he had imposed, thereby impoverishing the nation (*War* 2.55; cf. 2.48 and following). The picture of Idumean economic life that can be gleaned from the Zenon papyri shows that it was an important area in terms of Ptolemaic exploitation of Palestinian resources, and the general productivity of the region was not likely to have been diminished subsequently. Sidonian colonies at both Yavneh Yam and Marisa, dating from the Ptolemaic period, are a further indication of the commercial importance of the region (Isaac 1991). Even if eastern Idumea by the shores of the Dead Sea could not match the fertility of Galilee and its lake district, it nevertheless was rich in such exportable materials as bitumen, balsam, and dates, all of which are mentioned in the sources (Kokkinos 1998: 54–9). The Babatha archive gives an interesting insight into agricultural life in the region in the early second century C.E., and the picture is that of a relatively affluent environment, consisting of freeholding and crown properties side by side, involved in production and sale of various items such as olives, dates, and barley (Isaac 1992; Broshi 1992). On the coastal plain to the west the larger, Hellenistic-style estates were to be found, and these would have passed into Herodian hands from the previous rulers. On the basis of this evidence, therefore, I see no good reason to distinguish sharply between Galilee and Idumea in terms of the relative functioning of the economic system in the first century.

There is, however, one aspect under which the regions appear to differ, namely, the prevalence of banditry in Galilee, which Josephus mentions more than once. Much has been written on these *lestai*, particularly Richard Horsley's several articles, inspired by Eric Hobsbawm's model of social banditry (Horsley 1981; Horsley and Hanson 1985). However, this rather schematic model does not seem to fit all the instances of Galilean brigandage mentioned by Josephus, especially the claims that the brigands maintained close links with the peasants, assisting them in their struggles in a pre-revolutionary mode (Freyne 1988). In fact Josephus claims to have been able to do a deal with the bandits in upper Galilee on his arrival in the province, and on another occasion Jesus and his robber gang are prepared to assist the people of Sepphoris (*Life* 77–9, 105 and following). The other incidents might equally be examined in terms of how well they fit the proposed model. The question remains as to why Galilee would appear to have been the theatre for many of the incidents of brigandage that Josephus reports. These occurred not just during the immediate pre-Revolt period, but dating back to the young Herod's encounter with the *archilestes* Hezekiah, operating on the Syrian border. By contrast we do not hear of any acts of brigandage in Idumea, unless we include them in Josephus's generalized remarks about "the whole country being infested with brigands," often repeated throughout both *War* and *Antiquities* (Hengel 1961: 41–6; Rhoads 1976: 159–62; Shaw 1993: 204).

Perhaps it is merely a matter of perception, based on Josephus's desire to demonstrate the difficulties he encountered in Galilee. On the other hand the suggestion of Brent Shaw that this phenomenon, especially when it is associated with named leaders, must be seen within the context of power relations as these functioned in the east, where the institutional power of the state had often to take second place to and rely on personal power of certain local "big men" in order to maintain control of the region. In this regard, Shaw claims the Near East differed from the Greek city states where personal power had been co-opted in the service of the institution through the network of patron–client relationships that controlled the whole system. Roman policy in the east was to attempt the suppression of such centres of personal power, especially through the imposition of the provincial system with all the burdens that this entailed locally. Was this perhaps one of the reasons why bandit leaders and their gangs began to emerge in Judea throughout the first century, and in particular in the immediate pre-Revolt period in Galilee, just as the Roman noose began to tighten in the region?

Conclusion

For purposes of the argument of this chapter I have remained in the regions, never once visiting Jerusalem, since the perspective I wanted to explore was that of the periphery and how things might have looked for Jews living there, as distinct from those at the center, in terms of an encounter with Rome. What else might have been on their minds besides plans for a grand Revolt against Roman imperialism? To what extent were they likely to have felt that these local concerns were shared with other regions and therefore constituted a common cause for the Revolt? Or is it possible to talk with Seth Schwartz of a Judean war, a Galilean war, an Idumean war, and a Perean war? It seemed possible to show that some of the factors commonly put forward as "causes for the Jewish War" following Josephus would have played themselves out rather differently in the two regions that we have chosen to explore. It must be freely admitted that this perception, like so much else of our views of Roman Palestine, may have been due to Josephus's coloring of the various pictures he paints in his different works. Perhaps it is impossible after all to escape entirely from Josephus's clutches, *pace* McLaren, and it may in fact be both unnecessary and unwarranted to seek to do so.

When Idumeans flocked to Jerusalem to join the zealots in liberating the city, one of their leaders, Simon, is made by Josephus to use the language of kinship to complain about being excluded by those in control of the city, as Martin Goodman notes (*War* 2.478). The same Josephus chides the Sepphorites for their lack of *homophia* in not supporting the temple "that was common to us all" (*Life* 348). Clearly this notion of kinship was important as far as Josephus and the ruling class he represented were concerned in obtaining the loyalty of the regions for their point of view. Yet Josephus's reception in Galilee shows how problematic loyalty based on such ideas was, at least when uttered by a representative of the center. His most bitter enemy in Galilee, John of Gischala, led some of his Galilean followers to Jerusalem, notwithstanding his opposition to Josephus, however. Did the fact that he was John, son of Levi, have anything to do with his presence in Jerusalem, much to the chagrin of the Jerusalem priest Josephus? The accusation, in decidedly levitical language, of his having polluted the city, perhaps betrays Josephus's sense of what John's real motives were for going to Jerusalem. Despite the feeling of having been put upon by the Jerusalem aristocracy, it seems that there was sufficient attachment to the center to draw some survivors of the Galilean campaign there. Thus, the factors that had tended to make the events of 66–70 C.E. regional struggles had not obliterated totally the sense of loyalty to Jerusalem and what it symbolized.

The Idumeans too had been put upon by the provisional council in sending two priestly aristocrats to take charge of the region, thus compelling Niger the Perean, the previous governor, to submit to their command. The alacrity with which he seems to have responded to the cause despite his demotion is in sharp contrast to John's resentment of Josephus and his machinations in order to have him removed. Niger fell in the defence of Jerusalem and Josephus has no difficulty in reporting his bravery. It might just be possible to catch a glimpse of the differences felt in the two regions with regard to Josephus's notion of a *Jewish* War in these differing attitudes towards his ideology of the Revolt. But then, our discussion of the alledged causes of such a revolt has uncovered more evidence of their local impact in Galilee than in Idumea. Regionalism need not rule out nationalism, it would seem, despite the strains it can place upon it.

Bibliography

Aviam, M. (1993) "Galilee: the Hellenistic and Byzantine Periods," in E. Stern (ed.) *The New Encylopedia of Archaeological Excavations in the Holy Land,* 4 vols., Jerusalem: Israel Exploration Society.

Broshi, M. (1992) "Agriculture and Economy in Roman Palestine: Seven Notes on Babatha's Archive," *Israel Exploration Journal* 42: 230–40.

Freyne, S. (1988) "Bandits in Galilee. A Contribution to the Study of Social Conditions in First-Century Palestine," in J. Neusner *et al.* (eds.) *The Social World of Formative Christianity and Judaism. Essays in Tribute to Howard Clark Kee,* Philadelphia: Fortress Press.

—— (1995) "Herodian Economics in Galilee. Searching for a Suitable Model," in P. Esler (ed.) *Modeling Early Christianity. Social-Scientific Studies of the New Testament in its Context,* London and New York: Routledge.

—— (1999) "Behind the Names: Galileans, Samaritans, *Ioudaioi*," in E. Meyers (ed.) *Galilee through the Centuries. Confluence of Cultures*, Winona Lake IN: Eisenbrauns.

Goodman, M. (1987) *The Ruling Class of Judaea. The Origins of the Jewish Revolt against Rome A.D. 66–70,* Cambridge: Cambridge University Press.

Hengel, M. (1961) *Die Zeloten*, Leiden: Brill.

—— (1989) *The Zealots. Investigations into the Jewish Freedom Movement in the Period from Herod I until 70 A.D.,* Edinburgh: T. & T. Clark.

Horsley, R. (1981) "Ancient Jewish Banditry and the Revolt against Rome, A.D. 66–70," *Catholic Biblical Quarterly* 43: 409–32.

—— (1995) *Galilee. History, Politics People,* Valley Forge, PA: Trinity Press International.

Horsley, R. and Hanson, J. (1985) *Bandits, Prophets and Messiahs. Popular Movements at the Time of Jesus,* New York: Winston Press.

Isaac, B. (1991) "A Seleucid Inscription from Jamnia-on-the-Sea: Antiochus V Eupator and the Sidonians," *Israel Exploration Journal* 41: 132–44.

—— (1992) "The Babatha Archive. A Review Article," *Israel Exploration Journal* 42: 62–75.

Kasher, A. (1988) *Jews, Idumeans and Ancient Arabs. Relations between the Jews of Eretz-Israel with the Nations of the Frontier and the Desert during the Hellenistic and Roman Era*, Tubingen: J.C.B. Mohr.

Kokkinos, N. (1998) The *Herodian Dynasty. Origins, Role in Society and Eclipse*, Sheffield: Sheffield Academic Press.

Kreissig, H. (1970) *Die Sozialen Zusammenhange des Judäischen Krieges*, Berlin: Akademie Verlag.

McLaren, J. (1998) *Turbulent Times? Josephus and Scholarship on Judaea in the First Century*, Sheffield: Sheffield Academic Press.

Millar, F. (1987) "Empire, Community and Culture in the Roman Near East: Greeks, Syrians, Jews and Arabs," *Journal of Jewish Studies* 38: 143–64.

—— (1993) *The Roman Near East 31 B.C.–A.D. 337*, Cambridge, MA: Harvard University Press.

Rappaport, U. (1969) "Les Iduméens en Égypt," *Revue de Philologie* 43: 73–82.

—— (1981) "Jewish-Pagan Relations and the Revolt Against Rome in 66–70 C.E.," in L. Levine (ed.) *Jerusalem Cathedra* 2: 81–95.

Rhoads, D. (1976) *Israel in Revolution 6–74 C.E. A Political History Based on the Writings of Josephus*, Philadelphia: Fortress Press.

Ronen, I. (1988) "Formation of Jewish Nationalism among the Idumaeans," in A. Kasher, *Jews, Idumeans and Ancient Arabs*, Tubingen: J.C.B. Mohr.

Schäfer, P. (1997) *Judeophobia. Attitudes toward the Jews in the Ancient World*, Cambridge, MA: Harvard University Press.

Schwartz, S. (1991) "Israel and the Nations Roundabout: 1 Maccabees and the Hasmonean Expansion," *Journal of Jewish Studies* 41: 16–38.

—— (1993) "Josephus in Galilee: Rural Patronage and Social Breakdown," in F. Parente and J. Sievers (eds.) *Josephus and the History of the Greco-Roman Period. Essays in Memory of Morton Smith*, Leiden: E. J. Brill.

—— (1994) "Josephus in Galilee: Rural Patronage and Social Breakdown," in F. Parente and J. Sievers (eds.) *Josephus and the History of the Greco-Roman Period*, Leiden: E. J. Brill.

Shaw, B. (1993) "Tyrants, Bandits and Kings. Personal Power in Josephus," *Journal of Jewish Studies* 44: 176–204.

4 Romanization and anti-Romanization in pre-Revolt Galilee

Andrea M. Berlin

In his discussion of Judea, the Greek geographer Strabo, writing in the time of the emperor Augustus, records the interesting demographic aside that the country's northern regions are "inhabited in general ... by mixed stocks of people from Egyptian and Arabian and Phoenician tribes"; they live, he says further on, "mixed up thus" (16.2.34 § C760). Such a remark, made to and repeated by an outsider, likely reflects what at least some observers saw as significant about the region. Like any off-hand characterization of an entire area, it was surely as generally misleading as it was true, though those who lived in and knew northern Judea first-hand would have easily fleshed out the social picture behind the words. We stand at a disadvantage, trying to discern from words and disparate remains what such a remark might actually mean in terms of Galilean culture and society. Many historians and archaeologists have combed and compared the period's literary sources for answers to this fundamental question. In what follows, I hope to add a material thread to the picture they have developed. I will present new evidence that documents and clarifies the lifestyles and choices of the inhabitants of Galilee.

The archaeology of Galilee: presentation of the evidence

There is an astonishing amount of archaeological information from the Galilee (Meyers 1997: 57). The evidence includes all manner of material remains, from houses and reservoirs to paintings and cooking pots. The abundance and variety is surely one reason for the somewhat discrepant scholarly views of the region (*contra* Meyers 1995; Horsley and Hanson 1988: 51, 60–1, 72–3, 232–3; Freyne 1988: 165; and most recently Groh 1997: 30). This is, of course, the nature of the archaeological beast: practitioners increasingly overwhelmed by data are hard-put to devise coherent road maps, and non-specialists can easily lose their way. When the archaeological remains from Galilee have been considered on their own, it is often with an eye to evaluating whether they differ *in toto* from those of other regions (so Meyers 1976, 1985, 1995; Strange 1997: 43–7). An analysis that compares the region's abundant material remains within and among themselves is equally valuable, however; for the individual choices and decisions that the remains represent were more often made in a local, neighborly context (i.e. Galilean) than a country-wide, or international one (i.e. Judea, or the southern Levant). I propose first to summarize those archaeological remains that specifically reflect individual choices and priorities, and then to "read" these remains for insights into the contemporary culture. The kind of remains that can be adduced may be categorized into two large groups: house decor and arrangments, and the objects used within. The specific types of evidence that exist to be compared include: stucco decoration; wall painting; "special function" architecture (e.g., *mikva'ot*); table vessels; cooking vessels; and lamps. In support of this approach, I appeal to the authority of Fergus Millar (1993: 230): "any attempt to grasp the nature of culture and social formations in the region has to depend on representations by contemporaries, whether in literature, … in formal public documents such as inscriptions and coins, … or as embodied in buildings and artefacts." I will summarize the existing dated evidence from first century B.C.E. and first century C.E. (pre-Revolt) sites and contexts. I will then analyze the evidence by focusing on several specific dichotomies: local (i.e. Galilean produced) vs. imported (beyond the borders of Galilee); traditional (i.e. with stylistic and/or functional pre-decessors) vs. innovative; and finally, the obvious yet meaningful presence vs. absence (see Wells 1998b for a very similar methodology for late Iron Age Europe). Finally, I will discuss the implications of those changes that appear.

There are several ways to arrange the various sites of early Rooen Galilee and its environs: geographically, looking first at Lower Galilee, then Upper Galilee, and then the Golan (so originally Meyers 1976); typologically, looking first at cities, then villages, and then rural farms (so Meyers 1985; Strange 1992; Freyne 1997; but see Millar's comment on *War* 2.18.9 [1993: 269]); or culturally, looking first at known pagan sites, then those with mixed populations, and finally Jewish sites. I will give away the game by saying that, insofar as interior design or material accoutrements are concerned, neither the first approach nor the second produce consistent patterns or disparities, a result that I interpret as meaning that neither local topography nor settlement size made too much of a difference in terms of people's taste or acquisitions. Comparing remains according to the third format, however, reveals several consistent and, I believe, significant discrepancies.

Pagan sites

I begin with the material remains from sites whose inhabitants were certainly or probably Gentile. Excavated Gentile sites in the northern part of the country with first century B.C.E. remains are Tel Anafa and Pella; those with first century C.E. remains are Shiqmona, Tel Anafa, and Pella. Interior architectural accoutrements are attested in the first century B.C.E. house at Tel Anafa, but at none of the first century C.E. houses. The evidence from domestic assemblages of both the first century B.C.E. and the first century C.E. consists of abundant stores of red-slipped plates and bowls, Hellenistic or Roman-style mold-made lamps, and a variety of cooking pots, casseroles, and baking dishes. The only addition to the repertoire was the appearance of pan/bowls, a new shape reflecting a new cuisine (see p. 63). In one case only, at Pella, the spare knife-pared lamp typical of first century C.E. Judean contexts occurs in addition to mold-made discus lamps of the Roman style. The acquisition of household objects is marked by stylistic, and probably marketing, continuity.

Mixed sites

We may be underinformed about the religious constituencies of some settlements, but on present knowledge the only sites with attested Jewish and Gentile populations are the region's capital cities: Sepphoris, Tiberias, and Caesarea Philippi. First century B.C.E. or C.E. houses have not yet been excavated at Tiberias; no assemblages have been published from Sepphoris. As to domestic architecture, there are stepped pools in first century B.C.E. and C.E. contexts at Sepphoris, and painted houses in the first century C.E. No first century C.E. houses have yet been found at Caesarea Philippi, but excavations in the city center and up at the terrace of the Sanctuary of Pan allow us to identify available household goods. The same variety of red-slipped table vessels, mold-made lamps, and old and new-style cooking vessels are attested in both centuries, again reflecting both continuity of acquisition and some culinary innovation.

Jewish sites

The area's excavated sites with Jewish populations are Yodefat, Capernaum, Bethsaida, and Gamla. In these sites' first century B.C.E. levels no architectural adornment is attested; though at Yodefat and Gamla special-function architecture exists in the form of stepped plastered pools. During this same period, the household assemblages comprise the precise array seen at sites with Gentile and mixed populations: table settings of red-slipped plates and bowls, cooking pots and casseroles for preparation of meals, and mold-made lamps. Unlike sites with Gentile and mixed populations, however, in the first century C.E. there are many changes. At Yodefat and Gamla, a variety of classicizing interior decors, in the forms of stucco mouldings and plastered, painted walls appear. At every Jewish site but Bethsaida, the new pan/bowl is found in the cooking vessel assemblage. And finally, at every site, importation of red-slipped table vessels and mold-made lamps ceases. In each case, these last are replaced by plain, locally manufactured small bowls and saucers, chalk vessels, and knife-pared "Herodian"-style lamps.

Absolute quantities are unavailable for most of these sites. I can, however, present specific pottery counts from Gamla and Tel Anafa. I have personally counted and categorized every fragment of pottery that was saved from the 14 seasons of excavation at Gamla; and Kathleen Slane has counted and

Table 4.1 Architecture and pottery from first-century B.C.E. levels at northern sites with pagan, mixed, and Jewish populations

	Domestic architecture			Domestic assemblages		
	Moldings	Wall painting	Special architecture	Table vessels	Cooking vessels	Lamps
PAGAN Tel Anafa	Dentils, anta capitals	Masonry style	3-room bath complex	ESA plates and bowls	Cooking pots, casseroles	Mold-made
Pella	–	–	–	ESA plates and bowls	Cooking pots, baking dishes	Mold-made
MIXED Sepphoris	?	Vegetative schema	Stepped pools	?	?	?
Caesarea Philippi	–	–	–	ESA plates and bowls	Cooking pots, casseroles	Mold-made
JEWISH Yodefat	–	–	Stepped pools	?	Cooking pots, casseroles	Mold-made
Capernaum	–	–	–	ESA plates and bowls	Cooking pots, casseroles	Mold-made
Bethsaida	–	–	–	ESA plates and bowls	Cooking pots, casseroles	Mold-made
Gamla	–	–	Stepped pools	ESA plates and bowls	Cooking pots, casseroles	Mold-made

Sources: Tel Anafa: Herbert 1994; Slane 1997; Berlin 1997a; J. Dobbins, personal communication; Pella: McNicoll, Smith, and Hennessy 1982: 73–75, 83; Sepphoris: Hoglund and Meyers 1996: 40; Caesarea Philippi: V. Tzaferis and S. Israeli, personal communication; Yodefat: Adan-Bayewitz and Aviam 1997; Capernaum: Loffreda 1974, 1982a, 1982b; Bethsaida: Arav 1995, Fortner 1995, Tessaro 1995; Gamla: Gutman 1994: 118–22, 128, Berlin, personal study.

Table 4.2 Architecture and pottery from first-century C.E. levels at northern sites with pagan, mixed, and Jewish populations

	Domestic architecture			Domestic assemblages		
	Moldings	Wall painting	Special architecture	Table vessels	Cooking vessels	Lamps
P A G A N Shiqmona	–	–	–	ESA plates and bowls	Cooking pots, pans	Mold-made
Tel Anafa	–	–	–	ESA plates and bowls	Cooking pots, casseroles, pans	Mold-made
Pella	–	–	–	ESA plates and bowls	Cooking pots, casseroles	Mold-made, knife-pared
M I X E D Caesarea Philippi	–	–	–	ESA plates and bowls	Cooking pots, casseroles, pans	Mold-made
Sepphoris	–	Vegetative schema	Stepped pools	?	?	Knife-pared
J E W I S H Yodefat	–	Masonry style	Stepped pools	Plain ware and chalk vessels	Cooking pots, casseroles, pans	Knife-pared
Capernaum	–	–	–	Plain ware and chalk vessels	Cooking pots, casseroles, pans	Knife-paired
Bethsaida	–	–	–	Plain ware and chalk vessels	Cooking pots, casseroles	Knife-pared
Gamla	Greek-style moldings	Masonry style	Stepped pools	Plain ware and chalk vessels	Cooking pots, casseroles, pans	Knife-pared

Sources: Shiqmona: Elgavish 1997; Tel Anafa: Herbert 1994; Slane 1997; Berlin 1997a; J. Dobbins, personal communication; Pella: McNicoll, Smith, and Hennessy 1982: 73–5, 83; Sepphoris: Hoglund and Meyers 1996: 40; Caesarea Philippi: V. Tzaferis and S. Israeli, personal communication; Yodefat: Adan-Bayewitz and Aviam 1997; Capernaum: Loffreda 1974, 1982a, 1982b; Bethsaida: Arav 1995, Fortner 1995, Tessaro 1995; Gamla: Gutman 1994: 118–22, 128, Berlin, personal study.

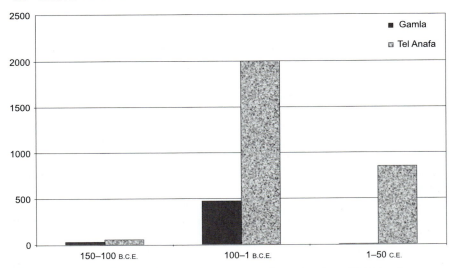

Figure 4.1 Quantities of red-slipped table vessels from Gamla and Tel Anafa.

categorized all of the fine ware found in five seasons of excavation at Tel Anafa. One fortunate feature of fine table wares are their inherent datability, regardless of context. In Figure 4.1, a bar graph details quantities by half century.

The archaeology of Galilee: discussion of the evidence

The situation may be summarized as follows. Throughout the north, from the later second through the later first centuries B.C.E., there is not much evidence either for interior decoration or "special-function" architecture: the only two examples are the stucco interiors and the bath complex at Tel Anafa and the mikve (Jewish ritual bath) from Gamla Area B. Household "high design" was apparently not yet widely desired. In this same period, however, Gentile and Jewish residents alike used what flashy household goods were then available, regardless of origin. At every site in the region, people set their tables with imported red-slipped plates and bowls and lit their homes with imported mold-made lamps. Further, at all sites throughout the region, people used both narrow-mouthed cooking pots and wide-mouthed casseroles for the preparation of food. In a previous study, I have shown that casseroles are particularly suited to a style of cuisine popularized in Greece in the fifth and fourth centuries B.C.E. (Berlin 1993: 41–2). The fact that casseroles appear at both Gentile and Jewish sites indicates that by the first century B.C.E. the stews and braised dishes originally associated with Greek cuisine had become a culinary commonplace throughout Galilee.

Several significant changes mark the archaeological record of the subsequent period. At some sites with gentile and mixed populations, as well as at two Jewish sites—Yodefat and Gamla—interior wall painting and stucco decoration are attested. The wall paintings emulate the well-known late Hellenistic masonry and architectural styles attested from Alexandria to Macedonia and as far west as Italy. The fact that they are not attested in this particular region before the Romans exerted political control (the villa at Tel Anafa being a singular exception) might suggest that their cultural association should in fact be read as "Roman" rather than "Hellenistic." A second interesting change supports that reading. The assemblages of cooking vessels found at every site include the new pan/bowl: a relatively shallow, flat-bottomed dish with straight or slightly rounded walls. There are three important aspects to this form's sudden appearance. First, it is sufficiently different from those of previously known vessels that it clearly accommodated different culinary preparations. Second, both this new form and at least some of the sorts of dishes for which it was suitable are Italian (Berlin 1993: 43–4). Third, all the examples known to me from Galilean sites— whether of Gentile, mixed, or Jewish population—were locally manufactured in at least three different Galilean locales. One of these was the Jewish manufactory of Kfar Hananiah. Another manufactory in the central Golan supplied some of these pan/bowls to Gamla. Pan/bowls from a third producer, in the Hula Valley, supplied the early first-century settlers of Tel Anafa (Berlin 1997a: 104–9). In other words, an innovative, Roman type of cooking vessel was adopted so enthusiastically across the region that many local suppliers began to manufacture it. Both of these changes might be read as the beginnings of a kind of "Romanization" in Galilee.

The last change that appears in the Galilean archaeological record around the end of the first century B.C.E. and the beginning of the first century C.E. is thus all the more surprising. Whereas the people living at Gentile and mixed sites continued to import red-slipped table vessels and mold-made lamps (now of early Roman rather than late Hellenistic styles), Jews stopped. Instead, Galilean Jews set their tables exclusively with locally manufactured, small, undecorated buff-colored saucers and bowls and white chalk vessels, and lit their homes with wheel-made knife-pared lamps. Table 4.3 summarizes the types of changes that characterize first century C.E. levels at Jewish sites in the Galilee.

Explanations, borders, and behavior

While variation is more readily established than explained, some mechanisms can be easily ruled out. One obvious possible explanation for these specific discrepancies is unevenness of supply, an erratic trade network. A glance at a map showing the distribution of red-slipped table vessels and mold-made lamps demonstrates that this is nonsense: why would residents of Tel Anafa and Caesarea Philippi be able to acquire such goods while residents of Capernaum, Bethsaida, and Gamla could not? Surely the Jews living at Yodefat were not cut off from the markets and suppliers of Sepphoris? (On

Table 4.3 Changes in architecture and pottery at first-century C.E. northern sites with Jewish populations

	Domestic architecture			Domestic assemblages		
	Moldings	Wall painting	Special architecture	Table vessels	Cooking vessels	Lamps
Yodefat	–	New Greco-Roman style	Local style	Local wares only	Local and new Roman forms	Local forms only
Capernaum	–	–	–	Local wares only	Local and new Roman forms	Local forms only
Bethsaida	–	–	–	Local wares only	Local forms only	Local forms only
Gamla	New Greco-Roman style	New Greco-Roman style	Local style	Local wares only	Local and new Roman forms	Local forms only

J
E
W
I
S
H

road networks and trade see Adan-Bayewitz 1993: 219, 228–34; Safrai 1994: 271–3, 286–7; Strange 1997: 39–42.) No, it is not the supply half of the equation that is in doubt. Suspicion then falls on the other half: demand. Specific demands, or the lack thereof, are easy to understand for some of the structures and objects whose distribution is confined to Jewish sites, such as *mikva'ot* and chalk vessels. These seem obviously dependent on contemporary halachic requirements, or at least some people's understanding thereof (Sanders 1992: 214–17). A similar explanation may underlie the acquisition of imported wine and oil: food commodities were susceptible to purity laws. This is well illustrated by Josephus's famous story of John of Gischala's scheme to corner the Syrian Jewish market for pure Galilean-produced olive oil. But while some scholars have recently asserted that halachic principles and kashrut regulations can explain the cessation of mold-made lamps and red-slipped plates and bowls (Adan-Bayewitz and Aviam 1997: 165), there is strong counter-evidence. Throughout Gamla Area B, a large residential district with a public mikve, every single individual household assemblage contains red-slipped table vessels, and several of these assemblages contain chalk vessels as well. Red-slipped table vessels appear at Gamla through the Augustan period, but then suddenly disappear in the early first century C.E. I would also point to the well-documented continued use of such vessels among the Jewish aristocracy in Jerusalem (Avigad 1980: 197–8, 202). So here we have some of Millar's eyewitness evidence of behavior, and the question is: what does it mean? Why did the previous, clear demand for these specific objects abruptly cease among the Jewish settlers of Galilee?

In addition to the general observations about Galilee's mixed population given by Strabo, with which I began, we have other specific information about the region's demographics from the *baraita* concerning the halachic boundaries of *Eretz Israel*. These boundaries define the regions where agricultural precepts were especially binding. There existed two categories: the land of *Eretz Israel* "*minima,*" and "permitted towns," whose residents, though technically living within the boundaries, were exempt from certain tithes and other obligations. Several complementary sources describe the halachic boundaries of *Eretz Israel*: two tractates of the Jerusalem Talmud (*Dem.* 2–22c–d and *Shevi'it* 6–36c); two Tannaitic sources (Tosefta *Shevi'it* 3 and *Sifre Deuteronomy* 51); and the Rehov synagogue inscription, which is both the earliest—the inscription belongs to the floor of the synagogue's second phase, dated late fifth century C.E.—and the fullest, as it contains a detailed topography of the towns in the immediate environs of Beth She'an, as well as a list of "permitted towns" in the region of Sebaste. While all of these sources are of course much later than the period under discussion here, they do preserve definitions and rulings derived from this period. What is interesting about this *baraita* is the great number of "permitted towns" in and immediately surrounding Galilee, in fact far more than all other regions combined. In other words, Jewish legal analyses recognized that this region was fundamentally mixed, religiously and culturally.

Anthropologists have identifed an interesting cultural adaptation of some people who live in areas of mixed population: they deliberately adopt specific, "identity-signalling" characteristics. The characteristics are generally material, rather than behavioral, and so they show up most clearly in archaeological (or modern physical) assemblages (Stevenson 1989; Moore 1987; see also the pertinent comments of Freyne 1997: 50). There is no rule or pattern or set of objects specific to the enterprise. People will adopt or reject whatever easily communicates or advertises affiliation. In other words, people will make a statement with whatever they can, when they feel the need to do so.

Of the several constituencies that Strabo identified as living in this region, we possess reliable literary and material evidence on one only: the Phoenicians. In several studies, Uriel Rappaport (1981, 1992) has discussed the considerable inimical effect of Hasmonean expansion on the Phoenicians. There is some interesting material evidence that supports Rappaport's observations. From the middle of the second to the early first century B.C.E., Phoenicians living at the extreme eastern edges of the Tyrian hinterland imported specific ceramic goods from the coast, though comparable objects were locally available. In a previous study, I discussed this phenomenon as a deliberate strategy of cultural identification, a likely, if minimal, reaction for a Gentile population at a time when Hasmonean rulers were fighting battles in and beginning to annex Tyrian territory (Berlin 1997b). The chronological coincidence is startling: the first Hasmonean battle within Phoenician territory was Jonathan's advance to Kedesh in 145 B.C.E. (1 Macc. 11.46–73); the pattern of ceramic importation first appears in archaeological contexts of the third quarter of the century.

During the first century B.C.E., relations worsened. Just after the middle of the century, conflicts arose across the northern border zone between the hinterland of Tyre (which extended to Kedesh in the Upper Galilee) and the region's Jewish settlements (Applebaum 1977: 382–3; for much of what follows *contra* Rhoads 1976). In 46 B.C.E. Herod, as governor of Galilee, put to death Hezekiah, "a bandit chief" for "overrunning the district adjoining Syria" (*War* 1.204–5); on this account Herod's praises were sung "in all the villages and towns." Just four years later, however, in 42 B.C.E., Mark Antony ordered the Tyrians to restore Jewish property seized during recent political upheavals (*Ant.* 14.314–18; does this refer to the villages seized by Marion in *War* 1.238? *Ant.* 14.304–23 have no parallel in the *War*). As is well known, hostilities did not abate (*War* 2.588, 4.84; Applebaum 1971; Applebaum 1977: 379–83; Horsley and Hanson 1988). When Judah of Gamla, the probable son of Hezekiah (Kennard 1945–6) "threw himself into the cause of rebellion" on account of the census (*War* 18.4), in 6/7 C.E. (on the dating see Schürer rev. ed. 1973, I: 399–427), he readily found followers in the area.

For the Jews of Galilee, therefore, Tyre and its villages were clearly a specific locus of animus. Marion's incursions and Antony's edict highlight the early stages, in which bad feeling may well have been exacerbated by

Herod's subsequent actions: he not only spared his captives but "even sen[t] some away laden with gifts" (*War* 1.238, trans. Williamson). Herod's subsequent lavish benefactions to Phoenician cities, in part financed by taxes on agricultural produce from Galilee, would have further alienated Galilean Jews (*War* 1.422; see also Roller 1998: 220, 222, 232, 235, 237). By the time Judah began organizing, anti-Tyrian sentiment was entrenched among the area's Jews. This background amplifies Josephus's characterization of Tyrian–Galilean relations on the eve of the Revolt; he describes Kedesh, the easternmost village of the Tyrians, as "always engaged in bitter strife with the Galileans" (*War* 4.104, trans. Williamson).

Romanization and anti-Romanization in Galilee: the loaded plate

Should we then read the archaeological shift that abruptly appears at the end of the first century B.C.E. as an anti-Tyrian statement? By rejecting red-slipped plates and bowls and mold-made lamps, were Galilean Jews thereby differentiating themselves from their Gentile neighbors and signaling their identity? Or, by shunning such items, were they making a more active, in fact a political statement? Abraham Wasserstein interpreted an analogous linguistic phenomenon, that the Dead Sea Scrolls contain practically no Greek loan words, as "deliberate avoidance" (1995: 119). In that case, the identity of the thing being avoided is clear: as Wasserstein notes, "the Qumran sectarians ... knew that these words were, by origin, not Hebrew or Aramaic but Greek, and they took great care to avoid using them" (1995: 120; on language as a political statement, see Chapter 10 by Eshel in this volume). In our case, the question is: precisely what did Galilean Jews think red-slipped plates and bowls and mold-made discus lamps represented?

It is tempting to "read" the Jewish rejection of these fancy household wares as an anti-Phoenician message. Tyre (and probably Ptolemais) had been the main points of origin and/or supply for most of the imported and luxury goods found at Galilean sites, from the later second through the first centuries B.C.E. (Berlin 1997b). Yet the archaeological evidence from first century B.C.E. sites does not support an "anti-Tyrian" interpretation. Throughout that century, Galilean Jews continued to import red-slipped table wares and mold-made lamps, as did their Gentile neighbors. By the middle of the century, these were the main ceramic goods available from Phoenician suppliers. Though social and political relations deteriorated, there is no evidence that this affected economic relations. Regional trading patterns continued. The change, abrupt and consistent, occurs towards the end or just after the rule of Herod the Great.

Did Rome introduce a specific change into the cultural landscape of this region around this time? Most emphatically so: in 15 B.C.E., on the old ruins of the Phoenician city Berytus, the Romans established a true veterans' *colonia*, the only such settlement outside of Italy, peopled by two legions

(Strabo 16.2.19 § 756; Millar 1990: 10–23). Berytus and its extensive hinterland, stretching to the Orontes River, constituted an "island of Romanisation, of Latin language and culture and of Roman law," as is proved by its distinctive epigraphic record, in which Latin is widely attested for both public and private uses, including an array of individual dedications to Roman deities (Millar 1990: 8). The colony's character is clear early on: one of the city's illustrious native sons was the Latin grammarian Valerius Probus, who lived during the first half of the first century C.E. This situation further degraded with the establishment of a second *colonia* at Ptolemais in 54 C.E. Such settlements had as profound and long-lasting an effect on the natives living in and around them as a meteor, striking earth, has on the local topography; Millar emphasizes "how considerable the changes brought about by Roman rule ... affected the personal and collective identities by which people lived" (Millar 1990: 56).

One benefit of the surge of studies focusing on Romanization is that we can now see how varied this phenomenon was throughout the Empire (for Britain: Hingley 1996; Meadows 1997; Millett 1990; for Germany: Wells 1995a, 1995b, 1998a, 1998b; Woolf 1998; for the Low Countries: Slofstra 1983; Brandt 1983; for Gaul: Bats 1988; for Sardinia: van Dommelen 1998; for Greece: Alcock 1993; Rotroff 1997; Abadie-Reynal 1995; and Wright 1980; for Syria: Schmidt-Colinet 1997; see also Curti, Dench, and Patterson 1996: 181–8). Even within a single country, individual and communal response to the advent and spread of Roman political control varied widely. I cite here just one of many possible examples. The Romans established a new colony at Corinth, in 44 B.C.E., and created the province of Achaia, comprising mainland Greece and the Peloponnese, in the year 27 B.C.E. Archaeological evidence reveals that local responses to this new political situation varied. In Corinth, where at least some of the inhabitants must have been Roman soldiers and their families, the importing and imitating of Italian table wares and lamps is well attested by the first decade of the first century C.E. (Wright 1980: 171–5). In Argos, however, only a short distance away, archaeological deposits from the beginning of the first century C.E. contain barely any Italian imports, and no imitations (Abadie-Reynal 1995: 2). Similarly, in Athens and Knossos, potters followed Greek ceramic traditions for another generation. At all three sites, Italian imitations and imports do not appear before the reign of Tiberius, and are not common until Claudian times (Abadie-Reynal 1995: 2–4; Rotroff 1997: 108–11; Sackett 1992). In each of these Greek cities, the residents could hear of heroic mythological traditions, see beautiful and long-lived temples and government buildings, and feel themselves inheritors of a renowned cultural tradition. Yet these characteristics apparently carried far more weight in Argos, Athens, and Knossos than in Corinth. It is clear that "Romanization" is a single word for what was, in reality, a series of individual choices on whether and how to affiliate or reject a new cultural paradigm.

Evidence for Romanization in Galilee is a mixed bag, and suggests that the new cultural paradigm was taken up in some ways and rejected in others. The local interpretation clearly did not proceed according to a single, pan-Mediterranean, script. Some new, "Romanized" decor and goods were adopted easily and widely, such as the fancy interior stucco and painting at Gamla and Yodefat, and the wholesale use of the new Roman-style cooking pans. Still other changes, such as the construction of stepped pools at Gamla and Yodefat, or the new industry in chalk vessels, being specific to Jewish needs, were irrelevant to Roman life, and tell us little about interactions or attitudes. But some aspects, such as the rejection of red-slipped table vessels and mold-made lamps at Jewish sites throughout the north, cannot be explained away either by economic or functional causes. I suggest that these were the result of individual choice; they were, in effect, a kind of statement. And I submit that the statement was anti-Roman.

What supports a reading of these formerly unobjectionable objects as suddenly anti-Roman? One explanation depends on the peculiar transformation that Roman culture underwent in eastern contexts. In the east, Greek modes, not Latin ones, prevailed. Greek culture, in the form of language, literature, and philosophical schooling, was used by and under the Romans as "a universally intelligible code" (Millar 1987: 149; Applebaum 1971: 164). This is nowhere better reflected than in the hugely disproportionate use of Greek *versus* Latin in inscriptions and papyri (Millar 1995; Cotton, Cockle and Millar 1995). In other words, in the Roman east, Greek styles were one manifestation of Roman control. Especially after a region received a Roman colonial foundation, local populations might readily retranslate generally foreign items as loci of Roman culture or control (Millar 1990: 7–10; contra Horsley, pp. 92ff. in this volume, who does not see evidence for anti-Roman sentiment in Galilee, but rather "anti-ruler"or even anti-Jerusalem).

I suggest that these fancy household items, often the only foreign and certainly the most noticeable goods found in a typical household assemblage, performed a convenient communicative role. Those bright, shiny red-slipped table vessels would be immediately visible within the small and simply planned first century B.C.E. and C.E. houses. As a manifestion of foreign and, I suggest, now specifically Roman, control, Galilean Jews rejected them. By this, they made a political statement of solidarity and affiliation with a traditional, simple, unadorned, Jewish lifestyle, as well as demonstrating a unified opposition to the newly looming Roman presence.

Conclusion

Material remains are a minefield: loaded and hidden at the same time. Abundance and sheer physicality make them appear to be straightforward documents of ancient life. But few things created and used by humans are so obvious—neither their writings, as all historians know, nor their physical accoutrements. It is human nature to seek, announce, and display one's identity and affiliation; to this end material display (or the lack thereof) can accomplish as much, if not more, than speech or writing. Susan Rotroff has examined this precise period as reflected in the Athenian ceramic record, and her comments are apt here: "Pottery is a poor guide to political and military events–but it can reflect other situations and developments that are also a part of what we call 'history.' ... [D]iffering fortunes ... are written in [people's] ceramics, if only we can be subtle enough to read them" (Rotroff 1997: 112, 113).

In the spring of the year 66 C.E. Vespasian led three legions through the Galilean countryside. Some of the region's Jews came forward to profess their loyalty; many gathered behind new fortifications in defiance. Battle lines were drawn. But for many Jews in Galilee, those lines followed much older cracks. Just as an earthquake moves most quickly along already existing fault lines, so too many Jews organized rapidly and readily against Vespasian's legions. Josephus fortified thirteen cities and towns; resistance was fierce. I submit that this response can be understood at least in part by the fact that overt resistance did not begin in 66, or 60, or 50 C.E. Rather, the archaeological evidence demonstrates that for over two generations, Galilean Jews resisted Rome—individually, collectively, consistently, and actively. For them, Vespasian's army was yet another, though the most serious, manifestation of a long-standing and very real threat.

Bibliography

Abadie-Reynal, C. (1995) "Céramique et romanisation de la Grèce: Argos aux Ier s. av. et ap. J.-C.," *Hellenistic and Roman Pottery in the Eastern Mediterranean— Advances in Scientific Studies, Acts of the II Nieborów Workshop*, Warsaw: Polish Academy of Sciences.

Adan-Bayewitz, D. (1993) *Common Pottery in Roman Galilee: A Study of Local Trade*, Ramat-Gan: Bar-Ilan University Press.

Adan-Bayewitz, D. and Aviam, M. (1997) "Jotapata, Josephus, and the Siege of 67: Preliminary Report on the 1992–94 seasons," *Journal of Roman Archaeology* 10: 131–65.

Alcock, S. (1993) *Graecia Capta: The Landscapes of Roman Greece*, Cambridge: Cambridge University Press.

Applebaum, S. (1971) "The Zealots: the Case for Revaluation," *Journal of Roman Studies* 61: 155–70.

—— (1977) "Judaea as a Roman Province; the Countryside as a Political and Economic Factor," *Aufstieg und Niedergang der Römischen Welt* 2.8: 355–66.

Arav, R. (1995) "Bethsaida Excavations: Preliminary Report 1987–1993," in R. Arav and R. Freund (eds.) *Bethsaida. A City by the North Shore of the Sea of Galilee*, Kirksville, MO: Thomas Jefferson University Press.

Avigad, N. (1980) *Discovering Jerusalem*, New York: Thomas Nelson Publishers.

Bats, M. (1988) *Vaiselle et alimentation à Olbia de Provence (v. 350–v. 50 av. J.-C.). Modèles culturel et catégories céramiques*, Revue Archéologique de narbonnaise, supplément 18.

Berlin, A. (1993) "Italian Cooking Vessels and Cuisine at Tel Anafa," *Israel Exploration Journal* 43: 35–44.

—— (1997a) *Tel Anafa* II, i. *The Hellenistic and Roman Pottery: The Plain Wares*, *Journal of Roman Archaeology*, Supplementary Series 10.2.1, Ann Arbor: Kelsey Museum of Archaeology.

—— (1997b) "From Monarchy to Markets: The Phoenicians in Hellenistic Palestine," *Bulletin of the American Schools of Oriental Research* 306: 75–88.

Brandt, R. (1983) "A Brief Encounter Along the Northern Frontier," in R. Brandt and J. Slofstra (eds.) *Roman and Native in the Low Countries*, British Archaeological Reports International Series 184.

Cotton, H., Cockle, W. and Millar, F. (1995) "The Papyrology of the Roman Near East: A Survey," *Journal of Roman Studies* 85: 214–35.

Crowfoot, J., Crowfoot, G. and Kenyon, K. (1957) *The Objects from Samaria*, London: Palestine Exploration Fund.

Curti, E., Dench, E. and Patterson, J. (1996) "The Archaeology of Central and Southern Roman Italy: Recent Trends and Approaches," *Journal of Roman Studies* 86: 170–89.

Elgavish, J. (1974) *Archaeological Excavations at Shiqmona, Report No. 2. The Level of the Hellenistic Period—Stratum H. Seasons 1963–1970*, Haifa: City Museum of Ancient Art (Heb.).

—— (1977) *Archaeological Excavations at Shiqmona. The Pottery of the Roman Period*, Haifa: City Museum of Ancient Art (Heb.).

Fortner, S. (1995) "Hellenistic and Roman Fineware from Bethsaida," in R. Arav and R. Freund (eds.) *Bethsaida. A City by the North Shore of the Sea of Galilee*, Kirksville, MO: Thomas Jefferson University Press.

Freyne, S. (1988) *Galilee, Jesus, and the Gospels. Literary Approaches and Historical Investigations*, Philadelphia: Fortress Press.

—— (1997) "Town and Country Once More: The Case of Roman Galilee," in D. Edwards and C. Thomas McCollough (eds.) *Archaeology and the Galilee: Texts and Contexts in the Graeco-Roman and Byzantine Periods*, Atlanta: Scholars Press.

Groh, Dennis E. (1997) "The Clash Between Literary and Archaeological Models of Provincial Palestine," in D. Edwards and C. Thomas McCollough (eds.) *Archaeology and the Galilee: Texts and Contexts in the Graeco-Roman and Byzantine Periods*, Atlanta: Scholars Press.

Gutman, S. (1994) *Gamla—A City in Rebellion*, Jerusalem: Israel Ministry of Defence (Heb.).

Herbert, S. (1994) *Tel Anafa I, ii. Final Report on Ten Years of Excavation at a Hellenistic and Roman Settlement in Northern Israel*, Journal of Roman Archaeology supplementary series 10.1, Ann Arbor: Kelsey Museum of Archaeology.

Hingley, R. (1996) "The 'Legacy' of Rome: the Rise and Fall of the Theory of Romanization," in J. Webster and N. Cooper (eds.) *Roman Imperialism: Post-Colonial Perspectives*, Leicester Archaeology Monographs 3: 35–48.

Hoglund, K. and Meyers, E. (1996) "The Residential Quarter on the Western Summit," in R. Nagy, C. Meyers, E. Meyers and Z. Weiss (eds.) *Sepphoris in Galilee: Crosscurrents of Culture*, Winona Lake, IN: Eisenbrauns.

Horsley, R. and Hanson, J. (1988) *Bandits, Prophets, and Messiahs. Popular Movements in the Time of Jesus*, San Francisco: Harper and Row.

Kennard, J. S. (1945–6) "Judas of Galilee and his Clan," *Jewish Quarterly Review* 36: 281–6.

Loffreda, S. (1974) *Cafarnao II. La Ceramica*. Publicazioni dello Studium Biblicum Franciscanum n. 19, Jerusalem: Franciscan Printing Press.

—— (1982a) "Documentazione preliminare degli oggetti della XIV campagna di scavi a Cafarnao," *Liber Annus* 32: 409–26.

—— (1982b) "Ceramica ellenistico-romana nel sottosuolo della sinagoga de Cafarnao," *Studia Hierosolymitana* III. Studium Biblicum Franciscanum collectio maior n. 30: 273–312.

McNicoll, A., Smith, R. and Hennessy, B. (1982) *Pella in Jordan 1*, Canberra: Australian National Gallery.

Meadows, K. (1997) "Much Ado about Nothing: The Social Context of Eating and Drinking in Early Roman Britain," in C. G. Cumberpatch and P. W. Blinkhorn (eds.) *Not So Much a Pot, More a Way of Life: Current Approaches to Artefact Analysis in Archaeology*, Oxbow Monograph 83, Oxford: Oxbow Books.

Meyers, E. (1976) "Galilean Regionalism as a Factor in Historical Reconstruction," *Bulletin of the American Schools of Oriental Research* 221: 93–101.

—— (1979) "The Cultural Setting of Galilee: The Case of Early Judaism," *Aufstieg und Niedergang der Römischen Welt* 2.19.1, Berlin: de Gruyter

—— (1985) "Galilean Regionalism: A Reappraisal," in W. Green (ed.) *Approaches to Ancient Judaism V*, Atlanta: Scholars Press.

—— (1995) "An Archaeological Response to a New Testament Scholar," *Bulletin of the American Schools of Oriental Research* 295: 17–26.

—— (1997) "Jesus and his Galilean Context," in D. Edwards and C. Thomas McCollough (eds.) *Archaeology and the Galilee: Texts and Contexts in the Graeco-Roman and Byzantine Periods*, Atlanta: Scholars Press.

Millar, F. (1987) "Empire, Community and Culture in the Roman Near East: Greeks, Syrians, Jews and Arabs," *Journal of Jewish Studies* 38: 143–64.

—— (1990) "The Roman *Coloniae* of the Near East: a Study of Cultural Relations," in H. Solin and M. Kajava (eds.) *Roman Eastern Policy and Other Studies. Proceedings of a Colloquium at Tvärminne 2–3 October 1987*, *Commentationes Humanarum Litteratum* 91: 7–58.

—— (1993) *The Roman Near East 31 B.C.–A.D. 337*, Cambridge, MA: Harvard University Press.

—— (1995) "Latin in the Epigraphy of the Roman Near East," in H. Solin, O. Salomies, and U.-M. Liertz (eds.) *Acta Colloquii Epigraphici Latini*. Commentationes Humanarum Litterarum 104: 403–19.

Millett, M. (1990) *The Romanization of Britain: An Essay in Archaeological Inter-pretation*, Cambridge: Cambridge University Press.

Moore, H. (1987) "Acculturation, Diffusion, and Migration as Social-Symbolic Processes," in I. Hodder (ed.) *Archaeology as Long-Term History*, Cambridge: Cambridge University Press.

Rappaport, U. (1981) "Jewish-Pagan Relations and the Revolt against Rome in 66–70 C.E.," in L. Levine (ed.) *Jerusalem Cathedra 1*, Jerusalem: Yad Itzhak Ben Zvi Institute.

—— (1992) "Phoenicia and Galilee: Economy, Territory and Political Relations," *Numismatique et histoire économique phéniciennes et puniques*, Studia Phoenicia 9 Louvain: Université Catholique de Louvain.

Reisner, G., Fisher, C. and Lyon, D. (1924) *Harvard Excavations at Samaria 1908–1910*, Cambridge, MA: Harvard University Press.

Rhoads, D. (1976) *Israel in Revolution 6–74 C.E.*, Philadelphia: Fortress Press.

Roller, D. (1998) *The Building Program of Herod the Great*, Berkeley: University of California Press.

Rotroff, S. (1997) "From Greek to Roman in Athenian Ceramics," in M. Hoff and S. Rotroff (eds.) *The Romanization of Athens*, Oxbow Monograph 94, pp. 97–116.

Sackett, L. H. (1992) "The Roman Pottery," *Knossos. From Greek City to Roman Colony. Excavations at the Unexplored Mansion II*, British School of Archaeology at Athens Supplementary Series 21, Athens: British School at Athens.

Safrai, Z. (1994) *The Economy of Roman Palestine*, London: Routledge.

Sanders, E. P. (1992) *Judaism. Practice and Belief 63 B.C.E.–66 C.E.*, Philadelphia: Trinity Press International.

Schmidt-Colinet, A. (1997) "Aspects of 'Romanization': The Tomb Architecture at Palmyra and its Decoration," in S. Alcock (ed.) *The Early Roman Empire in the East*, Oxbow Monograph 95, Oxford: Oxbow Books.

Schürer, E. (1973) *The History of the Jewish People in the Age of Jesus Christ (175 B.C.–A.D. 135)*. A new English version revised and edited by G. Vermes and F. Millar, 3 vols, Edinburgh: T. & T. Clark.

Slane, K. (1997) *Tel Anafa II, i. The Hellenistic and Roman Pottery: The Fine Wares*, Journal of Roman Archaeology Supplementary Series 10.2.1, Ann Arbor: Kelsey Museum of Archaeology.

Slofstra, J. (1983) "An Anthropological Approach to the Study of Romanization Processes," in R. Brandt and J. Slofstra (eds.) *Roman and Native in the Low Countries*, British Archaeological Reports International Series 184: 71–104.

Stevenson, M. G. (1989) "Sourdoughs and Cheechakos: The Formation of Identity-Signaling Social Groups," *Journal of Anthropological Archaeology* 8: 270–312.

Strange, J. F. (1992) "Some Implications of Archaeology for New Testament Studies," in J. Charlesworth (ed.) *What Has Archaeology to do with Faith?*, Philadelphia: Trinity Press.

—— (1997) "First Century Galilee from Archaeology and from the Texts," in D. Edwards and C. Thomas McCollough (eds.) *Archaeology and the Galilee: Texts and Contexts in the Graeco-Roman and Byzantine Periods*, Atlanta: Scholars Press.

Tessaro, T. (1995) "Hellenistic and Roman Ceramic Cooking Ware from Bethsaida," in R. Arav and R. Freund (eds.) *Bethsaida. A City by the North Shore of the Sea of Galilee*, Kirksville, MO: Thomas Jefferson University Press.

van Dommelen, P. (1998) "Punic Persistence: Colonialism and Cultural Identities in Roman Sardinia," in R. Laurence and J. Berry (eds.) *Cultural Identity in the Roman Empire*, New York: Routledge.

Wasserstein, A. (1995) "Non-Hellenized Jews in the Semi-Hellenized East," *Scripta Classical Israelica* 14: 111–37.

Wells, P. (1995a) "Identities, Material Culture, and Change: 'Celts' and 'Germans' in Late-Iron-Age Europe," *Journal of European Archaeology* 3.2: 169–85.

—— (1995b) "Manufactured Objects and the Construction of Identities in Late La Tène Europe," *Eirene* 31: 129–50.

—— (1998a)"Culture Contact, Identity, and Change in the European Provinces of the Roman Empire," in J. Cusick (ed.) *Studies in Culture Contact: Interaction, Culture Change, and Archaeology*, Carbondale: Southern Illinois University Press

—— (1998b) "Identity and Material Culture in the Later Prehistory of Central Europe," *Journal of Archaeological Research* 6.3: 239–98.

Woolf, A. (1998) "Romancing the Celts. A Segmentary Approach to Acculturation," in R. Laurence and J. Berry (eds.) *Cultural Identity in the Roman Empire*, New York: Routledge.

Wright, K. Slane. (1980) "A Tiberian Pottery Deposit from Corinth," *Hesperia* 49: 135–77.

5 Phoenicians and Jews

A ceramic case-study

Dina Avshalom-Gorni and Nimrod Getzov

We present a case-study of the Hellenistic and early Roman ceramic storage jars from Yodefat and Bet Zeneta. We have chosen to study the types and distribution of storage jars because, as the main receptacles for both domestic storage and commercial transport of foodstuffs, they are among the most common vessels found at ancient sites. Yodefat and Bet Zeneta are both located in the mountainous region of the Galilee. While both are situated in similar ecological niches, however, their ethnic surroundings differed. Yodefat is within Jewish Galilee, while Bet Zeneta lies close to the Phoenician coastal plain. According to Josephus, the border dividing Jewish Galilee from the Gentile west traversed Beq'a (Peqi'in), about 11 kilometers east of Bet Zeneta (*War* 3.3.40), thus situating it within Phoenicia proper.

Yodefat

Yodefat (map coordinates: 1763/2486) is located in the southern flanks of the hilly lower Galilee, approximately 22 kilometers southeast of Akko and 9 kilometers north of Zippori (Sepphoris) (Adan-Bayewitz and Aviam 1997). Yodefat is mentioned in a number of ancient sources but is discussed in greatest detail by Josephus (*War* 3.6–7). It was in Yodefat that Josephus established his seat as the leader of the Jewish revolt in the Galilee. In 67 C.E., after a forty-seven-day siege, Yodefat was captured and totally destroyed by the Roman army.

Seven seasons of excavations were undertaken in Yodefat (1992–7, 1999) in a joint project sponsored by the Israel Antiquities Authority and the University of Rochester (USA).[1] The results of these excavations show that there was a first, meager, occupation of the site during the Persian period. More substantial settlements occurred during the Hellenistic and early Roman periods. The archaeological findings—the defensive walls circumventing the city, weapons such as arrowheads and balista stones and the destruction resulting from battle—substantiate the account of the Roman conquest as related by Josephus. After the destruction carried out by the Roman army in 67 C.E., the site remained uninhabited (for details see Chapter 8 by Aviam in this volume).

The present study concerns the jars found in six separate ceramic assemblages from three different fields on the site[2]. These assemblages divide into two chronological groups: the first belonging to the Hellenistic period and the second to the early Roman period. Below, we describe the contexts of these assemblages according to the fields in which they were found.

The southeastern slope assemblage (Area XI)

The building complex where this assemblage was found consists of an open courtyard surrounded by five rooms, a cave utilized as a storage room, two water cisterns and two stepped pools (*miqva'ot*). The city wall and an adjoining street separating the wall from the complex were uncovered to the east. On the basis of the relevant finds, this complex was founded during the early Roman period in an area of the site that was previously uninhabited. It can thus be expected that the pottery findings in this complex are limited to a single period. The jar findings from three units in this complex will be examined:

(1) The storage cave (Locus O2010), in which a number of jars were found *in situ*.
(2) On the rock hewn floor of one room where a *tabun*, three nearby jars, and several other vessels were found *in situ* (Loci P3006, P3008). This floor was sealed by what appears to be the collapsed ceiling that contained lumps of burned earth and clay. The collapse was probably caused by the destruction and incineration of the structure at the time of the Roman conquest.
(3) Jars found in the accumulation on the hewn bedrock floor of the central courtyard (P2003, O2014).

The northwest fortifications (Area XV)

The hewn floor of a room that was destroyed by a fire was exposed within the northwestern fortification complex (Loci B16008, B16017, C16020, C15016, C15019, C15020). On the floor were vessels *in situ* dating to the Hellenistic period among which were storage jars, an imported Rhodian amphora with a stamped handle dated to the second half of the second century B.C.E. and a third century B.C.E. Ptolemaic coin.[3] The floor was sealed by a layer of ash upon which was constructed a massive wall which is dated to the late Hellenistic period (Hasmonean period).

The terraced fresco house on the eastern slope (Area XVI)

A small section of an impressive villa was exposed on the upper area of a terrace on the eastern slope. Its walls were covered with multicolored frescos executed in the Architectural (Second Pompeian) style and its floor was well plastered. Human bones and arrowheads on the floor suggest that the structure was probably destroyed at the time of the Roman conquest (Loci G15007, G15008, H15006, G15017, F15002).

A probe below the floor of the villa revealed its having been constructed on material dating to the Hellenistic period (Loci G15021, G15022, H15013).

Bet Zeneta[4]

Khirbet Bet Zeneta (1707/2697) is situated on the top of the sloping northern bank of Nahal Ga'aton and on a narrow hill that spreads between Nahal Ga'aton and Nahal Sha'al. It is identified with the Bet Zeneta that is mentioned in the description of the northwestern boundary of the area settled by Jewish "Babylonian immigrants" in the Mishnah *Breitat Hatkhumim* compiled at the end of the second century C.E. (Frankel and Finkelstein 1983: 43 and notes 2–4).

Although Bet Zeneta is mentioned as lying on the boundary of the Jewish settled area, it appears that in the early Roman period it was actually outside the Jewish area whose border at that time passed through Beq'a (Peqi'in), 11 kilometers to the east, as mentioned above. A salvage excavation, undertaken in 1993, revealed remains of a rural occupation dating to the Roman period. The ceramic evidence indicates that the site was occupied from the first century B.C.E. through the first century C.E. The approximate date of destruction may be determined on the basis of a cooking pot found inside a *tabun*. This cooking pot is identical to Kfar Hananiah cooking pot type 4B, which is dated from the second half of the first century C.E. to the first half of the second century C.E. (Adan-Bayewitz 1993: 126–7, Pl. 4B). A coin attributed to Claudius from the year 50–1 C.E. was found inside the pot, thus providing a specific *terminus post quem* for the site's destruction.

Ceramic evidence indicates earlier occupations of the site during the Iron Age I, Persian, and Hellenistic periods. Later Crusader construction destroyed almost all earlier remains down to the bedrock and left no sealed homogeneous earlier loci intact. The great contrast between the Crusader and early Roman ceramic vessels, however, enabled each period's material to be identified, even though found in heterogeneous accumulations.

The storage jars

Two groups of jars predominate among the archaeological finds from the Galilee and its adjacent regions during the early Roman period.[5] The first group (Fig. 5.1: 1–3) reflects the tradition of barrel-shaped jars whose roots may be traced to everted-rim jars of the Hellenistic period (Avshalom-Gorni 1998: 49–67; Guz-Zilberstein 1995: Fig. 36: 5–9). During the early Roman period their shape changed slightly, becoming even more barrel-shaped. The shoulder was widened, and became either round or flat. Occasionally a ridge runs around the jar circumference at the join of the shoulder to the body

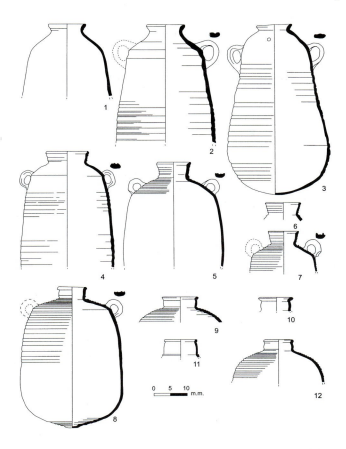

Figure 5.1 Storage jars from the Hellenistic and the early Roman period.

No.	Site	Locus	Basket	Fabric description
1.	Yodefat	B16019	XV.B16.85	White with many small black inclusions
2.	Yodefat	B16008	XV.B16.56	White with many small black inclusions
3.	Yodefat	C15020	XV.C15.62	White with many small black inclusions
4.	Yodefat	P2005	XII.P2.37	Brown-red
5.	Yodefat	L15011	XVI.L15.38	Brown-grey
6.	Yodefat	P3006	XI.P3.46	Brown-red
7.	Yodefat	Q3016	XI.Q3.74	Reddish brown
8.	Yodefat	O2010	XI.O2.31	Reddish brown
9.	Yodefat	P3005	XI.P3.22	Brown
10.	Bet Zeneta	119	1060/2	Reddish brown, grey slip
11.	Bet Zeneta	119	1060/3	Reddish brown
12.	Yodefat	O2010	XI.O2.31	Reddish brown, grey core

where a pair of round double ridged handles are attached. Dense ribbing appears on the lower third of the widened body and covers the rounded base as well.

Within this group of barrel-shaped jars, two variants are most prominent. The first is called the "Yodefat jar," after excavation of a pottery production area during the 1999 excavation season demonstrated that this particular variant of everted-rim jar was manufactured at Yodefat (Fig. 5.1: 4–7). This variant has a simple everted rim and an upright ribbed neck with a ridge around its base. It is dated from the second half of the first century B.C.E. until the middle of the first century C.E. (Diez Fernandez 1983: 136, Fig. 12: 14, 15; Adan-Bayewitz and Aviam 1997; Avshalom-Gorni 1998: 52, type 1.1.5). The second variant is differentiated by a stepped rim (Fig. 5.1: 8–12). The everted rounded rim has an internal step or shelf that probably supported a lid. The neck is concave and smooth with a ridge around its base (Loffreda 1974: Fig. 1.1; Avshalom-Gorni 1998: 53–5). This variant has been attributed to the pottery manufactury at Shikhin and is dated from 63 to 135 C.E. (Adan-Bayewitz and Wieder 1992: Fig. 5: 5).

The second group of storage jars continues the coastal Phoenician tradition (Fig. 5.2). Appearing first during the Iron II and continuing through to the middle Roman period,[6] this type is characterized by its thickened rim, conical body and two twisted handles (on which see Artzy 1980) (Fig. 5.2: 6). Four variants may be distinguished. The earliest, dated to the third and second centuries B.C.E., is the round-rim jar (Fig. 5.2: 1). This is a neckless jar with an externally thickened rim, half-round in section. Its drooping shoulder is defined by a ridge at its join to the jar body (Landgraff 1980: pl. 7: 8; Berlin 1997a: pl. 57; Berlin 1997b: 77–9). The three remaining variants, which all date to the Roman period, demonstrate a clear developmental progression (Avshalom-Gorni 1998: 68–72). The square-rim jar (Fig. 5.2: 2–5) differs from the earliest variant in its square and upright rim. The thickened-rim jar (Fig. 5.2: 6) has a thickened, inwardly turned, flat lying rim. Occasionally a wide channel, that often appears as a continuation of the body ribbing, defines the base of the rim. This vessel's profile, in contrast to the earliest Hellenistic type, has no ridge between the shoulder and body and presents instead a continuous sloping line from the rim to the top of the jar base. The last type is a channel-rim jar (Fig. 5.2: 7, 8) which is similar to the thickened rim type but whose rim carries a channel, perhaps intended for a stopper or lid, circumventing the inner edge.

Although it is impossible to precisely date each of these individual types, it is clear that all developed from Hellenistic period predecessors. Their relative chronology is also clear: the square-rim jar is the earliest, appearing at the beginning of the Roman period, followed by the thickened-rim and channel-rim jars. Based on the evidence from Shiqmona, they apparently continued in use at least up to the second century C.E. (Elgavish 1977: pl. 19: 142–4 for square-rim jar; pls. 5: 25, 19: 146–9 for thickened-rim jar; pl. 19: 145 for channel-rim jar).

Discussion

In Table 5.1, we summarize the number and distribution of these storage jars. A significant picture emerges, which is highlighted in Figure 5.3. As expected, the first group of barrel-shaped jars predominate at Yodefat

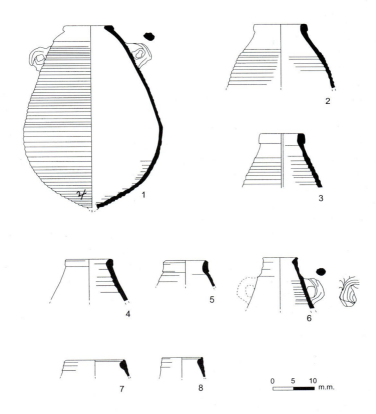

Figure 5.2 Coastal Phoenician storage jars from the Hellenistic and Roman periods.

No.	Site	Locus	Basket	Fabric description
1.	Yodefat	B16008	XV.B16.51	Orange-brown
2.	Yodefat	O2010	XI.O2.31	Reddish brown
3.	Yodefat	Q16014	XI.Q16.35	Light reddish brown
4.	Yodefat	O2014	XI.O2.38	Light reddish brown, light brown core
5.	Yodefat	O2010	XI.O2.31/1	Orange-brown
6.	Bet Zeneta	131	1153/2	Pinkish brown
7.	Bet Zeneta	177	1294/1	Pink-brown
8.	Bet Zeneta	146	1187/6	Pink-brown

Table 5.1 Quantities of Galilean storage jars by type at Yodefat and Bet Zeneta

	Yodefat Hellenistic contexts	Yodefat early Roman contexts	Bet Zeneta
Barrel-shaped body, everted rim	100	46	1
Barrel-shaped body, "Yodefat" type	7	73	0
Barrel-shaped body, stepped rim	4	44	7
Conical body, rounded rim	2	0	3
Conical body, square rim	–	6	7
Conical body, thickened rim	–	0	27
Conical body, channel rim	–	0	30
Miscellaneous	21	2	0
Total	134	171	75

throughout the different periods. Few jars from the Phoenician group were found and of these, only the two earliest types occur: the folded-rim jars from the Hellenistic period and the square-rim jars from the earliest Roman period. No examples of the two subsequent Phoenician jars were found, despite the fact that the site was occupied when these forms appeared. The absence of either thickened-rim or channel-rim jars probably indicates that they were not brought to Yodefat at all. In contrast to the findings at Yodefat, at contemporaneous Bet Zeneta Phoenician jars totally dominate. They are already prominent among the poor findings from the Hellenistic

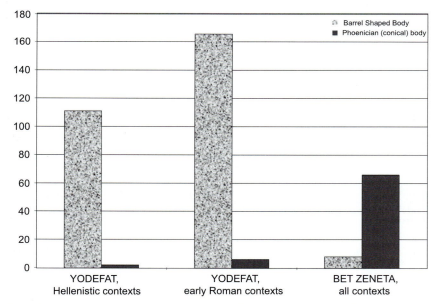

Figure 5.3 Quantities of storage jars by type from Yodefat and Bet Zeneta.

Phoenicians and Jews 81

period and comprise the main ceramic element from the Roman period. Notable here are the predominance of the thickened-rim and channel-rim jars, both of which are absent from the Yodefat assemblage.

This specific, separate distribution pattern may be taken as a reflection of the preferences of the two separate ethnic groups who lived at these sites. The Jewish population of Yodefat primarily used the traditional Galilean barrel-shaped jars. During the Hellenistic period, they did on occasion acquire goods from other, Gentile, regions—hence the few Phoenician jars found in Hellenistic contexts, as well as a few imported Aegean amphoras. The presence of these latter vessels show that the Jews did engage in some outside commerce, even if to a relatively small degree.[7]

It is interesting to note that only the earliest types of Phoenician jars were found in Yodefat. The subsequently developed thickened-rim and channel-rim jars, so common at contemporaneous Bet Zeneta, do not appear. The preference of the first century C.E. Jewish populace of Yodefat to prefer locally produced vessels may be understood in light of Jewish halachic, or legal, precepts that demanded strict adherence to ceramic vessel purity (Vitto 1986: 55–6; but see Chapter 4 by Berlin in this volume). Buyers were advised to witness the firing of the vessels in the kiln in order to be certain that no Gentile handled the vessel during its manufacture, thus rendering it impure (*Mishnah Para* 1.5). The specific place of the vessel in the kiln and even its row were seen to influence and assure the vessel's purity.

In the first century C.E., the Jewish population seems to have developed a growing adherence to religious dictates and commandments, which in turn caused them to become more insular and closed-in. If this assumption is correct then one can see in the material remains of Yodefat a progression from a somewhat more cosmopolitan spirit before and during the time of Herod the Great to one of religious separation and isolation. This separatist spirit is part of the background to, and perhaps foundation for, the Jewish rebellion.

Notes

1 The first season was directed by M. Aviam, D. Adan-Bayewitz and D. Edwards; the second season by M. Aviam and D. Adan-Bayewitz; the final seasons by M. Aviam. (Aviam, Edwards and Adan-Bayewitz 1995; Aviam and Adan-Bayewitz 1997; Adan-Bayewitz and Aviam 1997). The pottery restoration was done by L. Porat; the vessels were drawn by C. Tahan; both of the Israel Antiquities Authority.

2 All baskets were sifted and every vessel rim was saved. The complete ceramic assemblages will be dealt with in depth in the Yodefat final report.

3 Both the stamped handle and the coin were read and dated by D.T. Ariel of the Israel Antiquities Authority.

4 The excavation of the site was financed by the Public Works Department and was directed by N. Getzov and H. Abu-Uqsa on behalf of the Israel Antiquities Authority. The vessels were drawn by E. 'Amar. All recovered vessel rims were

counted although systematic sifting was not undertaken during the excavation. The final report is in preparation.

5 Additional jar types were found in the two excavations but since they are types common to other regions or are imported they are not relevant to the present discussion.

6 For the Iron II prototype see Raban 1980: 150; for its appearance in the Persian period see Stern 1982: 107–10; for the Hellenistic period see e.g. Elgavish 1974: Fig. XXIII: 251, 252 and Berlin 1997a: pl. 57; for the Roman period see Elgavish 1977: Fig. V: 24, 26 and Fig. XIX: 145, 146. The progressive development of this type from the Iron II was first pointed out by Frankel and Getzov as a result of their survey of the western Galilee (Frankel and Getzov 1997: 34–5).

7 Based on the dating of the stamped imported amphora, it appears that, subsequent to the Hasmonean conquest, no additional imported amphora reached Yodefat. This is in contrast to the Phoenician jars which continued in use. Evidence of this is a complete Phoenician jar found on a floor in a clear Hasmonean context (Fig. 5.2: 1).

Bibliography

Adan-Bayewitz, D. (1993) *Common Pottery in Roman Galilee: A Study of Local Trade*, Ramat Gan: Bar Ilan University.

Adan-Bayewitz, D. and Aviam, M. (1997) "Iotapata, Josephus, and the Siege of 67: Preliminary Report on the 1992–1994 Seasons," *Journal of Roman Archaeology* 10: 131–65.

—— (1998) "Yodefat—1993–1994," *Excavations and Surveys in Israel* 18: 16–18.

Adan-Bayewitz, D., Aviam, M. and Edwards, D. R. (1995) "Yodefat," *Excavations and Surveys in Israel* 16: 42–4.

Adan-Bayewitz, D. and Wieder, M. (1992) "Ceramics from Roman Galilee: A Comparison of Several Techniques for Fabric Characterization," *Journal of Field Archaeology* 19: 189–205.

Artzy, M. (1980) "The Utilitarian 'Persian' Storejar Handles," *Bulletin of the American Schools of Oriental Research* 238: 69–73.

Avshalom-Gorni, D. (1998) "Storage Jars from the Hellenistic, Roman and Byzantine Periods in Western Galilee—Chronological, Typological and Regional Aspects," unpublished M.A. thesis, Bar-Ilan University, Ramat-Gan (Heb.).

Berlin, A. (1997a) *Tel Anafa* II, i. *The Hellenistic and Roman Pottery: The Plain Wares*, *Journal of Roman Archaeology*, Supplementary Series 10.2.1, Ann Arbor: Kelsey Museum of Archaeology.

—— (1997b) "From Monarchy to Markets: The Phoenicians in Hellenistic Palestine," *Bulletin of the American Schools of Oriental Research* 306: 75–88.

Diez Fernandez, F. (1983) *Ceramica Comuna Romana de la Galilea*, Madrid: Escuela Biblica.

Elgavish, J. (1974) *Archaeological Excavations at Shikmona—Report No. 2: The Level of the Hellenistic Period—Stratum H*, Haifa: Haifa Museum of Art (Heb.).

—— (1977) *Archaeological Excavations at Shikmona: The Pottery of the Roman Period*, Haifa: Haifa Museum of Art (Heb.).

Frankel, R. and Finkelstein, I. (1983) "The Northwest Corner of Eretz-Israel' in the Baraita 'Boundaries of Eretz-Israel'," *Cathedra* 27: 39–46 (Heb.).

Frankel, R. and Getzov, N. (1997) *Archaeological Survey of Israel: Map of Akhziv (1); Map of Hanita (2)*, Jerusalem: Israel Antiquities Authority.

Guz-Zilberstein, B. (1995) "The Typology of the Hellenistic Coarse Ware and Selected Loci of the Hellenistic and Roman Periods," in E. Stern (ed.) *Excavations at Dor, Final Report—Volume I B; Areas A and C: The Finds*, Jerusalem: Israel Exploration Society.

Landgraff, J. (1980) "The Byzantine Pottery," in J. Briend and J-B. Humbert (eds.) *Tell Keisan (1971–1976)*, Paris: J. Gabalda.

Loffreda, S. (1974) *Cafarnao II. La Ceramica*. Publicazioni dello Studium Biblicum Franciscanum n. 19, Jerusalem: Franciscan Printing Press.

Raban, A. (1980) *The Commercial Jar in the Ancient Near East: Its Evidence for Interconnections amongst the Bible Lands*, unpublished Ph.D. dissertation, Hebrew University, Jerusalem (Heb.).

Stern, E. (1982) *Material Culture of the Land of the Bible in the Persian Period: 538–332 B.C.*, Warminster: Aris and Philips.

Vitto, F. (1986) "Potters and Pottery Manufacture in Roman Palestine," *Bulletin of the University of London Institute of Archaeology* 23: 47–64.

Part II

The first year in Galilee

6 Power vacuum and power struggle in 66–7 C.E.

Richard A. Horsley

The Great Revolt, whether in Judea or Galilee, was a complex series of events. It requires a multifaceted critical approach, a consideration of many factors and their interrelation. I will focus on three principal aspects: (1) our main sources, Josephus's histories, which must be read suspiciously and critically; (2) the political and economic structure of the Roman imperial order, particularly the fact that Rome worked initially through indirect rule in Judea and Galilee; (3) the developments and differences within the districts of Judea and Galilee. In sum, we must consider the interactions and effects between the distinct and various political and economic structures and particular histories of Roman Judea and Galilee as part of the contingent dynamics of key actors and unfolding events.

First principles: key structural and historical factors

The structure of ancient societies was such that religion was embedded in all aspects of daily life, including political and economic activities. Since the fundamental social forms were the household and village communities, it is difficult to identify structures that provided inter-village or regional coherence. While some peoples may have had a certain common awareness as *ethnoi*, "nationalism" is a modern concept that is anachronistic when applied to ancient societies. I understand the specific case of the Revolt, therefore, as a conflict rooted in a society with an interlocking religious–political–economic structure, which was under stress because Judeans and Galileans had experienced Roman conquest and reconquest three times in the sixty years from 63 to 4 B.C.E. In response to the severe Roman practices of scorched-earth slaughter and devastation, people fled to any place that seemed more secure (Yodefat, Yaffo, Gamla, Jerusalem); and rather than simply be slaughtered, some attempted to resist.

Some factors are pertinent particularly to the Revolt in Galilee. First, Galilee had been independent of Jerusalem and/or under a separate division of imperial administration for over 800 years prior to its takeover by the Hasmoneans and its rule by Herod. Significant aspects of Judean society and history, such as the centuries of interaction with the Temple and high priesthood and the Maccabean Revolt, were not part of Galilean collective memory. We must take seriously what anthropologists call the differences between the "great tradition" and the "little tradition," in this case the differences between elite and partially written traditions developed in the Jerusalem temple-state and the Israelite popular tradition that was presumably cultivated in Galilean village communities.

Judeans in Galilee during the first century B.C.E. and the first half of the first century C.E. were probably Hasmonean and then Herodian administrative officials and their service personnel. There is no evidence for institutionalized mechanisms by which Galileans would have been socialized into greater conformity with Jerusalem-based traditions. Galileans may well have had an ambivalent relation to the Temple and high priesthood. Further, there is clear evidence that Galileans, like their Judean cousins, were hostile to Herod and Herodian rulers generally.

This antipathy notwithstanding, after the death of Herod, for seventy years leading up to the Great Revolt, Galilee was controlled mostly by Herodian client kings. In establishing his rule directly in Galilee and building two major cities within twenty years, Antipas must have made a great impact on Galilean village society. Suddenly the rulers of the Galileans lived right in their midst, and a new or rebuilt capital city was accessible from nearly every village. Such major building projects required money from the only available source, the productive peasantry.

After the removal of Antipas, the Romans imposed frequent changes of rulers in Galilee—not exactly stable and consistent rule in a time first of drought and then social unrest. In their policy of indirect rule through client kings and temple-states, the Romans expected indigenous aristocracies such as the Jerusalem high priests to maintain order in the society under their charge. Once the Revolt erupted in the summer of 66 C.E., the only chance for the Jerusalem aristocracy to retain its position of power and privilege was to attempt to regain control of the society (Judea and Idumea). Presumably Agrippa II and his officials in Tiberias and Tarichaeae were faced with the same problem.

Josephus and his agenda as agent and historian

In approaching the Revolt in Galilee we face a dilemma that inevitably involves circular reasoning. In order to use our principal source, Josephus, a highly interested central participant in the events he portrays and so, with good reason, highly suspect in his portrayal of these events, we need to understand the role he was playing in Galilee. In order to understand that role, we must understand the character and strategy of the provisional government in Jerusalem that sent him to Galilee. Yet our only source for the latter is Josephus's own characterization of that provisional government, its circumstances, and its strategy. Nevertheless our situation is not utterly impossible. Considerable debate about how Josephus's histories should be read and critically assessed has led to fairly persuasive hypotheses about the merits of his different portrayals of events and about the character and agenda of the provisional government in Jerusalem.[1]

Josephus's *War* and his later *Life* are often seen to stand in conflict with regard to the formation of a provisional government in Jerusalem and, more importantly, that Jerusalem provisional governments' strategy with regard to the popular insurgency already underway against the Romans. In the *War* Josephus claims that "those who defeated Cestius, after going back to Jerusalem, attracted those who still supported the Romans to their side, some by force and others by persuasion and, gathered in the Temple, appointed several commanders for the war," among whom was Josephus, sent to Galilee (*War* 2.562). In the *Life*, on the other hand, "the principal men of Jerusalem" only pretend to go along with the Revolt in order to regain control of the country and stall for time until they can negotiate with the Romans. In that connection "they dispatched me [Josephus], with two other priests, to induce the disaffected [in Galilee] to lay down their arms and … to wait and see what action the Romans would take" (*Life* 28–9).[2]

If we read the *War* more completely and critically, however, its conflict with the *Life* is more apparent than real. Josephus indicates clearly in later passages in the *War* that the actual strategy of the aristocratic Jerusalem provisional government was exactly as claimed in the *Life*. In the assembly supposedly held in the Temple after the Roman military forces were expelled (*War* 2.562–8) the principal leaders of "those who defeated Cestius," in particular Simon bar Giora and Eleazar ben Simon, were—evidently on purpose—*not* appointed among the "generals to conduct the war." Further, the renegade high priestly temple captain Eleazar ben Ananias was sent to Idumea where he would have difficulty taking any further dramatic revolutionary initiatives. Those appointed to key positions, especially in Jerusalem itself, were stabilizing priestly aristocrats. Subsequently in the *War* Josephus indicates that the high priest Hanan, one of the two heads of the Jerusalem junta, took action to suppress the more insurrectionary forces in the countryside, in hopes of moderating the conflict, apparrently to buy time for an accommodation with the Romans (2.651, 652–4). Later, in Josephus's account of the aristocratic junta's struggles against the Zealots, a coalition of brigand bands from the Judean countryside who invaded Jerusalem in the winter of 67–8 C.E., and particularly in Josephus's encomium on Hanan (4.319–22), Josephus indicates that the real strategy of the high priests and leading Pharisees was to regain control of the society and negotiate a settlement with Rome (Horsley 1995: 72–5). Thus this cannot be dismissed either because it appears only in the later *Life* or because it is simply an "apology" by Josephus. As he indicates clearly in both versions of the Revolt and his role in it, the aristocratic junta was attempting to carry out what was in effect a "counter-revolution" in Jerusalem, and Josephus himself was sent to Galilee basically to assert control of the situation there.

Others have independently recognized similarly that the provisional government in Jerusalem was not all that revolutionary, indeed, was attempting to regain control of the volatile situation and reach accommodation with the Romans. Although he still characterizes it as "popular," Jossa notices that the provisional government in Jerusalem does not give positions of command to the very leaders of the defeat of Cestius (Jossa 1994: 269–72) and that Josephus's behavior in Galilee can hardly be characterized as anti-Roman (273–7). Instead, he adopted "the tactics of waiting and trying to keep open the possibility of a mutual understanding with the Romans" (277). Still working on the sense that the accounts in the *War* and the *Life* conflict, Rappaport recognizes that however "apologetic" the latter may be, it is by far the more credible account historically: in the *Life* Josephus is admitting that he and the aristocratic junta in Jerusalem were pursuing a two-faced policy, pretending to go along with the Revolt while hoping for negotiation with the Romans. Josephus had been forced into this admission by Justus of Tiberias' accusation, based partly on his self-portrayal as a revolutionary general in the *War*, that Josephus was responsible for drawing Tiberias into the appearance of revolt (Rappaport 1994: 282–5). Jossa (1994: 272) concludes that "it is impossible to share those scholars' opinions who want the Jewish aristocracy involved against the Romans together with the Zealots and victim only of their own weakness."

We can thus secure an hypothesis to build upon in reading Josephus's histories, our principal sources, that the provisional high priestly government in Jerusalem sent Josephus to Galilee as part of their general strategy of attempting to control the volatile situation at the end of the summer of 66 C.E. in order to regain the favor of the Romans and negotiate a settlement that would preserve their own positions as client rulers. That conclusion is confirmed by what Josephus did and did not do in Galilee, according to both of his accounts of his activities there. Although he portrays himself in the *War* as the great Jewish general, a worthy foe for the future Emperors Vespasian and Titus and much beloved by his own people, Josephus fails to portray himself engaging the Roman forces in battle in any significant way—with the notable exception of the siege of Jotapata. Interpreters have long since become suspicious of his claim to have fortified all those cities and villages (*War* 2.573). His grossly exaggerated claim about the size of his army have never been credible (576, 583). Except for Jotapata, Josephus and his military forces engaged the Roman's forces or Agrippa's royal forces rarely and then in relatively insignificant connections, as in checking each other's maneuvers. In what is virtually the only case (*Life* 115–18), Josephus and 2,000 infantry (he claims) skirmished briefly and tentatively with a small Roman force under the decurion Aebutius on the frontier between Galilee and the Great Plain near Besara and Herod's old military colony of Gaba.

Josephus did have military forces under his command in Galilee. But instead of using them against the Romans, he used them to control affairs in Galilee, in various connections. Whatever control Josephus was able to exercise in Galilee was based on his own, apparently private, army which he claims consisted of 4,500 mercenaries and a "body-guard" of 600 (*War* 2.583). Those figures are likely inflated, and even if these mercenaries were the same as the "brigands" he paid in Galilee (which I doubt), the effect was the same. While he did not use them against the Romans in any significant encounters, he did use them to control certain areas and general affairs in Galilee. Whatever his credibility, he claims to have "taken by storm" the cities of Gabara, Sepphoris (twice) and Tiberias (four times) as well as to have deployed his own hoplites (obviously 10,000 is a gross exaggeration) against Tiberias at one point (*Life* 82.321–31). He indicates at several points that he deployed a commander with troops to control Tiberias (*War* 2.616; *Life* 89.272). He kept most of his troops and bodyguard always with him, dismissing them only for the special occasion of the Sabbath (*Life* 159), relying on them for his own security and "forceful suasion" (e.g., the distinction in *Life* 240–2, 243). He effectively neutralized potential rival fighting forces, such as the brigand bands that formed in various regions of Galilee. Indeed he simultaneously co-opted both these brigands and the Galilean peasants by conning the latter into paying the former to serve as mercenaries—who of course were to take orders from him. He even adapted a standard use of military forces in ancient politics: as he candidly admits in the *Life* (79.228; cf. *War* 2.570) the Galileans who dined with him as his "friends" and served as envoys to Jerusalem (while under guard!) were really local Galilean magistrates ("those in office") whom he had taken as hostages for the acquiescence of the Galilean villagers and whom he could use to legitimate his actions.

Insofar as the provisional government in Jerusalem was attempting to control the active conflict that had erupted in 66 C.E. and insofar as the "general" they sent to Galilee was using his own military forces not to fight against the Romans but to control the Galileans and Galilean cities, events in (Judea and) Galilee cannot be understood in terms of a simple binary opposition of pro and anti-Roman forces or of "the peace party" and "the war party" (cf. Cohen 1979: 183–5). The Jerusalem provisional government delegated Josephus to take control of Galilee and he proceeded to do so with the help of the military forces at his disposal. But the Galilee already had Roman-installed rulers. Galilee had not been under the jurisdiction of Jerusalem authorities since the death of Herod the Great, at which point the Romans had placed Galilee under the rule of Antipas. Thereafter Galilee was ruled by Agrippa I and later partitioned, the western part of lower Galilee apparently under the control of the city of Sepphoris, itself accountable to the Roman governor in Caesarea, while eastern lower Galilee was under the client king Agrippa II from 54 C.E. on. Thus, after a century under Hasmonean and Herodian rule from 104 to 4 B.C.E., Galilee had not been under Jerusalem's jurisdiction for the following seventy years prior to the Revolt. In sending Josephus and his aristocratic priestly colleagues to attempt to take control of affairs in Galilee during the summer of 66 C.E., therefore, the high priestly provisional government in Jerusalem was reasserting Jerusalem rule over Galilee (*War* 2.562–8). Josephus's elaborate accounts of the attempts by the Jerusalem junta to replace him is further indication that the leading high priests and Pharisees believed that they should control affairs in Galilee (*War* 2.626–31; *Life* 189–335). As noted above, the high-priestly led provisional government in Jerusalem could have entertained no illusions that, in the long run, they were independent of Roman rule. Rather they were attempting to assert control over Galilee as part of their overall strategy to regain control of the Judean and Galilean people in order to regain the confidence of the Romans in their ability to maintain order. But they were clearly taking the opportunity of the vacuum of effective Roman control of Galilee through Sepphoris and Agrippa II's governing apparatus in Tiberias and Tarichaeae to intervene in an area not designated by Rome as under their jurisdiction.

What Josephus encountered and contributed to in Galilee and then subsequently portrayed in his histories was thus far more complex than a simple anti-Roman revolt. It was instead a variety of interrelated and overlapping conflicts including urban–rural hostilities, class conflict within the cities, hostility toward and acquiescence in Roman and/or Herodian rule, and response to and rejection of Jerusalem authority—including plenty of mutual manipulation and negotiation and shifting alliances. Far from examining the Revolt in Galilee in general, it is necessary to focus on particular cities, areas, or groups in order to begin to comprehend the shifting dynamics of the power struggles from the initial outbreak of the Revolt in the summer of 66 C.E. to the Roman reconquest in the summer of 67 C.E.

Galilee in 66–7 C.E.

Of the two rival capital cities, Sepphoris, Antipas' "ornament of all Galilee" and still "the greatest city of Galilee," remained unswervingly loyal to (and dependent on) Roman rule (see further, Chapter 7 by Meyers, in this volume). Through Josephus or otherwise, the high-priestly provisional government in Jerusalem attempted to assert its authority in Sepphoris. The capital city of western lower Galilee, however, for its part consistently resisted its advances, for example refusing to talk with either Josephus or with the priestly Pharisaic delegation Jerusalem sent to replace him in Galilee (*Life* 123–4). While waiting for the inevitable Roman reconquest of the area, Sepphoris therefore resourcefully engaged the brigand-chieftan Jesus and his horde of several hundred as mercenaries to protect it from the hostile Galileans (*Life* 104–11). Josephus would appear to have been engaged in some sort of mutually manipulative game with Sepphoris. It is not at all clear how to understand Josephus's accounts of his interaction with the city. He claims to have taken it by storm twice (*War* 2.646; *Life* 82, 374, 395–6). Yet he also claims to have served at one point as a mediator making it easier for

Sepphoris, as the only unit consistently loyal to Rome, to maintain its position and he came to a "mutual understanding" with Jesus the brigand-chief and his horde serving as the city's protectors (*Life* 30–1, 107–11). He also says that he was "inveigled into [further] fortifying the city"—which was already an exceptionally strong fortress (*Life* 347; *War* 3.61; cf. 3.34).

Tiberias, the other principal city in Galilee, was sharply divided along class lines between the "ten principal men" headed by Julius Capellus and the "party of sailors and the poor" led by Jesus son of Sapphias (*Life* 32–5, 64–7, 69, 296). The third party mentioned by Josephus, headed by his rival historian Justus son of Pistus (*Life* 36), does not appear to play much of a role in his subsequent accounts. Josephus himself repeatedly consulted and collaborated with Capellus and the "leading men," who were consistently pro-Roman and pro-Agrippa, repeatedly attempting to have royal troops take over the city. As the Roman reconquest worked its way toward Tiberias, these Herodian elite of Tiberias fled to Agrippa in the Roman camp and pleaded for Vespasian's mercy (*Life* 34, 155; *War* 2.632; 3.453–4). Jesus and the Tiberian "riff-raff," on the other hand, killed "all the Greeks" and burned and looted the royal palace at the beginning of the Revolt and at the end actively resisted the Roman army both at Tiberias and then at Tarichaeae (*Life* 66–7; *War* 3.450, 457–9). Josephus suggests that these two classes fought for control over Tiberias throughout the brief "revolt" in Galilee and led a pitched intra-city battle or a "purge" by one side or another as the Roman army marched closer (*Life* 353).

Josephus's main concern was his own control of Tiberias, the machinations of which complicate his narratives. After taking control he placed one of his own officers, Silas, in charge of the city (*Life* 89; *War* 2.616). Then for one reason or another, he repeatedly had to reassert his control, claiming to have taken the city by assault four times (*Life* 82, 155–74, 317–35; *War* 2.632–46). Josephus provides clear indications that his assertion of control over Tiberias was part of the general agenda of the provisional government in Jerusalem, headed by high priests and influenced increasingly by leading Pharisees such as Simon son of Gamaliel. When he first arrived, Josephus pressed upon the "council and principal men of the city" the orders of the Jerusalem *koinon* that the royal palace be demolished because it contained "representations of animals … forbidden by the [Judean] laws" (*Life* 64–5). Similarly Josephus's lengthy account of the Jerusalem priestly Pharisaic envoys' negotiations to replace him reveals the Jerusalem council's continuing agenda of control in Tiberias. However it may have accorded with that of the Jerusalem council, moreover, Josephus had his own agenda which he repeatedly had to disguise because it ran counter to the popular interests in Tiberias. He repeatedly collaborated with the Herodian upper class of Tiberias who were loyal to Agrippa, for example, handing over the spoil taken from the royal palace to Capellus and the leading men to hold in trust for the king, while effectively delaying the time when Agrippa would re-establish control.

Just as Sepphoris' loyalty to the Romans can be explained from its history, so the position of the "principal men" of Tiberias can be explained from the history of that royal city. Tiberias had been founded by Antipas only a half-century before the Revolt as a royal city of a Roman client king. At least among its Herodian elite, it seems to have retained its identity as a small royal administrative city, never having been under Jerusalem's jurisdiction and having experienced only about a decade of direct Roman rule. The Herodian elite, however, had reason for some resentment over the city's loss of status, since under Agrippa II it had become reduced to a toparchy capital, like Tarichaeae, and had lost the royal bank and archives (*Life* 37–9). That, along with the formidable opposition of the party of the poor and sailors led by the city magistrate Jesus, may explain why Tiberias was more vulnerable to Josephus's manipulations than was Sepphoris.

Tarichaeae (Magdala) just northwest of Tiberias along the shore of the Sea of Galilee, also the center of a toparchy under Agrippa II, appears to have been more solidly in the control of the leading residents who remained loyal to Agrippa. Two of the "leading men," Dassion and Jannaeus son of Levi ("the most powerful man of the Tarichaeans") were "very special friends of the king" and still secure in their positions (*Life* 131; *War* 2.597). Josephus entrusted them with goods taken from one of the king's officers in an ambush for safe return at the appropriate time. The interests of the dominant Tarichaeans were apparently similar to those of Josephus and those of the Jerusalem *koinon*. Tarichaeae proved his most dependable ally in Galilee, and his most comfortable "headquarters" (*Life* 97, 159–60, 276, 304). He benefited from their support particularly in difficult dealings with Tiberias (*War* 2.635–41; *Life* 97–8). Josephus distinguishes carefully between the dominant Tarichaeans and the refugees from other towns and peasants from the surrounding area who came together in and around Tarichaeae at times and were eager to resist royal or Roman rule, as well as Josephus's leadership (*War* 2.598–602). "The indigenous residents, intent on their property and city," had from the beginning opposed the war and were simply caught in the middle between the Roman attack and the resistance of the rebellious nearby peasants and Tiberian lower class (*War* 3.492, 500–1). Although they were taken captive, Vespasian restored these leading Tarichaeans to their town (*War* 3.532–5). Again as with Sepphoris and the Tiberian elite, their history helps explain the stance of the dominant Tarichaeans: their interests and orientation lay with the established imperial order.

For Josephus to have presented Gabara (about ten miles north of Sepphoris) as the third of the "chief cities of Galilee," it also must have been an administrative town (*Life* 82, 123, 203; identical with the village of Gabaroth? *Life* 229, 235, 240, 242–3). In the escalation of social conflict during the summer of 66 C.E., some people from Gabara joined with some from Sogane, Tyre, and Gadara (?) in attacking Gischala (Gush Halav) to the northeast, which proceeded to counterattack (*Life* 44). Once Simon, the leading resident of Gabara, became fast friends with John son of Levi, however, the two towns formed a lasting alliance (*Life* 123–4). Assuming that the "house of Jesus" was anything like the "great castle as imposing as a citadel" described by Josephus, there were some extremes of wealth and power in the area. Gabara stoutly resisted Josephus's attempt at taking control. Although Josephus claims to have taken Gabara by assault, he makes no mention of fortifying it (mentioning rather the village of Sogane, nearby). Vespasian's "first objective" as he launched his reconquest of Galilee was Gabara. Finding no combatants in the town, "he slew all the males who were of age … and also burned all the surrounding villages and towns," enslaving the remaining inhabitants (*War* 3.132–4).

What happened in Gischala (Gush Halav) and Upper Galilee during the Revolt cannot be separated from the rise to prominence of John son of Levi. It is difficult in the extreme, however, to reconstruct the rise of John from Josephus's polemics against his principal rival for control in Galilee. Gischala was a key regional town in the rugged hill country of Upper Galilee along the frontier with territory controlled by Tyre. As is usually the case during times of social conflict in a frontier region, fugitives gathered along the frontier near Gischala in 66 C.E. (*War* 2.588, 625; *Life* 372). Toward the outset of the widening disorder, as mentioned above, the towns of Gabara and Sogane to the southwest and some elements from Tyre had attacked Gischala, which then counterattacked and fortified itself (*Life* 43–5). Such are the circumstances from which John rose to become Josephus's principal rival in Galilee. Josephus's charge that John got his start as a brigand has at least some credibility, since it is in just such circumstances that communities (such as the city of Sepphoris) rely on strongmen for protection and leadership. Whatever his origins, John built a following from the fugitives along the Tyrian frontier (*War* 2.587–8). His first conflict with Josephus revolved around local autonomy and local leadership versus control from above (i.e., by Josephus as a representative of the Jerusalem junta). Josephus's complaints about both John's seizure of the imperial stores of grain in the villages of Upper Galilee and about John's scheme to supply pure olive oil to the Jewish inhabitants of Caesarea Philippi simply suggest that John had outmaneuvered him in bolstering his own local power as opposed to Josephus design to enhance his regional power. John and Gischala, however, next moved to challenge Josephus for influence in the rest of Galilee. John sought alliances in Tiberias, in active conflict with Josephus's attempt to control the city (*War* 2.6 14–25; *Life* 84–96; cf. 368–72). Gischala reversed the earlier conflict with Gabara, John cementing a friendship with the town's strongman, Simon (*Life* 123–4, 235). John also started cultivating central figures in the Jerusalem provisional government, supposedly establishing the second co-commander there, Jesus son of Gamala, as "an intimate friend" (*Life* 204) and forming links with leading Pharisees who played an increasingly influential role in the provisional government. The struggle in Galilee created unlikely bedfellows: peasants and refugees in upper Galilee forged alliances not only with their former enemies, the elite of Gabara, but with scribal officials as well as the lower class of Tiberias and, finally, the Pharisaic delegation from Jerusalem. Josephus almost met his match in maneuvering for control of Galilee.

Throughout both of Josephus's accounts of affairs in Galilee, "the Galileans" are consistently hostile to the cities and/or the urban elite of Sepphoris and Tiberias and to those who dominate Gabara and Tarichaeae as well. In both accounts "the Galileans" usually refers to the people from the countryside (*chora*), i.e., the peasantry, in a given area or in Galilee as a whole (e.g., *War* 2.602, 621–2; 3.199; *Life* 102, 243), often in distinction from the people of Tiberias and/or Sepphoris. Josephus uses *hoi galilaioi* to refer to the Galilean peasantry regardless of whether they are loyal to himself in the *Life* (30, 39, 66, 143, 177, 351) just as he had in the *War* (2.621–22; 3.110, 199, etc.). The only variation is that from a perspective beyond Galilee, "the Galileans" can refer to all residents of Galilee, including people in Sepphoris and Tiberias. Josephus thoroughly distorts his relationship with the Galilean peasants insofar as "the Galileans" figure as the key to his self-defense in the *Life*. He even has them acclaim him as "the benefactor and savior of their country" (244, 259) when the delegation arrives from the Jerusalem provisional government to displace him from his command. In moments of greater realism and candor, however, he admits several examples of how he co-opted the Galilean peasants in his attempts to control one or another of the cities or to counter John of Gischala and how he kept their leaders as hostages under guard because he did not trust them (e.g., *Life* 79, 228). Obviously we should be extremely suspicious of Josephus's apologetic narcissism and of his claims about the peasants' devotion to himself. Indeed, Josephus himself indicates at several points that, far from being deceived by and loyal to him, the Galileans distrusted, challenged, and opposed him. While he presented the Jerusalem provisional government's concerns to the Herodian elite in Tiberias, the Galilean peasants in the area were helping to loot the royal palace (*Life* 66). They were not fooled by his secret plan to return goods they had plundered from the king Agrippa's finance officer and they were suspicious of his protection of the foreign officers of the king (*War* 595–7; *Life* 126–31, 149–52). Not surprisingly, they suspected that his real intention was "to betray the country to the Romans," distrusted his protestations to the contrary, and even (he says, credibly enough) attempted to kill him (*Life* 132–48; *War* 2.598–610). While peasants often appear overly trusting of those seeking alliances with them in times of social disruption and revolt, the Galilean peasants appear to have been healthily skeptical of the "general" from Jerusalem, and appear to have cooperated mainly when it suited their own concerns.

The Galilean peasants' hostility to the cities and/or city elite in Sepphoris and Tiberias is indisputable. It must have been present and at times intense, or Josephus could not have exploited it for his own purposes, as he repeatedly claims to have done. "The Galileans ... had the same detestation for the Tiberians that they had for the Sepphorites" (*Life* 384). This hostility had built up for decades out of the people's resentment at the way they had been treated by their rulers in the cities (e.g., *Life* 30, 39, 177). Josephus's tirades against his rival historian Justus, who held some official administrative position in Tiberias, provides a specific example of the intensity of the peasant resentment as well as of the reason for it in their rulers' exploitative machinations: "The Galileans, resenting the miseries which he had inflicted on them before the war, were embittered against the Tiberians" (*Life* 392). Indeed, "the Galileans had cut off his brothers' hands on a charge of forging letters prior to the outbreak of the hostilities" (*Life* 177). Not surprisingly, the Galilean peasantry seized the opportunity of the collapse of effective Roman or Herodian royal rule to exercise their intense hostility against those whom they viewed as their exploiters in Sepphoris and Tiberias (e.g., *Life* 66–7, 374–8, 381–4). While claiming to have mitigated its most extreme potential manifestations, Josephus unabashedly admits that he used the Galileans' hostility to Sepphoris in his attempts to control that city (*Life* 30, 107, 374–7). As in the case of the burning and looting of the royal palace in Tiberias, the peasants in the area made common cause with the party of poor and sailors led by Jesus son of Sapphias inside the city against the Herodian elite who controlled the area on behalf of the king, just as their predecessors had for Antipas and Agrippa I. Given the political–economic structure of the Roman imperial order, Josephus's report that the peasantry's hostility to the Sepphoris and Tiberias elite was closely related to the latters' loyalty to Rome and/or king Agrippa II is highly credible. One incident concerning Tiberias should be sufficient to illustrate the conflicting power relations, in which their opposition to their ultimate rulers, the Romans, was connected with their hostility to their immediate rulers in the capital cities, in the very structure of the situation:

> The principal men from the council [of Tiberias] had written to the king inviting him to come and take over their city. The king promised to come, writing a letter in reply, which he handed Crispus, a groom of the bed-chamber, a Judean by race, to convey to the Tiberians. On his arrival with the letter he was recognized by the Galileans, who seized him and brought him to me. The news created general indignation and all were up in arms. On the following day large numbers flocked together from all quarters to the town of Asochis ... loudly denouncing the Tiberians as traitors and friendly to the king, and asking permission to go down and exterminate their city. For they had the same detestation for the Tiberians as for the Sepphorites.
>
> (*Life* 38.1–84)

The historical role of the cities in Galilee as elsewhere in the Roman imperial order can be seen in the eventual Roman reconquest, in which troops from bases in the city resubjected the countryside, re-establishing the traditional power-relations in no uncertain terms. Both infantry and cavalry "made constant sallies and overran the surrounding country devastating the plains and pillaging the property of the countryfolk, invariably killing all capable of bearing arms and enslaving the weak" (*War* 3.59–63, 110).

For all the intense Galilean peasant hostility to the cities of Tiberias and Sepphoris, however, there is little in Josephus's accounts to indicate that they were actively engaged in a revolution against the Rome-imposed political–economic order. To the extent that they were armed, they had done it on their own (Josephus's claims to have organized and armed an army being utterly incredible). Yet there is no evidence that they mounted major or frequent attacks against the cities, hence difficult to imagine that they would have except for Josephus's restraining influence. The only remotely "insurrectionary" activity Josephus describes was clearly an *ad hoc* local occurrence.

> Some adventurous young men of Dabaritta [a village on the western slope of Mount Tabor] lay in wait for the wife of Ptolemy, the king's overseer. She was travelling in great state, protected by an escort of cavalry, from territory subject to the royal administration, into the region of Roman dominion, when, as she was crossing the Great Plain, they suddenly fell upon the cavalcade, compelled the lady to fly, and plundered all her baggage. They then came to me at Tarichaeae with four mules laden with apparel and other articles, besides a large pile of silver and five hundred pieces of gold.
>
> (*Life* 126–7)

Indeed it would be difficult to argue that the Galilean peasants were actively engaged in a revolt or insurrection in any sustained and organized way, unless defending yourself against the intentionally punitive and retaliatory Roman reconquest can be construed as somehow revolutionary. Once the Roman military briefly "pacified" Galilee and then withdrew in the summer of 66 C.E., the Galilean villagers simply enjoyed the temporary realization of a typical peasant fantasy: living independent of taxation and other exploitation by landlords and rulers. Apparently the power-relations were such that the Roman agents in Sepphoris and the royal officers in Tiberias temporarily felt unable to carry out their usual duties of tax-collection and social control. Even villages in immediate proximity to the ruling cities were able, temporarily, to take a position remarkably independent of their once and future rulers. The village of Shikhin, for example, was resistant to direction from Jerusalem as well as temporarily independent of Sepphoris' and Roman rule (*Life* 230–3). Sepphorites, for their part, felt sufficiently vulnerable to potential attacks from the surrounding villagers that they hired the brigand Jesus and his horde of 800 to defend them. And the Herodian elite of Tiberias repeatedly attempted to arrange for Agrippa to reassert control there. But aside from the raid on the royal palace early on, we know of no organized popular assault on either city or on the urban elite (the attack on the Greeks in Tiberias was by the urban lower class there).[3]

Some villagers did resist the Roman reconquest, in which the Roman troops systematically slaughtered and enslaved the people and destroyed their villages without consideration of whether combatants were present. Many peasants simply fled to mountain strongholds such as labor or fortress towns like Jotapata or Gischala. Whatever Josephus's role there may have been historically, the Romans conducted a major siege and assault at Jotapata, so those gathered there did "go down fighting" (see Chapter 8 by Aviam in this volume). Josephus's recitation of the heroics of a few Galileans from nearby villages such as Saba and Rumah has a ring of credibility (*War* 3.229–33). Josephus claims that at Japha, "the largest village in Galilee," near Nazareth and Sepphoris, the villagers offered heroic resistance to the Romans' attack (*War* 3.289–306). Similarly at Tarichaeae, although the residents of the town were quiescent, Galileans from the nearby countryside offered resistance (*War* 3.492–502). And "a vast multitude" who had fled to Mount Tabor held out as long as possible against the relentless Roman attack (*War* 4.45–61).

Throughout Josephus's accounts of affairs in Galilee, it is clear that the Galilean peasants' activity was distinct from, if at points similar to, the actions of the large troops of brigands that formed out of the social dislocation leading up to the Revolt (Horsley 1995: 85–6, 264–8). Josephus's accounts, moreover, must be read critically in any attempt to discern banditry and to distinguish it from *ad hoc* insurrectionary activities by rebellious bands of peasants still based in villages (*contra* Schwartz 1994: 296–300). The behavior of brigand bands in 66–7 C.E. in Galilee appears to have been every bit as diverse as the other local and regional conflicts examined above, with the situation in and around Gischala being unique insofar as banditry can, but rarely does, flow directly into peasant revolt. Factors such as taxation, indebtedness, drought and famine, repressive political administration, and in Galilee in particular shifting political jurisdictions and frequent change of rulers during the 40s and 50s contributed to the social and economic difficulties of the peasantry and the rising incidence of banditry. In the years just prior to the outbreak of the revolt banditry escalated to epidemic proportions in Galilee as well as in Judea (see further Horsley 1979a; Horsley 1981; Isaac 1984: 176–83; Shaw 1984). In Galilee banditry was of relatively greater importance in the developing social turmoil, in contrast to Judea, with its diverse types of popular resistance, such as prophetic movements and "dagger men." Josephus's accounts indicate that the large brigand groups already in existence constituted one of two principal kinds of resistance to the initial Roman attempt to regain control of Galilee in the summer of 66 C.E. While Sepphoris was welcoming the Roman forces, "all the rebels and brigands fled to the mountains in the heart of Galilee" where they were able temporarily to hold off a Roman legion (*War* 2.511). As happened repeatedly later in Judea, the Roman practice of systematic devastation ironically generated the very insurrection they were supposedly suppressing by generating thousands of fugitives (e.g., *War*

2.504–5; cf. 3.60–3). Other fugitives from the Greek and Syrian cities' attacks on their Jewish inhabitants or dependent villages may also have swelled the ranks of the brigands (*War* 2.457–80; *Life* 77–8, 105).

Epidemic banditry, however, while perhaps an indication of social breakdown, is not necessarily revolutionary. Once Galilee slipped into political anarchy, it would be difficult to view the large brigand horde that formed as fitting Hobsbawm's model of "social banditry," flexible as his discussion is.[4] The large brigand bands appear rather to have become pawns in the struggles between the principal leaders and cities during the year leading up to the Roman reconquest. As already noted, Sepphoris, which remained loyal to its Roman patrons, hired Jesus and his band of 800 as mercenaries to defend them against the potential attacks of the Galilean peasants—and Josephus. (Presumably the Jesus hired by Sepphoris is different from "the Galilean named Jesus" mentioned later as "staying in Jerusalem with a company of 600 men under arms" whom the Jerusalem junta engaged to protect the Pharisaic delegation sent to displace Josephus in Galilee, *Life* 200.) The greatest manipulator of bandit groups in Galilee was probably Josephus himself. The source of the power he wielded in Galilee during 66–7 was surely his own mercenary force and bodyguards. But he also manipulated the peasants into a "protection racket," paying for their freedom from harassment from bands of brigands who then were to report to and take orders from Josephus:

> I also summoned the most stalwart of the brigands and, seeing that it would be impossible to disarm them, persuaded the people [to plethos] to pay them as mercenaries, remarking that it was better to give them a small sum voluntarily than to submit to raids upon their property. I then bound them by oath not to enter the district [*chora*] unless they were sent for or their pay was in arrears, and dismissed them with injunctions to refrain from attacking the Romans or their neighbors.
>
> (*Life* 77–8)

Throughout his manipulation of both peasants and brigand groups Josephus's "chief concern" was in effect counter-revolutionary: "the preservation of the peace in Galilee" (*Life* 78). Even if there was any revolutionary potential among the bandit groups of Lower Galilee, it was cut off by the city of Sepphoris, Josephus, and perhaps other local power-holders, who used them as mercenaries in the service of other interests.

Only in Upper Galilee around Gischala, so far as we know, did the escalating banditry flow into rebellion and perhaps even stimulate wider peasant revolt, rather than be manipulated by those attempting to restore the established order (see further Horsley 1981). Through Josephus's sharp hostility to his principal rival for influence in Galilee we can still discern two significant aspects of the relationship between John, the bandits in this frontier area, and the people of Gischala. Bandits, many of whom were fugitives from across the frontier in the villages of Tyre, constituted a significant part of the fighting force that provided the basis of John's expending influence in Galilee (e.g., *War* 2.588, 625; *Life* 94, 101, 233, 292, 301, 304, 371–2). However partially or completely John dictated their actions, his agenda appears to have been relatively revolutionary, especially when compared with that of Josephus. John's attempt to "seize the imperial grain stores in the villages of upper Galilee" was a clear act of revolt against Roman rule (*Life* 71–3). Moreover, in contrast to the capitulation of Tiberias and Josephus's self-serving surrender at Jotapata, John and his forces at Gischala resisted as long as they could, and then headed for what must have appeared as the center of revolt and a more defensible fortress in Jerusalem (*War* 4.98–120). In the introduction to his account of the Gischalans' final struggle to maintain their independence, Josephus himself explains how perhaps the escalation of banditry in the area stimulated the Gischalan peasants to revolt.

> In Gischala, a small town in Galilee, … the inhabitants were inclined to peace, being mainly farmers [*georgoi*] whose whole attention was devoted to the prospects of the harvest. But they had been afflicted by the invasion of numerous gangs of brigands, from whom some members of the community had caught the contagion.
>
> (*War* 4.84)

As Hobsbawm points out, although rare, this is exactly what can happen in certain circumstances. The earlier attacks on Gischala by Tyre, Gabara, and Sogane undoubtedly contributed both to the escalating banditry in the area and to the politicization of the peasants of Gischala. Thus from these and related factors, in contrast to what happened in Lower Galilee, the peasants and brigand groups in and around Gischala joined in common insurrection against Roman rule, as well as resisted Josephus's machinations as a representative of Jerusalem rule.

To summarize this survey of events in Galilee in 66–7 C.E.: there was no unifying ideology and no coherent anti-Roman revolt in Galilee (*contra* the archaeological evidence and suggestions of Berlin, Chapter 4, and Avshalom-Gorni and Getzov, Chapter 5, in this volume). There were, instead, a number of interrelated local or regionally based conflicts. Sepphoris remained consistently loyal to Rome. Tiberias split between its Herodian elite and a more revolutionary popular faction. "The Galileans," by which Josephus refers to the villagers of Lower Galilee, directed their hostilities against Sepphoris and the ruling elite of Tiberias, often making common cause with the popular party in the latter city. Although the elite of the toparchy capital Tarichaeae remained loyal to Agrippa II, there was less conflict with the surrounding villagers who were ready to resist Roman reconquest. Any "revolutionary" potential of the burgeoning brigand bands was vitiated by their hiring as mercenaries by Sepphoris and Josephus and perhaps others.

Distinctively in Upper Galilee in and around Gischala, Josephus's principal rival for influence in Galilee, John, led a coalition of peasants and brigand bands partly composed of refugees from the Tyrian frontier, and both challenged Josephus for domination of Galilee and resisted the Roman reconquest, finally fleeing to join the resistance in Jerusalem. With the exception of the Herodian "leading men" of Tiberias and the elite who dominated Tarichaeae, all of the various towns and groups successfully resisted Josephus's attempts to assert Jerusalem's or his own control in Galilee. In sum, I conclude that there was no coherent, unified, anti-Roman "revolt" in Galilee in 66–7 C.E., but rather a number of overlapping but independent conflicts, rooted in local and regional history within the broader structure of the Roman imperial order in Judea and Galilee. While local or regional in their particular manifestations, these conflicts' principal common division was between the rulers, who were based in cities, and the ruled, whether in cities or villages.

Judea and Jerusalem

It is pertinent to compare the conclusions of this analysis of multiple conflicts raging in Galilee in 66–7 C.E. with the patterns discernible in the Revolt in Judea and Jerusalem. Here also, although there was more of a coherent and sometimes coordinated revolt, local factors rooted in local history were of crucial importance. The principal division, again, was between urban-based rulers and village- or city-based ruled. The Revolt in Judea and Jerusalem, however, differs from that in Galilee, insofar as the former gained momentum and intensity long after the latter was fully suppressed by the Roman reconquest. Events in Galilee, moreover, were relatively remote and detached from events in Judea and Jerusalem. Ancestral Judean–Jerusalem institutions of the Temple and its high priesthood played little or no role in Galilee, while these were central to the Revolt in the the south.

It is important to distinguish the structural roots of the Revolt from its sequence and patterns. Judea was a temple-community headed by an ancestral high-priestly aristocracy. As is increasingly evident from recent analysis of post-exilic prophetic literature, apocalyptic literature, and Qumran literature, however, the imperially sponsored temple-state and high-priestly incumbents had never been completely accepted by all elements in Judean society, not even by the scribal retainers of the temple-state. Periodic conflicts had emerged among rival priestly groups, whether between rival high-priestly factions or between the ordinary priests and the incumbent high priests. Such recent recognitions must make us all the more uncertain about the basic loyalty of the Judean peasants to the Temple and supposedly hereditary high priesthood. The Hasmonean dynasty, itself an "illegitimate" upstart family of rebels who consolidated their position by arrangement with imperial regimes and wars of expansion, evoked substantial opposition and internal division, particularly in its last generations. After systematically eliminating the Hasmoneans, the Roman-installed client king Herod recon-stituted the priestly aristocracy from Jewish priestly families from Egypt and Babylon. These families had no previous relations either with the Judean priestly clans or with the region's ordinary people. Thus the priestly aristocracy that the Romans entrusted with control of Judea after Herod's death and the deposition of his son Archelaus had little legitimacy, their power depending on Roman patronage that worked primarily through Roman governors. The priestly aristocracy, moreover, became increasingly predatory on the people they ruled. They built themselves lavish mansions in the New City in Jerusalem while gradually manipulating Judean peasants into indebtedness, through which they could exploit their labor and extract their produce. This pattern of exploitation was further compounded by the remaining Herodian families who had established estates at various points, including the Judean hill country northwest of Jerusalem.

Social conflicts escalated steadily during the decades preceding the out-break of revolt in the summer of 66 C.E. In Jerusalem itself, where the populace was economically dependent on the temple apparatus, these in-cluded protests over the oppressive or insensitive actions of Roman governors (among many treatments, Horsley 1987: 90–120). The priestly aristocracy did little to mediate (Horsley 1985). In the countryside popular prophets led movements of liberation inspired by fantastic visions of a new exodus or new conquest (Theudas and the "Egyptian" Jewish prophet respectively). Parti-cularly after the drought and famine of the late 40s deepened the crisis for many Judean peasants, the always endemic social banditry became epidemic at times, a telling sign of the breakdown of social order (Horsley 1979a, 1987). Far from attempting to mitigate such circumstances and attend to the disintegrating social order, the four principal high priestly families exacerbated it, competing for influence with and appointment by the Roman governors and even gathering gangs of thugs which they used both to seize tithes from the threshing floors, depriving the ordinary priests of their living, and to attack each other (Horsley 1987: 46–7; Goodman 1987: 20 and *passim*). In this respect I appreciate and affirm the important, careful analysis of Martin Goodman in delineating the high-priestly factions and their struggle for power, particularly in the last decades prior to the Revolt, as one of the principal factors leading to its outbreak. The fundamental division was between the increasingly exploited peasantry and frustrated Jerusalem populace, on the one hand, and the high-priestly and Herodian aristocracy and Roman rulers, on the other. In order for a revolt to happen, however, as has been pointed out for modern times, the ruling class must come to a point where it can no longer effectively rule. And the struggle between various high-priestly factions compounded the illegitimacy of the priestly aristocracy and their alienation from the people and the ordinary priests sufficiently that by the mid-60s they could no longer control Judean society, to the specific extent that they were no longer able to collect the tribute for Rome, which was in arrears (*War* 2.405).

In Jerusalem and Judea the sequence of the Revolt unfolded in three phases: the initial eruption in the summer of 66 C.E.; the temporarily successful attempt by the high priestly aristocracy and leading Pharisees to control it from late 66 C.E. through early 68 C.E.; and the coalescence of popular forces from the Judean countryside and their entry into Jerusalem during 68 and 69 C.E., where they held out against the Roman reconquest until Jerusalem was destroyed in 70 C.E..

The first phase not only was concentrated in Jerusalem, but involved Jerusalemites, including ordinary priests and renegade high priests as leading participants. In the deteriorating series of events leading up to more revolutionary actions, the Jerusalem "crowd" engaged in protests over what they considered outrages and provocations by Florus, the Roman governor and his troops (*War* 293–332). Eventually the Jerusalemites began fighting back against the Roman troops unleashed to "pacify" the city (*War* 2.325–9), and Florus simply withdrew, leaving the ruling aristocracy to bail themselves out of the now uncontrollable situation (331–2). A more serious act was the symbolic one of the cessation of sacrifices for the emperor by the priests, led by the renegade high priest, the Temple-captain Eleazar son of Ananias (409). Despite abuse by Florus, the high priests, other "notables" and leading Pharisees desperately attempted to calm the crowd and keep minimal control on the deteriorating situation while attempting to obtain help from the Roman officials and Herodian client king Agrippa II (*War* 2.3 18, 320, 333–42, 410–21). The situation had degenerated into class warfare within the city, with the renegade Eleazar son of Ananias leading the rebellious ordinary priests and populace against his own father as well as other aristocrats in attacks on their mansions, the royal palaces and their garrisons, and the public archives where debt-records were kept—all significant targets of popular resentment against the ruling class (*War* 422–41). They were joined by the *sicarioi*, the terrorist group now led by Menahem (a descendant of the teacher Judas, who had organized the Fourth Philosophy and resistance to the Roman tribute in 6 C.E.) who were apparently intent on taking the leadership of the Revolt now underway in Jerusalem. The Jerusalemites and priests led by Eleazar, however, suspicious of Menahem's "messianic" pretentions, rejected their leadership (*War* 433–8). After the urban insurrectionaries massacred the Roman garrison, Cestius Gallus, the Legate of Syria, launched an expedition to put down the rebellion (*War* 499–500). At this point the rebellion spilled beyond the bounds of the city, as Judean rebel forces effectively opposed the Roman troops' march on the city, their attempt to take control of it, and their retreat, which turned into a rout. High-priestly elements attempted to turn the city over to the Romans but fighting forces apparently from the countryside now joined with urban elements to drive the Romans effectively out of the country (*War* 517–55).

Although it eventually involved surrounding villagers, the first phase of the Revolt in Judea was both based largely in Jerusalem and took place mainly in the city. The first phase was, moreover, as much a class war of the ordinary priests and populace of Jerusalem against their high priestly rulers as it was a rebellion against Roman overlords. In addition to battling Roman troops, the insurrectionaries attacked the public archives housing the records of debts and the mansions and even the persons of the high-priestly rulers and drove out King Agrippa II. The claim that the "ruling class" of Judea was actively involved in the revolt at this stage cannot be supported from a critical reading of Josephus's accounts. Eleazar son of Simon, who emerged from these battles in control of Roman spoil, may have been an ordinary priestly leader, but nothing indicates that he was from a high-priestly family. And Simon bar Giora, who captured much of the Romans' baggage in the rout of Cestius Gallus at Beth Horon, was not a priest, let alone a high priest, but a leader of popular forces generated from the province of Akrabatene. While a few renegade military officers of Roman client kings participated in these battles, there is no mention of any members of the Judean "ruling class" as involved in action against the Romans other than the Temple-captain Eleazar son of Ananias, who led cessation of sacrifices for the emperor and the attack on the public archives.[5]

In the second phase of the Revolt some of the high-priestly figures who had not already fled Jerusalem apparently managed to put together a provisional government in a desperate attempt to reassert control over their society (and then to reach some accommodation with the Romans). Given the Roman system of indirect rule through native elites, this was their only chance of retaining their position of power and privilege. As discussed above, Josephus's portrayal of the transition in *War* 2.562–8 is simply incredible, because it contradicts itself. It cannot have been "those who had pursued Cestius" who engineered the appointment of generals because those who pursued Cestius were either sent out to remote posts, as in the case of the high priest Eleazar son of Ananias, or excluded from any role in the provisional government and conduct of affairs, as in the case of both Eleazar son of Simon and Simon bar Giora. The provisional government was clearly dominated by high-priestly figures, headed by Ananus son of Ananus and Jesus son of Gamalas, and eventually included leading Pharisees such as Simon son of Gamaliel. Whether or not the high-priestly provisional government had to "pretend" to be organizing resistance to the inevitable Roman reconquest, they were clearly attempting to control the society. Not only did they push the earlier revolutionary leaders out of the way, but Ananus even sent an "army" into the district of Acrabatene to push Simon bar Giora out of the area where he was still "ransacking the houses of the wealthy" (*War* 2.652–3). The principal division remained that between the high priestly "coup" or "counter-revolution" and the popular urban and countryside rebels whom they were attempting to suppress or manipulate.

In the third phase of the Revolt in Judea and Jerusalem, popular forces emerged from various districts of the countryside and moved into Jerusalem both to take control of the city and to prepare for the Roman reconquest.

The emergence of these popular movements was either directly provoked by the Roman advance in 67–8 C.E. or made possible by their delay in advancing toward Jerusalem until 70 C.E., after Vespasian had secured his position as emperor. First, bands of what Josephus calls "brigands" forming in flight from the Roman "scorched-earth" practices in their advance toward Jerusalem through northwestern Judea coalesced in Jerusalem, forming a coalition calling itself the "Zealots" (Horsley 1986b). They attacked wealthy Herodians still in the city, probably because of their previous exploitation of the peasants in northwest Judea, where many Herodian estates were apparently located (*War* 4.138–42). When the leaders of the high-priestly provisional government became alarmed and attempted to check the Zealots, the latter invited forces from the Idumean countryside to enter the city. The latter eliminated the high-priestly leaders of the provisional government, Ananus and Jesus (*War* 4.228–35, 316), after which most of them withdrew again to Idumea. John of Gischala and his followers from Upper Galilee meanwhile moved into alliance with the Zealots, then split with them, in the principal factional strife among the popular forces now controlling Jerusalem from the summer of 68 C.E. to the summer of 69 C.E. Simon bar Giora, who had meanwhile been building his popular movement in southeastern Judea and Idumea, finally entered Jerusalem with the most numerous fighting force of all, and thereafter controlled most of the city outside of the Temple, still in the control of John and the Zealots (Horsley 1984). Each of these peasant forces from the countryside, moreover, attacked the Herodians and/or the priestly aristocrats who still remained in the city, thus continuing the class warfare from the first two phases of the Revolt.[6]

By the time the Romans finally mobilized their forces for the reconquest, there were thus four popular groups from different districts of the countryside in Jerusalem awaiting their assault: the Zealots from northwest Judea, the Idumeans from the south, John's smaller contingent from Upper Galilee, and finally the largest force, under Simon bar Giora, from southeastern Judea and Idumea. Their parallel but uncoordinated emergence may seem somewhat similar to popular insurrections in the twentieth century. In Mexico in 1910–14, in Algeria and Viet Nam in the 1950s and 1960s, and in El Salvador in the 1970s and 1980s, rebel movements emerged in several different areas of the countryside, at first separate if not competing and only gradually forming "national liberation fronts." In ancient Judea, similarly, even once they had all entered Jerusalem, as long as the Romans delayed their attack, these popular forces feuded with and fought each other. Not until the Romans advanced did they combine forces to resist the siege and eventual Roman attack. The third phase of the Revolt was thus carried out by several peasant movements, only they fought from the fortified city of Jerusalem, not by guerrilla warfare in the remote countryside, as had the Maccabees and their twentieth century counterparts.

Notes

1   It is interesting that several independent recent analyses of Josephus's histories, each working with a different reconstruction of the Jewish Revolt itself, have come to roughly the same conclusion about the relative reliability of Josephus's *War* and his *Life*: Horsley 1995: 72–6; Jossa 1994; Rappaport 1994.

2   Cohen (1979) provides an extended argument from comparison of key texts for the difference between the *War* and the later *Life* on this issue. Rajak (1983: chapters 4 and 6) and Bilde (1988: chapters 2 and 5) critique Cohen's identification of a conflict between the two histories and provide a critically established alternative reading that moves in the same direction as the argument here.

3   A critical, sceptical reading of *Life* 373–80 suggests that if Josephus did take Sepphoris by assault, he used his own trained mercenaries. Yet it would be credible that the Galilean peasants would only have needed a little encouragement and the occasion of such an assault to take out their resentment on the ruling elite of Sepphoris.

4   In a rather quantitative analysis of brigands supposedly involved in revolt in Galilee, Schwartz (1994: 297–300), while apparently following my earlier work on banditry in many key respects, states that it is "marred by the author's naive (or ideologically motivated) over-use of the "social bandit" model, derived from E. Hobsbawm (1959, 1969)," apparently preferring the analysis of Blok (1972). The analysis of the English social historian, however, is far more sophisticated and flexible in raising questions about and accommodating differences in political–economic circumstances and power relations than that of Blok.

5   Goodman's basic argument that "the power struggle within the Jewish ruling class" was a "crucial link in the chain of causation" (1987: 19) of the Revolt is a crucial supplement to discussion of the "causes" of the Revolt. His careful and detailed analysis agrees with my own limited analysis (1986a), as he comments in several notes. The contention that members of the Judean ruling class were involved in the Revolt, however, is based on only these three figures. His discussion seems inconsistently critical in rejecting or accepting particular accounts in Josephus's histories and involves inconsistently applied criteria for speculating about the class-standing of leaders such as Eleazar ben Simon and Simon bar Giora. Eleazar son of Ananias would rather appear to be the proverbial "exception that proves the rule"—in this case the sole renegade member of the high priestly aristocracy, and not a typical case from which a broader generalization can be made.

6   Goodman's historical construction of leading figures and their followers engaged in the Revolt (1987) seems to work on limiting assumptions about (insurrectionary) movements. He appears to assume that only figures from the ruling class are capable of leadership and, therefore, that any leader in the Jewish Revolt must have been from the ruling class. And he appears to assume that the principle or even only motive for leadership in revolt is the drive for power and the only motive for ordinary people to fight is monetary reward (and that men can be mobilized into fighting forces only after they have been transformed from peasants into bandits ready to respond to such monetary inducement). Comparative material from biblical history as well as modem "peasant revolts," however, indicate concrete revolts are formed in far more complex combinations. Most popular movements produce popular leaders from among their own ranks,

usually marginal figures previously involved in some contact with affairs outside the usual village relations who then make alliances with other leaders, including higher status figures. Often local "big-men," prominent local figures, take leading roles in a crisis situation, e.g., as leader of "peasant revolts" (e.g., Sheba, who led the second massive revolt against King David [2 Samuel 20]). Simon bar Giora and John of Gischala may well have been local "big-men" at the beginning of the Revolt. Sometimes, but rarely, an alienated ruling class figure becomes leader of a popular movement or revolt (e.g., David's son Absalom became leader of the first massive popular revolt against David [2 Samuel 15–19]; Jeroboam, Solomon's officer over forced labor for the tribe of Joseph, became leader of the ten northern tribes' rebellion from the Davidic monarchy [1 Kings 12]). The renegade Eleazar son of Ananias appears to have retained a following as long as he was operating within the city of Jerusalem, but disappeared from a serious leadership role once sent out to the remote district of Idumea. As I have attempted to demonstrate in several different cases (Horsley 1979a, 1984, 1985, 1986b), these are the sorts of social relations and social circumstances that should be taken into account in analysis of the various groups and leaders involved in the Jewish Revolt if we are to attain any precision in our historical construction.

Bibliography

Bilde, P. (1978) "The Roman Emperor Gaius (Caligula)'s Attempt to Erect his Statue in the Temple of Jerusalem," *Studia Theologica* 32: 67–93.

—— (1979) "The Causes of the Jewish *War* According to Josephus," *JSJ* 10: 179–202.

—— (1988) *Flavius Josephus between Jerusalem and Rome. His Life His Works, and Their Importance*, Sheffield: JSOT.

Blok, A. (1972) "The Peasant and Brigand: Social Banditry Reconsidered," *Comparative Studies in Society and History* 14: 494–503.

Cohen, S. J. D. (1979) *Josephus in Galilee and Rome. His Vita and Development As a Historian*, Leiden: E. J. Brill.

Dyson, S. L. (1971) "Native Revolts in the Roman Empire," *Historia* 20: 239–74.

—— (1975) "Native Revolt Patterns in the Roman Empire," *Aufstieg und Niedergang der römischen Welt* 11.3: 138–75.

Freyne, S. (1980a) *Galilee from Alexander the Great to Hadrian, 323 B.C.E. to 135 C.E.*, Notre Dame, IN: University of Notre Dame Press.

—— (1980b) "The Galileans in the Light of Josephus' *Vita*," *New Testament Studies* 26: 397–413.

Goodman, M. (1982) "The First Jewish Revolt: Social Conflict and the Problem of Debt," in G. Vermes and J. Neusner (eds.) *Essays in Honour of Yigael Yadin*, Oxford: Oxford Centre for Postgraduate Hebrew Studies.

—— (1987) *The Ruling Class of Judaea: The Origins of the Jewish Revolt Against Rome, A.D. 66–70*, Cambridge: Cambridge University Press.

Hobsbawm, E. (1959) *Primitive Rebels*, New York: Norton.

—— (1969) *Bandits*, New York: Delacorte Press.

Horsley, R. A. (1979a) "Josephus and the Bandits," *Journal for the Study of Judaism* 10: 37–63.

—— (1979b) "The Sicarii: Ancient Jewish 'Terrorists'," *Journal of Religion* 59: 435–58.

—— (1981) "Ancient Jewish Banditry and the Revolt Against Rome, A.D. 66–70," *Catholic Bible Quarterly* 43: 409–32.

—— (1984) "Popular Messianic Movements around the Time of Jesus," *Catholic Bible Quarterly* 46: 471–95.

—— (1985) "Menahem in Jerusalem. A Brief Messianic Episode among the Sicarii—Not 'Zealot Messianism'," *Novus Testamentum* 27: 334–48.

—— (1986a) "High Priests and the Politics of Roman Palestine," *Journal for the Study of Judaism* 17: 23–55.

—— (1986b) "The Zealots. Their Origin, Relationships and Importance in the Jewish Revolt," *Novus Testamentum* 2: 159–92.

—— (1987) *Jesus and the Spiral of Violence: Popular Jewish Resistance in Roman Palestine*, San Francisco: Harper & Row.

—— (1995) *Galilee: History. Politics, People*, Harrisburg, PA: Trinity Press International.

—— (1996) *Archaeology, History, and Society in Galilee*, Harrisburg, PA: Trinity Press International.

Isaac, B. (1984) "Bandits in Judaea and Arabia," *Harvard Studies in Classical Philology* 88: 171–203.

Jossa, G. (1994) "Josephus' Actions in the Galilee During the Jewish War," in F. Parente and J. Sievers (eds.), *Josephus and the History of the Graeco-Roman Period*, Leiden: Brill, pp. 265–78.

Rajak, T. (1983) *Josephus. The Historian and His Society*, Philadelphia: Fortress Press.

Rappaport, U. (1994) "Where was Josephus Lying – in His Life or in the War?" in F. Parente and J. Sievers (eds.) *Josephus and the History of the Graeco-Roman Period*, Leiden: Brill, pp. 280–9.

Schwartz, S. (1994) "Josephus in Galilee: Rural Patronage and Social Breakdown," in F. Parente and J. Sievers (eds.), *Josephus and the History of the Graeco-Roman Period*, Leiden: Brill, pp. 289–307.

Shaw, B. D. (1984) "Bandits in the Roman Empire," *Past and Present* 105: 3–52.

7 Sepphoris

City of peace

Eric M. Meyers

The role of Sepphoris in the Great Revolt of 66–73 C.E., or lack of one, is a point of special interest due to the city's decision to adopt a pro-Roman policy, official at least from the spring of 68 C.E. onwards, or just prior to the death of the emperor Nero on June 9, 68 C.E. (Meyers 1999). I speak of this short time span specifically since we have several coins minted in Sepphoris under Nero with the sobriquet *Eirenopolis* on its legend ("City of Peace"). Allowing the second largest Jewish city (after Jerusalem) to mint coins at so late a date is surely significant since even King Agrippa II ceased to mint coins during the Revolt, resuming only after it was suppressed in 73 C.E. (Meshorer 1996). But this is getting a bit ahead in our story.

Explaining what was going on at Sepphoris at this time has become a matter of urgent interpretive interest in view of the identification of a large complex on the western summit known as Unit I or 85.3 as a fort (Meyers, Meyers, and Hoglund 1996).[1] The fort, which is late Hellenistic in date, is completely covered by a huge, intentional earthen fill, in which the latest pottery is "late Herodian" in date (with a *terminus ad quem* of ca. 70 C.E.) and the latest object is a coin of Agrippa II, dated to 53 C.E. The filling activity itself therefore must have occurred between 53 and 70 C.E., but the circumstances leading up to that time are very complex, and I will attempt to describe a scenario for understanding the fill, which has to do with the most unusual behavior of the citizens of Sepphoris during the war.

While the exact nature of the community that occupied Sepphoris in the Hellenistic period is not known, the archaeological record nicely supplements the Josephan narrative of events there in this period. The city is known as a center of Galilee from Maccabean times onward. Josephus first mentions Sepphoris in the context of Ptolemy Lathyrus' unsuccessful attempt to capture Sepphoris in his pursuit of Alexander Jannaeus (*Life* 337–8). Lathyrus, son of Cleopatra III and then governor of Cyprus, lost many men at Sepphoris, and pursued Jannaeus down to the Jordan River (Weiss 1993; Meyers 1996; Meyers and Meyers 1997; Miller 1996; Weiss and Netzer 1996)

Sepphoris is subsequently incorporated as an administrative center in the aftermath of the Roman takeover of Palestine in 57 B.C.E. (*Ant.* 14.91), when Gabinius, the legate of Pompey in Syria, made it a council along with

Jerusalem, Gadara, Amathus, and Jericho *(synedria)* *(War* 1.170). It is note-worthy that Sepphoris is the only city of the five outside of Judea (Horsley 1995: 164–5). No doubt Sepphoris was selected because of its past record of military accomplishment and its strategic location. The extent of its victory over Ptolemy suggests that it was fortified at the time. The nature of the population at Sepphoris in late Hellenistic times is clarified by an artifact of great significance from the western summit. While there is a paucity of small finds from the late Hellenistic period, of special interest there is an ostracon, painted on a jar fragment with handle found on the western summit, just some meters to the west of what we are calling Unit I (85.3) and interpreted as having a possible military function. The inscription is in Hebrew square letters, written beneath the handle, in a script that Naveh (1996: 170) describes as "typical of the second century B.C.E." The first five letters read *'pmls,* probably from the Greek word *epimeletes,* which Naveh understands to come from the word "manager" or "overseer," i.e., one who is in charge. Though there are other letters after an apparent break, it is impossible to read them. Despite the absence of the letter *tet,* because the term is attested in a Palmyrene inscription and in rabbinic literature, Naveh concludes that the term may thus refer to a treasurer, manager, or *gabbay* of the Jewish community. But the term may also have a broader connotation as well, as it seems to have in several places in Josephus: namely, that it is at least possible, if not probable, that some sort of settlement at Sepphoris had been there for some time—a supposition also supported by considerable ceramic data. Antipater, father of Herod the Great is called *epimeletes* of the Jews, translated "governor" in the Loeb edition *(Ant.* 14.127), though translated "procurator" elsewhere *(Ant.* 14.139); Herod himself is appointed *epimeletes* of all Syria *(War* 1.225), though he is called *strategos* elsewhere *(Ant.* 14.280); and Marcellus, appointed temporary procurator of Judea when Pontius Pilate is called to Rome, is also called *epimeletes* *(Ant.* 18.89). It is therefore quite possible that there was in the time of Jannaeus a military presence at Sepphoris with its own quartermaster or leader of *epimeletes;* no doubt this leader was Jewish, else there would be no reason to use the Hebrew script for a Greek term. I would also lower the date of the inscription closer to ca. 100 B.C.E., in part because we are uncertain about the makeup of the community in the second century B.C.E. The ceramic type may allow a slightly later date as well.

Because the area of the western summit is built on bedrock it is very difficult to recover all phases of use. What is attested stratigraphically, how-ever, is late Hellenistic (late second century–first century B.C.E.), while its date of construction and earliest use must remain conjectural. The character of the Galilee in the pre-Hasmonean era is hotly debated. Suffice it to say that it is at least feasible to consider the possibility that some of the popu-lation growth in the early Hellenistic period (third–second centuries B.C.E.) may be attributed to new Jewish settlements.[2] Most of the data pertinent to this discussion comes from archaeological surveys, many of which remain unpublished. But the literary data leaves the clear impression that the Galilee was repopulated and well administered by the end of the Hellenistic period.

The evidence for establishing Sepphoris as a major administrative location in the Galilee if not the major center in Galilee by the first century B.C.E. is incontrovertible. With the establishment of the five councils' *synedria,* however, the Romans sought to limit Hasmonean rule to Temple affairs alone. Pompey had taken away Hyrcanus II's title of king and the councils were ruled by the aristocracy (*Ant.* 14.91). The reorganization apparently did not last very long; the last of the Hasmonean kings, Antigonus, had a garrison installed in Sepphoris. Herod, probably, in the winter of 38 B.C.E. entered Sepphoris with a view towards eliminating the garrison only to find that it was gone, but Herod did find "an abundance of provisions" that were undoubtedly put to good use (*Ant.* 14.414–16). From Sepphoris Herod pursued a group of brigands who were holed up in the cliffs near Arbel (416). It is therefore quite clear that Sepphoris had been a military and administrative outpost in the Galilee for some time before the activities normally associated with it. It is precisely its military association for this early period that we choose to emphasize in light of the character of the archaeological remains preserved in Unit I (85.3).

The death of Herod in 4 B.C.E. led to a great deal of uncertainty regarding the kingdom and Sepphoris in particular was the scene of a major insurgency. Apparently one Judas, son of Ezekias the brigand, having aspirations to the Jewish crown, led a group of desperate men in an assault on the royal palace at Sepphoris where he succeeded in arming his own soldiers with weapons that had been stockpiled there (*War* 2.56, *Ant.* 17.271). In order to quell the rebellion Varus, the Syrian legate set out for Ptolemais with a force of two legions. At Sepphoris Josephus reports that the city was burned to the ground and its inhabitants enslaved (*Ant.* 17.289, *War* 2.68). Josephus no doubt is exaggerating a good deal as he does about many things, but only the Florida expedition has thus far reported a burning that might be attributed to this time. Staying with the literary evidence of Josephus for now, whatever the truth of the report regarding Varus, Sepphoris is universally thought to have recovered and gained a good deal of its reputation under Herod Antipas (4 B.C.E. to 39 C.E.) who reportedly fortified the city, renamed it *autocratoris* and made it "the ornament of all Galilee" (*Ant.* 18.27). It is not clear what *autocratoris* means, whether referring to the emperor or indicating that Sepphoris was granted autonomy. From the archaeology there are no signs of the fortifications, unless we understand him to have rebuilt the garrison on the summit, possible for troops and arms (see *Ant.* 18.251–52). But the archaeology of Unit 1 (85.3) shows conclusively that the area was already being transformed into non-military space. Stuart Miller (1996) has convincingly clarified the meaning of "ornament" *(proschema),* by explaining it as signifying the impregnable nature of the city. Meanwhile, Antipas's reign as tetrarch in Galilee and

Peraea ended in failure and tragedy. Emperor Caligula assigned Agrippa I the royal title and granted lands to Philip in his second year of office (38–9 C.E.). Agrippa was the brother-in-law of Antipas; he went to Palestine that year, and his sister Herodias was jealous for her husband, wanting a royal title for him too. Agrippa, upon hearing this turn of events, set out to discredit Antipas, accusing him of collaborating with the enemy and of stockpiling weapons at Sepphoris (*Ant.* 17.252, *War* 2.183). Antipas and Herodias were both exiled, where they either died or were executed.

Surprisingly, Josephus is silent about the period between the reign of Herod Antipas and the onset of the Great Revolt in 66 C.E. Archaeological evidence for the first century C.E. is abundant however; each of the areas on the western summits provide substantial remains from this period, though it is very difficult to pinpoint the period from Antipas to 66 C.E. The Florida expedition, as already noted, believes they can identify pre- and post-Varus material, though the Duke expedition and the Hebrew University expedition have been unable to do so. There is no doubt, however, that substantial building and renovation was being undertaken during the middle of the first century C.E.

Josephus's remaining comments on Sepphoris are confined to *War* and *Life*; he resumes his narrative on Sepphoris with an account of the arrival of Caesennius Gallus' expeditionary force to Galilee to ensure that it would not revolt. Once again reiterating that Sepphoris was the "strongest city in all Galilee" Josephus notes that Sepphoris welcomed Gallus to its midst, allowing him to pursue the remaining rebels and brigands as far as Mt. Asamon (*War* 2.510–11). It is significant that this first mention of Sepphoris in the resumed narrative mentions what is so unusual about Sepphoris, namely, that it was pro-Roman from the outset of hostilities, or at least we might say that significant portions of the city were. The problem, however, is that Josephus is not at all consistent in his reports about the city's role in the Revolt. Undoubtedly Josephus's inconsistencies arise from his own ambivalent attitude: first as commander of the Galilean forces (66–8 C.E.) and then as advocate of a pro-Roman, at least co-operative posture vis-à-vis Rome.[3]

We encounter Josephus's inconsistencies in *War* after he reports accepting the command of the forces in Upper and Lower Galilee and Gamala, which was part of Peraea, and undertook to fortify several towns in the region (*War* 2.572–3). But it is in this context, early in his command, probably in 66 C.E., that he reports that the Sepphoreans were ready and eager for war to such an extent that they were allowed to put up their own walls (*War* 2.574). Though two of the Sepphoris expeditions have thought they found such a wall no one has been sufficiently convinced of it to have published such an identification. Sepphoris' warlike attitude is reflected in the report that the city went over to the side of the rebel leader John of Gischala who challenged Josephus's Galilee command (*War* 2.629). The Tiberians also had difficulties with Josephus's command and they appealed to Agrippa II for support (*War* 2.636–45), ultimately joining others who opposed him. Josephus's activities as commander of the "official" Galilean forces sent by the Jerusalem establishment continued and in his attempts to subdue towns and villages that were disloyal to his command, he made an unsuccessful attack on Sepphoris because "he [Josephus] had himself so strongly fortified it as to render it practically impregnable even to Romans" (*War* 2.61). Josephus also mentions in this context that he had already "abandoned the Galilean cause."

Some have suggested that Josephus has exaggerated the resistance he encountered at the hands of the Sepphoreans in order to make his accomplishments on behalf of the war effort seem even greater. Since he was ultimately to adopt a pro-Roman stance he may well have wanted the reader to be assured that he did all he could to prevent Sepphoris from becoming pro-Roman as well. But it is also quite possible that Sepphoris was of a mixed mind in the matter in early 67 C.E., since its large population no doubt reflected a variety of opinions. It is even quite possible that Josephus's change of mind reflected an honest inner turmoil that resulted in his own pro-Roman, peace policy. Hence, the pro-Roman policies of the citizens of Sepphoris probably came gradually, in 67 C.E., after much debate and interaction with Josephus and his troops.

Overtures of allegiance had been made to Cestius Gallus by the Sepphoreans shortly after Josephus's arrival in 66 C.E. when other Galilean revolutionaries threatened the city because of their pro-Roman tendencies. Josephus's role in calming the city of Sepphoris at this key moment (*Life* 30–1) in the early years of the Revolt is indicative of his views generally throughout his autobiography that he was a mediator and ultimately a pro-Roman spokesman. Josephus also secured permission for the Sepphoreans to communicate with the hostages who were being held in Dora, no doubt as a guarantee of co-operation with the Sepphoreans. The population of Tiberias was also divided over the war (*Life* 32–42). Justus of Tiberias fanned the fires of jealousy when he suggested that Tiberias had always been the intended capital of Galilee, but now Sepphoris was once again made capital as a result of its changed, pro-Roman views, while Justus understandably urged the Tiberians on to fight with other Galileans against Rome and against Sepphoris (*Life* 38–40; on Galilean conflicts see also Chapter 6 by Horsley, in this volume).

There are still more inconsistencies in Josephus but we may better understand them if we accept that *War* and *Life* were written at different times and with different points of view. In addition, the Sepphoreans appear to be quite independent-minded, resisting attempts from both Josephus and the Jerusalem government to assert their authority over them. The citizens of Sepphoris even refused to listen to Josephus or a Pharisaic delegation sent to replace him (*Life* 123–4). Disputes over the war among the Sepphoreans persisted throughout the year 67, and possibly into 68 C.E. among the Galileans. There is the story of the Sepphoreans' flirtation with the brigand named Jesus who, with support from the city, nearly captured Josephus (*Life*

104–14) who was still involved with the war effort, while the inhabitants of the city remained "loyal to Rome" (*Life* 104). Apparently the Sepphoreans had hired Jesus to protect them (*Life* 104–11). Particularly puzzling in Josephus's account of this period is his report that the residents of Sepphoris requested assistance in fortifying the city and were "eager for hostilities" against Rome (*War* 2.574). Josephus credits himself with fortifing the city (*Life* 188), but he also reports that he had considerable trouble with John of Gischala (*Life* 203, 232–3; *War* 2.629), who was prepared to attack Josephus with assistance from some Sepphoreans and Justus of Tiberias (*Life* 346–54). Justus might also have changed his position on the war after the trauma at Jotapata—the Tiberians ultimately appealed to Agrippa II for support (*War* 2.636–45). Josephus goes on to question the accuracy and reliability of Justus's account of the war (*Life* 357–67). Both cities eventually joined hands in opposing Josephus's authority.

Josephus's account of invading Sepphoris after Vespasian had promised military assistance (*War* 3.59–62) and the story of his attack on Sepphoris (*Life* 373–80) before the Roman troops had arrived are very complicated, especially when Josephus himself is supposed to have fortified the city earlier. Despite conflicting stories that indicate the citizens of Sepphoris held both pro-Roman and anti-Roman or pro-war positions, it is the Hellenistic heritage of the city as capital that nurtured and gave support to the pro-Roman policies ultimately adopted. From Hellenistic times onward the Jerusalem political establishment had supported leaders who were either beholden to the Herodian royal family or the Hasmoneans before them. The picture we gain of Sepphoris in the first century C.E., therefore, is one of an expanding city with its priestly caste intact. The fact that Sepphoris is associated with both the royalists—see the story about Herod Antipas's birthday in Mark 6.21–9—and priestly families certainly explains why a majority of the city would argue for a pro-Roman position.

In any case, the pro-Roman stance of the citizenry of Sepphoris that eventually wins out is not unique and resembles most closely the city of Paneas, home of Agrippa II (Schürer 1973: 491–513). This ascendant view is best commemorated in the coins minted in 68 C.E. which bear the legend "Eirenopolis–Neronias–Sepphoris."[4] These coins date to the fourteenth year of the emperor Nero, in which the inhabitants of Sepphoris declared loyalty to Vespasian and the senate. They provide striking visual testimonies to the unique role the city came to play in the course of the war. Moreover, Josephus's own change of heart vis-à-vis the war in 68 C.E. must be taken into account when evaluating the frequent mentions in *Life* of Sepphoris's support of Rome (30, 38, 104, 124, 232, 346–8, 373–80, 394–6, 411) with which *War* usually agrees (2.511; 3.30–4, 59). Along with the lingering doubts as to the full meaning of the revolutionary attitudes attested among some of the inhabitants of Sepphoris (e.g., *War* 2.574, 629; *Life* 188, 203), at the very least it suggests that some Sepphoreans supported the war effort early on, but by Nero's fourteenth year Sepphoris had adopted as formal policy its pro-Roman political stance, one that had apparently predominated all along but that now became official.

It is precisely in this connection, in relation to some vacilliation in attitude or internal disagreement that we turn to the archaeology of the site. First, the numismatic evidence shows unequivocally that a unified position had been ironed out by 68 C.E. Adopting such an extraordinary position of peaceful co-operation with the enemy is truly reflected on the coins of Sepphoris. Although Seyrig thought that the sobriquet "City of Peace" was taken in honor of the closing of the Gate of Janus in Rome in 64 C.E. as an act of *pax romana*, we accept the observation that it was adopted because Sepphoris alone of all cities and villages welcomed Vespasian and his army in peace. It may also be a play on the expression in Zechariah (8:3) "City of Truth," which is there applied to Jerusalem. Meshorer (1982) has correctly pointed out that Sepphoris certainly was a principal city of Agrippa II. In this connection there were doubtless many royalists living there who supported an accommodationist stance toward Rome. Moreover, the fact that both Caesarea Maritima and Sepphoris chose to honor Vespasian on their coins of 68 C.E. shows the extent of his popularity and power in the east. Josephus's subsequent prediction, after he was taken prisoner, that Vespasian would become emperor after Nero (*War* 3.399–401) shows the pragmatic and political aspects of his persona. One other interesting point about the Sepphoris "City of Peace" coins is that they also mention the emperor Nero. Paneas (or Baneas), or Caesarea Phillipi, was dedicated to Nero in 61 C.E. and renamed Neronias and served as the capital city of Agrippa II (*Ant.* 20.211; cf. *Life* 9.37–9). Though it was usual to continue the name of the emperor on coins after his death for some years, due to the fact of Nero's condemnation by the Senate and the Roman people, his name disappeared immediately after his death on June 9, 68 C.E. Of special interest is the coin of Agrippa II struck at Paneas in 67 C.E.: it shares with Sepphoris the dedication to Nero, as well as including the symbols of the double cornucopia and caduceus. The coins of Sepphoris that bear the tripartite nomenclature in honor of Vespasian, Nero, and "City of Peace" also imitate the coin of Agrippa II from Paneas from the year before, 67 C.E., and hence send forth the message very clearly of the particular point of view of the city, which by 68 C.E. had resolved its internal political differences, at least for public consumption.[5] Meshorer believes that the choice of symbols and absence of the image of the Roman emperor means that the Sepphoris coins and those of Paneas were struck by Jewish authorities, though in suggesting this he is inclined to understand the double cornucopia and caduceus symbols as being Jewish, because they were used by Herod and Herod Archelaus, a suggestion that we reject. These symbols, however, had a much broader usage in the Mediterranean world. What is most striking about the design is the absence of the image of Nero, no doubt omitted in deference to Jewish sensibilities, and the utilization of pagan symbols that were associated with peaceful times.

The minting of these coins, especially the coins of Sepphoris, proclaimed the clear message that in addition to Agrippa II there were other important elements in Jewish life prepared to adopt a pacific stance toward Rome in public. No doubt there were many elements in the Roman military and imperial administration who doubted that such a tendency could counter-balance the weight of rebellion being promulgated in virtually every quarter. Especially prior to the change in Josephus's own position, from a Roman perspective, a pro-Roman stand reflected in some of the teachings of some pious Pharisees or priests could hardly convince them that the Jews were of a mixed mind on the Great Revolt. Even in the case of Sepphoris, in reference to which we have found literary evidence (in Josephus) of a divided opinion in the matter of collaborating with the Romans, the year 68 C.E. would have been an appropriate time for a public gesture from its inhabitants to convince the Romans that their city was united: such a public action might have been the intentional filling in of the area that had served for more than a century and a half as the *castra* of the military garrison. Such a hypothesis brings us back to the mute or anepigraphic archaeological record, and it is to that we now turn.

We have already suggested that the fort on the western summit, dated initially to the late Hellenistic period, probably functioned in a military way up to the reign of Herod Antipas. Prior to this time the area had the appearance of a barrack or outpost, which took full advantage of Sepphoris's favorable physical location high on the mound and overlooking the Natufian Valley to the north. A cache of weaving tools found in this area suggests that the area was not used for military purposes in the first part of the first century C.E., which is the context for the finds. Prior to that time some ballistas, arrowheads, and several *mikva'ot* dating to the Hellenistic period were identified. While our archaeological investigations do not present evidence for active military use during the reign of Herod Antipas and after, we may certainly conclude that the large structure gave the appearance of a garrison even if it were empty.

During the excavation of this area, Unit I (85.3), the staff became painfully aware of two archaeological realia that made digging there very difficult: (1) the presence of a huge artificial earthen and pebble-laden fill that covered the area; and (2) an unusual north–south "retaining" wall that was plastered solid from the outside, or western, face. Both of these con-structions could only be understood as being intentionally laid-in, the former on top of the area of the fort, the latter built to contain the fill on its western, exterior side, especially during the rainy season. Apparently at some point in the second half of the first century—the latest coin on the floor of the structure being one of Agrippa II and dated to 53 C.E.—the area of the fort was converted into an open plaza that in elevation rose a bit steeply above the surrounding first century buildings to the west. In my view, this tremendous filling and leveling operation was undertaken by the citizens of Sepphoris as an outward demonstration of their policy of co-operation with

Rome. By such an action the appearance on the summit would have been dramatically changed and the large fort once used to house troops and provisions would have been dismantled to foundation levels and filled in for civilian use.

It is interesting in light of the differing views of the population residing in Sepphoris to speculate whether this action occurred before or after Josephus gave up his command at Jotapata. In any case Sepphoris assumed the title of "City of Peace" sometime in the year 68 C.E. before Nero's death in June. If Josephus's quixotic change in position regarding the war is difficult for modern readers to accept it should be remembered that many Pharisees and priests opposed the war for theological or selfish reasons. Obviously, from Josephus's writings we know that significant debate and disagreement over this subject occurred and divided the city. By 68 C.E., however, the die had been cast, in recognition of which the majority decided to make a public gesture to the Romans that could not be mistaken.

The result was dramatic and memorable: Sepphoris adopted a pro-Roman stance early on in the Revolt, sending a message to the Galileans who were fully committed to the war effort and to fellow Jews who had misgivings about it. To the Romans who were prosecuting the war, having Sepphoris officially in the peace camp must have caused great jubilation at home and in Judea. The pro-Roman policies of the middle Roman period of Rabbi Judah the Patriarch should be understood in light of the extraordinary position adopted by Sepphoris in the early Roman period. The policy of detente articulated at Sepphoris during the Revolt was implemented during the next century when co-operation with Rome allowed one of the most fertile and creative periods in Jewish history to prosper. The Mishnah is the centerpiece of that legacy.

Notes

1 I am grateful to Professors Melissa Aubin and Juergen Zangenberg for their field work in this area as well as for their valuable interpretive suggestions.
2 The question of the Judaization of the Galilee is at the heart of Horsley's study on Galilee (1995) in which he makes an elaborate case for the independence of the Galilean community as a result of the Assyrian conquests in the eighth century B.C.E. The Hasmonean attempt to incorporate the Galileans was doomed to fail because of this longstanding tradition of independence. For another point of view on this important issue see Chancy 1999.
3 Compare Horsley's remarks (1995: 165–9). It is noteworthy that Horsley's understanding of the social makeup of the population of Sepphoris supports our contention that influential members of the community brought about the pro-Roman stance that was adopted. He identifies priestly and wealthy citizens, both of Judean if not Jerusalem extraction (168).
4 These coins do not bear the image of the emperor, which on later issues is standard. The symbols used, namely, the double cornucopia with caduceus

between them is quite rare, appearing only on coins of Herod the Great, Archelaus, and Agrippa II, and some non-Jewish Palestinian issues such as Ashkelon (Meshorer 1982: vol. 2, 27). But it is the coins of Paneas (Caesarea Philippi), renamed Neronias in 61 C.E., residence of Agrippa II, that apparently inspired the Sepphoris mint and its pro-Roman posture (Seyrig 1950; Meshorer 1982: vol. 2, n. 2).

5 Hamburger (1970) suggests that Vespasian issued these coins to pay for his troops in the field; see also Meshorer 1967: 66–7.

Bibliography

Chancey, M. (1999) *The Myth of a Gentile Galilee: The Population of Galilee and New Testament Studies*, unpublished Ph.D. dissertation, Duke University.

Hamburger, H. (1970) "The Coin Issues of the Roman Administration from the Mint of Caesarea," *Israel Exploration Journal* 20: 81–91.

Hoglund, K. G. and Meyers, E. M. (1996) "The Residential Quarter on the Western Summit," in R. M. Nagy, C. L. Meyers, E. M. Meyers and Z. Weiss (eds.) *Sepphoris in Galilee: Crosscurrents of Culture*, Raleigh: The North Carolina Museum of Art.

Horsley, R. A. (1995) *Galilee. History, Politics, People*, Valley Forge, PA: Trinity Press International.

Meshorer, Y. (1967) *Jewish Coins of the Second Temple Period*, Tel Aviv: Am Hasyer.

—— (1982) *Ancient Jewish Coins*, Dix Hills, NY: Amphora.

—— (1996) "Coins of Sepphoris" in R. M. Nagy, C. L. Meyers, E. M. Meyers and Z. Weiss (eds.) *Sepphoris in Galilee: Crosscurrents of Culture*, Raleigh: The North Carolina Museum of Art.

Meyers, C. L. (1996) "Sepphoris and Lower Galilee: Earliest Times through the Persian Period," in R. M. Nagy, C. L. Meyers, E. M. Meyers and Z. Weiss (eds.) *Sepphoris in Galilee: Crosscurrents of Culture*, Raleigh: The North Carolina Museum of Art.

Meyers, C. L. and Meyers, E. M. (1997) "Sepphoris," in E. M. Meyers (ed.) *The Oxford Encyclopedia of Archaeology in the Near East*, Oxford: Clarendon Press.

Meyers, E. M. (1999) "Sepphoris on the Eve of the Great Revolt (67–65 C.E.): Archaeology and Josephus," in E. M. Meyers (ed.) *Galilee Through the Centuries: Confluence of Cultures*, Winona Lake, IN: Eisenbrauns.

Meyers, E. M., Meyers, C. L. and Hoglund, K. (1996) "Notes and News: Sepphoris (Sippori), 1996," *Israel Exploration Journal* 47: 264–8.

Miller, S. (1996) "Hellenistic and Roman Sepphoris: The Historical Evidence," in R. M. Nagy, C. L. Meyers, E .M. Meyers and Z. Weiss (eds.) *Sepphoris in Galilee: Crosscurrents of Culture*, Raleigh: The North Carolina Museum of Art.

Naveh, Y. (1996), "Jar Fragment with Inscription in Hebrew," in R. M. Nagy, C. L. Meyers, E. M. Meyers and Z. Weiss (eds.) *Sepphoris in Galilee: Crosscurrents of Culture*, Raleigh: The North Carolina Museum of Art.

Schürer, B. (1973) *The History of the Jewish People in the Time of Jesus Christ (175 B.C. – A.D. 135*, revised and edited by G. Vermes and F. Millar, Edinburgh: T. & T. Clark.

Seyrig, H. (1950) "Irenopolis–Neronias–Sepphoris," *Numismatic Chronicle* 10: 284–9.

Weiss, Z. (1993) "Sepphoris," in E. Stern (ed.) *The New Encyclopedia of Archaeological Excavations in the Holy Land*, Jerusalem: Israel Exploration Society.

8 Yodefat/Jotapata

The archaeology of the first battle

Mordechai Aviam

Josephus names Yodefat as the first town on the list of fortified settlements in the Galilee *(War* 20.6), and he mentions it many times thereafter in the *War* as well as in his *Life*. The site is located on an isolated hill in the Lower Galilee near the modern Moshav Yodefat (Fig. 8.1). Although the site was identified in the last century, it was not excavated until 1992, primarily because scholars thought that it had been badly destroyed and further eroded by nature. In six seasons of excavations beginning in 1992, however, we uncovered the remains of a fourteen-acre town occupied from late Hellenistic through early Roman times (Adan-Bayewitz and Aviam 1997). About one-third of the town was built on four or five large terraces on the steep eastern slope, another third of it was built on the crest of the rounded hill and its southern slope, and the rest on the southern plateau (Fig. 8.2). Five residential areas were excavated, containing modest private dwellings with cisterns, ritual baths *(miqva'ot)*, storage areas, cooking ovens, pressing installations, loom weights, spindle whorls, clay and stone vessels, and coins. We also excavated pottery kilns, an oil press in a cave, and part of a luxurious mansion with frescoed walls and floors. The latest securely identifiable object found throughout these areas is a coin found on one of the floors from the reign of the Roman emperor Nero. This piece of datable evidence correlates precisely with the story of the battle of Yodefat—its siege, fall, and the aftermath, which is the second longest battle description given by Josephus (the battle of Jerusalem is the longest) *(War* 141–218, 316–408, 432–42). The battle of Yodefat, as described by Josephus, is also the second bloodiest of the battles of the Revolt, again after Jerusalem, as well as the third longest siege, after Jerusalem and Masada. Many scholars have noted that the attention that Josephus lavished on his account may well be suspect, considering his own role in the city's defensive preparations as well as his subsequent and infamous behavior (see the detailed discussion in Chapter 6 by Horsely in this volume). It is reasonable, therefore, to examine the archaeological evidence for the siege, the battle, and the city's demise in tandem with Josephus's narrative, in order that specific discrepancies and/or points of agreement be made clear.

The fortifications

> But this quarter, too, Josephus, when he fortified the city, had enclosed within his wall … Under this screen the builders, working in security day and night, raised the wall to a height of twenty cubits, erected numerous towers, and crowned the whole with a stout parapet.
>
> (*War* 3.158–9, 174–5)

Josephus lists Yodefat as one of the towns that he fortified. Our excavations revealed two phases of fortifications on the mound's northern, accessible side, which is the weakest point of the town's natural fortifications. The earlier phase, which dates to the late Hellenistic period, consists of two parallel walls that probably joined to a single wall beyond the summit. There is a massive tower in the center and a smaller tower to the west (Figs 8.1 and 8.2). This late Hellenistic wall was probably preserved to different levels and seems to have been reused as the foundation for the second phase of fortifications. This later phase, which is datable to the middle of the first century C.E., is probably to be identified with the efforts described by Josephus.

The second phase of the fortifications was identified in two different areas on the northern side. First, there was a long and narrow wall that we exposed to a length of 20 meters. This probably served as a second fortification line behind the earlier walls. Second, there was a portion of a casemate wall (4.9 meters wide) that was built above the earlier Hellenistic wall. Two and a half

Figure 8.1 View of Yodefat, looking south.

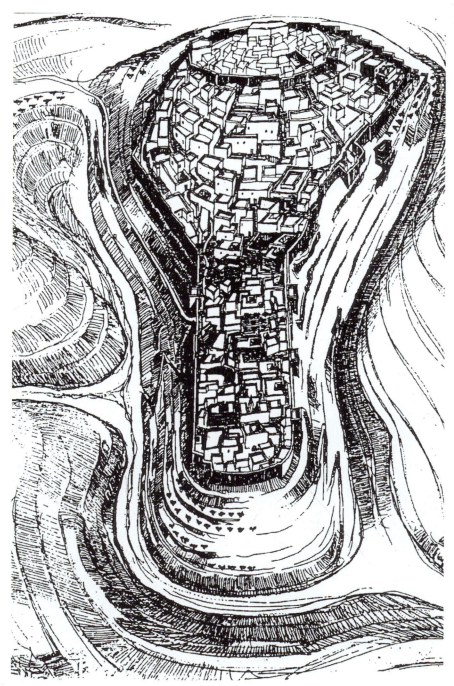

Figure 8.2 Reconstruction of Yodefat, looking north.

rooms of this casemate wall survived. Its outer wall was built directly on a layer of limestone quarry chips, without further foundations. The inner wall, on the other hand, was firmly founded on top of the collapsed Hellenistic tower. In the northwest corner of the western casemate, we found a massive fill of large boulders laid as "headers" with different sized stones behind them. This fill was situated in such a way as to leave enough space to open the door of the room and enable its use. Inside the fill, we found a ballista stone, indicating that it dated to the days of the actual war. I believe that the fill was made by the town's defenders in order to prevent the battering ram from breaking through the wall. A similar phenomenon has been identified at Gamla (see Chapter 9 by Syon in this volume).

We excavated other portions of the town's fortifications in four other areas around the mound. We discovered both that the early Roman period fortifications were more extensive than the earlier, Hellenistic ones, and also that these later fortifications were constructed differently across the site. In Field XIV we identified the point where the second, early Roman period wall abuts the earlier Hellenistic one. From that point, the early Roman period wall runs downhill to the southwest and surrounds the southern plateau. On the eastern side of that plateau (Field VII) we excavated on both sides of the wall. At this point the width of the wall is only 0.7 meters. In Field XI, where the outer face of the wall was exposed at the surface, we uncovered the inner face and found that the wall's width here was 0.9 meters. In Field XVI we uncovered the point where the wall curved up the northeastern side of the hill to the highest point in the north, probably to

Figure 8.3 Wide wall on west, built above early Roman house.

control the town's main approach road. At this point, the width of the wall is 1.8 meters.

In the 1999 season we excavated three more areas of the early Roman period wall circuit, and discovered additional evidence of hasty, "emergency-style" construction. In one area were the foundations of what seems to be a private house. Two of its western rooms had been filled up with soil and stones, and these served as foundations for the wall (Fig. 8.3). In another area, we excavated three casemates, all surviving only to their foundations and with no indication of doorways. In the westernmost room, we discovered a short, narrow shaft leading to a narrow tunnel with a gabled roof that opened into three rock-cut chambers (Fig. 8.4). These are clearly hideouts. The rooms themselves yielded a complete storage jar and several jar lids, all of the early Roman period. We also found an iron arrowhead, two ballista stones, and twenty coins, of which twelve are silver. Preliminary field readings assign them to the emperor Nero, and one dates to the year 60 C.E., only seven years before the battle of Yodefat. In another area we discovered two pottery kilns, the larger of which was covered by the wall (Fig. 8.5). (This kiln contained store of the "Yodefat" type, on which see Chapter 5 by Avshalom-Gorni and Getzov in this volume.) Stratigraphical evidence indicates that the second, smaller kiln was built after this larger kiln was covered. Everywhere that we excavated along the perimeter of the wall, we were able to date the construction to the early Roman period.

In sum, the early Roman fortification wall was built according to the topography of the hill, differently across the site. Along the eastern side of

Figure 8.4 Entrance to underground chamber.

the plateau the wall was built as a casemate system, whereas along the western slope it was a solid wall that even directly abutted some buildings. These changes are likely the result of the short time and the stressful

Figure 8.5 Wide wall on east, built on top of early Roman kiln (under sandbags).

situation under which construction occurred. This also explains why the wall line followed the topography so closely (just as at Gamla, on which see Chapter 9 by Syon in this volume). The underground hideout adds another piece to this picture of urgent operations.

The assault ramp

> It was decided to erect earthworks against the accessible portion of the wall, whereupon the whole army was sent out to procure the necessary materials. The mountain forests surrounding the town were stripped and, besides timber, enormous masses of stones were collected.
>
> (*War* 3.163–5)

We excavated two squares on the northern slope of Yodefat. The reason to open these squares was that on the surface we had identified some unusual chunks of mortar that included a lot of crushed pottery. The excavation revealed a layer about 1 meter deep of red-brown soil with many fieldstones. On top of this, there was a patchy mortar surface that we originally identified as a natural calcareous crust (Adan-Bayewitz and Aviam 1997: 147, n. 15), though this is not certain. Within both the red-brown soil layer and the mortar surface we found dozens of iron bow and catapult arrowheads, some of which had banded tips or tails, as well as two tiny nails of the Roman army shoe (*calligae*) and a large rolling stone (Figs. 8.6 and 8.7).

Figure 8.6 Two arrowheads from Roman assault ramp (right arrowhead embedded in mortar).

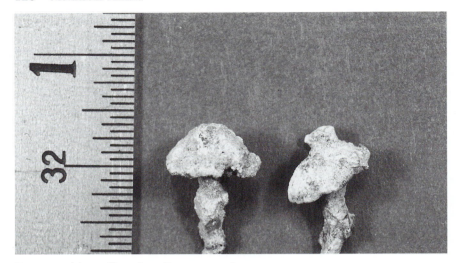

Figure 8.7 Two *calligae* from Roman assault ramp.

These finds suggest that these two layers of stony soil and mortar are the remains of the Roman assault ramp, built during active battle. This ramp is very different from the well-known Roman siege ramp at Masada. At Yodefat, the ramp is essentially a levelling coat on the natural slope of the hill, built to create a moderate and easy angle to push up the siege machines.

The weapons

Arrowheads

> And at a given signal arrows poured from all quarters, intercepting the light.
>
> (*War* 3.266–7)

We found more than seventy bow arrowheads during the excavations: eighteen in the two squares on the northern slope; twenty-six from the squares along the northern fortifications; twenty-seven from the residential areas, including five on the floor of the frescoed room (Fig. 8.8). Most of the arrowheads are of the common iron trilobate type (5 grams) though a couple are of the pyramidal type. In addition to the smaller bow arrowheads, we also found about fifteen catapult arrowheads all over the site. These were various sizes and weights, from 8 to 15 centimeters long and from 20 to 30 grams.

Ballista stones

> Vespasian now had his artillery engines, numbering in all one hundred and sixty, brought into position round the spot and gave orders to fire

upon the defenders on the wall … Thus the missiles from the "quick-
fires" came with such force as to strike down whole files, and the whizz-
ing stones hurled by the engine carried away the battlements and broke
off the angles of the towers. Indeed, there is no body of troops, however
strong, which the force and mass of these stones cannot lay low to the
last rank.

(*War* 3.196–7, 242–5)

About thirty-five ballista stones were found during the excavations (Fig. 8.
9). Almost every excavated area yielded a few of them. All are made of
local limestone and are hand chiseled with a pointed chisel. The largest is
23 centimeters in diameter and weighs 2 kilograms, while the smallest is 8
centimeters in diameter and weighs 0.65 kilograms.

Human remains

At length, when the whole army had poured in, they started up, only to
realize their calamity; the blade at their throat brought home to them
that Jotapata was taken. The Romans, remembering what they had
borne during the siege, showed no quarter or pity for any, but thrust the
people down the steep slope from the citadel in a general massacre. Even
those still able to fight found themselves deprived of the means of
defense by the difficulties of the ground. Crushed in the narrow alleys
and slipping down the declivity, they were engulfed in the wave of
carnage that streamed from the citadel … On that day the Romans
massacred all who showed themselves: on the ensuing day they searched
the hiding-places and wreaked their vengeance on those who had sought

Figure 8.8 Bow and catapult arrowheads.

Figure 8.9 Ballista stones.

refuge in subterranean vaults and caverns, sparing none, whatever their age, save infants and women. The prisoners thus collected were twelve hundred: the total number of dead whether killed in the final assault or in previous combats, was computed at thirty thousand.

(*War* 3.329–32)

The problem of human remains from battle sites of the Revolt is well known. Besides Yodefat, three such sites have been excavated: Masada, Gamla, and Jerusalem. Only a very few human remains have been found at each. At Masada, a few skeletal remains were found in the northern palace and some complete skeletons were found in a cave below the cliff (Yadin 1966; Zias, Segal, and Carmi 1994; Zias 1998). From Jerusalem, only the bones of a human arm were found (at the "Burnt House"; Avigad 1980: 123). From Gamla there is one human jawbone (see p. 151). The preliminary finds from Yodefat were somewhat more numerous, though not substantially so. We found a few human bones, some of which were burnt, in the weight pit of the oil-press cave. At the bottom of the cistern in Field XI we found a burial, in which the remains of two adults and a child were surrounded by a low wall of fieldstones. In the upper level of another cistern in Field XI, we also found a few human bones.

Then in the 1999 excavation season, we excavated a large cistern in the residential area in the northern part of Field XI. On the surface of the cistern fill, we uncovered the top of a thin wall, a single stone in width, that encircled a small area (3 by 1.5 meters) along the western wall. Within the enclosed area were many human bones, as well as skulls (Fig. 8.10). Anthropological analysis concluded that the bones belonged to about twenty different persons: twelve adults, including four females, eight males, and eight children below eighteen years of age. Preliminary study suggests that there is evidence of violent marks on some of the bones. The cistern was not totally excavated, so it is possible that there are more burials here. Other finds from the fill included early to mid-first century C.E. pottery as well as a heavy ballista stone.

The combination of this single concentration of human remains, along with the relatively wide scatter of such remains elsewhere at Yodefat, requires explanation. I believe that many of the bodies of the slaughtered were left unburied for more than a year, while the Roman army continued its march. Eventually, however, some Jews were allowed to come back, and they gathered the bones from the streets, yards, and destroyed houses, and buried them in cisterns and caves. In some cases, they surrounded the gathered bones with low walls, and in others they only put them into caves. Some of the cisterns they filled up with soil and stones from the destroyed houses.

The number of the dead given by Josephus is without doubt highly exaggerated. Based on the size of the site I would estimate the population in a peaceful time at around 1,500 to 2,000. We may assume that about 5,000 refugees fled into the walled town from neighboring villages, thus raising the population of Yodefat to about 7,000 people by the beginning of the siege. The number of 1,200 captives given by Josephus is reasonable, and leaves several thousands who probably died during battle, of hunger and disease, or in the final conquest and massacre.

Figure 8.10 Human bones from cistern.

Let each man fight not as the savior of his native place, but as its avenger, as though it were lost already. Let him picture to himself the fate of the children and women at the hands of the foe, momentarily impending. Let the anticipation of these threatened calamities arouse his concentrated fury, and let him vent it upon the would-be perpetrators.

(*War* 3. 259–62)

One final discovery bears mention. This is a small (8 by 11 centimeter) stone, found in Field Xl, flat on both sides, and covered on each with lightly scratched drawings made with a pointed tool (Fig. 8.11). On one side is etched a building with a triangular shaped roof atop a podium of three steps. On one side of the roof is a small tree and on the other a harp. This is so similar to inscribed depictions of mausolea that appear in tombs and on ossuaries from Judea dated to the first and second century C.E. that it is surely the same sort of thing (Rahmani 1994: 31). The trees may symbolize the "tree of life" or else indicate trees standing beside a tomb. On the other side of the stone there is an abstract depiction of a crab, which is the astrological symbol of the Hebrew month of *Tamuz* (July). I believe that this stone carries a graphic description of impending death, made by a besieged Jew. The absence of writing may suggest that the artist was actually illiterate, and so chose to express his sense that he would die in the month of *Tamuz* by these drawings. Yodefat fell on 20 July, 67 C.E. It was the first day of *Tamuz*.

Conclusion

The story of the battle of Yodefat is one of the most detailed descriptions of a Revolt battle. Our excavations have succeeded in documenting many of the

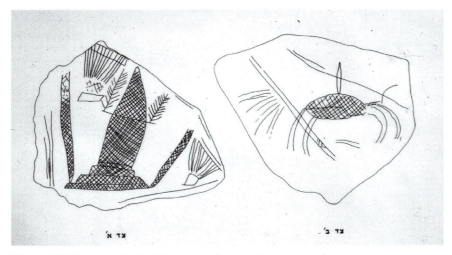

Figure 8.11 Stone etched with images of mausoleum and crab.

aspects of Josephus's narrative: (1) there was indeed a heavy battle around the hill of Yodefat in the mid-first century C.E.; (2) the town was surrounded with a wall hurriedly built in the early Roman period; (3) an earthwork was made on the northern slope of the town; (4) weaponry, including bow and catapult arrows and ballista stones were shot into the town from all around; (5) many people died during the siege, battle, and fall. Our excavations have also demonstrated aspects that Josephus did not describe, including the gathering of bones into graves long afterwards.

In the end, however, there is a difference between the excavation's realia and the historian's narrative. The length and detail of Josephus's account may in part be attributed to the fact that he wanted to justify both the city's and his own eventual fall into Roman hands. Surely, however, the extraordinary poignancy of his description cannot be explained by such considerations alone. Assigned to fortify the city, seen by some at least as the embodiment of its defence, commander of the battle, and eyewitness to the fall, Josephus had the most immediate and personal of reasons to expand on the horrors at Yodefat. It was the only battle in which he experienced the trauma himself.

Bibliography

Adan-Bayewitz, D. and Aviam M. (1997) "Jotapata, Josephus and the Siege of 67: Preliminary Report on the 1992–1994 Seasons," *Journal of Roman Archaeology* 10: 131–65.

Avigad, N. (1980) *Discovering Jerusalem*, New York: Thomas Nelson Publishers.

Rahmani L. Y. (1994) *A Catalogue of Jewish Ossuaries in the Collections of the State of Israel*, Jerusalem: Israel Exploration Society.

Yadin, Y. (1966) *Masada*, New York: Random House.

Zias, J. (1998) "Whose Bones?" *Biblical Archaeology Review* 24.6: 41–65.

Zias, J., Segal, L. and Carmi, L. (1994) "Human Skeletal Remains," in J. Aviram, G. Foerster and E. Netzer (eds.) *Masada* IV, Jerusalem: Israel Exploration Society.

9   Gamla

City of refuge

Danny Syon

The siege and battle of Gamla are described in detail by Josephus (*War* 4.1–83). Elsewhere (*Life* 11, 24, 35, 37, 58–61, 71–2; *War* 2.20.6) Josephus tells of the prelude to these events: how Gamla was initially loyal to the Romans because it was in the hands of Agrippa II; how it turned rebellious under the influence of the refugees flowing in; how Josephus helped the inhabitants fortify the city and how Agrippa besieged it. He also tells of the skirmish between him and Sylla, general of Agrippa II, who tried to block the roads leading from Galilee to the Golan, and especially to Gamla. In the following pages I will attempt to assess the events at Gamla during the Revolt, as reported by Josephus and filtered through the archaeological evidence.[1]

The identification of Gamla

To consider the events at Gamla in light of the archaeological discoveries, a brief discussion on the identification of the site is in order, as this question has not yet been fully discussed in English (Syon 1995; *contra* Bar-Kochva 1976). The passage in *War* provides the key for the identification of the site, which "moved around" between several sites in the last quarter of the nineteenth century. The previously accepted identification of Gamla with the site of Tel ed-Dra', in the Rukkad river-bed, now on the border of Israel with Syria, was proposed by Konrad Furrer in 1889.[2] This identification was based on the presumed preservation of the name Gamla in the name of the nearby village Jamleh, plus two faulty assumptions. One was that Tarichaeae, which is, according to Josephus, "across from Gamla on the far side of the lake," is at the southern extremity of the Sea of Galilee, at the modern site of Beth Yerach. The second was that *across* from Gamla should mean *on the same geographical latitude*. Tarichaeae is now identified with certainty at Magdala, on the northwest shore of the lake, and Josephus can hardly be credited with familiarity with geographical latitudes in the first century C.E. Gustav Dalman later "corroborated" Furrer's identification, based on a visit to the site (Dalman 1911).

The present site was first suggested in 1968. On older maps it is called es-Salam or es-Sanam (the hump) and it accords well with the particulars of Josephus's description: the site of Taricheae is clearly visible from es-Salam (hereafter referred to as Gamla); the ridge at Gamla resembles a reclining camel from certain angles; the approach to the ridge is possible only over a narrow saddle connecting it to the plateau to the east; the ruins are found only on the southern slope of the ridge and a wall separates the ruins from the saddle on the east; there is no other wall around the site. Finds from the Hasmonean period accord with the brief reference to Alexander Jannaeus' activity at Gamla (*War* 1.103–6; *Ant.* 13.394). The typically Jewish finds attest to the city's character: a synagogue, four ritual baths (*miqva'ot*), many hundreds of knife-pared lamps (the so-called Herodian lamps), fragments of limestone cups and thousands of Hasmonean coins, mostly those of Jannaeus. The site of Tel ed-Dra' on the other hand, has not been surveyed well, and its identity remains a mystery. However, a fragment of a stele or architectural fragment depicting a winged deity—possibly Victory—discovered there (Dalman 1913: 50, Fig. 5) is inconsistent with the Jewish city Josephus describes, and is certainly later than the first century C.E.

Gamla is mentioned in some later rabbinical sources, evidently in connection with events that took place in the Second Temple period. The excavations proved without a doubt that the site was indeed abandoned in the second half of the first century C.E.; the latest coins date to 64 C.E. The excavations corroborated Josephus's account on many more points and finally, the archaeological finds relating to the Revolt, described below, leave no doubt as to the site's identification as Gamla.

Josephus as the historical source

Modern scholars have frequently questioned the reliability of Josephus. I believe that the approach to his testimony should be pragmatic, as Rappaport has suggested (1992: 99–100): each case should be assessed separately, with as few general assumptions and preconceptions as possible. At Gamla, while the recounting by Josephus of some of the *events* should be taken with a pinch of salt, the reliability of his *description* of the site is remarkable. Indeed, some of the archaeological discoveries help clarify his statements concerning the events during the siege and battles.

Josephus knew Gamla well. His description of the city discloses an intimate acquaintance with it, made no doubt when he answered the call of the inhabitants to send an army and workmen to build the walls (*Life* 37). Here I beg to differ with Rappaport (1992: 100–1), who claims that Gamla was too distant to be under Josephus's command, and that he did not fortify it at all. During the siege of Vespasian Josephus was already a prisoner of war, having fallen into Roman hands a few months earlier at Yodefat (Jotapata), in one of the most controversial episodes of Jewish history (*War* 3.333–407). Josephus persuaded Vespasian not to send him to Nero in Rome, but to keep him as his own prisoner (*War* 3.407). Josephus's detailed description of Vespasian's moves after the fall of Yodefat suggests that he remained in the train of the general and was an eyewitness to the events at Gamla. Thus, we are in a position to compare point by point the finds with this primary historical source and add our own observations.

The archaeological evidence

Gamla, alongside Yodefat, is one of the few examples of a battle site of the first century C.E. in the Roman Empire that was left as it was abandoned. Since the site was never resettled, it provides an almost unparalleled glimpse of Jewish life in the last decades of the Second Temple period. Shmarya Gutman, the first serious explorer of Masada, led the excavations at Gamla for fourteen seasons (1976–89). After participating in the Yadin excavations at Masada, he saw Gamla as the "missing link" in the history of the Revolt. Notwithstanding the major importance of Gamla as the best preserved example of a Jewish town that flourished in the last two centuries of the Second Temple period, Gutman invested his major efforts in studying the siege and the battle. What follows reflects primarily his findings and conclusions, with some modifications based on new data or new interpretation.

The Roman camps

> Unable to put an unbroken ring of men round the town because of its situation, [Vespasian] posted sentries wherever he could and occupied the hill that overlooked it. When the legions had fortified their camps in the usual way on its slopes, he began to construct platforms at the tail end.
>
> (*War* 3.12–13)

It is probably futile to look for the remains of the Roman camps. Attempts by Gutman to locate them on the plateau north and south of Gamla have not yielded results. Any comparison with the well-preserved stone-built camps at Masada is equally meaningless. Vespasian did not plan to spend much time at Gamla and the camps and sentry posts would have been constructed of perishable wood. Even if their foundations were of stone, these were long ago dismantled by agricultural and building activity during the subsequent centuries, especially from the Byzantine period onwards.

The wall

One of the most striking findings at Gamla was the immense number of weapons and military objects recovered (see p. 141). The vast majority were found along the city wall, inside and outside. Although only about five percent of the built-up area of the city has been excavated, the distribution of the weapons in the city clearly shows that most of the fighting took place within a circumscribed band (ca. 50 meters wide) along the wall.

This wall was one of the surprises of the excavation. Josephus's claim that he *built* the city wall (*Life* 37; *War* 4.9) had been understood to mean that he *strengthened* and *reinforced* an existing wall, because the impression gained from his description was that of a fortified city. The archaeological picture is quite different, however. The wall visible today is, in fact, a patchwork of pre-existing buildings at the eastern extremity of the city, with evidence of hasty construction closing the gaps between them. When viewed on a plan (Fig. 9.1) the wall is anything but a straight line: it bulges, zigzags, projects, and retracts. Thus, the fortification by Josephus included closing gaps between existing buildings (e.g., Fig. 9.1, numbers 4 and 6) and the thickening of existing building walls facing east by the construction of a second wall behind them (as in the breach, see p. 140 and Fig. 9.1, number 10). It also included the filling-in with stones of rooms along the course of the wall, such as the "study room" next to the synagogue hall (Fig. 9.1, number 3) and a room in Area T (Fig. 9.1, numbers 8a and 11). Buildings, perhaps weak or old ones, were dismantled to construct the wall over them (e.g., Fig. 9.1, number 1). The round tower, at the highest point of the wall, was apparently built at an earlier period; the wall abuts it and is not joined to it. At all points along its length, the wall is distinguished from the pre-existing buildings of higher quality by its hasty, simple, field stone construction. It should be added however, that about midway along the wall (Fig. 9.1, Area M) a pair of well-constructed towers was discovered, flanking a narrow passage. At present it is unclear if this was an "official" entrance into the city before the war, or whether it was built as part of the fortifications in anticipation of the Roman siege. In any case, the towers were constructed over an earlier building, probably of the Hasmonean period. At the bottom of the wall (Fig. 9.1, Area T, number 12) yet another pair of square buildings, eight meters apart, may be towers, but they could equally be pre-existing buildings incorporated in the wall. The gap between these towers may be an opening, termed by Gutman the "water gate," with reference to what appears to be a small reservoir just below this spot, outside the wall. However, nineteenth and twentieth-century activity here in the form of a shepherd's hut and corral makes it near impossible to assess the evidence. Enigmatically, relatively few arrowheads and ballista balls were found along the lower parts of the wall, suggesting that the Romans concentrated their siege efforts at the top half of the wall, perhaps because it was more easily accessible to them.

The trench and the ramp

Outside of the wall, and parallel to it, is a depression running more or less in a straight line down to the stream below. This is an unlikely place for a

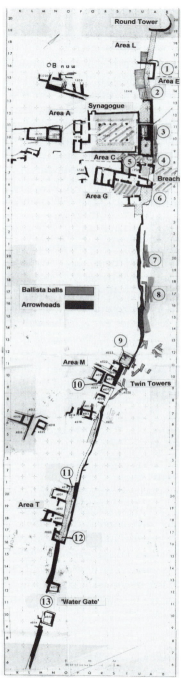

Figure 9.1 Plan of excavated areas at Gamla.

natural wash to form, as it does not originate at the lowest point of the saddle connecting the hill of Gamla to the plateau above. Instead, it is probably the "trench" referred to by Josephus that the inhabitants dug across the saddle and down the slope: "But here too, by digging a trench across, the inhabitants made access very difficult" (*War* 4.6). Although this feature was not excavated systematically, it is still prominent in the landscape.

The top of this trench, where it should have crossed the crest of the saddle, is filled up to an unknown depth. This is probably the ramp that Josephus cites: "With so many skilled hands the platforms (χωμάτων) were soon finished and the engines brought up" (*War* 4.17). While χωμάτων is variously translated as "earthworks" (Thackeray), "banks" (Whiston) and simply "the necessary works" (Bradshaw), it appears that the Romans constructed an earthen ramp at this spot, consisting of the flat space stretching from below the round tower to the nearest cliff, some 30 meters to the east. Although not formally excavated, over the years many ballista balls, coins and various other objects have surfaced in this area, which served as the expedition camp for fourteen seasons. This place was the only logical choice for Vespasian to build a siege ramp.

The round tower

Very little of the tower was found in the excavation. About half of the lowest course was uncovered from the point the wall abuts the tower, going around a rock outcrop, together with parts of two to three not very well built additional courses (the tower seen today is largely reconstructed). Three things, however, were clear even from the little that was found: (1) what remained of the tower was constructed mostly (but not exclusively) of headers; (2) it was a complete and separate structure, against which the wall abutted but did not bond; (3) it was built directly on the soft chalk that makes up the hill of Gamla, without any discernible foundation.

The first two points hint at an early date for the construction of the tower, perhaps in the Hellenistic period. Header construction, especially in military architecture, was common in this period, as illustrated by the splendid tower at Samaria (Crowfoot, Kenyon, and Sukenik 1942: pl. 36). Josephus's builders then used it, incorporating it as the highest terminus of their fortification.[3] The third point brings us to a passage that is usually looked upon as fantasy. It happened just before the second Roman assault on the city: "Working in silence, the [three] soldiers [of the Fifteenth legion] rolled away five stones forming the base. As they jumped out of the way the tower fell with a resounding crash, bringing the sentries down with it" (*War* 4.62–9). While by no means conclusive, the fact that the tower had no foundations and that its entire northern side was missing lends some credibility to this story, as it would have been relatively easy to dislodge stones from a structure built directly on soft chalk.

The breaches

According to Josephus, the Romans applied battering rams at three points along the wall (*War* 4.20). How many breaches they actually made is quite another question. The surviving Greek manuscripts state "των ερειφθεντων" literally "those [parts] that were torn down." The translations, again, vary: "breach" (Bradshaw), "broke through the wall" (Thackeray), "breaches" (Williamson), and "parts of the wall that were thrown down" (Whiston). Further on, recounting the events after the first assault, Josephus states that "the bolder spirits guarded the gaps in the wall" (*War* 4.51), so we may assume that there was more than one breach, though how many exactly remains unclear.

Although Gutman always referred to three breaches, as did Gichon (1987: 79) the excavations show clearly only one: in a building below the synagogue (Fig. 9.1, Area G; Fig. 9.2). Here the wall was found broken down almost to its foundation and a huge number of arrowheads (some 300) and ballista balls (some 180) were found inside and outside of it. The wall is breached in a room of a domestic building. The original thickness of the wall was 0.70 meters, and it was thickened to 2.05 meters. by the addition of a secondary wall behind it, built mostly of fieldstones. Even at two meters, it was one of the weakest points in the wall; just south of it the wall is four meters thick. Did the Romans have information on the easiest point to breach the walls? As the room probably had no roof at this point in time, it may have been

Figure 9.2 The main breach.

possible for someone standing on the cliffs above to judge the thickness of the wall. Furthermore, the information may have been extracted from a prisoner, a fugitive, or told by Josephus himself.

Another possible breach is located about midway along the wall (Fig. 9.1, number 7) where a small concentration of arrowheads was found in front of a 3.5 meter-wide section where the wall was missing. A third place is situated just above the synagogue, where an unusually carelessly patched-up passage through the wall was found (Fig. 9.1, number 2), which might be a breach that was re-closed by the defenders after the first attack. Here not many arrowheads were found, but some 100 ballista balls tell of an artillery barrage. Thus, there does not seem to be a correlation between missing sections of the wall and concentrations of ammunition, and the actual number of breaches will, unfortunately, remain conjectural.

The weapons [4]

Units from three legions took part in the siege and conquest of Gamla: the fifth Macedonica, the tenth Fretensis and the fifteenth Apollinaris. From the (mainly epigraphic) sources we know that the tenth and probably much of the fifteenth legions were composed of Syrian troops (Mann 1983: 41–2). There is of course no way to assign the material remains to specific units, but the weapons and other gear found at the site are typical of the general make-up of Roman military equipment of the first century C.E. As far as I have been able to ascertain, the sheer quantity of arrowheads and ballista balls found at Gamla is unsurpassed anywhere in the Roman Empire. A preliminary analysis shows that except at the main breach and the synagogue area, the major concentrations of arrowheads and ballista balls along the wall do not overlap.

Ballista balls

Some 2000 basalt ballista balls (some still strewn along the wall remain unrecorded) have been found to date. As opposed to arrowheads, which would have been collected (see p. 144), this probably represents more or less the complete inventory of ballista balls that were deployed at Gamla. The concentration of ballista balls and arrowheads was greatest in and around the large breach, where clearly an artillery barrage took place (see p. 140), but most buildings next to the wall, including the synagogue hall, were filled with them, providing a dramatic visualization of the siege. In the synagogue hall itself 157 balls were collected (Fig. 9.3). Near the round tower there were about 130, while near the entrance just above the synagogue (Fig. 9.1, number 2) there were about 100.

At the foot of the twin towers of Area M (Fig. 9.1, number 9), on the inside, a concentration of several dozen ballista balls was found (Fig. 9.4). Apparently, at night the defenders would gather the balls that had fallen in the city and hurl them back by hand at the Romans the following day. *Ballistae* had an effective range of ca. 350–450 meters at most (Holley 1994: 361). The furthest balls were found just east of Area B, some 60 meters from the wall. The balls found here were among the smaller ones found, as

Figure 9.3 Ballista balls on the synagogue steps.

Figure 9.4 Concentration of ballista balls inside the wall.

lighter balls would have traveled farther. Thus, the *ballistae* themselves were placed at most some 300 meters from the wall. There were probably several emplacements along the wall, though it cannot be determined exactly where. The edge of the Deir Qaruh spur that has been suggested (Gichon 1987: 79) is probably beyond firing range. In the cut made in the mountainside during the construction of the service road to the expedition camp, a large pile of ballista balls was discovered. It is situated ca. 300 meters from the wall, so it could be a ballista emplacement, but it could just as well be the spot where the balls were manufactured from locally collected basalt.

Arrowheads

Some 1,600 iron arrowheads have been found to date (Fig. 9.5). Since the Romans would have collected any spent arrows that they found after the battle for reuse, this number probably represents only a fraction of the arrows spent—those hidden by debris or vegetation, or that penetrated deep into the ground and escaped being corroded to powder. As the majority of arrowheads were found *outside* the wall (Fig. 9.1), it appears that those in the city were more easily recovered. Apart from the breach, two other concentrations of arrowheads were found. About 120 were collected outside the wall of the synagogue around the passage just below (Fig. 9.1, number 5), and nearly 300 were found about 50 meters north of the twin towers, again, outside the wall (Fig. 9.1, number 8).

Figure 9.5 Types of arrowheads and catapult bolts.

Aside from the standard trilobate arrowhead (with its variants), which is the most common in this period (91 percent), two other forms are represented: a flat type (7 percent) and a pyramidal type (2 percent). A preliminary study shows that these latter were found in three concentrations. The flat type was found near the upper entrance (Fig. 9.1, number 2, thirty-five arrowheads) and in Area T, near the bottom end of the wall (twenty-eight arrowheads). The pyramidal type was found in one concentration, near the breach, outside the wall (fourteen arrowheads). Although far from conclusive, these specific distributions may be evidence of auxiliary ethnic archer units (*sagittarii*), some of which may have used "traditional" arrowheads alongside the "standard" Roman issue. Josephus explicitly refers, for example, to Arab (Nabatean) bowmen at the siege of Yodefat (*War* 3.211).[5] Some hundred catapult bolts were also found along the length of the wall, including two concentrations, suggesting an "artillery barrage." One concentration occurred in the breach area (sixty-three bolts) and a smaller one near the twin towers in Area M (twelve bolts). Some of these found their way to the western areas of the city, some 300 meters west of the wall, underscoring the immense power of the catapults.[6]

Other weapons

An unusual concentration of Roman military equipment was found in Area M, in a very narrow alley between the inner side of the twin towers and the wall of a building (Fig. 9.1, number 9, locus 4019). Here was found what appear to be discarded or lost pieces of the equipment of a Roman officer. The concentration includes a helmet visor and a silver-plated cheek-guard, a gold-plated scabbard chape and parts of *lorica segmentata* armor, this last a rare find in the eastern provinces. It would not be stretching the imagination too far to see a trapped Roman officer during the failed first attack, who tried to escape from the city and lost or dropped parts of his equipment in his attempt to flee the city.

A dramatic illustration of the assault at the breach was a siege-hook found on the breach itself, used both for stabbing and hooking onto the wall for climbing. At other points along the fighting zone, as well as elsewhere in the city, there were a small number of armor scales (as opposed to the hundreds found at Masada), several other scabbard chapes, sheet bronze identification tags affixed to various pieces of equipment, possible *pilum* (the Roman spear) points, an *umbo* (the central bronze boss of a shield), military buttons, harness decorations, and pendants. Since the Jews used essentially the same kinds of weapons and equipment as the Romans, it is impossible to assign the finds to either group.[7]

Another class of "weapons" is heavy objects that the defenders threw from the wall on to the Romans. Except reused ballista balls (see p. 142), all kinds of stones and architectural elements were used, most of which cannot be told apart from the stones of the collapsed wall. A few, though, can be recognized:

several round millstones and about ten roof rollers that were found along the wall. About four of these rollers were found next to the breach. These objects could roll, thus causing more damage than a square block that would come to rest as soon as it hit the ground.

City of refuge

> For the town was crowded with refugees because of the protection it offered, which was proved by the fact that the forces previously sent by Agrippa to besiege it had made no headway after seven months.
>
> (*War* 4.10)

We have no accurate information on the origin of the refugees, but it can be safely assumed that they were of two kinds. Rebels from Galilee proper, escaping the Roman army, and villagers from the vicinity of Gamla, who sought refuge behind its wall, as was normal practice in antiquity when a town was about to come under siege. Two areas in the city provided evidence for public places used by refugees. In the western quarters of the town (Area R) remains of baking ovens, cookpots, and storage jars were found on a stone-paved public square—certainly not the normal location for these. The synagogue itself appears to have been converted to a dwelling for refugees, as evidenced by the dramatic find of a number of meager fireplaces and large quantities of cookpots and storage jars found along the platform next to the northern wall. These were all covered with the ballista balls that smashed the place (Fig. 9.6).[8]

The coins minted at Gamla

Perhaps the most intriguing single find at Gamla is a coin (Fig. 9.7). Only six of its kind are known, all of them found in the western quarters at Gamla, and all from the same pair of dies. It is a very crudely made bronze coin, obviously minted under improvised conditions and by an unskilled artisan. The obverse shows a cup, in clear imitation of the famous Jerusalem silver shekels which made their first appearance in the winter of 66 C.E., which are generally accepted as showing one of the Temple utensils (Meshorer 1982: 106–8). No doubt one of the Jerusalem coins served as a prototype for the Gamla coin, though no examples of the "models" have been found to date. The inscription starts around the cup and ends on the reverse, which carries no design. It states, in a mixture of paleo-Hebrew (biblical) and Aramaic (square) characters: "For the redemption of Jerusalem the H(oly)."[9] Ironically, a coin of Akko-Ptolemais was found together with one of these, minted in honor of Vespasian when he landed there some months earlier on his way to crush the Revolt.

No doubt these coins were produced during the siege or immediately preceding it, more as a propaganda effort than as currency, to make a

Figure 9.6 The synagogue hall during excavations (1976).

political statement to the Jews, and possibly to the Romans. This coin challenges the traditional view of a fragmented Jewish front that was pre-occupied mainly with internal strife and the defense of isolated sites by pockets of rebels, presenting Vespasian with an easy prey of towns and strong-holds instead of a unified front (Rappaport 1992: 101–2). It shows that even

Obverse

Reverse

Figure 9.7 Obverse and reverse of Gamla coin.

under the most difficult conditions, the people of Gamla still remembered the original aims of the Revolt, symbolized by "the redemption of Holy Jerusalem."

The final moments

Two other points pertinent to Josephus's battle narrative remain. While neither can be documented by hard archaeological evidence, I raise them for discussion as someone who has spent a great amount of time at Gamla and has come to know it intimately.[10] They concern the final moments of the defenders at the top of the ridge. While Josephus clearly allowed himself some latitude of literary liberty describing this episode, I would like to corroborate one of his accounts and to demolish a second, which at least among the public, has become an accepted myth.

The tempest

> But to ensure [the Jews'] destruction they were struck full in the face by a miraculous tempest, which carried the Roman shafts up to them but checked their own and turned them aside. So violent was the blast that they could neither keep their feet on the narrow ledges, having no proper foothold, nor see the approaching enemy.
>
> (*War* 4.76–7)

The fall of Gamla was in the month of *Hyperberetaios* (*Tishri*—September–October), a time of year characterized by occasional but predictable eastern winds, sometimes approaching gale force. In most seasons we were still in the field at this time, experiencing at first hand the immense strength of these winds, which at Gamla accelerate even more because of the effect of the narrow gorge. Sporadic blasts of these winds can stop one from breathing, blow clouds of dust and make almost anything that is not tied down or made of stone airborne. Thus, the description of Josephus, even if embellished, is no doubt based on fact. A similar incident is described at Masada, where the wall was set on fire by the Romans and the wind first blew the fire back towards them, but then, "as if by divine providence" the fire veered back and consumed the wall (*War* 7.315–18).

The final stand

The most dramatic episode is no doubt the last stand of the defenders of Gamla. In this context, Gamla is sometimes called "Masada of the Golan" or "Masada of the North." This is a falacious analogy, though one embraced by the general public. Even the late Menachem Stern (1982: 384) was under the impression that a mass suicide took place at Gamla, just as at Masada. True, at both sites dramatic episodes of the Revolt were played out. Furthermore, both are symbols of heroism for the modern state of Israel and both are important historical and archaeological sites. But here the similarities end.

Masada was conceived of and built as a desert fortress and served as such throughout its existence. During the Revolt it was held by a group of several hundred *sicarii* and their families. Gamla on the other hand, evolved as a city and existed as such, relying mainly on natural fortifications. Josephus's recurring reference to the "citadel" of Gamla (*Life* 11, 24, 36) is misleading. I suggested above that Gamla may have been a fortified Seleucid outpost until the days of Alexander Jannaeus, but during the first centuries B.C.E. and C.E. it was an unfortified city and certainly not a citadel. Although the crest of the ridge at Gamla was not excavated, thorough surveys have not revealed any remains of a citadel (*akra*) in the sense of a fortified building. There are a few scattered building stones on the ridge, and a single column drum lies just below the crest above the western quarters, but the remains are not substantial enough to reconstruct a massive defensive building. Had one existed, it would be difficult to account for Josephus's complete silence about it, especially as a refuge or a last stand for the defenders. Thus *akra* at Gamla simply refers to the crest of the ridge.

> No matter how critically or uncritically we read the suicide story of Eleazar Ben-Yair and his comrades (*War* 7.8:2–9:2), at Masada no actual battle was fought. At Gamla however, a very real battle took place, at the end of which, when there was no more hope, they flung their wives and children and themselves too into the immensely deep artificial ravine that yawned under the citadel. In fact, the fury of the victors seemed less destructive than the suicidal frenzy of the trapped men; 4000 fell by Roman swords, but those who plunged to destruction proved to be over 5000.
>
> (*War* 4.79–80)

Discussion on mass suicide in the Hellenistic–Roman world, real or literary, is beyond the scope of this paper, but has been amply discussed elsewhere (Stern 1982; Hankoff 1977; Hooff 1990). Here I propose to take a more pragmatic two-step approach to disproving the suicide story.

First, the only place along the crest of the ridge where there is a vertical cliff high enough for someone falling off it to die with reasonable certainty is at the summit, which can only be reached with some difficulty, by clambering over large boulders. Today the summit area can accommodate a few score people at most. In antiquity it may indeed have been larger, as earthquakes certainly brought down some massive boulders, but not by much. Even if we accept only 500 people, not 5000, standing on the ridge, it would be physically impossible for all but a few to reach the summit and jump headlong to their deaths. The rest would not have made it. The remainder of the ridge on the north simply slopes down, though steeply indeed, to the gorge below.

Second, contrary to the time afforded to Eleazar Ben-Yair on Masada to make his speech and persuade his comrades to commit suicide, it is hard to imagine that the people at Gamla would have had the presence of mind in the midst of the fighting to decide on carrying out a mass suicide. The truth must be that the remaining defenders and townspeople were trying to flee down the steep northern slope in panic, with the inevitable result that many were trampled underfoot and died. Some of the more agile may have actually reached the gorge and thence safety. For an observer (Josephus?) standing on the Deir Qaruh ridge and looking at this drama unfolding, it may have appeared as a mass suicide. Josephus's description may be read as an honest, though erroneous, interpretation, a deliberate distortion, or simply a literary "touch up."

The dead

In fourteen seasons of excavation at Gamla, we never found a single human skeleton. Among the thousands of animal bones recovered in all areas excavated, only a single lower human jawbone was found together with an arrowhead in Area S, in the western quarter of the city, far from the main events of the battle. One explanation, while not completely satisfactory, lies in the supreme importance of the Jewish religious command for the burial of the dead. The Romans, possibly leaving a temporary garrison, would have allowed Jews to return and bury the dead, doing themselves a service at the same time in the way of sanitation. The Romans too would have collected their dead because of reasons of morale and cremated them, which was the standard Roman military practice. The dead were probably buried in mass graves somewhere in or near the city; their discovery could only come about by sheer luck.

While the existence of a garrison remains a matter of speculation, the recent dramatic find of the mass burial in a cistern at Yodefat (see p. 131) unexpectedly affirms this explanation, while at the same time increasing the affinity of these two tragic sites.[11]

Notes

1 So far, the only general English presentations about Gamla are Gutman and Shanks 1979, Syon 1992, and the entry in *The New Encyclopedia of Archaeological Excavations in the Holy Land* (Gutman 1985). A detailed presentation of the site in Hebrew is given by Gutman 1994. A full report of the excavations of Shmarya Gutman is due to appear in the near future.

2 Furrer published two articles; in the first one he suggested the village of Jamleh, on the bank of the Rukkad (1879). In the second article he suggested Tel-ed-Dra', also known as Tel el-Ehdeb, in the riverbed below Jamleh (1889).

3 Though not strictly relevant to the topic under discussion, the numismatic evidence (and it alone, so far) points to an appreciable presence at Gamla as early as the days of Antiochus IV (175–164 B.C.E.). The campaign of Jannaeus to

capture the "strong fort" of Gamla indicates a military presence there in his days (*War* I, 4, 8 §(103–6), *Ant.* XIII, 394) and perhaps the tower was constructed hastily to face his attack. Contrary to the belief of Gutman, who saw in Gamla a Jewish foundation from the start, I now tend to accept the suggestion made by Moti Aviam, that Gamla may have started out as a Seleucid fort in one of the later Syrian wars of the third century B.C.E. For a suggested line of Hellenistic fortifications in the Golan see M'aoz 1983.

4 The weapons from Gamla are being prepared for publication by J. Magness (the arrowheads and other projectile points); A. Holley (the ballista balls) and G. Stiebel (all other weapons and military items). I thank them for some insights while preparing this paper. For the situation on Masada, see Magness 1992.

5 See also Magness, forthcoming and Syon 1990: 99–100. With rare exceptions, there were no organic archery units in a Roman legion. The Romans did not excel as archers and they preferred using auxiliary units composed of ethnic groups from the East, who were known as excellent archers (Davies 1981: 260–2).

6 No such bolts were found at Masada and only a few at Yodefat though at the latter site their percentage is greater in relation to the overall number found.

7 On Masada, what appears to be a zealot workshop for forging arrowheads was found, of exactly the same type as the Roman standard military issue (Magness 1992: 60–3).

8 Incidentally, the discovery that Gamla was not fortified before the war sheds light on a talmudic passage which states that Gamla was consecrated as a city of refuge instead of Kedesh (Cadasa) in Galilee (*JT* Makkot 2,7; *Tos.* Makkot 3(2), 2). From another passage (*Sifre* for Deut.180) it appears that only an unfortified city—which Gamla indeed had been—qualifies as a "city of refuge."

9 The inscription was originally read by Joseph Naveh. See also Syon 1992–3: 40–1.

10 I would like to stress again that in all that follows I am but a spokesman of the whole excavation team: Shmarya Gutman, Zvi Yavor, David Goren, and myself.

11 I dedicate this chapter to the memory of Shmarya Gutman (1909–1996).

Bibliography

The editions of Flavius Josephus quoted:

(1798) *The Wars of the Jews. The Whole Works of Flavius Josephus*, Thomas Bradshaw (trans.), London: Alex Hogg.

(1822) *Wars of the Jews. The Whole Genuine Works of Flavius Josephus*, William Whiston (trans.), Edinburgh: Allman.

(1968) *The Jewish War*, H. St. J. Thackeray (trans.), Loeb Classical Library, Cambridge: Harvard University Press.

(1959) *The Jewish War*, G.A. Williamson (trans.), London: Penguin.

Bar-Kochva, B. (1976) "Gamla in Gaulanitis," *Zeischrift für Deutschen Palästina Vereins* 92: 54–71.

Crowfoot, J. W., Kenyon, K. M. and Sukenik, E. L. (1942) *The Buildings at Samaria*, London: Palestine Exploration Fund.

Dalman, G. (1911) "Jahresbericht des Instituts," *Palästina Jahrbuch* 7: 1–31.

—— (1913) "Jahresbericht des Instituts," *Palästina Jahrbuch* 8: 52.

Davies, J. L. (1981) "Roman Arrowheads from Dinorben and the Sagittarii of the Roman Army," *Britannia* 12: 257–70.

Furrer, K. (1879) "Die Ortschaften am See Genezareth," *Zeischrift für Deutschen Palästina Vereins* 2: 52–74.

—— (1889) "Tarichaea und Gamala," *Zeischrift für Deutschen Palästina Vereins* 12: 148–51.

Gichon, M. (1987) "The Golan and the Battle of Gamla," in M. Inbar and E. Schiller (eds.) *Ramat Ha-Golan, Ariel* 50–1: 77–81 (Heb.).

Gutman, S. (1985) "Gamla," in E. Stern (ed.) *Encyclopedia of Archaeological Excavations in the Holy Land*, Jerusalam: Israel Exploration Society, pp. 459–63.

—— (1993) "Gamla," in E. Stern (ed.) *The New Encyclopaedia of Archaeological Excavations in the Holy Land*, Jerusalem: Israel Exploration Society.

—— (1994) *Gamla—A City in Rebellion*, Tel Aviv: Ministry of Defense Publishing House (Heb.).

Gutman, S. and Shanks, H. (1979) "Gamla—Masada of the North," *Biblical Archaeology Review* 5.1: 12–27.

Hankoff, L. D. (1977), "Flavius Josephus—First Century A.D. View of Suicide," *New York State Journal of Medicine* (October): 1986–92.

Holley, A. (1994) "The Ballista Balls from Masada," *Masada IV. The Yigael Yadin Excavations 1963–1965 Final Reports*, Jerusalem: Israel Exploration Society, pp. 349–65.

Hooff, A. J. L. (1990) *From Autothanasia to Suicide: Self Killing in Classical Antiquity*, London: Routledge.

Magness, J. (1992) "Masada: Arms and the Man," *Biblical Archaeology Review* 18.4: 58–67.

—— (forthcoming) *The Arrowheads and Projectile Points from Gamla*.

Mann, J. C. (1983) *Legionary Recruitment and Veteran Settlement during the Principate*, London: Institute of Archaeology Occasional Papers 7.

M'aoz, U. Z. (1983) "The Hellenistic Fortification System on the Golan and the Conquests of Jannaeus," *Eretz Hagolan* 81: 14–17 (Heb.).

Meshorer, Y. (1982) *Ancient Jewish Coinage*, New York: Dix Hills.

Rappaport, U. (1992) "How Anti-Roman was the Galilee?" in Lee. I. Levine (ed.) *The Galilee in Late Antiquity*, New York: Jewish Theological Seminary.

Stern, M. (1982) "The Suicide of Eleazar Ben-Yair and His Men at Masada, and the 'Fourth Philosophy,' " *Zion* 47: 367–97 (Heb.).

Syon, D. (1990) "The Arrowhead," in S. Wachsmann (ed.) *An Ancient Boat in the Sea of Galilee, 'Atiqot* 19: 99–100.

—— (1992) "Gamla: Portrait of a Rebellion," *Biblical Archaeology Review* 18.1: 20–37.

—— (1992–3) "The Coins from Gamla—an Interim Report," *Israel Numismatic Journal* 12: 34–55.

—— (1995) "The Identification of Gamla—Through the Sources and by Results of the Excavations," *Cathedra* 78: 3–24 (Heb.; English summary on p. 195).

Part III

From archaeology and history to ideology

10 Documents of the First Jewish Revolt from the Judean desert

Hanan Eshel

The caves of Wadi Murabba'at are located near the water holes of Nahal Dragot (Wadi Darajeh). These caves were used as temporary dwelling quarters from the Chalcolithic period to the 1950s. The presence of water during the winter months, and the wadi's remoteness from any permanent settlements, made its caves an ideal refuge throughout history. More than 175 documents have been found in the caves of Wadi Murabba'at (Benoit, Milik, and de Vaux 1960). The earliest (Mur. 17) was brought to the desert in the sixth century B.C.E., at the time of the Babylonian conquest and the destruction of the First Temple (Milik 1960: 93–100; Cross 1962) whereas the latest documents (Mur. 169–73) date to the tenth century C.E. (Grohmann 1960: 284–90).

In this paper I will discuss seven documents from Wadi Murabba'at. Most of the documents found in Wadi Murabba'at were brought to the caves at the end of the Second Jewish Revolt (i.e. in 135 C.E). It is hard to determine the exact date when the Bar Kokhba revolt ended. From various sources we know that the Revolt lasted three and a half years (Schäfer 1981: 10–28). Mishnah *Ta'anit* (4:6) avers that Beitar, the last stronghold of the Revolt, fell on the ninth of Ab, namely in the middle of the summer. Four papyri found in Wadi Murabba'at have been used by some scholars to prove that Bar Kokhba captured Jerusalem and that the Revolt lasted into the winter of 135 C.E. (Koffmann 1968: 178; Applebaum 1983: 254). One of the problems much debated by students of the Second Jewish Revolt is whether Bar Kokhba captured and occupied Jerusalem (Isaac and Oppenheimer 1985: 54–5).

The four documents in question are, first, an Aramaic deed of land sale (Mur. 25) dated "On the [ ] day of Marheshvan, year three to the freedom of Jerusalem." Milik ascribed this papyrus to November 133 C.E. (Milik 1960: 134–7). The second document is another deed of sale (Mur. 29) written in Hebrew and dated: "The fourteenth of Elul, year two to the redemption of Israel in Jerusalem." The vendor in this deed is Kleapos son of Eutrapelos from Jerusalem. According to Milik this document is to be dated to early 133 C.E. (Milik 1960: 140–4, 205). Neither document is well preserved and there is no indication what the nature of the business they were meant to record was, but it is quite probable that they deal with real estate. Third is a Hebrew deed recording the sale of a field (Mur. 30), written "On the twenty-first of Tishri, year four to the redemption of Israel in Jerusalem." The twenty first of Tishri is at the end of the feast of Tabernacles. In this deed the vendor Dosthos sold a field to a man whose name was not preserved. Milik dated this deed to late 134 C.E. (Milik 1960: 144–8, 205). The fourth document is in Hebrew (Mur. 22) and its opening clause is "On the fourteenth of Marheshvan, year four to the redemption of Israel." This deed records the sale of real estate, dated about a month after the Feast of Tabernacles in the fourth year of the Revolt (Milik 1960: 118–22).[1]

The negligible number of Bar Kokhba coins found in Jerusalem (Ariel 1982: 293; Gitler 1996: 328) has led many scholars to conclude that Jerusalem did not fall into the hands of the insurgents (Applebaum 1976: 27; Mildenberg 1980: 320; Schäfer 1981: 87–8). Based on historical considerations some scholars reject Milik's reading "Jerusalem" in Mur. 25, 29 and 30 (Herr 1978: 9, n. 44; Schäfer 1981: 119; Isaac and Oppenheimer 1985: 54, n. 95; Mor 1991: 157). An interesting situation emerges from the study of the Bar Kokhba revolt. The three epigraphists who studied the Murabba'at documents read "Jerusalem" in Mur. 25, 29 and 30 and assumed that the rebels captured the city (Milik 1960: 205; Yardeni 1991: 12–14; Misgav 1996) while the archaeologists and most historians were of the opinion that Jerusalem was never conquered. Therefore, doubts concerning this reading were raised.

In 1997 I found two Aelia Capitolina coins together with four Bar Kokhba coins in the el-Jai Cave, a refuge cave used by Jews who fled from the Roman army in 135 C.E. These finds clearly led to the conclusion that Aelia was founded in 130 C.E. during Hadrian's visit to Judea, and coins were minted in Aelia before 135 C.E. Clearly, the rebels could not have held Jerusalem during 133–5 C.E. (Eshel 1997; Eshel, Zissu and Frumkin 1998).

As the name of Simeon son of Khosiba is not mentioned in the dating formulas of Mur. 22, 25, 29 and 30, we decided to check the possibility that those documents may date to the First Revolt, i.e. to 68–9 C.E. A Carbon 14 analysis performed on two of the documents (Mur. 22 and 29) indicated that they were written before 78 C.E.; accordingly, they were written during the First Jewish Revolt (Eshel, Broshi and Jull 1998). These documents can now be added to two other documents from Wadi Murabba'at whose connection to the First Revolt was established long ago. The first is Mur. 18, a bill dating to Nero's second year, i.e. to 55–6 C.E. written in Sobah, in which Zachariah son of Yehohanan from Kesalon declares that he owes Absalom son of Hanum 20 denarii. Both Sobah and Kesalon are located near Jerusalem, to the west (Milik 1960: 100–4).

The second document is Mur. 19, a bill of divorce (*get*) written in the year 6 at Masada. In this document, Joseph son of Naksan, who was at Masada for a time, divorced Miriam daughter of Jonathan of his free will. Milik proposed that this document is dated according to the era of Provincia Arabia, which was established by Trajan in 106 C.E. This means that this document should be dated to 111 C.E. (Milik 1960: 104–9). However, Yadin, who discerned no evidence of a Jewish presence at Masada after the First Jewish Revolt, suggested that this document is dated according to the era of that revolt. He therefore dated the document to 71 C.E., and concluded that Miriam left Masada one year after the fall of Jerusalem and took her bill of divorce to Wadi Murabba'at. Yadin assumed that the Jewish rebels who occupied Masada after the destruction of the Temple continued to use the era initiated at the beginning of the Revolt. However, they could not write "Year 6 to the Redemption of Israel" or "Year 6 to the Freedom of Jerusalem," because Judea was already under Roman rule and the Temple had been destroyed. Therefore, they simply wrote "Year 6" (Yadin 1965: 119, n. 112). This document attests to the messianic expectations and aspirations of the occupants of Masada, who continued to use the era initiated at the time of the First Revolt even after the destruction of Jerusalem and the Temple. Whoever dated this bill of divorce according to this era assumed that this date would also be understood by people outside Masada, and hoped in 71 C.E. that the situation would still change for the better. Miriam left Masada after her divorce, before the Roman army besieged the fortress in 73 or 74 C.E. (Eshel, forthcoming).

A seventh document is 4Q348. Recently Cotton and Yardeni published the economic documents from the Seyal Collection (Cotton and Yardeni 1997). As an appendix, nineteen additional economic documents were published. These documents were purchased by the Jordanians from the Bedouin, who claimed they were found in Cave 4 at Qumran (Cotton and Yardeni 1997: 283–317). Yardeni and Cotton are of the opinion however, that these documents originated from Nahal Hever (*op. cit.* 283). Ada Yardeni, who edited the Hebrew and Aramaic documents, read in 4Q348, one of the double documents of this collection, the words: "[...]WS High Priest" (Cotton and Yardeni 1997: 300–3). Since these words appear in the first line of the open part of the deed, they seem to be part of the dating formula. The document is fragmentary, but some names can be read, among them "שמעון משוק הקורות", or "Simon of the beam (or the timber) market." The "timber market" in Jerusalem was mentioned by Josephus (*War* 2.530). This market was burned together with the new city by Cestius Gallus, at the beginning of the Revolt. The timber market was probably located in the northern part of Jerusalem, as part of the area surrounded by the Third Wall (Price 1992: 362). Therefore we may conclude that 4Q348 was probably written in Jerusalem. It seems that we shall read the name "קומ[ו]דיוס" in the first line of 4Q348 and date this document to the time of Joseph son of Camydus, who served as the high priest from 46 to 47 C.E.

If our dating of this document to the years of the high priest is acceptable, we may conclude that some Jews of the Second Temple period avoided dating documents according to the Roman emperors, as we found in Mur. 18 mentioned above. The people who wrote 4Q348 probably belonged to

Temple circles, and they counted years according to the service of the high priests. Some of them later joined the rebels and fled to the Judean desert.

Although we cannot rule out the possibility that the document under discussion (4Q348) was brought to the cave in which it was found at the end of the Bar Kokhba Revolt, i.e. in 135 C.E., it seems more reasonable to assume it was brought there shortly after the destruction of the Temple. Therefore, I believe that this document was found in the caves of Wadi Murabba'at that were used as refuge caves at the end of the First Revolt.[2]

We may conclude that, in all, there are seven documents that were brought to the desert at the end of the First Revolt. Six of these documents were published by Milik (1960) including one which dates to 55/56 C.E. (Mur. 18). The other five (Mur. 19, 22, 25, 29, 30) were written during the course of the Revolt. A seventh document (4Q348) that is also probably from Wadi Murabba'at, published by Cotton and Yardeni (1997), apparently belongs to this group as well. Like Mur. 18, it dates to the years before the Revolt. Six of these documents were brought to Wadi Murabba'at by refugees who fled from Jerusalem and the villages of Sobah and Kisalon (west of Jerusalem). The seventh (Mur. 19) was brought to Wadi Murabba'at by Miriam daughter of Jonathan, a woman who left Masada after divorcing her husband Joseph son of Naksan.

Although we are dealing with a small group of documents, it is possible to glean from them details about the social history of the First Revolt. During the course of the Bar Kokhba Revolt, the leaders issued an order to use the Hebrew language, apparently for nationalistic reasons. This can be seen in letter no. 3, which was discovered by Yadin in Nahal Hever. This letter deals with the transport of *ethrogim* (citrons) from Ein Gedi to the Jewish camp. A clause in the letter specifies that "it (the letter) was written in Greek because of no means having been found to write it in Hebrew" (Yadin 1961: 42–3; Lifshitz 1962: 241–8; Yadin 1971: 130–1). Mur. 42 is in an intermediate status between a letter and an economic document. It was sent from the administrators of the village of Beth Mashcho to Yeshua Ben Galgula, the commander at Herodion. The administrators tried to write in Hebrew, but incorporated Aramaic words and Aramaic syntax into the document, a fact which reflects the difficulty they had in expressing themselves in Hebrew (Milik 1960: 155–9).

Two of the documents written during the course of the First Jewish Revolt are in Aramaic (Mur. 19, and 25) and three are in Hebrew (Mur. 22, 29, and 30). Of the two written before the Revolt, one (Mur. 18) is in Aramaic and it is dated according to Nero's reign. The other (4Q348) is probably written in Hebrew and it is dated according to the service of the high priest. These documents indicate that Hebrew was used as an expression of nationalistic feeling during the First Revolt; some circles tried to use Hebrew even before the outbreak of the Revolt. This can be seen not only from 4Q348 but from the ostracon found at Qumran in 1996 as well. On this ostracon a draft of a deed of a gift is written in Hebrew (Cross and Eshel 1997).[3]

Mur. 29 and Mur. 30 are unique in having a list of members of a judicial court at their beginning. The court signed and ratified the deals specified below. Such an arrangement is not found in any of the economic documents unequivocally dated to the Bar Kokhba Revolt (Misgav 1996). 4Q348 is written in a similar way (Cotton and Yardeni 1997: 301–2). We may assume that such a legal institution (Jewish Courts of Law) did not exist after the destruction of Jerusalem in 70 C.E.

The three Hebrew documents that were written during the First Revolt bear the following dates: Year 2 (Mur. 29) or Year 4 (Mur. 22, 30) "for the Redemption of Israel." One of the Aramaic documents (Mur. 25) is dated to "Year 3 for the Freedom of Jerusalem." The bronze coins from the second year of the First Jewish Revolt bear the inscription, "Freedom of Zion," (Meshorer 1982: 109–10) while the coins from the fourth year of the Revolt bear the inscription "For the Redemption of Zion" (Meshorer 1982: 122–3). No examples of the use of the slogan "For the Redemption of Israel" or "For the Freedom of Jerusalem" are attested on the coins. From this we can see that there is no correlation between the slogans that appear on the coins and those that appear on the documents, which were all used simultaneously.

In the excavations of Masada hundreds of ostraca and jar inscriptions in Hebrew and Aramaic were found (Yadin and Naveh 1989), as well as fifteen Hebrew manuscripts, fourteen of which are written on parchment and one on papyrus (Talmon 1999). Nevertheless although three fragmentary letters were found in Masada written on ostraca (Yadin and Naveh 1989: 49–51) no private economic documents of Jews written during the First Revolt were found in Masada. This is probably only a question of luck since private documents of Roman soldiers stationed on Masada were found in the fortress (Cotton and Geiger 1989). In this paper I have tried to show that seven documents that were brought to the Judean desert at the end of the First Revolt were found in Wadi Murabba'at. These documents shed some light on the Revolt's social history.

Notes

1 Milik read in Mur. 22 "year one" and dated this deed to 131 C.E. (Milik 1960: 118–22). However A. Yardeni, who re-examined the reading of the Murabba'at documents, is certain that Mur. 22 belongs to the fourth year (Yardeni 1991: 12–14).

2 One cannot rule out the possibility that 4Q348 was actually found in Qumran cave 4.

3 The editors suggest three possible reconstructions to line 1 of this deed: "ל[בשנת שתים." The first is to restore a name of a Jewish ruler, presumably Agrippa. The second is to restore a name of a Roman emperor, as Mur. 18. The last is to restore לחרות ציון or לגאלת ציון and to date it to 67 C.E. (Cross and Eshel 1997: 20). If we accept the last suggestion then this ostracon is from the First Revolt as well. Based on 4Q348 one should consider the possibility that this ostracon was dated according to the service of a high priest. The

authors wrote: "Most of the economic documents dated to the Second Temple period which were found in the Judean Desert were written in Aramaic. In the period between the First and the Second Revolt deeds were written in Greek or in Aramaic and only during the Second Revolt were some deeds written in Hebrew" (Cross and Eshel 1997: 26–7). In light of the evidence brought about this statement can now be corrected.

Bibliography

Applebaum, S. (1976) *Prolegomena to the Study of the Second Jewish Revolt*, Oxford, British Archaelogical Reports, Supplemental Series 7.

—— (1983) "The Bar Kokhba Revolt and Its Aftermath," in U. Rappaport (ed.) *Judea and Rome—The Jewish Revolts*, Jerusalem: Masada (Heb.).

Ariel, D. T. (1982) "A Survey of the Coin Finds in Jerusalem (Until the End of the Byzantine Period)," *Liber Annuus* 32: 273–326.

Benoit, P., Milik, J. T. and de Vaux, R. (1960) *Les Grottes de Murabba'at*. Discoveries in the Judean Desert 2, Oxford: Clarendon Press.

Cotton, H. M. and Geiger, J. (1989) "The Latin and Greek Documents," in *Masada II: The Yigael Yadin Excavations 1963–1965 Final Report*, Jerusalem: Israel Exploration Society.

Cotton, H. M. and Yardeni, A. (1997) *Aramaic, Hebrew and Greek Documentary Texts from Nahal Hever and Other Sites*, Discoveries in the Judean Desert 27, Oxford: Clarendon Press.

Cross, F. M. (1962) "Epigraphic Notes on Hebrew Documents of the Eighth–Sixth Centuries B.C.: II. The Murabba'at Papyrus and the Letter Found Near Yabneh-Yam," *Bulletin of the American Schools of Oriental Research* 165: 34–46.

Cross F. M. and Eshel, E. (1997) "Ostraca from Khirbet Qumran," *Israel Exploration Journal* 47: 17–28.

Eshel, H. (forthcoming) "Josephus' View on Judaism without the Temple," in A. Lange, B. Ego and P. Pilhofer (eds.) *Gemeinde ohne Temple*, Tübingen: Mohr.

—— (1997) "Aelia Capitolina, Jerusalem No More," *Biblical Archaeology Review* 22.6: 46–8, 73.

Eshel, H., Broshi, M. and Jull, T. A. J. (1998) "Documents from Wadi Mura'abat and the Status of Jerusalem during the War," in H. Eshel and D. Amit (eds.) *Refuge Caves of the Bar Kokhba Revolt*, Tel-Aviv: Israel Exploration Society (Heb.).

Eshel, H., Zissu, B. and Frumkin, A. (1998) "Two Refuge Caves in Wadi Suweinit," in H. Eshel and D. Amit (eds.) *Refuge Caves of the Bar Kokhba Revolt*, Tel-Aviv: Israel Exploration Society (Heb.).

Gitler, H. (1996), "A Comparative Study of Numismatic Evidence from Excavations in Jerusalem," *Liber Annuus* 46: 317–62.

Grohmann, A. D. (1960), "Textes Arabes," in P. Benoit, J. T. Milik, and R. de Vaux (eds.) *Les Grottes de Murabba'at*, Discoveries in the Judean Desert 2, Oxford: Clarendon Press.

Herr, M. D. (1978), "The Causes of the Bar-Kokhba War," *Zion* 43: 1–11 (Heb.).

Isaac, B. and Oppenheimer, A. (1985) "The Revolt of Bar Kokhba: Ideology and Modern Scholarship," *Journal of Jewish Studies* 36: 33–60.

Koffmann, E. (1968) *Die Doppelurkunden aus der Wuste Juda*. Leiden: E. J. Brill.

Lifshitz, B. (1962) "Papyrus grecs du desert Judea," *Aegyptus* 42: 241–8.

Meshorer, Y. (1982) *Ancient Jewish Coinage*, vol. 2, New York: Amphora.

Mildenberg, L. (1980) "Bar Kokhba Coins and Documents," *Harvard Studies in Classical Philology* 84: 311–35.

Milik, J. T. (1960) "Textes Hebreux et Arameens," in P. Benoit, J.T. Milik, and R. de Vaux (eds.) *Les Grottes de Murabba'at*, Discoveries in the Judean Desert 2, Oxford: Clarendon Press.

Misgav, H. (1996) "Jewish Courts of Law as Reflected in Documents from the Dead Sea," *Cathedra* 82: 17–24 (Heb.).

Mor, M. (1991) *The Bar Kochba Revolt. Its Extent and Effect*, Jerusalem: Yad Itzhak Ben Tsvi.

Price, J. J. (1992) *Jerusalem Under Siege: The Collapse of the Jewish State, 66–70* C.E., Leiden: E. J. Brill.

Schäfer, P. (1981) *Der Bar Kokhba Aufstand*, Tübingen: Mohr.

Talmon, S. (1999) "Hebrew Fragments from Masada," in *Masada* VI: *The Yigael Yadin Excavations 1963–1965, Final Report*, Jerusalem: Israel Exploration Society.

Yadin, Y. (1961) "Expedition D," *Israel Exploration Journal* 11: 36–52.

—— (1965) "The Excavation of Masada 1963–64: Preliminary Report," *Israel Exploration Journal* 15: 1–120.

—— (1971) *Bar-Kokhba*, London: Weidenfeld & Nicolson.

Yadin Y. and Naveh, J. (1989) "The Aramaic and Hebrew Ostraca and Jar Inscriptions," in *Masada* I: *The Yigael Yadin Excavations 1963–1965 Final Report*, Jerusalem: Israel Exploration Society.

Yardeni, A. (1991) *The Aramaic and Hebrew Documents in Cursive Script from Wadi Murabaat, Nahal Hever and Related Material: A Paleographic and Epigraphic Examination*, unpublished Ph.D. thesis, Hebrew University, Jerusalem (Heb.).

11 Jewish millenarian expectations

Tessa Rajak

Introduction

In the course of the first two centuries, the Jews revolted three times against Rome within a period of some seventy years. These revolts caused considerable disruption, engaged substantial Roman forces and senior commanders each time for several years, and had a major impact on the history of the empire at the very highest level, being primary causes of Nero's fall, of the Flavian ascent to power and of Trajan's Parthian disaster. Yet the Jews—in the eyes of any rational observer—were bound in the end to be defeated. To explain both their determination and their foolhardiness it has been all too easy to invoke the messianic temper of the times and to suppose that the rebels acted in the assurance of the expected destruction of the Gentiles, the promised victory of Israel, the translation of an elect group and, if not the End of Time, at least the opening of the final act of the drama. Such reasoning underlies numerous interpretations, especially perhaps those offered by historians of Rome.[1] Thus the outbreak of revolt is explained less in terms of the nature of Roman rule and more primarily by the peculiar character of this subject population.

To be sure, such views are not entirely without some support in the sources; but that support is all of it problematic. Overtones of messianism—of whatever kind—have been detected by interpreters of all three revolts, in relation both to the claims of the leaders and the responses of the followers.[2] Gager (1998) speaks of a "messianic reflex." For the revolt under Trajan (115–17 C.E.), such interpretations center on the scant evidence of a leader of the revolt in Cyrene, named Lukuas by Eusebius (*HE* 4.2.3–4), and described as a king. Cassius Dio (68.32) in fact gives a different name Andreas, for this man, while for the Revolt leader in Cyprus, Dio offers no more than another bare name, Artemion. To this Horbury (1996) would add as messianic indicators the sudden outbreak, the tenacity of the rebels, the destruction of shrines and the understanding of rebel movements as an intended return from exile. He also cites the textual evidence of messianism in the liturgy, while Hengel finds a messianic background in the fourth and fifth Sibylline oracles.[3]

But messianism is associated particularly with the leadership of Bar Kokhba in the third, Hadrianic rebellion in Judea (132–5 c.e.). Coins and documents reveal his adoption of the title of *nasi* and the use of a calendar counted in terms of the "years of redemption." A little less ambiguous is the rabbinic attestation for recognition of Bar Kokhba as saviour by a pre-eminent rabbinic figure, R. Akiva, himself to be ultimately executed (together with other rabbis) by the Roman authorities.[4] Yet it should be noted that the Talmudic story also exposes the scathing response of another rabbi. And for our purposes, the paucity of the information and the ambiguity of the prophecy ascribed to Akiva require underlining. Recently, both the hailing of Bar Kokhba as King Messiah and the application to him of Balaam's prophecy in *Numbers* 12.1 that "a sceptre shall rise out of Israel" have been cogently interpreted as political statements, assertions of the revival of the Davidic dynasty (Oppenheimer 1983: 158–9). Oppenheimer, in fact, depicts Akiva as not a prophet but an activist.

The First Revolt, however, offers documentation of an altogether different order. Historical questions can therefore be asked and more precise definitions sought. What is the real connection between the huge interest of those times in the last things and concerted political action? Was messianism a language for the expression of political ideas, for envisaging social and political change? Did the thoughts and the actions emanate from the same circles? Was messianic expectation at the heart of the movement, or on its fringes? And again, what exactly was expected? The beginning of the End? Or the end of the beginning? How was the possible onset of a new age identified? By the presence of a leader? By signs? By the arrival of a certain pre-ordained date? Millenarianism has always come in many shapes and sizes. The scenario could be abrupt or gradual: in later periods, streams calling themselves post- and pre-millenarians differed about the significance of the second coming of Christ, that is to say whether it would inaugurate the thousand felicitous years of Revelation or whether it would come after them as something yet greater. Comparative study reveals that the End might be a minority concern, or it might sweep a society off its feet. It might be an academic interest or an engine for social change. It might be sophisticated in conception or a widespread popular belief. It might, but it need not, arise out of a historical crisis.

A comparable range of possibilities exists for our period. Scholars concerned with the origins of Christianity naturally interest themselves in this aspect of contemporary Jewish thinking, and for many such scholars Jewish messianism looms large and monolithic. For some of these scholars, and for others too, the messianic component is endorsed by the very distinct social dimension in the Great Revolt against Rome, with its twin struggle against internal oppression and external domination. Messianism springs, often enough, out of times of crisis, and the first century seems admirably to fit the bill.[5] Simply because a connection with an apocalyptic environment is readily made, however, does not mean that the connection is true. First we must explore some of the many different strands, not always separable, that make up first century preoccupation with the Last Days. Only then can we set the Revolt against the context of that diversity.

Messianic caution

"Three things come unawares," says the Babylonian Talmud, "the Messiah, a found article and a scorpion" (*Sanhedrin* 97b). This was not a new view. A similar reaction can be found in earlier Jewish contexts and also in Christian writing. Thus Mark and Matthew put a warning at the heart of Jesus' prophetic teachings in chapter 24, the so-called "little apocalypse": "But about that day and hour no one knows, neither the angels of heaven, nor the Son, but only the Father ... Keep awake therefore, for you do not know on what day your Lord is coming" (Matthew 24.36, 42; cf. Mark 13.32–3; Luke 21.8–28).

There was a comparable view at Qumran: "God told Habakkuk to write down what would happen to the *dor aharon* (last generation), but did not inform him about the end of that *ketz* (block of time)" (1QP*Habakkuk* 7.1–4; 9.1–7).

There are good reasons always for leaving shrouded in vagueness the exact extent of the Last Days and, within that period, of the exact time of arrival of the expected messianic figure or figures. The consequences of non-fulfillment are the most obvious hazard. The history of later millennial movements throws up many examples, one of the best known being the foundation, on the east coast of the United States, of the Seventh Day Adventist Church, as a consequence of the "Great Disappointment" when the Millerite predictions of the end of the world failed to materialize in 1843 and 1844.[6] Lists of failed dates from the annals of the Jehovah's Witnesses' prophecies are relished by a scornful public. The Babylonian rabbis had no illusions about the risk: according to a Talmudic tradition about a bird called *raham* (vulture), if it settles on the ground and hisses the Messiah will come. But one Babylonian rabbi said to another "but didn't [a *raham*] once settle on a ploughed field and hiss when a stone fell and severed its head?" The other rabbi replied "that one is a liar." (BT *Hullin* 63a; Urbach 1975: 1004, n. 29). In the important excursus on messianic matters in tractate *Sanhedrin* from which I quoted above, the point is ascribed to a Tannaitic authority and made explicitly:

> Rabbi Shmuel ben Nahmani declared in the name of Rabbi Jonathan "blasted be the bones of those who calculate the End, for they used to say 'since the time of his arrival has arrived and he has not come he will never come'."
>
> (BT *Sanhedrin* 97b; Urbach 1975: 680 and n.16)

In this respect at least there is continuity between pre-70 attitudes and the rabbinic period. Alexander (1998: 473) speaks of "a considerable baggage of messianic speculation from the Second Temple period" carried by the rabbis. Thus, the Qumran *Habakkuk* commentary has itself been interpreted by some as a response composed at the very moment when the expected End did not materialize. The authors of this *pesher* were regrouping, it is thought, in the face of disappointment (Talmon 1987: 127; García Martínez in J. Collins 1999: 177–8). They are forced to conclude, Talmon (1987: 127) writes, that "the *ketz aharon* shall be prolonged more than the prophets have told, for the mysteries of God are astounding." Reassurance is provided: "the Torah shall not slacken in the service of truth, for all the divine ages will come in their destined order, as He has decreed in his unfathomable wisdom."

Charges of false prophecy and of spurious messiahship abound in the Second Temple period. Josephus and Matthew share a common distaste though, it need hardly be said, for different reasons:

> Beware that no one leads you astray. For many will come in my name, saying, "I am the Messiah!" and they will lead many astray. And you will hear of wars and rumours of wars; see that you are not alarmed; for this must take place, but the end is not yet.
>
> (Matthew 24.4–5; cf. Mark 13.5–6)

There is also a larger reason for leaving matters open. Jewish meditation on redemption generally belongs in the sphere of mystical speculation, and about the acceptability of mysticism itself there is characteristic and continuing concern (Gruenwald 1980: 73–97). That the secret things of God should be studied only by the elect becomes a recurrent theme in rabbinic literature: "What is above, what is below, what has been beforehand, what is to come are four things to which one ought not to give one's mind" (*M. Hagigah* 2.1). The attitude is epitomized by the famous *pardes* story, according to which four rabbis entered the high realms of interpretation, for which the letters of the word *pardes* (orchard) are an acronym, but only one, R. Akiva, emerged physically and spiritually intact, while ben Azzai, ben Zoma, and Aher were all in one way or another damaged (Rowland 1982: 309–23; Gruenwald 1980: 86–7).

The location of apocalyptic and eschatology

At the same time, it is commonly agreed that post-exilic Palestine produced a new way of thinking and a new way of writing, conveniently subsumed under the modern description "apocalyptic." But there is room for disagreement over the extent of its continuity with biblical prophecy. When the biblical prophets looked forward to redemption and expatiated upon it, that was primarily a national victory. For Hosea, Amos and Isaiah, the ruling

House of David, now in ruins, would be re-established at a time described as *ketz hayamim*; there would be everlasting peace and a turning away from heathen cults and images. Apocalypticism in post-exilic Palestine is something more than this. The apocalyptic agenda is now generally defined in terms such as "revelations of God's hidden knowledge" or as "the disclosure of divine secrets" and indeed "revelation" is the root meaning of the word. Anything involving "mysteries beyond the bounds of human knowledge" is fit subject matter for apocalypse, including nature, cosmology and the geography of the heavens (Rowland 1982; Gruenwald 1980: 3–72; McGinn 1994: 6–17; Himmelfarb 1993; J. Collins 1997: 1–138; 1998: 1–14). Writings wholly or partly devoted to these themes proliferated, offering a language for the unfathomable, a way of making sense of the world in its cosmic entirety, and a vehicle through which a range of moods and reactions can be conveyed, from expressions of despair to outbursts of passionate anger. Within that mode, there is a privileged place for knowledge of the End, and yet it is always important to keep in mind the many other concerns in apocalyptic revelation besides eschatology. If, then, we ask what is new in all this, we discover at the very least that biblical prophets receive revelations but do not go on tours of heaven under the guidance of angels, that they stand "in the council of the Lord," but do not know the names of the angels, that they see history as moving towards a goal but do not conceive of the rewards and punishments of individuals, that they have some conception of a messianic redeemer but spend little energy on fleshing it out.[7]

The new vantage point, and the genre of literature which incorporates it, are indeed seen by scholars as a defining feature of the period. They represent a particularly powerful current in both Judaism and Christianity from the third century B.C.E. (when this thinking is already present at Qumran) down to late antiquity; and, of course, they continue in existence far beyond (McGinn 1994). And yet we remain unable to judge whether that distinctive apocalypticism, even in its most inclusive sense, constituted a central and general way of thinking in Second Temple society, or whether rather these tendencies flourished in limited, if perhaps vocal, circles. Rowland's *Open Heaven* (1982: 443) leaves the question unresolved. Indulgence in full-blown eschatology may well have been even more restricted.[8]

Another approach is to look closely at the concept of eschatology itself. A valuable distinction has been proposed by Barton (1986: 218–23) between first, second and third order eschatology. With this tool, he distinguishes incisively between, on the one hand, a general sense that history will pass through programmed phases to reach an end or goal (first order) and, on the other hand, an urgent expectation of the coming of that end by the much smaller number of people who think they have already seen some of the signs (second order), that is to say, between the non-imminent and the imminent. This is a central distinction, but a third phenomenon is also related to eschatology and sometimes allowed the same name, and that is the biblical prophets' reading of certain historical events as being heavy with meaning.

For them, a phrase like "the day of Yahweh" does not seem to have referred to the End of the World or even necessarily to the culmination of Israel's history. On both sides, the borders of second order eschatology are far from firm. Ambiguity, quite simply, goes with the territory. But the main point is that not every look forward to cataclysmic events is necessarily involved with a sense of the approach of final things. Far from it. The most we can say, I suppose, is that any look forward is likely to induce at least a degree of tension.

The main question for us, however, relates to second order eschatology and concerns the correlation between event and belief. There is a tendency to take for granted that there is a nexus in Jewish society between troubled times and messianic expectation. There is a real risk here of circular argument: writings with a messianic flavour will tend to be so dated as to link them with moments of crisis. The prophecies in Daniel, with their demonstrable linkage to Antiochus IV's desecration of the Temple, may be invoked in support of such claims. Even in this case, however, commentators have differed widely in the extent to which they read those prophecies in millenarian terms and the text itself allows such divergence, as we shall shortly see. Further serious complications arise from the consideration that the book of Daniel appears to be a collection of older material.[9]

Evidence of the end

What assurances, then, might observers look for in difficult times, to permit messianism to go beyond the realm of desire, hope and dreams into that of conviction of a truly imminent End? In the popular mind, signs and wonders are the primary indicator. And yet signs often—or perhaps always—mislead, and they are regularly open to charlatanry of every kind. Extreme caution is essential:

> Then if anyone says to you, "Look! Here is the Messiah!" or "There he is!" do not believe it. For false messiahs and false prophets will appear and produce great signs and omens, to lead astray, if possible, even the elect. Take note, I have told you beforehand. So, if they say to you, "Look! He is in the wilderness," do not go out. If they say, "Look! He is in the inner rooms," do not believe it.
>
> (Matthew 24.23–6)

Yet, if signs are delusive, people are left to identify in some other way the beginning of the era of troubles and disasters, as indeed they constantly do. There is scarcely a moment in history which could not be seen to fit the bill somewhere or other, and of course there are countless crises that have been made to fit. The second main aid, which like the first method relies on guidelines in an authoritative text and which can indeed be combined with the first, is chronological reckoning, bringing to bear on the problem some kind of "allegorical arithmetic," to use Russell's memorable term (Russell 1974; J. Collins 1997: 55–138). Here the difficulties are perhaps even greater, and there are obvious hazards and complications in excessive precision. As Volz observed long ago (1934: 142), it is in fact quite uncommon to find "ein bestimmtes Datum" in early Judaism. Key configurations were available for people to conjure with. In fact, however, at all times, much second order eschatology lacks any kind of determinacy about dates and times.

Daniel's messianic chronologies

The underpinning of eschatological chronology is the capacity, or indeed the need, of prophecy to build upon earlier prophecy, so that predictions are endlessly recycled and the same texts applied to any number of new sets of circumstances.[10] This is certainly the case with the *fons et origo* itself of all subsequent millennial speculation, the visions that an angel dictated to the prophet Daniel, supposedly at the Persian court, and which are recorded in chapters 7–12 of his book, the latest to be included in the Bible. In fact, precisely because prophecy builds on earlier prophecy, even this remarkable creation had an earlier biblical derivation. For in chapter 9, the angel interpreted for Daniel the true meaning of Jeremiah's prophecy that the Jews would serve the king of Babylon and their land lie desolate for seventy years, after which they would return (Jeremiah 25.11–12; 29.10; J. Collins 1997: 58–60). And Daniel worked explicitly from Jeremiah's seventy year exile (Daniel 9.2) for his own key prediction of seventy weeks of years for the length of the metaphorical exile. Since 70 times 7 yields 490, this will be the length of the vicissitudes to be endured by the people and the holy city.[11]

> Seventy weeks are decreed for your people and your holy city: to finish the transgression, to put an end to sin, and to atone for iniquity, to bring in everlasting righteousness, to seal both vision and prophet, and to anoint a most holy place.
>
> (Daniel 9.24)

This stretch of time is then divided into sections according to a timetable: seven weeks of years will pass before the appearance of "an annointed one"; 62 weeks, i.e., 434 years (9.25), will be a time of restoration; and then one week will be a critical period of havoc, deluge and horrors. As it happens, if the figure of 434 was meant to be the length of time from the savior monarch Cyrus to Antiochus IV, when the prophet's troubled final week is thought to have begun, then the calculation is quite far out, and it has not proved easy to propose explanations for the precise figure offered. Most commentators simply suppose that Daniel's reckoning is faulty.

However, this was not Daniel's sole venture into arithmetic. He also set a ball rolling when he specified (7.25) "a time, two times and half a time," i.e., three and a half years, for the period of the greatest distress of all, during which the holy ones will be delivered into the power of the fourth beast of Belshazzar's vision. The persecution of Antiochus, taken to be the historical crisis from the very midst of which Daniel was actually writing (Millar 1997) lasted, in the event, somewhat less. But here was another number to be extrapolated to new situations and contexts, where its messianic coloring could be intensified.

At Daniel 8.14: yet another chronology is presented: in connection with Belshazzar's second vision, and thus linked to the book's historical mise en scène, it is predicted that horrors of all kinds will last 2,300 evenings and mornings, "then the holy place shall emerge victorious." And finally, the book of Daniel reaches its conclusion with these words:

> from the time when the regular offering is abolished and the abomination of desolation is set up there shall be an interval of 1,290 days. Happy the man who lives to see the completion of 1,335 days. But go your way to the end and rest and you shall arise to your destiny at the end of the age.
>
> (Daniel 12.11–12)

This is clearly a reference to the prophet's own time. I shall not decode the figures, though it is worth observing that 1,335 days, are 1,290 plus 45, and one suggestion is that the lower figure is lunar, the higher solar. Others have understood the second date as a gloss added after the failure of the first prediction to materialize (Hartman and di Lella 1978: 313–4). These totals are somewhere in the region of the earlier sum of three and a half years and probably refer to the same thing. But whether the End of Days comes at the end of that time, or whether there is longer, perhaps much longer, to wait for the final events, remains shrouded in enigma (Kosmala 1963: 30–1; Steudel 1993).

Daniel's book was popular from the start, as we can tell from the survival in the Septuagint corpus of two rival translations, from the book's propensity to acquire lively accretions, such as the story of Susanna and the tales of Bel and the Dragon, and from the use as a reference point of the image of the three young men in the burning fiery furnace in subsequent martyr literature. Daniel is also much represented in early Christian art, an image of salvation and a familiar figure.[12]

It is interesting that Josephus has special praise for Daniel precisely because he puts dates to his prophecies:

> For the books which he wrote and left behind are still read by now even now, and we are convinced by them that Daniel spoke with God, for he did not only regularly prophesy future events, but he also defined precisely when these events would happen.
>
> (*Ant.* 10.268)

This judgment, moreover, is later reinforced in book 10 of the *Antiquities* by the historian's acknowledgement of Daniel's accurate foretelling of the desolation of the Temple by Antiochus Epiphanes, 480 years, in Josephus's view, before the event (12.322; Mason 1994: 174). Bockmuehl's (1990: 84) general observation that "Josephus shows a recurring interest in the specific intervals which elapsed between a prophet's prediction and its fulfillment" enables us to make sense of this admiration for Daniel in terms of the historian's outlook.

Timetables for the Last Days

The book of Revelation joins Daniel as the key supplier of messianic time-tables in the Christian sphere. It is evident that Revelation is heavily dependent on Daniel for many things, not least its scenario of redemption. For 42 months, or 1,260 days, i.e. Daniel's three and a half years, the Holy City will be trodden underfoot. According to this author, that is when Antichrist will be overthrown (Rev. 11.3; McGinn 1994: 21–3; A.Y. Collins 1996: 118–38 with references to recent literature; A.Y. Collins in J. Collins ed. 1999: 384–414). In chapter 20, Revelation produces the most crucial of all figures, the millennium in the true sense, which is the 1,000 years during which Satan is to be held in chains before being released for the final battle.

This round figure no doubt derives from Jewish tradition. For a second main numerical preoccupation of apocalypticism is that of figuring out the total duration of life on earth, and this much larger stretch of time is usually conceived of in millennia. There are different ways in which importance is attached to intervals of 1,000 years or its multiples. Volz (1934: 143–4) has a useful, though unchronological, list of the range of estimates on offer, from which I select a few examples: a period of 7,000 years appears in *Pseudo-Philo* (28.8) and later texts, including a *baraita* found in some Babylonian Talmud manuscripts and discussed below; 6,000 years occurs in the Life of Adam (42); 5,000 years is the span in the Assumption of Moses (10.12). The idea that our world has 2,000 years of the total left to run is widespread. Calculation on such a basis is necessarily opaque, by virtue of the simple fact that its starting point, the date of creation, has to be speculative.

The messianism of early Jewish texts involves a standard scenario even if not all the ingredients are always present. The "systematic presentation" of the messianic drama constructed by Schürer (1979: 514–46) guides us through the key stages in the unfolding of the future. By a conflation of sources, we put together the following sequence: final ordeal and confusion, coming of the Messiah, last assault of the hostile powers, destruction of the hostile powers, renewal of Jerusalem, gathering of the dispersed, kingdom of glory in the holy land, renewal of the world, general resurrection, and last judgement with consequent eternal bliss and damnation. So it is not a simple business, nor a quick one. In is important to notice that the messianic era is only really a beginning, to last, it seems, until the end of this world, but by no means into eternity.

It is the initial stage of all this that emerges most clearly and, for our purposes, the really crucial element is the time of wrath and confusion. That period is sometimes described as the pains or birth pangs of the Messiah, in a concretization of prophetic language.[13] The period makes a momentary but clear appearance in Daniel 12.1: "There shall be a time of anguish, such as has never occurred since nations first came into existence." Ingredients of this phase may be war, earthquake and famine. Ezekiel's battle against Gog in the land of Magog is seen as its final enactment, not only in Revelation, but also according to the Third Sibylline Oracle (the most Jewish of this curious collection of Greek hexameters from different periods):

> Woe to thee, land of Gog and Magog, in the midst of the rivers of Ethiopia!
> What a stream of blood shall flow out upon thee! And thou shall be called among men the house of judgement, and they shall drink and be drenched with red blood
>
> (319–22)

Matthew (24.8) and Mark (13.8) invoke the classic scheme:

> And you will hear of wars and rumours of wars; see that you are not alarmed; for this must take place, but the end is not yet. For nation will rise against nation, and kingdom against kingdom, and there will be famines and earthquakes in various places: all this is but the beginning of the birth pangs.

And it is perhaps worth noting that the Messiah's appearance, the destruction of the wicked, the appearance of the heavenly Jerusalem, the ingathering of the exiles and the era of joy, peace and fruitfulness, are particularly graphically depicted in those apocryphal works which are usually dated to the years immediately after 70 C.E., 4 Ezra and 2 Baruch (Schürer 1979: 511). The time of troubles enables such schemas to be used as explanations of suffering and as a form of theodicy, a vindication of divine justice:

> For the most High will surely hasten his times, and he will certainly cause his periods to arrive. And he will judge those who are in the world, and he will truly inquire into everything with regard to all their works which were sins. He will certainly investigate the secret thoughts and everything which is lying in the inner chambers of all the members of those who are in sin.
>
> (2 Baruch 83.1–3)

We can observe throughout continued interest in the precise enumeration of the phases in the protracted End of Days era itself. An early schema, which seems to predate Daniel, is the sequence of ten weeks (of years) or ten generations known to us from *I Enoch*'s Apocalypse of Weeks (91–105). A fragment of what seems to be a commentary on the Apocalypse of Weeks was found at Qumran (4Q 247; Broshi 1995: 187–91; Milik 1976). Significantly, a group of righteous persons make their appearance in the seventh week (J. Collins 1998: 21). And seven-day schemas were to be a particularly long lasting tradition (A.Y. Collins 1996: 87–8). Thus, in the apocryphal 2 Baruch, the final events unfold day by day through a week and there are also various seven-day schemas in rabbinic literature. From the Mishnah we learn that

> R. Akiba used to say: there are five things that endure for twelve months: "the generation of the flood ... the judgement of Job ... the judgement of the Egyptians ... the judgement of Gog and Magog which is to come ... and the judgement of the unrighteous in Gehenna shall endure twelve months. For it is written "it will be from one month until its same month" [Isaiah 66.23].
>
> (Mishnah *Eduyot* 2.10)

But there was a dissenting voice in the shape of R. Johanan ben Nuri who insisted "[only as long as] from Passover to Pentecost [i.e., seven weeks], for it is written: 'from one sabbath until its [next] sabbath'" (Mishnah *Eduyot* 2.10). In these opinions, the theme that links the disparate events is evidently that of judgement, in a patterning where past and future are invoked indiscriminately. And Johanan ben Nuri's dissenting view depends on the widespread seven-day schema, here, as often, interpreted as seven weeks.

Periodization

During the Second Temple period, it seems to have been normal for scholars—if not for the plain man—to conceive of the entire stretch from Creation to the End as a continuum.[14] Josephus is part of a long tradition of working out dates for the creation, the flood, the Exodus, the destruction of the First Temple and the return from Exile. These are a framework for history (Russell 1974: 208). While these structures implicitly encompass the future as well as the past, their builders do not always make it their business to explore the former (cf. Rowland 1982: 137; Barton 1986: 228–9). At the same time, those whose view of the march of history stretches forward as well as back are bound sometimes to consider what is to come. So one of the concerns which enhanced the millenarian culture of the day (in the broad sense of that word), without necessarily inducing agitation about an imminent End, was precisely this periodization, the division of time, past and future, into a sequence of stages and the exploration of its patterns (A.Y. Collins 1996: 69–86).

While a framework of this kind may well underpin the conviction that the End is nigh (Barton 1986: 228–30), it is in itself something altogether larger, an important theme in its own right (see J. Collins 1997: chapter 4).

It was noted by Gershom Scholem (1971: 6) that in the *Antiquities* (1.60) Josephus represents Adam as able to predict universal flood and fire in the time to come. Scholem reads into this remark the implication that the first man could look forward from Noah through the whole sweep of history to the conflagration at the End of Days, an interpretation no doubt justified in Scholem's mind by the figure of the visionary Adam familiar from apocalyptic texts. To put it simply, eschatology is a part of history, more often, perhaps, than a "retreat from history," in the term commonly invoked (Rowland 1982: 444–5). In the book of Jubilees (not generally classed among the Apocalypses), Moses on the mountain is shown "the first things and the last things" and commanded to write down all the weeks of years, according to Jubilees, till eternity, when God will descend and dwell with his people (1.26). And yet that last stage is for this author far away indeed.

In sectarian texts from Qumran, we find doctrines about the way the world was created, the process of history and the workings of predestination regularly presented through an exposition of "periods," dividing history into blocks of time, *kitzim*, or "generations," *dorot*, which run from the creation. The destruction of the First Temple is usually the watershed. The end is obscure. This pattern of thought is visible in the Habakkuk *pesher*, the Community Rule, the Damascus document, the *Hodayot*, and elsewhere. The periods seem to be the main concern of a remarkable fragmentary text, the so-called "Pesher on the Periods" or "Ages of Creation" (4Q180), whose opening line announces that God created the periods with the end of each one in view and that the meaning and activities of each are engraved on tablets—probably the heavenly tablets of *Enoch* 93.2. The author pays close attention to biblical chronology and appears to run through the ten biblical generations familiar, from *I Enoch*'s "Apocalypse of Weeks".[15]

There is ample suggestion in the texts that the Qumran sectarians interpreted the periods in such a way as to include the Last Days and to locate their own lives in the approach to that era. This was clearly within, not outside history. Thus Talmon writes:

> the covenanters conceived of the 'Messianic Age,' *aharit hayamim*, the preordained period in which the two anointed shall ring in the new aeon ... as one further link in the chain of historical epochs. The anointed will come not at the end of time, but rather after a turn of times, after a profound crisis in history.
>
> (Talmon 1987: 128)

The sect along with its enemies belong to the last generation, which will move seamlessly into the End of Days. Yet the End of Days, though a radical transformation of the existing order, is by no means the final end of time. Indeed, commentators have observed an inclination in the sect to envisage an indeterminate prolongation of the End of Days era (as in 1QpHab.7.–13), running alongside the certainty that there would come a final conclusion in the shape of God's intervention in the world.[16] Steudel 1993 shows how the reference of the term *aharit hayamim* at Qumran depends on the writer's standpoint and may be to past, present or future. Yet the theme of an era already launched recurs, finding clear expression in the document known as "Some Precepts from the Torah" (4QMMT) and in the "Rule of the Congregation of Israel in the Last Days" (1Qsa).

Delimited periods of time are closely linked with yet another distinct phenomenon, the "political prophecy" which is Barton's third type. This form of expression harks back to the ringing denunciations of Israel's enemies by the biblical prophets. It covers the schemata of the destruction and succession of empires and the rise and fall of rulers. Barton's first order eschatology is already quite close to political prophecy but the latter, while using much of the same language, sets its sights even lower. The cosmic significance of political prophecy rarely gets fully articulated. We shall come later to the question of its relation to action.

Lastly, it is worth giving a moment's thought to the role played by much of this calculation. Michael Stone (1980: 42) has argued that what he calls "speculative interests"—cosmology, astronomy, calendar—are a core element of the apocalypses. Science, understanding the shape of things; is a motivation for many of the authors (though Stone rightly points out that Daniel itself seems to be not quite in this category). Of course, investigation of the highest seriousness was involved. But there could also be satisfaction in the exercise of this learning, the satisfaction that lies in the making of patterns with meaning, as for example in the passage from Mishnah *Eduyot* 2.10 quoted above (p. 174).[17]

Josephus's evidence

We come to our central problem, how we should classify the rebels of 66–73/4 C.E. within the setting which we have mapped out. In what sense, if any, are they to be judged millenarian? The issues are complex, but a stark question can be put. We may ask, quite simply, whether there are grounds for envisaging the participants in the Great Revolt, or at least their leaders and core supporters, as fired for their struggle by the certainty that the End was at hand? In many accounts, such expectation is a motivating force, or even perhaps the prime motivating force, which led the Jews to rebellion. The case needs examination.

Our familiarity with the entire history of these events derives from the pages of a historian, Flavius Josephus, who was unsympathetic to the rebels (to say the least), contemptuous of the masses, indifferent, if not hostile, to explicit apocalyptic expression, and permanently wary of upsetting his Roman overlords. The perennial problem in dealing with Josephus is just how far to go in reading between his lines, whether glimpses of a suppressed world should be sought through and behind his narrative? Josephus's version is the crux of any interpretation of the Revolt and his opacity is the obstacle.

Almost all of Josephus's possible testimony to messianic elements in the Revolt can be interpreted in more than one way. But it is illegitimate simply to proceed from the untested assumption that we are dealing with a partisan writer who so far rejected the vision shared by his fellow citizens, for political or other reasons, that he contrived systematically to conceal its influence, and that he did this throughout his recital both of the action and of the participants' words and motivations, thereby expunging from the record one whole dimension of the events (for a skeptical reading, see Bilde 1988: 126–57; 191–200).

It is at one's peril that one assaults Martin Hengel's classic reconstruction (1989a) of the beliefs and ideas of the Zealots (by which he means the whole spectrum of revolutionaries). Something usually comes up to hit one in the face. Yet it is, I think, fair to say that the speculative edifice constructed to support the attribution to the revolutionaries of a thoroughgoing and urgent messianism, expressed in traditional Jewish terms and steeped in biblical and midrashic reference, is the most controversial part of Hengel's creative and vastly learned reconstruction. Though wide-ranging, and acutely aware of the Second Temple thought-world, it is a reconstruction rooted in a particular understanding of Josephus—and so indeed it should be. For apart from the bronze revolt coins, with their ambiguous declarations of liberation/redemption (*herut, ge'ulah*) which alone do not take us very far, there is no direct expression outside Josephus of the ideology of revolt (Rajak 1983: 78–107).

In any assessment, it must first be appreciated that Josephus is not to be taken as a wholly hostile witness. His attitudes are not as simple as they may seem. Bilde (1998) has brought out the historian's interest in various phenomena which we would describe as "apocalyptic." It is not insignificant that, throughout his writing, Josephus does, one way or another, give coverage, by no means all negative, to visions of the future, prediction and prophecy. Rebecca Gray (1993) has demonstrated that, while the historian believed the line of prophetic books to have ended, he was not pointing in this assertion to the demise of the kind of prophecy that looked into the future. Prophecy of this kind was for him a living possibility, even if quite a lot of what passed as such was in his eyes charlatanry. Thus it has been noted that we find in Josephus a positive evaluation of Essene prophecy, to an extent which would seem to go beyond his penchant for idealizing a philosophical sect for the benefit of his Greco-Roman readers (Blenkinsopp 1974; Bockmuehl 1990: 82–9; Beckwith 1996: 251–2). Again, prophecy and priesthood, including his own, are for Josephus closely connected phenomena (Blenkinsopp 1974; Horsley and Hanson 1985: 172–87; Feldman 1990: 419–21; Himmelfarb 1993: 96).

Prophets

What Josephus has to tell us is that prophecy abounded in the period leading up to the outbreak of revolt, all of it, in his eyes, either false or misinterpreted. The predictors of doom were in the pay of the "demagogues," and, moreover, deeply destructive in that they talked the people into awaiting "help from God." It may be suggested that Josephus has concealed the deep meaning of those teachers' message, to obscure an underlying intimate connection between them and the Revolt. Yet, while a messianic interpretation is by no means demanded for the "sign prophets," to adopt a term coined in New Testament scholarship, their announcements concerned miracles of divine assistance, and these miracles related to immediate confrontations. It is worth noting that Gray takes good care not to go any further than this.[18] Josephus's specific point is quite intelligible: it is simply that the prophets, by contributing to the general restlessness and encouraging a lack of realism among the people, turned out to have served all too well the disruptive purposes of the rebels. We may add to this a telling occasion where Josephus, reflecting on the sins of the rebels, unequivocally presents them as not only quite detached from the prophets but highly contemptuous, something which is here, of course, by no means to the rebels' credit (*War* 4.385). The historian tells us enough for us to see that these prophets behaved in the fashion characteristic of their breed; but they were neither messianic forerunners nor self-appointed messiahs (for the distinction see Saperstein 1992: 3–4).

Such prophecies continued into the final moments of the Temple (*War* 6.286), when 6,000 unfortunate individuals gathered in the last surviving portico where a pseudo-prophet (in Josephus's eyes) had announced that God would give them "signs of deliverance." This character would seem to be a typical sign prophet. But Hengel detects something more. For, at this point, into the fourth year of the War, he ingeniously proposes that Daniel's three and a half years may have been seen as coming to their conclusion. He further suggests that the approach of 10 *Av*, when the First Temple was destroyed and Daniel's seventy weeks of years began, will have added to the tension in the city (Hengel 1989a: 242). In a parallel attempt, Beckwith (1996: 265–9) seeks to reconstruct a "Pharisaic" chronology (as he calls it) where the last of the 70 weeks since the exile falls between 63 and 70 C.E. Here then are conceivable links between the moment of the political eruption, and a real and concrete expectation of the End. Yet we must realize that no hint of interest among any of the rebel factions in speculative or numerological thinking of the required kind is to be found in the sources.

There is one strange individual who impresses even Josephus. This is the peasant Jesus son of Ananias (*War* 6.300–5), who was arrested at the Temple for his denunciations and predictions of calamity during Tabernacles in the years before the outbreak of war. Ananias was undeterred by flogging and punishment at the hands of either the Jewish authorities or the procurator Albinus, not even by a spell in prison. Albinus concluded that he was mad. Ananias remained single-minded. He would wander the streets, talking to none, but echoing Jeremiah's cries of woe, which reached a crescendo at festivals, when his audience would have been at its greatest. Ananias was eventually killed by a stone from a Roman *ballista*. Josephus was willing to admit this extraordinary phenomenon as a true portent of the destruction of the Temple.

We may wonder that the historian is able to give the length of Ananias' career with extraordinary precision: the time was seven years and five months, and we might be tempted to slot those seven months into the pre-messianic scenario of the seven days. Even then, this prophecy will belong to what we have labeled the "political" genre. What we are actually told is less evocative of apocalyptic or eschatological revelation than, with its explicit echoes of Jeremiah, of the spirit of the biblical prophets' denunciations of the nations and predictions of their coming doom and of Israel's ultimate triumph. This spirit lives on, and I found the vignette of Ananias uncannily echoed in an American magazine report of November 1999 concerned with tension surrounding the approaching end of our own last millennium:

> This fall the Israelis quietly expelled an American street preacher known only as Elijah. Wearing a long gray beard, he had been wandering Jerusalem's Old City for more than a decade, insisting he was in fact the biblical prophet—as well as one of the "two witnesses" mentioned in chapter 11 of the Book of Revelation. In recent months, his apocalyptic preaching began to attract a group of disciples. Israeli police picked him up for questioning, gave him a psychiatric evaluation and quietly persuaded him to leave the country … Critics say Israel is overreacting. Elijah never bothered anyone—and, until the millennium bug bit, no one bothered him either.
>
> (*Newsweek*, Nov 15: 81, report by Matt Rees)

By far the best known of all Josephus's predictions is the one that concerns a ruler destined to emerge from Judea, much quoted and often indeed dubbed the "messianic prophecy" (De Jonge 1974: 206–12; Rajak 1983: 185–92; Levine 1987: 150–1). We are told that it circulated widely and that this idea, more than any other thing, incited the people to revolt. Josephus notoriously tells us that he himself, by contrast, applied the prophecy to Vespasian. This proved correct when Vespasian rose to the purple, thereby securing the imprisoned Jew's liberation. He specifies that the text in question was "an ambiguous oracle, which was found in the sacred texts" concerning the present time (*War* 6.312–15). The prediction, so valuable in the propaganda of the new Flavian house, hit the headlines in antiquity: it is almost certainly quoted by Tacitus (*Histories* 5.13) as well as in Suetonius' *Life of Vespasian* (4), and in both cases direct transmission from Josephus is possible. And "ambiguous" is just what this oracle is. The renegade rebel–historian is thought to have disgraced himself by insisting on its application to the rise of the Flavian house, and to Vespasian's acclamation as *imperator* by the legions of the east. For us, the oracle's interest lies in two other points: its alleged source, the Bible, and, even more, its application, however managed, to the immediate moment. Many intelligent people mistook its meaning, Josephus tells us, going on to condemn the public's inclination to interpret signs in an arbitrary way, exactly as they liked. Unfortunately Josephus does not indicate which specific biblical passage is in question: both Daniel's "son of man" prophecy (7.13) and Balaam's prediction about the star that is to come out from Jacob and the sceptre from Israel (Numbers 24.17), later to be associated, as we saw, with Bar Kokhba, have been supplied by commentators. Nor, again, does the historian expand upon what delusions as to the oracle's meaning were entertained by the masses. But evidently there was significant common ground, in that both parties read the text as pointing to an event which lay on the visible horizon. Thus it is fair to say quite simply that, for his contemporaries just as much as for Josephus himself, the prediction was about a change of government. In other words, this prediction belongs to the category of political prophecy. Their interpretation gave support and succor to those swept up by the dreadful tide of events, but it was a long way from a full-blown messianic announcement.[19] We recall that political prophecy, which focuses on the succession of empires, shares with other systems both the notion of a grand plan and the immediacy of the imminent event. But in political prophecy only the home stretch is accessible to the prophet or relevant to his hearers.

The rebels during the Revolt

We come now to the conduct of the revolutionaries during the war itself. Messianic claims have often been detected behind reports of the royal pretensions ascribed by Josephus to two leaders in particular, Menahem, who led the *sicarii*, and Simon bar Giora. Menahem is said to have made himself a "tyrant" and the immediate trigger of his assassination was his flaunting himself in public in royal robes (*War* 2.441–6). Simon too is charged with tyranny by Josephus, in the same breath indeed as is Simon's (and Josephus's) rival John of Gischala, and both rebel chiefs are said to be dominated by lust for power (*War* 4.556–65). Horsley (1992: 100) suggests that the unusual strength and courage ascribed to Simon are "charismatic" (messianic?) qualities. To evade capture after the fall of the Temple, or perhaps in order to ensure that he was captured in style, Simon caused a diversion by emerging from his subterranean refuge in white tunic and purple mantle at the precise spot where the Temple had stood (*War* 7.29). The episode is a curious one, but it is scarcely credible that at this moment of desperation Simon can have had any coherent stance to offer the city's doomed survivors. Horsley (1992: 99–102) seeks further to lend significance to Simon's death in Rome (*War* 7.153–5) by describing it as a ritual execution of the king of the Jews. Sadly, however, the entire modern ascription of messianism to the rebel leaders rests on no more than the crude assimilation, which we have already encountered, of supposed kingship claims to the king-messiah traditions of Judaism (*War* 2.433–8; 7.26–36; Horsley and Hanson 1985: 226; Price 1992: 15–17;

25–7; for effective criticism see Levine 1987: 148). And indeed, in the case of the First Revolt, even the ascription of assumed kingship to the rebel chiefs is dubious, in view of the visible contribution such assertions make to Josephus's invective against them. It is perhaps relevant to remember at this point that at the heart of rebel thinking had been that ideal of the *sicarii*, labelled by Josephus the "Fourth Philosophy," which allowed legitimacy to no ruler but God.

A redemptive movement does not necessarily need a Messianic figure, but it does need enthusiasts (Saperstein 1992: 3–4). And in our search for such a movement's supporters, Hengel's interpretation again offers a challenge, when he gives the apparently self-defeating incineration by the rebels of supplies and food inside besieged Jerusalem a theological twist and understands this action as expressly designed by its perpetrators to exacerbate the woes that ushered in the End Time. To justify such a reading, it is necessary for Hengel to offer attestation for the idea that human agency might encourage or in some way force the end by active intervention. The belief that human conduct can speed things along indeed did become a commonplace in the rabbinic period. Aphorisms are spun around this doctrine, for example the well known statement in *Exodus Rabbah* (25.16): "if Israel would repent even for a single day they would be instantly redeemed and the son of David would instantly come. For it says (*Psalm* 95.7) 'today, if you will listen to his voice.'"[20] Similar dicta have keeping the Sabbath as instrumental. In all such ideas, however, the longed-for salvation is brought about through piety not militancy and, even more crucial, this effect be achieved by Israel as a whole, not by a dissident faction. As Hengel (1989a) pointed out, if the typically rabbinic "keeping of the Sabbath" is replaced by the concept "breaking with foreign rule," we have a genuinely Zealot idea. But the shift is far from trivial. Keeping the Sabbath, the highest of *mitzvot,* is a commitment *sui generis*; here, moreover, the Sabbath serves as a characteristically rabbinic metaphor for observance of the full halakhah. Hengel's "Zealots" are a Jewish party for whom casting off the Gentile yoke was the pre-eminent act of sanctification, but it is a large step from that to constructing a serious form of first-century Jewish piety, commanding the required wide support, where militancy was the sole and unique requirement for a share in the world to come.

Finally, we should look at a dramatic moment in book 6 of the *War* (364) when, "with the city aflame, the rebels declare with joyful faces that they cheerfully awaited the end." A strong eschatological reading has been offered: the rebels' joy arose out of their certainty that out of the city's agony would come prompt redemption. Yet we note that Josephus's chosen word for "end" in this passage is the prosaic τελευτη, rather than the highly charged τελοs. What is more, the author offers his own unequivocal explanation, on an entirely different level, of the defeated rebels' joy: their satisfaction came from the thought that the total destruction would leave absolutely nothing to the enemy. This sentiment will be matched precisely by the mentality ascribed to the Masada suicides, and put into the mouth of the leader of the *sicarii*, Eleazar ben Yair, in one of the two speeches attributed to him (*War* 7.335). Here we have a case where a messianic interpretation is not just questionable but erroneous.

Conclusions

In the light of my initial survey, the results of this analysis of the Revolt should not surprise. Expectation of an imminent End, as distinct from a wider interest in the progress of time—future as well as present—was not the normal mind set of first-century Judaism, even if it existed as an ever-present resource. It may well be that a sense of a world undergoing total transformation was embedded in select groups; yet even in relation to such circles—Christian, Jewish–Christian, or Qumranic—a nuanced account of the role and prominence of these ideas is desirable. It is wrong to imagine either apocalypticism or millenarianism to have been everywhere in the air, still less that such thinking automatically translated itself into action. The revolutionaries of 66–73 C.E. were indeed responding to political and economic oppression, to various forms of humiliation, but that does not justify classifying them as a millenarian grouping in any full sense. Saperstein rightly warns (1992: 3) that "the assumption that any movement challenging the established order must necessarily be messianic is certainly one that needs to be tested." What we can observe in the pages of Josephus is the active production in pre-revolt Jerusalem, often by lone individuals, of political prophecies that followed a pattern quite familiar from the Bible. We can see that this mode of thought was by no means confined to simple people; Josephus certainly shared in its presuppositions. On the other hand, the evidence scarcely allows a close association between those prophetic individuals and the activists. Among the latter, if we allow that accusations of pretensions to royal grandeur do not amount to claims of messianic status, then no leaders convincingly emerge as would-be messiahs, while to find messianic ardour among the followers requires contortions. In short, we cannot pin down revolutionaries motivated in their militancy by a conviction that they were welcoming the Messiah or ushering in the End of Time.

It is hoped that the context sketched in the first part of this paper supports the reading of Josephus in the second part. The guarded stance taken towards any exact anticipation of the End of Days, which finds widespread attestation among the later rabbis, was probably already in the making before 70 C.E. Furthermore, even for those who did contemplate the final events, there were no easy routes to determining the time of their onset. When practiced, such determination was a specialized, perhaps esoteric activity, a science linked with calendrical lore and speculation. A connection with public developments is again lacking.[21] There remains much to clarify about the location of messianic hope in Second Temple Judaism. There is ample material and there is room for debate. But the simple equation, long favored by both historians and theologians, between intense expectation of immediate redemption and organized Jewish resistance, collapses under scrutiny.

Notes

1 Horbury (1996: 301) draws attention to this unsatisfactory reasoning, observing that "recognition of messianic characteristics in a revolt does no ... necessarily imply that it must have been an otherwise inexplicable outbreak."

2 For a strong messianic interpretation for the revolts, though one that co-exists with a socio-economic explanation, see Horsley and Hanson 1985: 88–134. Gager is brief and neat (1988: 40–6), but note the reserve of VanderKam 1999: 222–3.

3 See Horbury 1996: 295–403 and Hengel 1989b. Even Barnes (1989: 161–2) downplaying the role of "otherworldly yearnings," regards the messianic aspirations of Lukuas as undeniable.

4 See especially JT *Taanit* 4.8, 63d. Full sources in Schäfer 1981: 55–72. Discussion in Oppenheimer 1983. Oppenheimer (1995: 156–68) draws a contrast with Bar Kokhba's overt self-description as Messiah in the more distant version in the Babylonian Talmud.

5 Though Baumgarten 1998 sees the Jewish tradition in different terms and proposes connections between success and messianism in this period. This paper was revised in the congenial environment of the Institute for Advanced Studies in the Hebrew University, Jerusalem. The revision benefited greatly from the expertise of Prof. Hanan Eshel, who guided me through new issues in Qumran eschatology and through the complexities of the bibliography.

6 On these events within the world of eighteenth- and nineteenth-century millenarianism, see the classic study by Harrison 1979.

7 Barton's book (1986) is essentially concerned with continuities. The debate has a considerable history. On positions taken by von Rad, Plöger and others, see Lambert's brief but apt comments (1978: 4).

8 On the problems of locating Jewish apocalypticism, see Gruenwald 1982: 96.

9 For a summary of relevant aspects of Daniel, see Mason 1994: 161–7. The issues are more fully set out in the editions of Hartman and di Lella 1978: 11–14, and J. Collins 1993: 33–8. See also the analysis by Broshi and Eshel 1997 of a Qumran fragment which seemingly refers to Antiochus IV and is proposed as a source for Daniel.

10 Tabor's analysis (1998) covers both ancient and modern manifestations. For the latter, see Boyer's full-length study (1992).

11 On the Babylonian and Persian traditions which Daniel combines with the Hebrew prophets to generate his political prophecies, Lambert 1978 is still enlightening. For a new survey, see Clifford 1999 and Hultgård 1999.

12 At least twelve fragments related to Daniel are known from Qumran and the book's influence is visible there. For Daniel 11.40 in Qumran literature, see Flusser 1980. On Josephus and Daniel, see Mason 1994; Vermes 1991; Adler 1996: 210–17 (tracing the influence of the chronology of Daniel 9 in the *Antiquities*); Bilde 1998a. For a summary of Daniel's immediate influence, Millar 1997: 94–7. For the seventy week prophecy in Christian writing, Adler 1996.

13 See especially Hosea 13.13: "the pangs of childbirth come for him, but he is an unwise son; for at the proper time he does not present himself at the mouth of the womb."

14 Interestingly, this mode of thought does not seem to been important among the rabbis (a point I owe to Dr. Sacha Stern).

15 Allegro 1968: 77–80; García Martínez and Eibert 1997: 370–4; Vermes 1997: 520; Milik 1976: 248–53; corrections to Milik and discussion in Dimant 1979. Cf. Talmon 1987: 126–7. The fragment's publishers join the text with 4Q 181, which concerns the "sons of heaven" and their deliverance, "each according to his lot," but neither Dimant nor Vermes make this connection.

16 For helpful expositions, see J. Collins 1998: 64–8; F. García Martínez in J. Collins 1999: 162–92. It is salutary to appreciate what very different complexions have been put on Qumran eschatology as a whole. The meaning of the final war between the Sons of Light and the Sons of Darkness in 1QM remains disputed, as does the connection between its militancy and the sect's apparent pacifism: see J. Collins 1998: chapter 6. For a fully fledged apocalyptic reading, with reference to Daniel, see Flusser 1980: 450–2. Again, Collins rightly hesitates to interpret CD 20.14 as suggesting that the End was expected by the sect forty years after the death of the Teacher of Righteousness and he notes a lack of "evidence that anyone at Qumran ever counted the days ... or that their expectation ever focused on a particular day, or year." At the same time, Collins accepts that there was a "lively expectation" in this "apocalyptic community." For possible connections between the redemption doctrine of the Damascus Document and *Daniel* 9.24–7, see Eshel 1999.

17 Russell 1974: 207–8 has instructive comments. Urbach 1975: 680 discusses "calculators" of a later period. See also Silver 1959: 243–59 and Patai 1979: introduction, xxxvii–xl.

18 But contrast Aune (1983: 127–9) who insists that only the destruction of the entire existing order could bring salvation in the eyes of the sign prophets who are in his view a "revolutionist response."

19 Horsley (1992: 105–6) carefully distinguishes the messianism that he ascribes to the rebels from popular prophetic movements.

20 Scholem 1971: 11 and Barton 1986. For other expressions of the idea, see Urbach 1975: 672–3. Parente 1984–5 understands the idea of forcing the End, expressed in diverse ways, as shared by all the various revolutionary factions in the years leading up to the First Revolt.

21 Hill 1992 ascribes a comparable quietism to the chiliastic doctrines of the early Church.

Bibliography

Adler, William (1996) "The Apocalyptic Survey of History Adapted by Christians: Daniel's Prophecy of 70 Weeks," in J. C. VanderKam and W. Adler (eds.) *The Jewish Apocalyptic Heritage in Early Christianity*, Compendia Rerum Iudaicarum ad Novum Testamentum III.4, Minneapolis: Fortress Press.

Alexander, Philip S. (1998) "The King Messiah in Rabbinic Judaism," in J. Day (ed.) *King and Messiah in Israel and the Ancient Near East.* Proceedings of the Oxford Old Testament Seminar, JSOT Supplement Series 270: 456–73.

Allegro, John (1968) *Qumran Cave 4.I (4Q158–4Q186)*, Oxford: Clarendon Press.

Aune, David E. (1983) *Prophecy in Early Christianity and the Ancient Mediterranean World*, Grand Rapids, MI: Eerdmans.

Barnes, T. D. (1989) "Trajan and the Jews," *Journal of Jewish Studies* 40: 145–62.

Barstad, Hans M. (1994) "Prophecy at Qumran," in K. Jeppesen, K. Nielsen, B. Rosendal (eds.) *In the Last Days: On Jewish and Christian Apocalyptic and its Period*, Aarhus: Aarhus University Press.

Barton, John (1986) *Oracles of God: Perceptions of Ancient Prophecy in Israel after the Exile*, New York: Oxford University Press.

Baumgarten, Albert I. (1998) "The Pursuit of the Millennium in Judaism," in G. Stanton and G. Stroumsa (eds.) *Tolerance and Intolerance in Early Judaism and Christianity*, Cambridge: Cambridge University Press.

Beckwith, Roger, T. (1996) *Calendar and Chronology, Jewish and Christian: Biblical, Intertestamental and Patristic Studies*, Leiden: E. J. Brill.

Bilde, P. (1988) *Flavius Josephus between Jerusalem and Rome. His Life, His Works and Their Importance,* Journal for the Study of the Pseudepigrapha, Supplementary Series 2, Sheffield: JSOT.

—— (1998) "Josephus and Jewish Apocalypticism," in S. Mason (ed.) *Understanding Josephus: Seven Perspectives*, Journal for the Study of the Pseudepigrapha, Supplementary Series 32, Sheffield: Sheffield Academic Press.

Blenkinsopp, J. (1974) "Prophecy and Priesthood in Josephus," *Journal of Jewish Studies* 25: 239–62.

Bockmuehl, M. (1990) *Revelation and Mystery in Ancient Judaism and Pauline Christianity*, WUNT 2.36, Tübingen: Mohr.

Boyer, P. (1992) *When Time Shall Be No More. Prophecy and Belief in Modern American Culture*, Cambridge, MA: Belknap Press.

Broshi, M. (1995) *Qumran Cave 4.XIV, Parabiblical Texts, Part 2,* Oxford: Clarendon Press.

Broshi, M. and Eshel, E. (1997) "The Great King is Antiochus IV (4Q Historical Text = 4Q248)," *Journal of Jewish Studies* 48: 120–9.

Bruce, F. F. (1965) "Josephus and Daniel," *ASTI* 4: 148–62.

Charlesworth, James H. (ed.) (1983) *The Old Testament Pseudepigrapha*, 2 vols., Garden City, NJ: Doubleday.

Clifford, R. J. (1999) "The Roots of Apocalypticism in Near Eastern Myth," in J. Collins (ed.) *The Encyclopedia of Apocalypticism, vol.1, The Origins of Apocalypticism in Judaism and Christianity*, New York: Continuum, pp. 3–38.

Collins, A. Y. (1996) *Cosmology and Eschatology in Jewish and Christian Apocalypticism*, Leiden: E. J. Brill.

—— (1999) "The Book of Revelation" in J. Collins (ed.) *The Encyclopedia of Apocalypticism, vol.1, The Origins of Apocalypticism in Judaism and Christianity*, New York: Continuum, pp. 384–414.

Collins, J. (1993) *Daniel. A Commentary on the Book of Daniel*, Philadelphia: Hermeneia.

—— (1997) *Apocalypticism in the Dead Sea Scrolls*, London: Routledge.

—— (1998) *The Apocalyptic Imagination: An Introduction to Jewish Apocalyptic*, 2nd edition, Grand Rapids MI: Eerdmans.

—— (1999) *The Encyclopedia of Apocalypticism,* New York: Continuum.

—— (ed.) (1999) *The Encyclopedia of Apocalypticism*, Vol. I, *The Origins of Apocalypticism in Judaism and Christianity*, New York: Continuum.

Dimant, D. (1979) "The 'Pesher on the Periods' (4Q180) and 4Q181," *Israel Oriental Studies* 9: 77–102.

Eshel, H. (1999) "The Meaning and Significance of CD 20, 13–15," in D.W. Parry and E. Ulrich (eds.), *The Provo International Conference on the Dead Sea Scrolls. Technological Innovations, New Texts and Reformulated Issues*, Leiden: E. J. Brill.

Feldman, L. H. (1990) "Prophets and Prophecy in Josephus," *JTS* 41: 386–422.

Flint, P. W. (1997) "The Daniel Tradition at Qumran," in C. A. Evans and P. W. Flint (eds.) *Eschatology, Messianism and the Dead Sea Scrolls*, Grand Rapids, MI: Eerdmans.

Flusser, D. (1980) "Apocalyptic Elements in the War Scroll," in A. Oppenheimer, U. Rappaport and M. Stern (eds.) *Jerusalem in the Second Temple Period. Abraham Schalit Memorial Volume*, Jerusalem: Israel Exploration Society (Heb.).

Gager, J. (1998) "Messiahs and Their Followers," in P. Schäfer and M. R. Cohen (eds.) *Toward the Millennium: Messianic Expectation from the Bible to Waco*, Leiden: E. J. Brill.

García Martínez, F. and T. and Eibert, J. C. (1997) *The Dead Sea Scrolls Study Edition*, Leiden: E. J. Brill.

Goodman, Martin (1987) *The Ruling Class of Judaea,* Cambridge: Cambridge University Press.

Gray, R. (1993) *Prophetic Figures in Late Second Temple Jewish Palestine. The Evidence from Josephus*, New York: Oxford University Press.

Gruenwald, I. (1982) *Apocalyptic and Merkavah Mysticism*, Leiden: E. J. Brill.

Harrison, J. F. C. (1979) *The Second Coming. Popular Millenarianism 1780–1850*, New Brunswick, NJ: Rutgers University Press.

Hartman, I. F. and di Lella, A. (1978) *The Book of Daniel*, Garden City, NY: Doubleday.

Hengel, M. (1989a) *The Zealots: Investigations into the Jewish Freedom Movement in the Period from Herod until 70 A.D.*, Edinburgh: T & T Clark.

—— (1989b) "Messianische Hoffnung und politischer 'Radikalismus' in der jüdisch-hellenistischen Diaspora. Zur Frage der Voraussetzungen der jüdischen Aufstandes unter Trajan 115–7 n. Chr.," in D. Hellholm (ed.) *Apocalypticism in the Ancient Mediterranean World and the Near East*, Proceedings of the International Colloquium at Uppsala 1979, Tübingen: Mohr.

Hill, C. (1992) *Regnum Caelorum: Patterns of Future Hope in Early Christianity*, Oxford: Clarendon Press.

Himmelfarb, M. (1993) *Ascent to Heaven in Jewish and Christian Apocalypses*, New York: Oxford University Press.

Horbury, W. (1996) "The Beginnings of the Jewish Revolt under Trajan," in H. Cancik, H. Lichtenberger, and P. Schäfer (eds.) *Geschichte–Tradition–Reflexion. Festschrift für Martin Hengel zum 70 Geburtstag*, Tübingen: Mohr.

Horsley, R. A. (1984) "Popular Messianic Movements around the Time of Jesus," *Catholic Bible Quarterly* 46: 471–95.

—— (1992) *Jesus and the Spiral of Violence*, Minneapolis: Fortress Press.

Horsley, R. A. and Hanson, J. S. (1985) *Bandits, Prophets and Messiahs: Popular Movements in the Time of Jesus*, Minneapolis: Fortress Press.

Hultgård, A. (1999) "Persian Apocalypticism," in J. Collins (ed.) *The Encyclopedia of Apocalypticism, vol.1, The Origins of Apocalypticism in Judaism and Christianity*, New York: Continuum, pp. 39–83.

Idel, M. (1998) *Messianic Mystics*, New Haven: Yale University Press.

De Jonge, M. (1974) "Josephus und die Zukunftserwartung seines Volkes," in

O. Betz, K. Haacker and M. Hengel (eds.) *Josephus-Studien: Untersuchungen zu Josephus, dem antiken Judentum und dem Neuen Testament Otto Michel zum 70. Geburtstag gewidmet*, Göttingen: Vandenhoeck und Ruprecht.

Klausner, J. (1956) *The Messianic Idea in Israel*, New York: Macmillan.

Knohl, I. (1998) "On the 'Son of God', Armilus and Messiah son of Joseph," *Tarbiz* 58.1: 13–38 (Heb.).

Kosmala, H. (1963) "'At the End of Days'," *ASTI* 2: 277–312.

Lambert, W. G. (1978) *The Background of Jewish Apocalyptic*, London: Athlone Press.

Levine, I. (1983) "Messianic Tendencies at the End of the Second Temple Period," in Z. Baras (ed.) *Messianism and Eschatology*, Jerusalem: Merkaz Zalman Shazar (Heb.).

Levine, L. (ed.) (1987) *The Synagogue in Late Antiquity*, Philadelphia: ASOR.

Mason, S. (1994) "Josephus, Daniel and the Flavian House," in F. Parente and J. Sievers (eds.) *Josephus and the History of the Greco-Roman Period. Essays in Memory of Morton Smith*, Leiden: E. J. Brill.

McGinn, B. (1994) *Apocalypticism in the Western Tradition*, Brookfield, VT: Variorum.

Milik, J.T. (1976) *The Books of Enoch. Aramaic Fragments of Qumran Cave 4*, Oxford: Clarendon Press.

Millar, Fergus (1997) "Hellenistic History in a Near Eastern Perspective: The Book of Daniel," in P. Cartledge, P. Garnsey and E. Gruen (eds.) *Hellenistic Constructs. Essays in Culture, History and Historiography*, Berkeley: University of California Press.

Neusner, J. (1987) "Mishnah and Messiah," in J. Neusner, W. S. Green and E. S. Frerichs (eds.) *Judaisms and their Messiahs at the Turn of the Christian Era*, New York: Cambridge University Press.

—— (1994) *Messiah in Context: Israel's History and Destiny in Formative Judaism*, Philadelphia: Fortress Press.

Oppenheimer, A. (1983) "The Messianism of Bar Kokhba," in Z. Baras (ed.) *Messianism and Eschatology*, Jerusalem: Merkaz Zalman Shazar.

—— (1995) "Leadership and Messianism in the Time of the Mishnah," in H. G. Reventlow (ed.) *Eschatology in the Bible and in Jewish and Christian Tradition*, JSOT Supplement 243, Sheffield: Sheffield Academic Press.

Parente, F. (1984–5) "Flavius Josephus' Account of the Anti-Roman Riots Preceding the 66–70 War and its Relevance for the Reconstruction of Jewish Eschatology during the First Century A.D.," *Journal of the Ancient Near Eastern Society* 16–17: 183–205.

Patai, R. (1979) *The Messianic Texts. Jewish Legends for 3,000 Years*, Detroit: Wayne State University Press.

Price, J. J. (1992) *Jerusalem under Siege: The Collapse of the Jewish State 66–70 C.E.*, Leiden: E. J. Brill.

Rajak, T. (1983) *Josephus. The Historian and His Society*, Philadelphia: Fortress Press.

Rowland, C. (1982) *The Open Heaven. A Study of Apocalyptic in Judaism and Early Christianity*, New York: Crossroad.

Russell, D. S. (1974) *The Method and Message of Jewish Apocalyptic: 200 B.C.–200 A.D.*, Philadelphia: Westminster Press.

Saperstein, M. (ed.) (1992) *Essential Papers on Messianic Movements and Personalities in Jewish History*, New York: New York University Press.

Schäfer, P. (1981) *Der Bar Kokhba Aufstand. Studien zum zweiten jüdischen Krieges*, Tübingen: Mohr.

Scholem, G. (1971) *The Messianic Idea in Judaism and other Essays on Jewish Spirituality*, New York: Schocken Books.

Schürer, E. (1979) *The History of the Jewish People in the Age of Jesus Christ*. A New English Edition, vol. 2, revised and edited by G. Vermes, F. Millar and M. Black, Edinburgh: T & T Clark.

Silver, A. H. (1959) *A History of Messianic Speculation in Israel*, Boston: Beacon Press.

Steudel, A. (1993) "'*aharit hayyamim*' in the Texts from Qumran," *Revue de Qumran* 16: 225–46.

Stone, M. (1980) *Scriptures, Sects and Visions: A Profile of Judaism from Ezra to the Jewish Revolts*, Cleveland: Collins.

Tabor, J. D. (1998) "Patterns of the End: Textual Weaving from Qumran to Waco," in P. Schäfer and M. R. Cohen (eds.) *Toward the Millennium: Messianic Expectation from the Bible to Waco*, Leiden: E. J. Brill.

Talmon, S. (1987) "Waiting for the Messiah in the Spiritual Universe of the Qumran Covenanters," in J. Neusner, W .S. Green and E. S. Frerichs (eds.) *Judaisms and their Messiahs at the Turn of the Christian Era*, New York: Cambridge University Press.

Urbach, E. (1975) *The Sages: Their Concepts and Beliefs*, I. Abrahams (trans.), Jerusalem: Magnes Press.

VanderKam, J. C. (1998) *Calendars in the Dead Sea Scrolls: Measuring Time,* London: Routledge.

Vermes, G. (1991) "Josephus' Treatment of the Book of Daniel," *Journal of Jewish Studies* 42: 149–66.

—— (1997) *The Complete Dead Sea Scrolls in English*, New York: Penguin Press.

Volz, P. (1934) *Die Eschatologie der jüdischen Gemeinde im neutestamenlichen Zeitalter nach den Quellen der rabbinischen, apokalyptischen und apokryphischen Literatur dargestellt*, Tübingen: Mohr.

12 In the footsteps of the Tenth Roman Legion in Judea

Jodi Magness

In the first century B.C.E., Herod the Great, client king of Judea, built a fortress and lavishly decorated palaces on top of the mountain of Masada, by the southwest shore of the Dead Sea. Seventy years after his death, in 66 C.E., the Jews of Judea rose up in revolt against Roman rule. A band of 960 Jewish rebels (*sicarii*) took over the top of the mountain and occupied it for the duration of the Revolt. They continued to hold out against the Romans even after the fall of Jerusalem in 70 C.E. In 72 or 73 C.E., the Tenth Roman Legion (Legio X Fretensis) arrived at the foot of Masada and set up a siege. The conquest of the mountain by the Romans, which ended with the famous and controversial mass suicide of the Jewish rebels, is related in dramatic detail by the ancient historian Flavius Josephus.[1] After the fall of Masada, the Tenth Legion was stationed in Jerusalem until it was transferred to Aila (modern Aqaba) in about 300.[2]

Josephus does not provide many details of the day-to-day activities of the Tenth Legion while stationed at Masada, and no ancient sources discuss their subsequent actions in Jerusalem. A study of the pottery associated with the Legion at both sites, however, provides valuable insights on the manner in which the Roman army operated while in the field and when stationed in permanent camps.

Masada

The siege camps at Masada are probably the best-preserved examples anywhere in the Roman world (Richmond 1962; Yadin 1966: 208–31; Magness 1996). A 4,000-yard long circumvallation wall and eight camps, labelled A–H, encircle the base of Masada. The wall was intended to prevent people from entering or escaping the mountain. The camps provided living quarters and protection for the soldiers, and dominated possible routes of escape. There are two large camps and six small ones. The large ones are B in the east and F in the west, each measuring approximately 150 by 170 yards. The main strength of the Tenth Legion (numbering about 5,000 men) is believed to have been housed in these two camps. A smaller camp (F2) in the southwest corner of Camp F was occupied briefly by a garrison after the fall of

Masada. The six smaller camps apparently housed auxiliary troops. Based on the size of the camps, the total number of soldiers who participated in the siege at Masada is estimated at about eight to nine thousand (Roth 1995).

The most complete survey of the Roman siege camps at Masada was carried out by Richmond (1962). A few years later, Yadin conducted a small sounding in a corner of Camp F, but the results were never fully published (Yadin 1966: 218–19). In 1995, I was invited to co-direct the first systematic excavations of the Roman siege works at Masada, together with Professor Gideon Foerster of the Hebrew University of Jerusalem, Dr. Haim Goldfus (Ben-Gurion University in Beersheba), and Mr. Benny Arubas of the Hebrew University. We focused on Camp F, which is located by the foot of the Roman siege ramp on the northwestern side of Masada, close to the top of the mountain (Magness 1996). Camp F is a roughly rectangular enclosure with the classic layout of a Roman military camp. Its dry stone walls, which originally stood about 10 feet high, enclosed a roughly rectangular area. Four gates, one on each side, gave access to the two main roads inside the camp. They converged in the center of the camp, where the officers' quarters (*praetorium*) and headquarters (*principia*) were located. The units inside the camp had dry stone walls that were about 3–4 feet high. These served as the bases for leather tents which, when spread, would have provided a cool, breezy refuge from the desert heat. Among the units we uncovered in 1995 in the center of Camp F was a huge, three-sided, rectilinear structure that opened towards the east, apparently the officers' mess (*triclinium*). Nearby were the remains of a large tent unit which presumably served as the officers' living quarters, judging from its size, location, and unusually rich finds. The last included large, restorable fragments of painted Nabataean bowls (see p. 191), and luxury glass imported from Italy. A raised, square stone podium next to this unit apparently represents the *tribunal*, from which the commander addressed his troops and reviewed parades. The headquarters are probably represented by another unit uncovered just to the west, which had beautifully plastered walls and was partly covered by the later wall of Camp F2.

Roman legions were subdivided into smaller units reflecting battle formations and camping arrangements. Each group of eight men formed a mess-unit (*contubernium*), eating together and sharing a tent in the field (e.g., Webster 1998: 109). We excavated a row of *contubernia* in the rear half of Camp F (within Camp F2). Each consisted of a small rectangular room encircled on three sides by earth and stone benches, on which the soldiers ate and slept. At the front of each room was a small vestibule or anteroom, with hearths where food was cooked in the corners.

The finds from our excavations were unexpectedly abundant. Because the surface of the camp appears to be barren, we were astonished at the large quantities of broken potsherds that covered the floors of the soldiers' tent units. Almost all of the pottery was saved and sent for restoration. The fact that few vessels were completely restorable (that is, in almost all cases some pieces were missing) suggests that they were broken before being discarded.

The vast majority of the pottery is local (Judean), and nearly all of it consists of storage jars, with a few cooking pots (Fig. 12.1:3–7).[3] However, there are also a number of painted Nabataean bowls (Fig. 12.1:1), and a few Roman ceramic types such as thin-walled beakers and a painted amphoriskos (Fig. 12.1:2).[4] Most of these came from the area around the officers' living quarters. Military equipment was relatively rare in our excavations, consising mostly of *caliga* nails and a few arrowheads, although we did find a complete cheekpiece from a helmet.[5] There were also piles of natural river pebbles about the size of large eggs by the entrances to some of the units, which apparently represent slingshot stones (Griffiths 1989: 258).

Jerusalem

After the fall of Masada in 73 or 74 C.E., the Tenth Legion was stationed on Jerusalem's western hill, in the area of the modern Citadel and Armenian Garden. The kiln site where the legion's pottery, bricks, and rooftiles were manufactured is located at Binyanei Ha'uma, modern Jerusalem's convention center. Before 1948 the site was known by its Arabic name Sheikh Bader; it is also sometimes called Givat Ram, after the spur of the hill on which it is located. Binyanei Ha'uma lies about one and a half Roman miles from the ancient city of Jerusalem, close to the Roman road from Jaffa. Two small-scale salvage excavations were carried out at the site by Avi-Yonah in 1949 and 1967.[6] In 1992, a large-scale salvage excavation was conducted by Goldfus and Arubas (Arubas and Goldfus 1995). After the excavation ended, the site was destroyed to make way for the convention center's new parking lot.

The remains revealed in the 1992 excavations included a clay preparation area, a potter's workshop with a potter's wheel still *in situ*, and a series of kilns. Two main stratigraphic phases could be distinguished in the kilns. In the earlier phase, a group of at least five kilns was arranged in a row running southwest–northeast (1–5). Later, two new kilns (6–7) were built at the northern end of the earlier group, and another one (8) was added to the south. The excavators are preparing the publication of the hundreds of bricks and rooftiles recovered in the excavations, many of which bear stamps of the Tenth Legion. The fact that they include types that have been dated by Barag from the period between 70–135 C.E., as well as types dated to the reigns of Caracalla and Elagabalus indicates that the site was used by the legion from the period after the fall of Jerusalem in 70 C.E. until at least the first quarter of the third century (Arubas and Goldfus 1995; Barag 1967).[7]

The parallels for most of the ceramic types represented at Binyanei Ha'uma come from Roman sites, especially military kiln sites and camps throughout Europe. However, petrographic analysis has indicated that all of the Roman pottery from Binyanei Ha'uma is made of local Motza clay and was therefore manufactured at the site.[8] The ceramic assemblage from the 1992 excavations can be divided into two main categories: fine table wares (including oil

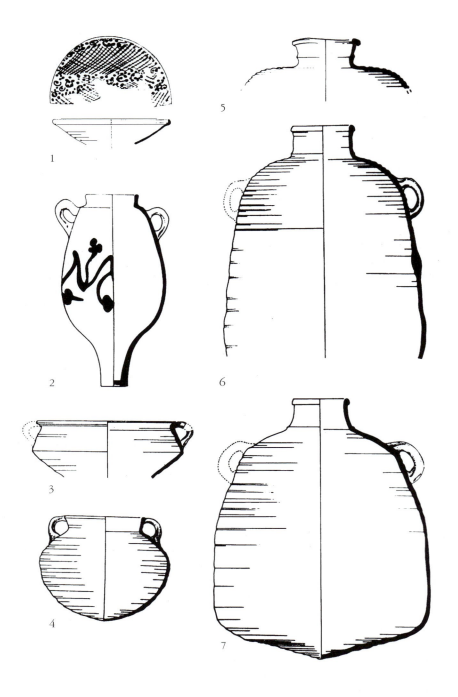

Figure 12.1 Examples of pottery vessels from Camp F at Masada.

lamps), and coarse cooking and kitchen wares. Storage vessels are almost totally absent. I base the following descriptions on my preliminary study of these wares.

Table wares

The fine table wares from Binyanei Ha'uma are made of a very soft, smooth, well-levigated, light brown to orange-brown fabric that I call Ware 1. Those covered with a red slip are clearly local imitations in form, ware, and surface treatment of western sigillata (known also as Samian). Western sigillata was produced from the first century B.C.E. onwards at sites in Italy (such as Arezzo), Gaul, and Spain (Hayes 1997: 41). The highest quality red slip attested at Binyanei Ha'uma is dark, even, and lustrous. Some of the vessels are covered with a dull, uneven, mottled orange-red to orange-brown slip that apparently represents a variant of the marbled treatment common on western sigillata, and which is also attested on some eastern wares. Marbled wares appeared in the western Mediterranean in the Augustan period and peaked during the reigns of Claudius and Nero, with some German variants produced until the third century (Swan 1988: 12; Greene 1977: 114; Ettlinger 1951: 105; Bettermann 1934).[9] The form and surface treatment of mottled wares and other western sigillata vessels reflect the inspiration of metal and glass prototypes.

There are almost no examples from Binyanei Ha'uma of vessels decorated with figured relief scenes (so-called decorated Samian) that are so common at sites in Europe (e.g., Hayes 1997: 51, pl. 19: 1–2; Grimes 1930: figs. 34–51). Our finest piece is the rim and wall of a deep bowl or chalice on which three human figures can be seen (Fig. 12.2:1). A standing female figure on the left holds a tall, leafy stalk. To the right a standing male figure plays a flute, while another male figure reclining below him looks up at the female with an outstretched arm. This scene may be cultic. A remarkably similar fragment, which looks like it comes from the same vessel or was made in the same mould, is published from Avi-Yonah's 1949 excavations at the site (Herschkovitz 1987: 320, Fig. 11.8, which also appears to depict a cultic scene; the form is identified as Dragendorff Ih).

Almost all of the red-slipped vessels from Binyanei Ha'uma are locally produced versions of a class called plain or undecorated sigillata or samian in Europe, since they do not have figured relief scenes. However, many of them are decorated in other ways, including with rouletting, stamped patterns, and moldmade or applied barbotine designs (made by trailing a thickened clay slip across the surface of the vessel; see Kendrick 1990). The distinctive profile of a number of bowls, which have flaring walls and rounded moldings below the rim, can easily be identified as an undecorated variant of a common western sigillata form called Dragendorff 29 (one example is illustrated in Fig. 12.2:2).[10] A variant of another Dragendorff form (33) is represented by a bowl covered with a lustrous, dark orange-red slip that is encircled by barbotine ivy leaves (Fig. 12.2:3; cf. Faber 1994: 229–31, pl. 10.95–107; Stefan 1945–7: 126, fig. 9.1–2; Grimes 1930: 222, fig. 70.165). Although most of the fine, red-slipped table wares consist of bowls, cups,

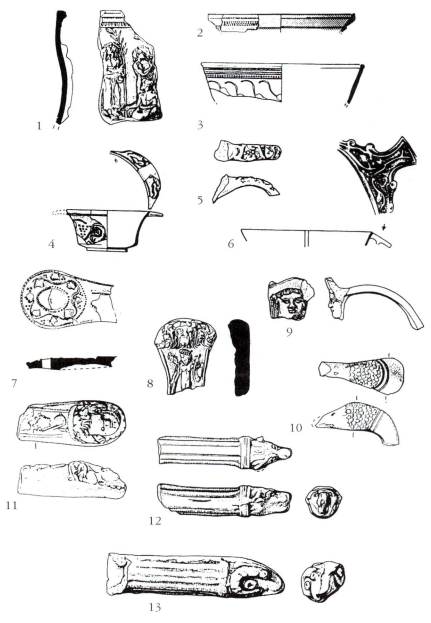

Figure 12.2 Examples of pottery vessels from Binyanei Ha'uma.

and chalices, a small number of lids, jars, and jugs are also represented. Some of the unslipped tablewares from Binyanei Ha'uma are clearly related to the red-slipped wares, as indicated by the fact that many of the same vessel shapes occur both with and without red slip.

The red-slipped sigillata dishes were complemented, for table use, by a class of drinking vessels in a very thin and light-weight fabric usually referred to as thin-walled or eggshell ware. Their eggshell-thin walls and relief decoration represent conscious copies of metal and glass vessels. Although this type was invented in Italy, during the first century C.E. imitations were produced in provincial workshops in Gaul, Spain, and the Rhineland. The delicately formed handles are sometimes elaborately treated with decorative thumb-rests and spurs (Hayes 1997: 67–8; for thin-walled wares from Cosa with these handles, see Moevs 1973: Forms XXVIII–XXIX). The eggshell ware at Binyanei Ha'uma (which is made of unslipped Ware 1) is clearly related in form, ware, and decoration to the red-slipped vessels. The walls and handles of many of the pieces are decorated in relief with delicate, swirling, grape or ivy leaves and bunches of grapes (Fig. 12.2:4–6; for a bronze jug handle with a vine pattern from Wadi ed-Daliyeh see Lapp and Nickelsburg 1974: pl. 35). The decoration on the walls is in the barbotine technique, while on the handles it is moldmade. Two antithetical *putti* recline on the top of one ledge handle (Fig. 12.2:6). Molds for ledge handles like ours have been found at the legionary kiln site at Holdeurn in the Netherlands, and at Brigetio in Hungary (Holwerda 1946: pl. 20.2.2; Bonis 1977: abb. 2: 1 and 7: 1; for similar handles from Holdeurn see Holwerda 1944: pls. I: 1–1a; XI: 13–13a).[11] The tip of one flat handle from Binyanei Ha'uma is pierced by a crescent-shaped hole (Fig. 12.2:7). It is outlined by raised dots that frame a delicate grapevine pattern. This handle belongs to a kind of multi-purpose vessel, usually referred to as a casserole or saucepan (probably *trulla* in Latin), that could be used as a cup, beaker, dipper or ladle, frying pan, cooking pot, or saucepan. Saucepans have a long, flat handle attached to a hemispherical body with a flattened base, and would have been hung or carried by a string or rope tied through a hole at the handle's end (den Boesterd 1956: xx). Plain versions of these vessels served as the mess-tin that was the standard issue among Roman soldiers.[12] The fine ware and decoration of our piece suggest that it was part of a drinking-set for mixing wine, water, and herbs (see Koster 1997: 56; den Boesterd 1956: xxi). A complete bronze saucepan was buried under the floor of one of the casemate rooms on Masada (Yadin 1966: 148, top; its precise provenience is not provided, and it is not clear if it was found together with the bronze jug next to it in the photograph; for other bronze and ceramic saucepans see den Boersterd 1956: 4–7, pl. I: 12–13; Koster 1997: 57, no. 66; Bettermann 1934: abb. 14; Radnoti 1938: 39–49, pl. 3: 11–13; Junkelmann 1997: pls. 10, 11.1; Deimel 1987: pl. 25).

Another flat handle is decorated in relief with a frontally standing nude male wearing a garland or headdress, perhaps consisting of ivy or grape leaves (Fig. 12.2:8). He holds a flat circular object with a raised central boss in his left hand, and a tall, slightly curved staff with a thickened tip (apparently a thyrsus) in his right hand.[13] A bearded mask floats above his head, at the top of the handle. The pose of the nude, slender, and youthful body, and his clean-shaven face and garlanded head are reminiscent of a marble statue of Dionysus from the recent excavations at Beth Shean (Foerster and Tsafrir 1990). The fact that this handle probably belongs to a wine-dipper or strainer supports the interpretation of this imagery as Dionysiac. Wine-dippers and strainers are related to saucepans, from which they differ in having thinner walls, a longer handle, and a rounded base. Like saucepans, they could be made of metal or clay. In the bronze examples, a perforated strainer of similar shape is often found inside the dipper. These sets were used to ladle and strain undiluted or spiced wine (den Boerstered 1956: xxi; Koster 1997: 46; Junkelmann 1997: 180–1). Our piece could represent a variant with a long, fan-shaped handle, or may belong to a saucepan, like similar clay and metal handles from Frankfurt (see den Boesterd 1956: pl. 3.53–60; Koster 1997: 47–8, nos. 42–4; Radnoti 1938: pls. 5.24, 6.25–6, 24.5, 9, 25; Bettermann 1934: 120, abb. 12, 14).

Two red-slipped handles that terminate in frontal human faces or masks decorated the tips of high oil lamp handles or the tops of jug handles (Fig. 12.2:9; for examples of bronze jug handles see den Boesterd 1956: pl. 12.282; Koster 1997: 77, no. 103; Yadin 1963: fig. 28). A similar handle of Hadrianic to Antonine date decorated with a Medusa head is published from the potters' quarter at Kurucdomb in Brigetio (Hungary), where it is identified as an oil lamp (Bonis 1977: abb. 2.14, 6.5). Oil lamp handles terminating in mask-like human visages are also published from the late first to second century potters' workshop at Gerasa in Jordan (Ilife 1944–5: pl. 7.118; Rosenthal and Sivan 1978: 90–1, nos. 368–9; the arrangement of the hair and headdress on no. 368, which is tentatively identified as Dionysus or Pan, is especially close to our specimens). However, the two closest parallels come from Mazar's excavations around the Temple Mount in Jerusalem and Avigad's excavations in the Jewish Quarter (Ben-Dov 1985: 204; Mazar 1971: 36, fig. 19; Avigad 1983: 204, no. 251). Although these handles and the two from Binyanei Ha'uma were manufactured in different molds, they are remarkably similar. In all four, the face is framed by wavy bangs and curls of hair, and is capped by a peaked headdress or crown.

A solid duck or swan-shaped head covered with a light brown slip has precisely incised lines indicating the feathers, eyes, bill, and nostrils (Fig. 12.2:10). Identical heads come from Avi-Yonah's 1949 excavations at Binyanei Ha'uma, and from Tushingham's excavations in the Armenian Garden (Hershkovitz 1987: 322, fig. 16; Tushingham 1985: fig. 25: 21). Another parallel, not as fine, is published from Brigetio in Hungary (Bonis 1977: 124; abb. 2: 13 and 6: 1). These heads may belong to figurines or zoomorphic vessels, or could have been protomes attached to deep bowls or kraters (e.g., Ilife 1944–5: fig. 6.87–93; Hershkovitz 1987: 322, 325 nn.

56–8; Deimel 1987: pl. 21.13). Duck and swan heads sometimes decorated the edges of handle attachments encircling jug rims (e.g., Deimel 1987: pls. 17.4–5, 24.1; den Boesterd 1956: pl. 3.67; Radnoti 1938: pl. 18.2; also see Koster 1997: 37, no. 22). It is also possible that our specimens are the tips of high oil lamp handles (for examples of ceramic lamp handles with animal heads see Ilife 1944–5: pl. 7: 116–17; Rosenthal and Sivan 1978: 90–1, nos. 370–2; Loeschcke 1919: 340, abb. 22; for bronze examples see Szentleleky 1969: nos. 277, 279, 284; none of these is a bird's head). However, I believe that the duck or swan heads from Jerusalem were probably the handle tips of a type of small ladle with a long vertical handle (*simpula*) that was used for offering wine at a sacrifice. Bronze ladles of this type dating to the first century have been found at sites in Europe and are also represented at Pompeii (den Boesterd 1956: 34, pl. 4.96–96a; Koster 1997: 44–5, no. 36; Radnoti 1938: pls. 5.23, 24.4, 28.4).

A series of solid handles from Binyanei Ha'uma which terminate in human heads or masks and animal heads would have been attached to a shallow dish with a rounded base. Such dishes (perhaps the Latin *trulleum*, often referred to as *paterae* in modern literature), were used for ritual and everyday handwashing, and for ceremonial purposes, when wine was offered as a libation (Koster 1997: 74; Hayes 1997: 73; Junkelmann 1997: pl. 13, fig. 88; den Boesterd 1956: xxii). They formed a set with a jug or pitcher (an *urceus*; see Koster 1997: 4; den Boesterd 1956: xxii).[14] The ridges along the length of our handles, and the orange or brown slip on some, clearly reflect the reeded handles and bronze color of the metal prototypes. One handle from Binyanei Ha'uma is made of porous, orange-brown ware with a yellow-brown slip (Fig. 12.2:11). A basket and curved stick are visible in the center at the top of the handle, above the human head at its tip. The basket can be identified as a *liknon*, a fruit-laden winnowing basket associated with Dionysus, and the curved stick as a *pedum*, the shepherd's staff that was an attribute of Pan (e.g., Godwin 1981: 134–5, 141; Turcan 1996: 308–9; for a *pedum* on the handle of a bronze *urceus*, see Koster 1997: 76, no. 101). A grotesque and clean-shaven human head with red-brown hair gazed up at the person grasping the handle. This visage probably represents the face or mask of a satyr or perhaps Pan.[15] Molds for similar handles are published from Holdeurn and Brigetio (Holwerda 1946: pl. 20: 1; Bonis 1977: abb. 2: 9 and 9: 3).[16] Two more handles from Binyanei Ha'uma (one with a red-slip) are decorated with dog's heads and may have been manufactured in the same mold (Fig. 12.2:12). A mold for a similar handle is published from Brigetio, and there are close parallels of bronze from Nijmegen (Bonis 1977: abb. 9.1; den Boesterd 1956: 28–9, pl. 4.73–5; Koster 1997: 78–9, no. 194; also Radnoti 1938: pls. 6.31, 26.4, 28.2–3). Another handle from Binyanei Ha'uma is covered with a flaky, orange-brown slip and terminates in a ram's head (Fig. 12.2:13). It is paralleled by a bronze bowl with a reeded ram's head handle from the time of the Bar Kokhba Revolt that was found by Yadin in the Cave of the Letters in Nahal Hever. The latter was part of a hoard of bronze vessels that were clearly of Roman—probably Italian— origin (see Yadin 1963: 58–62).[17]

Relatively few oil lamps were found at Binyanei Ha'uma. A number of fragments, made of red-slipped Ware 1, represent Broneer Type XXI/ Loeschcke Type III. This type, which has a sunken, circular discus and an elongated nozzle or multiple nozzles flanked by volutes, was common in Italy from Augustan to Flavian times. Some of our examples have large, leaf-shaped handles, which on the bronze prototypes would have served as a heat shield and reflector (Fig. 12.3:1–2). Close parallels to our handles come from the late first to second century potter's workshop at Gerasa, and from Tushingham's excavations in the Armenian Garden in Jerusalem (Rosenthal and Sivan 1978: 93–4, nos. 378–86; Ilife 1944–5: pl. 7.119, 125–7; also see Loeschcke 1919: 223, abb. 3; Robinson 1959: pl. 47.G149).[18]

Another common Roman type, the round lamp with a decorated discus (Broneer Type XXV/Loeschcke Type VIII), is also represented at Binyanei Ha'uma. Lamps of this type were produced around the Mediterranean from the second third of the first century through the second century. Syro–Palestinian variants, which differ from the western Mediterranean examples in lacking a handle, continued to be manufactured into the third century (Rosenthal and Sivan 1978: 36, 85; Fitch and Goldman 1994: 148–83 [described as "fat lamps"]). The only discus preserved from Binyanei Ha'uma, which is made of unslipped Ware 1 and is decorated with a maenad holding a thyrsus (Fig. 12.3:4), has a close parallel in the Schloessinger Collection (Rosenthal and Sivan 1978: 87, no. 355).[19]

One example of a Roman factory lamp (firmalampe), made of unslipped Ware 1, was found at Binyanei Ha'uma (Fig. 12.3:3). Factory lamps have a flat, sunken discus that is separated from a sloping rim by a ridge. Ours corresponds with Loeschcke Type X (the fully developed Normalform, or standard form), in which the ridge continues onto the nozzle, forming a channel that also surrounds the wick-hole. Factory lamps often have a potter's signature or factory mark in Latin on the base, which is not preserved on our piece. This type appeared at Pompeii shortly before its destruction in 79 C.E., and continued to be manufactured into the third century. Factory lamps are common in Italy and the western provinces, where they were mass-produced. However, the only examples from the Roman east listed by Rosenthal and Sivan, aside from those in the Schloessinger collection, are western imports from Antioch and Corinth (Rosenthal and Sivan 1978: 49).[20] Ours represents the first example of this type that is of known eastern origin.

Cooking and kitchen wares

The cooking vessels from Binyanei Ha'uma include a large number of flat-bottomed pans and a smaller number of lids, which represent locally produced versions or derivatives of Pompeian Red Ware (Fig. 12.3:5–6).[21]

Pompeian Red Ware is named after the color of the slip, which created a smooth, non-stick coating on the interior of the pans. The dull, streaky, orange-brown or red-brown slip that coats many of the pans from Binyanei

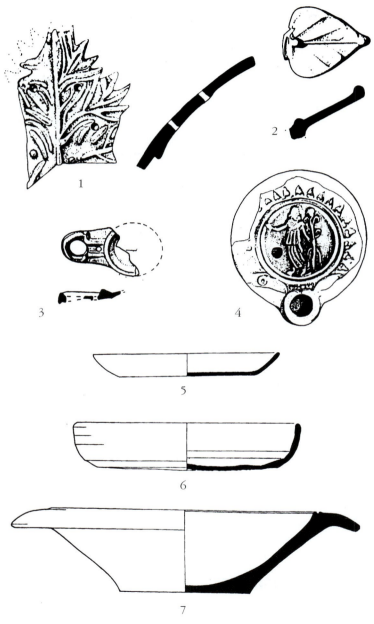

Figure 12.3 Examples of pottery vessels from Binyanei Ha'uma.

Ha'uma is easily distinguishable from the thick, lustrous, dark-red slip characteristic of the classic Pompeian Red Ware, which apparently originated in Italy.[22] Berlin has noted that food cooked in flat-bottomed pans, which are broad and shallow, would have taken on a defined form, unlike the globular cooking pots and casseroles characteristic of the Levant, which were used for boiling soups and stews. Flat-bottomed pans were especially suitable for the preparation of *patinae*, a type of Roman quiche in which layers of chopped fish, vegetables, and/or fruit were covered with a poured egg mixture and then baked (Berlin 1993: 43–4; Junkelmann 1997: 198, abb. 89). They were also used for baking the flat cakes of bread that were one of the main components of the Roman soldier's diet; the other was porridge or gruel (puls), which could resemble polenta (Berlin 1993: 39; Junkelmann 1997: 128–9). Flat-bottomed pans, including imports and locally produced versions, are attested at a number of sites around Palestine.[23] However, they are rare in Judea, with the only previously published examples coming from Jerusalem.[24]

The mortaria from Binyanei Ha'uma are made of a thick, gritty, orange or yellow-brown fabric which resembles that of the rooftiles (Fig. 12.3:7).[25] Grinding inside the bases of some has exposed dark stone chips or pebbles embedded in the fabric. The mortaria have rounded walls, broad flaring rims with a grooved or slightly projecting (beaded) lip, and flat bases. Some have a spout, although there are no examples of the makers' stamps often found on Roman mortaria. The Romans, who liked highly spiced foods, used mortaria for grinding nuts, garlic, and herbs. The remains of some spices have even been discovered in excavations in Roman military camps in Europe (Junkelmann 1997: 145–9; Edwards 1986: xi). Mortaria were essential for preparing the sauces, dressings and pesto-like pastes that were a component of many Roman recipes (see for example Junkelmann 1997: 200, abb. 90, taf. 17.2). For example, one of Apicius' recipes for potted salad (*aliter sala cattabia apiciana*) begins as follows: "In a mortar, mix celery seed, dried pennyroyal, dried mint, ginger, green coriander, seedless raisins, honey, vinegar, olive oil, and wine" (Edwards 1986: 38). Mortaria are very common at Roman sites in Europe, and have been found at Paphos on Cyprus and at Tarsus.[26] In Palestine, examples are published from Caesarea, Tel Dor, and Jerusalem (Bar-Nathan and Adato 1986: fig. 3: 4; Guz-Zilberstein 1995: fig. 6.49: 4; Hamilton 1944: fig. 6: 11).[27]

Conclusion

Many of the fine table wares from Binyanei Ha'uma connected with the offering and/or consumption of wine are decorated with appropriate imagery. The relative frequency of Dionysiac motifs suggests that this cult enjoyed great popularity among the Roman soldiers of Aelia Capitolina. In fact, Dionysus is depicted on many of the city coins of Aelia, and the attributes of his cult, including the thyrsus, wine cup, ivy leaves, and grapes and grape leaves were used as mint-marks (Meshorer 1989: 26).

The ceramic types used by the Tenth Legion during its siege at Masada and those produced in the kiln works that supplied its permanent camp in Jerusalem are strikingly different. At Masada, nearly all of the pottery consists of local (Judean) storage jars, with a few local cooking pots and painted Nabataean bowls. At Binyanei Ha'uma, the locally manufactured assemblage consists of types characteristic of Roman sites in Europe, which are rare or unattested in Palestine and elsewhere in the East. Why are the ceramic assemblages used by the same legion at these two Judean sites completely different? Since pottery vessels reflect cooking and dining habits, could it be that the soldiers prepared their food differently, and ate different kinds of foods, depending on whether they were on campaign in the field or stationed in permanent camps? Because we know that the Roman army operated in a standardized manner in other respects, it is reasonable to assume that Roman soldiers customarily prepared their food in the same manner, and ate the same kinds of food (although not necessarily with the same variety), under all circumstances. The differences between the Masada and Binyanei Ha'uma ceramic assemblages can be accounted for by comparing their composition. At Masada, the assemblage consists almost entirely of storage jars, that is, vessels used for transporting and storing grain, wine, and oil. Most of the examples of fine ceramic table wares consist of painted Nabataean bowls, which come from the officers' living quarters. As Greene has noted, the absence of pottery is characteristic of temporary Roman marching camps, since an army of conquest had little need of pottery (Greene 1979: 99; also see Whittaker 1989: 72). When in the field, the soldiers used sets of metal cooking vessels and dishes that were part of their mess-kits. Such metal cooking pots and mess-tins can be seen dangling from the forked sticks carried by the soldiers on the Column of Trajan (Greene 1979: 99; Fuentes 1991: 65, 78). When the siege at Masada ended, the soldiers took their mess-kits with them (Breeze 1977: 138–9). Thus, what remains in the siege camps at Masada are the containers used to import and store the army's supplies, instead of the vessels used to prepare and serve the food. On the other hand, the potters at Binyanei Ha'uma produced the fine table wares and cooking vessels required by an army of occupation stationed in a permanent camp.

Many of the distinctive ceramic forms and surface treatments or decorative techniques that are characteristic of legionary pottery industries in Europe, such as the use of red slip, marbling, barbotine, rouletting, and stamped and molded designs are attested at Binyanei Ha'uma (Greene 1977: 113–14). At most legionary fortresses in Britain and Europe some fine wares were usually imported, and many of the other types show native influence in form and decoration (Greene 1979: 100–1). The native influence is due to the fact that at least some of the pottery was manufactured by civilian potters, who either followed the legions or were locals (Swan 1988: 7). This is not the case at Binyanei Ha'uma, where the pottery supply arrangements are paralleled instead at the first century legionary fortresses at Wroxeter, Usk, and

Inchtuthil in Great Britain. The pottery at these fortresses was locally made, of continental type without native influence, under the control of the respective legions. This means that the potters at these sites produced all of the vessel types necessary for the legion's requirements (Darling 1977: 59). Wroxeter, Usk, and Inchtuthil differ from most other legionary fortresses in that all of the pottery was apparently made on the spot by military potters who were part of the legion (Darling 1977: 59–63). Military potters were not a regular part of the Roman army, which involved itself in making pottery only when it was unavoidable (Darling 1977: 64, 67, 68; Breeze 1977: 136–7, 141; Greene 1977: 125; Swan 1988: 8). At Wroxeter, Usk, and Inchtuthil, large garrisons were concentrated in hostile territories with poor ceramic traditions. The cost of transporting imported fine wares so far inland would have been prohibitive. The location of these fortresses in hostile areas would have deterred civilian potters from willingly following the legions (Darling 1977: 63). Thus, once the Roman army became established beyond areas of competent ceramic production, it was forced to make its own, or acquire it from further afield (Greene 1979: 103). Jerusalem, like these three British fortresses, lay in a remote, hostile territory where the native potters were not trained in the Roman ceramic tradition (see Darling 1977: 69). The Italian and Gaulish fine wares that are ubiquitous at Roman military sites around Europe are virtually unknown in Jerusalem and other sites in Palestine, apparently due to the high cost of transport.

Palestine also differs from Britain and the continent, where the principal response of native potters to the Roman occupation was to extend the range of their products to include the ceramic types that were introduced by the army and soon spread among the civilian population (Greene 1979: 101; Marsh 1978: 206; Darling 1977: 69; Swan 1988: 7–9). Although many civilian potters' products in Europe were sold in large quantities to the army, they were rarely made exclusively for military use. Instead, the military market constituted a small part of the Romanized demand for new forms alongside traditional vessels (Greene 1979: 102–3). In contrast, the ceramic types manufactured at Binyanei Ha'uma had a very limited distribution and little observable influence on the local repertoire.[28] This does not, however, mean that the native aristocracy of Judea never developed the tastes and culinary habits that required fine Roman table wares and Roman types of cooking and kitchen wares. Instead, the local demand for Roman types of table and kitchen wares may have been supplied largely by imports, such as African Red Slip Wares (which appeared in increasing quantities mainly from the third century on; see Hayes 1972) and North Syrian mortaria (dated by Hayes from the latter part of the third century on; see Hayes 1967: 347). These were apparently supplemented by locally produced types such as Jerusalem rouletted bowls, rilled-rim basins, and perhaps casseroles, all of which appeared by the end of the third century (Magness 1993).

It is probably not a coincidence that these imports and local types appeared or became common at about the same time the kiln works at

Binyanei Ha'uma ceased production. It is not clear whether there is some chronological overlap, or whether the importation and local production of these types began after the kiln works at Binyanei Ha'uma closed. The chronology of the ceramic types suggests to me that the latter is more likely. After the Tenth Legion was transferred to Aila, the demand for table and kitchen wares among the Judean population (including and perhaps especially the Roman veterans settled in Aelia Capitolina) was apparently supplied partly by imports, and partly by local potters, who now added to their repertoire some new types of Roman inspiration.

Notes

1 For Yadin's excavations at Masada, see his popular book (1966), and the six final report volumes which have appeared in print since his death (Aviram, Foerster, and Netzer 1989–99). For a recent summary of the debate about whether Masada fell in 73 or 74 C.E., see Barag and Hershkovitz 1994: 3, n. 1. The problem of the historicity of Josephus's account of the mass suicide at Masada lies beyond the scope of this paper; for a summary with references, see Silberman 1989: 87–101, 261–2.

2 The legion was apparently transferred to Aila in the time of Diocletian; see Geva 1984: 253; Isaac 1993: 325.

3 For parallels to the most common types of storage jars represented in Camp F, see Loffreda 1996: 47–50, Groups 13–14); Bar-Nathan 1981: 54–6, ("bell-shaped jars"); Lapp and Nickelsburg 1974: pl. 25. These types date from the first century C.E. at least through the time of the Bar Kokhba Revolt. Although the final report on the pottery has not yet been published, photographs in Yadin's popular book indicate that these types were also found in his excavations at Masada; see for example Yadin 1966: 95. This is a complete example of the type of storage jar that predominates in Camp F, which is characterized by a bag-shaped, somewhat cylindrical body; a tall neck with a ridge at the base and a rounded, thickened rim; and hard-fired, dark grey or brown ware covered with a flakey, green-yellow or yellow-brown slip.

For parallels to the most common types of cooking pots represented in Camp F, see Loffreda 1996: 75–6 (Group 40), 79–80 (Group 44), 81–3 (Group 46); Bar-Nathan 1981: pl. 5.1–6, 11–22; Lapp and Nickelsburg 1974: pl. 29; Yadin 1963: fig. 41. Like the storage jars, these types date from the first century C.E. at least through the time of the Bar Kokhba Revolt.

Most of the oil lamp fragments represented in Camp F are of the knife-pared, wheel-made ("Herodian") type (Barag and Hershkovitz 1994: 24–53). Although these lamps are typical of the first century C.E., the fact that they are common in caves occupied at the time of the Bar Kokhba Revolt indicates that the type continued into the first half of the second century (e.g., Eshel and Amit 1998: 197, pl. 4: 55–7; Avigad 1962: 176–7, fig. 5: 19–20).

4 The thin-walled beaker fragments were retrieved through sifting and are too small to draw; for this type in general see Moevs 1973. Although the painted decoration on the amphoriskos is vaguely reminiscent of Nabataean pottery (see for example Negev 1986: 40, nos. 280–1), the closest parallels I have

found are fragments of early or middle Roman kitchen wares from Tarsus with similar dark brown ivy leaf patterns; see Jones 1950: pl. 162, nos. 799–801. The Nabataean bowls from Camp F are decorated with a combination of painted criss-crosses, dots, and/or trellises, and most have a shallow body and rounded base with a sharply incurved rim; for parallels see Negev 1986: 44, no. 316, 55: no. 399. For an example from Yadin's excavations see Yadin 1966: 225. Interestingly, fine red-slipped wares were represented in Camp F by only a few tiny, worn fragments of Eastern Sigillata A. We also recovered a few pieces of imported amphoras.

5 The military equipment from our excavations will be published by Arubas and Goldfus.

6 The pottery from Avi-Yonah's 1967 excavations will be published by Rosenthal-Heginbottom. For the pottery from Avi-Yonah's 1949 excavations, see Hershkovitz 1987.

7 One of the biggest mysteries about the pottery from Binyanei Ha'uma is its limited distribution. The large quantities of pottery recovered in the excavations and the fact that the kiln works were active over the course of about two hundred years are not reflected in archaeological finds around Jerusalem. Only a small amount of Roman pottery has been discovered in excavations in and around Jerusalem, with nearly all of it coming from the Armenian Garden and the Jewish Quarter (for example, none of the Roman table or kitchen wares from Binyanei Ha'uma are represented at Ramat Rahel, where stamped tiles attest to the presence of the Tenth Legion; see Aharoni 1962, 1964).

8 Petrographic analysis of representative examples of the vessel types was conducted by Dr. Yuval Goren of Tel Aviv University; the results will be published as part of the final excavation report. Motza (Colonia) is located about 3 kilometers to the west of Binyanei Ha'uma (Arubas and Goldfus 1995: 107, n. 15).

9 For an eastern variant of mottled ware from Tarsus see Jones 1950: 183–4; fig. 145.518–22; for examples of western marbled ware from Corinth see Ilife 1942: 34–5. This treatment also occurs on Eastern Sigillata A; see Hayes 1976: pl. 11: 89. For a similar treatment on thin-walled wares of the first century B.C.E./first century C.E. see Moevs 1973: 123.

10 This follows a classification system that was devised by Dragendorff (usually abbreviated to Drag. or Dr.; see Dragendorff 1895; Hayes 1997: 42). For a more recent classification system focusing on the undecorated Samian see Ettlinger *et al.* 1990. An undecorated North African variant of Drag. 29 is common in second century contexts from Spain to Greece, but not in Palestine; see Hayes 1972: 15, 32–5; African Red Slip Form 8, dated ca. 80/90 to second half of the second century. For other examples of Drag. 29 see Peacock 1982: 115, pl. 29; Hayes 1997: 48, pl. 16; Swan 1988: 13, 62, fig. 2.117; Marsh 1978: 177, fig. 66.19, Type 44.1, 7; Darling 1977: figs. 6.5: 21 (from Usk), 6.7: 21–2 (from Wroxeter); 6.8: 2 (from Kingsholm); Faber 1994: 240 (numerous examples, mostly of Flavian date); Holwerda 1944: pl. 1: 15–16. Only one example is attested from Holt; see Grimes 1930: 98; 161, no. 156.

11 For examples of cups and beakers with similar forms and decoration see Stefan 1945–7: 128, fig. 10.5; Ettlinger 1951: 106, fig. 9.9. Red-slipped ledge handles of first- to second-century date made of "Roman Pergamene" fabric are published from Tarsus; see Jones 1950: fig. 155.687–9. For similar ledge handles without struts from Nijmegen see den Boesterd 1956: pl. 3.65–7.

12 For a ceramic rim and pierced handle made of blackened cooking ware that might belong to such a mess-tin from a second century C.E. context at Shiqmona, see Elgavish 1977: pl. 4.23.

13 The circular object looks like a shield. However, since that would be inconsistent with the identification of this figure as Dionysus, perhaps it represents a cymbal or tympanum; see for example Godwin 1981: 140.

14 It is interesting to note that a bronze set of this type, consisting of a saucepan and handleless jug, may have been found buried beneath the floor of one of the casemate rooms on Masada; see Yadin 1966: 148 top. However, since their precise provenience is not provided, and the bronze vessels from Yadin's excavations have not yet been published, it is impossible to determine whether the saucepan and jug were found together. A bronze jug found buried beneath the floor of a casemate room (L1196) is illustrated in Netzer 1991: 517, ill. 807, but there is no reference to the saucepan, and it is unclear whether this is the same jug illustrated by Yadin.

15 For an altar of 141/42 C.E. from Beth Shean decorated with Dionysiac imagery see Di Segni, Foerster, and Tsafrir 1999; they note (67, n. 11) that "the Romans do not seem to have made a distinction between masks and heads."

16 There are many examples of bronze handles that terminate in human heads or masks which, like ours, are positioned to gaze up at the person grasping it (e.g., den Boesterd 1956: pl. 26–7; pl. 4.70; Koster 1997: 74–5, no. 100 [a female head perhaps representing Omphale]; 79–81, nos. 106, 109 [Medusa heads]; Radnoti 1938: pls. 6.28, 26.Ib [bust and torso of a cupid]).

17 For other examples of bronze handles with ram's heads see Deimel 1987: pl 26.5, 9; Junkelmann 1997: pl. 13; Radnoti 1938: pls. 6.29, 7.30, 26.2, 3, 5, 28.1; den Boesterd 1956: 25–6, with a list of parallels, pl. 4: 68, 80. For examples of ceramic animal's head handles see Stefan 1945–7: 133, fig. 14: 1; Grimes 1930: 212, fig. 60: 4; Marsh 1978: 163, fig. 6.14, type 32.4; Bettermann 1934: abb. 14 top; Radnoti 1938: pl. 61: 1. Koster (1997: 74) noted that handles terminating in animal's heads seem to be most common in the western provinces and are almost absent elsewhere, perhaps reflecting the production of this type of libation set in Gaul. However, animal's head handles were apparently not uncommon in the eastern Mediterranean. Hayes illustrates two examples with ram's heads of second-century date which are made of Knidian fabric (1997: 72, pl. 26 bottom). According to Robinson, bowls with animal's head handles were popular in Athens in the fourth century (1959: 103, nos. M209, M210, pls. 26, 71; another example with a lion's head of fourth-century date is illustrated by Hayes 1997: 92, pl. 38). These animal heads are much cruder than those on the earlier handles, and were attached to a thick-walled bowl with a ledge rim and ring base, instead of to a shallow bowl with a rounded base.

18 The published description of a leaf-shaped handle from the Armenian Garden in Jerusalem indicates that it may have been produced at Binyanei Ha'uma (see Tushingham 1985: fig. 49.13 which is described as made of "smooth, light yellow brownish [ware] with a faint red core; slightly glossy orange-brown slip all over" (189). For imported lamps with leaf-shaped handles from Masada see Bailey 1994: 82–3, nos. 153, 154, 156, 157. Many of the leaf-shaped handles from Masada and Europe differ from ours in having a triangular outline with relief decoration on the upper surface; for examples see Fitch and Goldman 1994: 145, fig. 74; Rosenthal and Sivan 1978: 19–22, nos. 40, 41, 47, 48, 53;

Evelein 1928: pl. 28; Szentleleky 1969: nos. 56–63. The finds from Binyanei Ha'uma also include lunate handles that belong to the same type of oil lamp, which are not included in this discussion.

19 For other examples of oil lamps of this type from Jerusalem, see Herschkovitz 1987: 320, fig. 11.5–7, 321, figs. 12–13; Avigad 1983: 204, no. 252; Mazar 1971: fig. 9.3–6; Ben-Dov 1985: 198–9. This type was also produced in the potter's workshop at Gerasa; see Ilife 1944–5: pls. 8.140–5, 9.134–9; Rosenthal and Sivan 1978: 96, nos. 387–8.

20 An imported factory lamp representing Loeschcke Type IX is published from Masada; see Bailey 1994: 93, no 201. I am grateful to Professor Dan Barag for bringing this piece to my attention. For factory lamps in Italy and Europe see Loeschcke 1919: 255–98; Fitch and Goldman 1994: 194–200; Grimes 1930: fig. 75: 1–4 (apparently manufactured at Holt); Marsh 1978: 189–92; Holwerda 1946: pl. 20.1.2–8 (lamps), pl. 21.1.a–b (mold); Stefan 1945–7: fig. 16.3; Walke 1965: pls. 86.6, 87, 88, 92.4–7; Bonis 1977: abb. 1.4, 8–11, abb. 4 (all molds, including one signed by Fortis); Evelein 1928: pls. 7–9; Szentleleky 1969: nos. 120–35.

21 To distinguish them from the Italian imports, the term Pompeian Red Ware will not be used to describe the pans and lids from Binyanei Ha'uma.

22 Peacock (1977) has distinguished a number of different fabrics of Pompeian Red Ware, which apparently originated in different production centers. His Fabric 1, which is the most common and widespread throughout the Mediterranean, is characterized by the typical, thick, lustrous red slip of Pompeian Red color. Pans of this fabric are believed to have originated in Italy, perhaps in the bay of Naples. Peacock suggested that the eruption of Mount Vesuvius in 79 C.E. ended the production of the Fabric 1 workshops. The fact that the descriptions of some published examples from Palestine match Peacock's Fabric 1 suggests that they are Italian imports; see Berlin 1993; Hayes 1985: 185, 194, no. 8, fig. 60.7–16 (It is interesting that these examples, which come from the western hill in Jerusalem, apparently antedate the destruction of the city in 70 C.E.); Guz-Zilberstein 1995: fig. 6.49.8; Kenyon 1957: 298, fig. 68.10–11. Some of the other fabrics described by Peacock continued to be manufactured as late as the early to mid-third century (1977: 159, Fabrics 6, 7). Other variants of flat-bottomed pans and lids were produced in North African workshops during the second half of the second century and first half of the third century (Hayes 1972: 200–4, African Red Slip Ware Forms 181, 185). Peacock also proposed a typology by associating different pan forms with the seven fabrics (1977: 156–8). Almost all of the forms he illustrated are represented at Binyanei Ha'uma (the only exceptions are pans with an everted rim, and pans with a disc base; see Peacock 1977: fig. 3.14–15). For another typology of Pompeian Red Ware pans see De Laet and Thoen 1969. The Binyanei Ha'uma pans correspond in form with their Types 6 (Göse 244) and 7 (Göse 245), which are dated from the Flavian period to the mid-third century. As in the case of Peacock's typology, the earlier pans published by De Laet and Thoen differ from ours in having straight or concave walls, a flaring or everted rim, or a thickened, disc base (their Types 1–5).

23 In addition to the imports noted above (n. 21), see Berlin 1997: 104–6 (from Tel Anafa; mostly local products of Roman date); Reisner, Fischer, and Lyon 1924: 304, fig. 174.54–6 (from Samaria); Riley 1975: 45–6, no. 90 (from Caesarea); Bar-Nathan and Adato 1986: 164, fig. 2.20 (from Caesarea); Blakely 1987: fig.

20.46 (from Caesarea; a lid); Elgavish 1977: 53, 69, pls. 10: 72–3, 82–3, 18.137 (from Shiqmona); Avigad 1955: 6, fig. 3.16–17 (from Beth Shearim); Guz-Zilberstein 1995: 322; 403, fig. 6.49.3, 6, 7 (pans), 13 (a lid) (from Tel Dor); Fisher 1938: 557–8, fig. 36.1, 2, 5, 565, fig. 42.11, 569, fig. 46.42 (from Gerasa); Hayes 1997: 78–9, fig. 32: 1 (from Petra).

24 Aside from the Italian imports of first century date from the Armenian Garden (above, n. 21), see Tushingham 1985: fig. 25.35, 36, which come from post-70 C.E. contexts and are described as "local imitations" (Hayes 1985: 185); Hamilton 1944: fig. 22: 30, from a third- to fourth-century context. The form, ware and context of these pieces indicate that they could be products of the kiln works at Binyanei Ha'uma.

In Galilee, flat-bottomed pans apparently inspired the long-lived and locally produced Galilean bowl series (Berlin 1997: 105, n. 235; for Galilean bowls see Adan-Bayewitz 1993: 88–109). For Judean casseroles, which appeared by the end of the third century but usually have rounded bases, see Magness 1993: 211–14.

25 Hayes (1997: 80) has noted that the similarity between the makers' stamps on Roman mortaria and those on bricks and tiles suggests that they were manufactured in the same workshops.

26 For examples see Stefan 1945–7: 128, fig. 10: 2 (from Drajna-de-Sus); Faber 1994: beilage 20, 21, 22.269–72 (from Regensburg); Grunewald 1979: taf. 37: 1–3 (from Carnuntum); Grimes 1930: 146–9, 213, fig. 61 (from Holt); Swan 1988: 20–4 (Great Britain); Hartley 1977 (Great Britain); Jones 1950: fig. 201: A, 706; fig. 204: A, 778 (from Tarsus); Hayes 1977: fig. 6: 10 (from Paphos).

27 Hayes (1967) has noted that a different type of mortarium, which apparently originated in northern Syria, is found at sites in the Levant from the third to sixth centuries. This variant is distinguished by its dark red-brown ware, and by the rectangular or arched rim profile; for a more recent study see Blakely and Vitaliano 1992. The example in Bar-Nathan and Adato 1986: fig. 3: 4 is mistakenly identified as this variant.

28 It is likely that rouletted bowls and rilled-rim basins, which are characteristic of the Jerusalem area beginning in the late third to early fourth century, were influenced by the types manufactured at Binyanei Ha'uma; see Magness 1993: 185–92, 203–4. This may also be true of the red-slipping that is common on Jerusalem pottery in the late Roman period; see Magness 1993: 185.

Bibliography

Adan-Bayewitz, D. (1993) *Common Pottery in Roman Galilee, A Study of Local Trade*, Ramat-Gan: Bar Ilan University Press.

Aharoni, Y. (1962) *Excavations at Ramat Rahel I*, Rome: Centro di studi semitici.

—— (1964) *Excavations at Ramat Rahel II*, Rome: Centro di studi semitici.

Arubas, B. and Goldfus, H. (1995) "The Kilnworks of the Tenth Legion Fretensis," in J. H. Humphrey (ed.) *The Roman and Byzantine Near East: Some Recent Archaeological Research, Journal of Roman Archaeology*, Supplementary Series Number 14, Ann Arbor MI: Kelsey Museum of Archaeology.

Avigad, N. (1955) *Excavations at Beth Shearim, 1954, Preliminary Report*, Jerusalem: Israel Exploration Society (Heb.).

—— (1962) "Expedition A—Nahal David," *Israel Exploration Journal* 12: 169–83.

—— (1983) *Discovering Jerusalem*, Nashville: T. Nelson.

Aviram, J., Foerster, G. and Netzer, E. (eds.) (1989–99) *Masada I–VI, The Yigael Yadin Excavations 1963–1965*, Jerusalem: Israel Exploration Society.

Bailey, D. M. (1994) "Imported Lamps and Local Copies," in J. Aviram, G. Foerster, and E. Netzer (eds.) *Masada IV, The Yigael Yadin Excavations 1963–1965, Final Reports*, Jerusalem: Israel Exploration Society.

Barag, D. (1967) "Brick Stamp-Impressions of the Legio X Fretensis," *Bonner Jahrbucher* 167: 244–67.

Barag, D. and Hershkovitz, M. (1994) "Lamps from Masada," in J. Aviram, G. Foerster, and E. Netzer (eds.) *Masada IV, The Yigael Yadin Excavations 1963–1965, Final Reports*, Jerusalem: Israel Exploration Society.

Bar-Nathan, R. (1981) "Pottery and Stone Vessels of the Herodian Period," in E. Netzer (ed.) *Greater Herodium*, Qedem 13, Jerusalem: Israel Exploration Society.

Bar-Nathan, R. and Adato, M. (1986) "Pottery," in L.I. Levine and E. Netzer (eds.) *Excavations at Caesarea Maritima, 1975, 1976, 1979—Final Report*, Qedem 21, Jerusalem: Israel Exploration Society.

Ben-Dov, M. (1985) *In the Shadow of the Temple, The Discovery of Ancient Jerusalem*, New York: Harper and Row.

Berlin, A. (1993) "Italian Cooking Vessels and Cuisine from Tel Anafa," *Israel Exploration Journal* 43: 35–44.

—— (1997) *Tel Anafa* II, i. *The Hellenistic and Roman Pottery: The Plain Wares*, *Journal of Roman Archaeology*, Supplementary Series 10.2.1, Ann Arbor, MI: Kelsey Museum of Archaeology.

Bettermann, K. (1934) "Die bemalte Keramik der fruhen romischen Kaiserzeit im rheinischen Germanien," *Saalburg Jahrbuch* 8: 97–129.

Blakely, J. A. (1987) *Caesarea Maritima, The Pottery and Dating of Vault 1: Horreum, Mithraeum, and Later Uses*, Lewiston, NY: Edwin Mellen Press.

Blakely, J. A. and Vitaliano, C. J. (1992) "Roman Mortaria and Basins from a Sequence at Caesarea: Fabrics and Sources," in R. L. Vann (ed.) *Caesarea Papers, Straton's Tower, Herod's Harbour, and Roman and Byzantine Caesarea*, *Journal of Roman Archaeology*, Supplementary Series Number 5, Ann Arbor, MI: Kelsey Museum of Archaeology.

den Boesterd, M. H. P. (1956) *Description of the Collections in the Rijksmuseum G. M Kam at Nijmegen, V: The Bronze Vessels*, Nijmegen: Uitgegeven in Opdracht van het Departement van Onderwijs, Kunsten en Wetenschappen.

Bonis, E. A. (1977) "Das Topferviertel am Kurucdomb von Brigetio," *Folia Archaeologica* 28: 105–39.

Breeze, D. J. (1977) "The Fort at Bearsden and the Supply of Pottery to the Roman Army," in J. Dore and K. Greene (eds.) *Roman Pottery Studies in Britain and Beyond, Papers Presented to John Gillam, July 1977*, Oxford: BAR International Series 30.

Darling, M. J. (1977) "Pottery from Early Military Sites in Western Britain," in J. Dore and K. Greene (eds.) *Roman Pottery Studies in Britain and Beyond, Papers Presented to John Gillam, July 1977*, Oxford: BAR International Series 30.

Deimel, M. (1987) *Die Bronzekleinfunde vom Magdalensberg*, Klagenfurt: Verlag des Landesmuseums für Karnten.

De Laet, S. J. and Thoen, H. (1969) "La céramique 'à enduit rouge-pompeien'," *Helinium* 9: 29–38.

Di Segni, L., Foerster, G. and Tsafrir, Y. (1999) "The Basilica and Altar to Dionysos at Nysa-Scythopolis," in J. H. Humphrey (ed.) *The Roman and Byzantine Near East*, Volume 2, *Some Recent Archaeological Research, Journal of Roman Archaeology*, Supplementary Studies Number 31, Ann Arbor, MI: Kelsey Museum of Archaeology.

Dragendorff, H. (1895) "Ein Beitrag zur Geschichte der griechischen und romischen Keramik," *Bonner Jahrbuch* 96–7: 18–155.

Dyson, S. L. (1976) *Cosa: The Utilitarian Pottery*, Rome: American Academy at Rome.

Edwards, J. (1986) *Roman Cookery Revised*, Point Roberts, WA: Hartley and Marks.

Elgavish, J. (1977) *Archaeological Excavations at Shikmona, The Pottery of the Roman Period*, Haifa: Haifa Museum of Art (Heb.).

Eshel, H. and Amit, D. (1998) *Refuge Caves of the Bar Kokhba Revolt*, Tel Aviv: Israel Exploration Society (Heb.).

Ettlinger, E. (1951) "Legionary Pottery from Vindonissa," *Journal of Roman Studies* 41: 105–11.

Ettlinger, E. *et al.* (1990) *Conspectus Formarum Terrae Sigillatae Italico Modo Confectae*, Bonn: Dr. Rudolf Habelt GMBH.

Evelein, M. A. (1928) *De Romeinsche Lampen, Beschrijving van de Verzameling van Het Museum G. M. Kam*, Nijmegen: 'S-Gravenhage, Algemeene landsdrukkerij.

Faber, A. (1994) *Das Romische Auxiliarkastell und der Vicus von Regensburg-Kumpfmuhl*, Munich: C. H. Beck.

Fisher, C. S. (1938) "Tombs," in C. H. Kraeling (ed.) *Gerasa, City of the Decapolis*, New Haven: Yale University Press.

Fitch, C. R. and Goldman, N. W. (1994) *Cosa: The Lamps*, Memoirs of the American Academy in Rome 39, Ann Arbor, MI: University of Michigan Press.

Foerster, G. and Tsafrir, Y. (1990) "A Statue of Dionysus as a Youth Recently Discovered at Beth Shean," *Qadmoniot* 89–90: 52–4 (Heb.).

Fuentes, N. (1991) "The Mule of a Soldier," *Journal of Roman Military Equipment Studies* 2: 65–99.

Geva, H. (1984) "The Camp of the Tenth Legion in Jerusalem: An Archaeological Reconsideration," *Israel Exploration Journal* 34: 239–54.

Godwin, J. (1981) *Mystery Religions in the Ancient World*, San Francisco: Harper and Row.

Greene, K. (1977) "Legionary Pottery, and the Significance of Holt," in J. Dore and K. Greene (eds.) *Roman Pottery Studies in Britain and Beyond, Papers Presented to John Gillam, July 1977*, Oxford: BAR International Series 30.

—— (1979) "Invasion and Response: Pottery and the Roman Army," in B. C. Burnham and H. B. Johnson (eds.) *Invasion and Response, The Case of Roman Britain*, Oxford: BAR International Series 73.

Griffiths, W. B. (1989) "The Sling and Its Place in the Roman Imperial Army," in C. van Driel-Murray (ed.) *Roman Military Equipment: the Sources of Evidence, Proceedings of the Fifth Roman Military Equipment Conference*, Oxford: BAR International Series 476.

Grimes, W. F. (1930) "Holt, Denbighshire: The Works-Depot of the Twentieth Legion at Castle Lyons," *Y Cymmrodor* 41, London: The Society.

Grunewald, M. (1979) *Die Gefasskeramik des Legionslagers von Carnuntum (Grabungen 1968–1974)*, Vienna: Verlag der Österreichischen Akadamie der Wissenschaften.

Guz-Zilberstein, B. (1995) "The Typology of the Hellenistic Coarse Ware and Selected Loci of the Hellenistic and Roman Periods," in E. Stern (ed.) *Excavations at Dor, Final Report Volume IB, Areas A and C: The Finds*, Qedem Reports Volume 2, Jerusalem: Israel Exploration Society.

Hamilton, R. W. (1944) "Excavations Against the North Wall of Jerusalem," *Quarterly of the Department of Antiquities in Palestine* 10: 1–54.

Hartley, K. F. (1977) "Two Major Potteries Producing Mortaria in the First Century A.D.," in J. Dore and K. Greene (eds.) *Roman Pottery Studies in Europe and Beyond, Papers Presented to John Gillam, July 1977*, Oxford: BAR International Series 30.

Hayes, J. W. (1967) "North Syrian Mortaria," *Hesperia* 36: 337–47.

—— (1972) *Late Roman Pottery*, London: British School at Rome.

—— (1976) *Roman Pottery in the Royal Ontario Museum*, Toronto: Royal Ontario Museum.

—— (1977) "Early Roman Wares from the House of Dionysos, Paphos," *Rei Cretariae Romanae Fautorum Acta* 17/18: 96–108.

—— (1985) "Hellenistic to Byzantine Fine Wares and Derivatives in the Jerusalem Corpus," in A. D. Tushingham (ed.) *Excavations in Jerusalem 1961–1967*, volume I, Toronto: Royal Ontario Museum.

—— (1997) *Handbook of Mediterranean Roman Pottery*, Norman, OK: University of Oklahoma Press.

Hershkovitz, M. (1987) "The Pottery of the First and Second Centuries C.E. from Giv`at Ram," *Eretz-Israel* 19: 314–25 (Heb., English summary on p. 83).

Holwerda, J. H. (1944) *Het in de Pottenbakkerij van de Holdeurn Gefabriceerde Aardewerk uit de Nijmeegsche Grafvelden*, Leiden: E. J. Brill.

—— (1946) *De Holdeurn Bij Berg en Dal*, Leiden: E. J. Brill.

Ilife, J. H. (1942) "Sigillata Wares in the Near East. II," *Quarterly of the Department of Antiquities in Palestine* 9: 31–46.

—— (1944–5) "Imperial Art in Transjordan," *Quarterly of the Department of Antiquities in Palestine* 11: 1–26.

Isaac, B. (1993) *The Limits of Empire, The Roman Army in the East*, Oxford: Clarendon Press.

Jones, F. F. (1950) "The Pottery," in H. Goldman (ed.) *Excavations at Gözlü Küle, Tarsus, Volume I, The Hellenistic and Roman Periods*, Princeton: Princeton University Press.

Junkelmann, M. (1997) *Panis Militaris. Die Ernahrung des romischen Soldaten oder der Grundstoff der Macht*, Mainz am Rhein: P. von Zabern.

Kendrick, P. M. (1990) "The Use of Decoration on 'Plain' Italian Sigillata," in E. Ettlinger *et al.*, *Conspectus Formarum Terrae Sigillatae Italico Modo Confectae*, Bonn: Dr. Rudolf Habelt GMBH.

Kenyon, K. M. (1957) "Roman and Later Wares: Stratified Groups," in J. W. Crowfoot, G. M. Crowfoot, and K. M. Kenyon, *The Objects from Samaria*, London: Palestine Exploration Fund.

Koster, A. (1997) *Description of the Collections in the Provinciaal Museum G. M. Kam at Nijmegen, Volume XIII: The Bronze Vessels, 2, Acquisitions 1954–1996*, Nijmegen: Provincie Gelderland.

Lapp, N. L. and Nickelsburg, Jr., G. W. E. (1974) "The Roman Occupation and Pottery of 'Araq en-Na'saneh," in P. W. Lapp and N. L. Lapp (eds.) *Discoveries in the Wadi ed-Daliyeh*, *Annals of the American Schools of Oriental Research* 41, Cambridge, MA.

Loeschcke, S. (1919) *Lampen aus Vindonissa*, Zurich: In Kommission bei Beer und Cie.

Loffreda, S. (1996) *La ceramica di Macheronte e dell'Herodion (90 a.c.–135 d.c.)*, Jerusalem: Studium Biblicum Franciscanum.

Magness, J. (1993) *Jerusalem Ceramic Chronology circa 200–800 C.E.*, Sheffield: Sheffield Academic Press.

—— (1996) "Masada 1995: Discoveries at Camp F," *Biblical Archaeologist* 59: 181.

Marsh, G. (1978) "Early Second Century Fine Wares in the London Area," in P. Arthur and G. Marsh (eds.) *Early Fine Wares in Roman Britain*, Oxford: British Archaeological Reports British Series 57.

Mazar, B. (1971) *The Excavations in the Old City of Jerusalem Near the Temple Mount, Preliminary Report of the Second and Third Seasons, 1969–1970*, Jerusalem: Israel Exploration Society.

Meshorer, Y. (1989) *The Coinage of Aelia Capitolina*, Jerusalem: The Israel Museum.

Moevs, M. T. M. (1973) *The Roman Thin Walled Pottery from Cosa (1948–1954)*, Memoirs of the American Academy at Rome 32, Rome.

Negev, A. (1986) *The Late Hellenistic and Early Roman Pottery of Nabatean Oboda, Final Report*, Qedem 22, Jerusalem: Israel Exploration Society.

Netzer, E. (1991) *Masada III, The Yigael Yadin Excavations 1963–1965. The Buildings, Stratigraphy and Architecture*, Jerusalem: Israel Exploration Society.

Peacock, D. P .S. (1977) "Pompeian Red Ware," in D. P. S. Peacock (ed.) *Pottery and Early Commerce*, New York: Academic Press.

—— (1982) *Pottery in the Roman World, An Ethnoarchaeological Approach*, New York: Longman.

Radnoti, A. (1938) *Die Romischen Bronzegefasse von Pannonien*, Budapest: Institut für munzkunde und archäologie der P. Pazmany-Universität.

Reisner, G. A., Fisher, C. S. and Lyon, D. G. (1924) *Harvard Excavations at Samaria, 1908–1910*, Volume I. *Text*, Cambridge, MA: Harvard University Press.

Richmond, I. A. (1962) "The Roman Siege-Works of Masada, Israel," *Journal of Roman Studies* 52: 143–55.

Riley, J. A. (1975) "The Pottery from the First Session of Excavation in the Caesarea Hippodrome," *Bulletin of the American Schools of Oriental Research* 218: 25–63.

Robinson, H. S. (1959) *The Athenian Agora* Volume V: *Pottery of the Roman Period*, Princeton: American School of Classical Studies at Athens.

Rosenthal, R. and Sivan, R. (1978) *Ancient Lamps in the Schloessinger Collection*, Qedem 8, Jerusalem: Israel Exploration Society.

Roth, J. (1995) "The Length of the Siege of Masada," *Scripta Classica Israelica* 14: 87–110.

Silberman, N. A. (1989) *Between Past and Present, Archaeology, Ideology, and Nationalism in the Modern Middle East*, New York: H. Holt.

Stefan, G. (1945–7) "Le Camp Romain de Drajna-de-Sus," *Dacia* 11–12: 115–44.

Swan, W. G. (1988) *Pottery in Roman Britain*, Haverfordwest, UK: Shire.

Szentleleky, T. (1969) *Ancient Lamps*, Amsterdam: Adolf M. Hakkert.

Turcan, R. (1996) *The Cults of the Roman Empire*, Cambridge, MA: Blackwell.

Tushingham, A. D. (1985) *Excavations in Jerusalem 1961–1967*, volume I, Toronto: Royal Ontario Museum.

Walke, N. (1965) *Das Romische Donaukastell Straubing-Sorviodurum*, Berlin: Mann.

Webster, G. (1998) *The Roman Imperial Army of the First and Second Centuries A.D.*, Norman, OK: University of Oklahoma Press.

Whittaker, C. R. (1989) "Supplying the System: Frontiers and Beyond," in J. C. Barrett, A. P. Fitzpatrick, and L. Macinnes (eds.) *Barbarians and Romans in North-*

West Europe from the Later Republic to Late Antiquity, Oxford: British Archaeological Reports International Series 471.

Yadin, Y. (1963) *The Finds from the Bar Kokhba Period in the Cave of Letters*, Jerusalem: Israel Exploration Society.

—— (1966) *Masada, Herod's Fortress and the Zealots' Last Stand*, London: Phoenix Illustrated.

13 The First Revolt and Flavian politics

J. Andrew Overman

The broader political and cultural context within which the Revolt and its first wave of interpreters existed is Flavian Rome. Whenever we are discussing the Revolt we are confronting Flavian writers, propagandists, and sources, all of whom were shaped by their particular political context. Outside of the archaeological evidence, what we know about the Revolt has been primarily refracted through the lens of Flavian policies and proclivities. This is as true of reports of the Revolt as of much of the literature—Roman, Rabbinic, and early Christian—that follows in its wake. This has been often overlooked, and it is understandably tempting to focus completely on the events in Judea around the time of the Revolt. Viewing the Revolt from the point of view of Flavian goals, problems, and propaganda, however, is revealing and instructive.

First, from the point of view of the Roman writers, the Revolt is mentioned in the larger context of Vespasian's activity in the east. The point is less the Revolt, and more Vespasian's preparations to move against Vitellius and his subsequent reception by the eastern troops as Caesar. While the siege of Jotopata/Yodefat is deservedly famous, and numbers among one of the most intense and longer narratives within the *War*, it is from Flavian writers other than Josephus that we learn of Vespasian being hailed as Emperor first in Egypt (Tacitus, *Histories* 2.79; Suetonius, *Vespasian* 2). Indeed, both Suetonius and Tacitus discuss Vespasian's ascension in the broader, and for them more critical context, of the eastern troops throwing their support to the Flavians over against Vitellius. The third legion, called "the Gallic" by Dio (64.14ff.), was not far behind and maybe even slightly ahead of Tiberias Alexander, prefect of Egypt. They strongly urged the troops of Moesia to put their support behind Vespasian after having wintered in Syria. Early on they marked their standards with Vespasian's name, replacing Vitellius'. Suetonius attempts to be precise by assigning July 1, 69 as the date Vespasian is sworn the oath in Alexandria, and July 11 as the date that the troops in Judea pledge allegiance in person (*Vespasian* 6). By July 15, according to Tacitus, all of Syria had hailed him as Emperor (*Histories* 2.81). The discussions about who hailed Vespasian as Emperor then is treated as virtually a single process where the resourceful and influential eastern provinces came, according to the famous omen, to give rise to a world ruler (*War* 6.312f.; Suetonius, *Vespasian* 4.5; Tacitus, *Histories* 5.13.4f.).

The narratives regarding Vespasian's ascension spell out the crucial process of garnering support in the east so that he can realistically rival Vitellius whose strength at the time was concentrated in Germany. It may have been "happy augury" that Nero decided on Vespasian to put down the Jewish Revolt and therefore sent him packing to the east (Dio 63.22). But it is worth noting that, at least according to Suetonius, Nero shows little concern and demonstrates less action with regard to the Gallic Revolt under Julius Vindex (*Nero* 40). Vespasian's position in the east is reasonably understood as some combination of an imperial response to unrest in Judea and Vespasian's own awareness of and experience with what it would take to be successful in "his bid for power" (Tacitus, *Agricola* 7). His knowledge of and background in the region makes such a plan sensible. While governor of Judea it was Vespasian who administered the oath of allegiance to the Judean troops on Otho's behalf (*Histories* 1.76). If this scenario is correct, then Vespasian is in step with a fairly well-established Roman political pattern of building both one's reputation and financial and military support out east before returning to Rome to assume or accept power. His support and acclaim would have to come from the east, especially Syria and Egypt, though we know he also enjoyed the promise of support from the Parthian King Vologaesus. And it is clear from Tacitus that Vespasian was in Egypt to gather resources as well as support. While the civil strife in Judea was a problem to be faced, and success there would be important for any aspiring world ruler, the Judean struggles took place within a larger context of laying the foundation for Flavian success and subsequent Flavian rule. Between Syrian, Egyptian, and Parthian support, Vespasian, as Suetonius wrote, "was well prepared for civil war" (*Vespasian* 7). That the youthful and inexperienced Titus was charged with taking care of the Revolt while Vespasian took leave for other places supports the claim that the real issue and concern in 68–9 C.E.. was preparing for possible civil war and laying a serious claim to the throne.[1] Vespasian had other things on his mind. When Vespasian did assume power and the Flavian line was securely established, then the role and characterization of the Revolt seems to have changed.

What were some of those changes? First, as we might expect, once enthroned Vespasian is portrayed as the ruler who brought *Pax* to the world by Flavian literary figures. After the fact, and after Vespasian is the undisputed ruler, he is credited with restoring a world that was in upheaval. "All the world," according to Tacitus, "was in civil war." This started, in his view, in Gaul and in the Spanish provinces, it spread to both Germanies, to the Balkans, and finally traversed Egypt, Judea, and Syria (*Histories* 4.3).[2] The trouble in Judea is mentioned, but it is one of many regions and provinces where Vespasian restored order and peace. Like all good emperors, Vespasian and Titus were credited with bringing stability to an unsettled period and empire. This should not come as a surprise to Romans since this was putatively portented since Vespasian's youth (*Vespasian* 5). At this stage of Flavian development and propaganda Judea serves as one piece of the restoration and *Pax* that Vespasian especially provided. This may explain why neither Vespasian nor Titus assume the title *Judaicus*. To do that would risk emphasizing the regional or parochial nature of the conflict and thereby fail to make the most out of the victory by Vespasian and particularly Titus.

In time, however, within the broader Roman–Flavian orbit this role and dimension for the Jewish Revolt changed. The Flavian political machinery and network began to promote the triumph over the Jews in widespread ways that ultimately contributed to an over-emphasis on the Revolt and finally on the Jews themselves. Goodman (1987: 235) is certainly correct that "the Flavian dynasty needed a great victory to give it prestige." Vespasian's mean background and family line compared to the notable Vitellians was an issue (though writers like Suetonius try to make it a virtue). After the Flavian ascension the question remained: what did Vespasian and his son accomplish to warrant the throne outside of simply seizing it amid a vacuum? The answer that emerged to that question was the Flavian defeat of the Jews.

The promotion began with the so-called Judea Capta coins. While the utilization of coins in the political and cultural wars of Rome was not anything new, most provincial or regional defeats leading up to the Flavians had not been celebrated in coins.[3] The Judea Capta coins had a 10–12-year run, and were a prominent part of a nearly empire-wide promotion by the Flavian administration. They are quite rightly understood as representing "the official commentary" on Vespasian's, and especially Titus' involvement with the Jewish war (Hart 1952). The series very obviously stressed Flavian power and rule, the subjugation of the Jews, and the triumph of Flavian Rome with the aid of Nike/Victoria. The images of Vespasian or Titus are regular features of the coins, as is Iudea, usually symbolized by a woman, bound, kneeling, or even blindfolded before Nike. Meshorer (1962: 98) has argued that the Caesarea mint varied the series and slogan, and deleted some of the images that might be potentially offensive to Judeans, like the image of the half naked captive. This may have put more emphasis on the Roman victory and less on the Judean defeat. Fundamentally, however, the message of the coins was consistent. The Judea Capta series especially stresses Titus who figures prominently on a majority of the coins (Edwards 1992: 203).[4]

The propaganda value of the victory in Judea was especially important in the case of Titus. Since establishing trust in a stable and peaceful succession was crucial, a line or gens had to be established for the Flavians. "My sons will succeed me or no one will," Vespasian told the senate (*Vespasian* 25). Titus and Domitian, as the children of Vespasian, in theory provided the security of a line that would re-establish tradition and a stable imperium. Flavian coins featured busts of Vespasian's sons facing each other and describing them as *Caesar Augusti filius* (Mattingly 1923: II, xxxii). Tacitus and Josephus both mention the theme of succession as something Vespasian exploited in attempting to garner support during the civil war against Vitellius. It was crucial for Roman stability as well as personal expediency that the two Flavian leaders were so often depicted together.

Nonetheless, with respect to Titus, a problem persisted: what really had he done? The defeat of the Jewish rebels had to assume primacy within the Flavian propaganda program. As Syme (1929: 135) reminded us, "sacking Jerusalem was Titus' sole claim to glory." And that defeat had to be interpreted as an event that had empire-wide implications, not a local disturbance or parochial *seditio*, though many may have viewed it thus. The defeat of the Jews had to become a world event worthy of imperial pursuits and great leaders. This would become the single most prominent argument for Flavian selection, rule, and succession. The Jewish Revolt is transformed from one albeit significant event among many in the career of a would-be ruler (e.g., Vespasian), to the paramount accomplishment of the Flavian line under Titus.

This stage of development is reflected in several ways. The literary record of Flavian clients vigorously fostered this perception. The prooemium of Valerius' *Argonautica* captures this development with this insertion about Titus: "Your son tells of the overthrow of Idume, for he is able, and his brother begrimed with the dust of Jerusalem, scattered firebrands and causing havoc in every turret" (Taylor 1994). And the impact of Josephus himself on this score is not to be overlooked. He was known, or known of, by the leading figures of the Flavian literary circle. Suetonius mentions Josephus by name (*Vespasian* 6), as does Dio, and Titus himself apparently signed Josephus's writings (*Life* 361). Josephus's own account of the siege and surrender of Jerusalem was known to some, and he served as an important historical source not long after the publication of his work. In the emergence of Josephus's renown, there is the following circularity. The Jewish War was a vital part of Flavian policy and propaganda, which grew in importance as the Flavian period unfolded. This in turn increased the importance of Josephus and the value of his writings. Josephus's treatment of the Jewish people, various aspects of the Revolt, and the siege of Jerusalem suited the Flavians well. Vespasian and Titus emerge as the chosen winners of a difficult and protracted campaign. The Revolt is a world-class theological and military struggle. Thus, Josephus's role in the development of Flavian policy is substantial. He was an important source for Flavian and immediate post-Flavian writers who were actively developing the images and narrative around the Revolt which proved so important to the Flavian line.

Flavian building projects also played an important role in emphasizing the magnitude of the Jewish Revolt. First, and not insignificantly, the reconstruction of the Temple of Jupiter Optimus Maxiumus was financed with the *fiscus Judaicus*, the tax imposed on Jews by Vespasian following the Revolt. "All Jews," Josephus wrote, "paid to the Capitoline god what they had previously paid to the Jerusalem temple" (*War* 7.218). Second, there was the Temple of Peace, which was inaugurated in 75 C.E. (Darwall-Smith 1996:

55ff.). Vespasian financed this enormous new project with some of the spoils from the Jerusalem Temple; others were displayed there (*War* 7.159–62). Thus the rewards for the victory over the Jews mingled with the benefits and many guises of the goddess Pax. Finally there was the first Arch of Titus in the Circus Maximus, datable by inscription to 80/81 C.E. (Darwall-Smith 1996: 69).[5] This stood as a dramatic symbol of Roman–Flavian subjugation of the Jewish rebels. These structures sent a single, powerful message promoting the Flavians in their monumental struggle with the Jews on behalf of Rome and Roman imperium.

These developments moved the Jews of Galilee, Judea, and Jerusalem onto a prominent, if not central stage of Roman political and cultural life. By the start of Domitian's reign a struggle that began in Judea during the reign of Nero, and which fortuitously played a role in Vespasian's ascent to the throne, became an event of empire-wide magnitude and importance. I do not believe that Vespasian saw it that way when he left Titus in charge of the Jewish War. He was preoccupied with the dominant event of the day, namely the civil war with Vitellius. But during his rule the victory over the Jews emerged as an important and potent part of Flavian policy and programs, so that by 75 C.E., with the building of the Temple of Peace, the Flavian victory over the Jews was an event owned, as it were, by the entire Roman world. The return of order, imperium, stability, and peace was displayed for all to see.

The last stage in the development of the Flavian program occurred under Domitian. In the program and development described above, Domitian played a secondary role. He did not figure directly in the Jewish defeat, though he was an iconographic part of the Flavian message that stressed Vespasian's heirs and successors. At one point Domitian was said to have been acting so much like the Emperor that Vespasian sent word thanking him for allowing Vespasian to keep his office! Upon his actual succession, however, Domitian not only continued but even augmented Flavian programs and policies. Judea Capta coins continued to be minted and distributed. Most importantly, the succession of monuments linked to the Revolt continued, with the dedication of perhaps the most vivid surviving expression: the Arch of Titus.

The inscription from the Arch of Titus is itself a bold expression of the Flavian propaganda line:

> The Roman Senate and people [dedicate this] to the Emperor Titus Caesar Vespasian Augustus, son of the deified Vespasian, pontifex maximus, holding the tribunician power for the tenth year, acclaimed imperator seventeen times, consul eight times, father of his country, their princeps, because with the guidance and plans of his father, and under his auspices, he subdued the Jewish people and destroyed the city of Jerusalem, which all generals, kings, and peoples before him had either attacked without success or left entirely unassailed.
>
> (CIL VI, no. 994) (Lewis and Reinhold 1990: 15)

This inscription characterizes the victory over the Jews as accomplished by Titus, "with the guidance and plans of his father" as one of the greatest military victories in Rome's history. The Jewish people and the city of Jerusalem combined were one of the most obstinate and difficult of Roman enemies. Many kings and generals, apparently too many to name or count, had failed where Titus had succeeded. The inscription is banking on a short memory on the part of the audience. Even Tacitus recalled Pompey's triumph in Jerusalem (*Histories* 5.9). But this hyperbole helped move the Revolt from a particular event that led to Vespasian's rule to a unifying and remarkable feat for which few parallels existed in Rome's magnificent military and imperial history.

Domitian's own attitude toward the Jews appears to have developed a sharper edge than existed during the reign of his father or brother (on Roman attitudes in the years before and just after the Revolt, see Gruen in this volume). Above all, he was noted for the ferocity with which he collected the Jewish tax (Thompson 1982; Williams 1990), as notably reflected by Suetonius' disturbing and humiliating vignette about the 90-year-old man strip-searched in public because he was suspected of trying to avoid the fiscus (*Domitian* 12). Certainly Suetonius is indicating that Domitian has gone too far with respect to the Jews. The momentum of imperial Roman anti-Judaism had been building in the aftermath of the Revolt, due in large part to the effectiveness and extent of the well orchestrated Flavian program concerning their victory. But even in light of these attitudes, Domitian went too far. This is best indicated by the subsequent actions of Nerva, who removed the *calumnia* of the *fiscus Judaicus*, clearly in response to abuses under Domitian (Goodman 1989). By the time of Nerva's response, however, much damage had been done. Roman attitudes had developed, even hardened.

One final effect of the Flavian program remains to be described. The end-stage of the development described above, from local rebellion to world-renowned victory to specific anti-Judaism, took root within certain circles in early Christianity. Perhaps the most obvious and influential early Christian document in this regard is the Gospel of John. It is here that one reads, for the first time in first and early second-century Christian literature, about "the Jews," whom this author (alone among the Gospel writers) describes as Jesus' opponents (von Wahlde 1981/2; Ashton 1985). It is the *Ioudaioi* who convince Pilate, though he finds him innocent, to put Jesus to death (John 18: 38ff.). But these "Jews" are also portrayed as seditious, schismatics, and, in many respects, a threat to the stability of the nation. While the author is familiar with various Jewish groups (Pharisees, priests, etc.), these blur into one general, and basically negative group. And the depiction of this group in the Fourth Gospel bears some striking and unfortunate similarities to the image of the Jews that had developed by the later Flavian period.

It is the *Ioudaioi* who collectively speak the revealing sentence to Pilate, "if you release this man you are no friend of Caesar; everyone who makes himself out to be a king opposes Caesar" (John 19:12). From a strictly Roman point of view, of course, this makes perfect sense. And "the Jews" are speaking the truth. But this is early Christian, sectarian literature. The audience is not yet the Roman elite. Here the author of the Fourth Gospel has adopted terminology, language, and the general depiction of the Jews in the broader late Flavian culture and employed it for his own purposes. Here "the Jews" are portrayed in a manner that resonates with their depiction in the larger and more popular literary and material scene. They are dishonest and responsible for a lot of trouble, whether it is the destruction of the Temple in Jerusalem or the death of Jesus. Following the resurrection the group behind the Fourth Gospel is hiding in a room, "for fear of the Jews" (John 21:19). With imagery and terminology that would not have been unusual in the broader Roman world at the close of the Flavian period (ca. 100 C.E.), we can see early sectarian Christianity characterizing "Jews" as threats, enemies, and an influence to avoid, if not counter. Such a characterization also moves early, sectarian Christianity another step away from traditional Jewish culture and a step closer to Rome.

This language and attitude, though rooted in an imperial policy to exploit and expand early military success, no matter how parochial, ultimately blossomed into an expansive and explosive early Christian anti-Judaism. Perhaps Domitian and his unnecessary and excessive exploitation of the Jews, Judaism, and the Jewish tax in particular began this process. In any event, by the close of the Flavian period the Jews had moved from a group that represented a local but timely victory for an aspiring Caesar, in a part of the world most Romans knew little about, into a group henceforth depicted as a threat across the whole Roman world.

Notes

1 Dio, curiously, in one place (64.13–14) does not even mention Titus. He simply states that Vespasian "entrusted the war with the Jews to others, he proceeded to Egypt." That Vespasian so quickly leaves the youthful and inexperienced Titus in charge of putting down the Revolt, apparently on the heels of the battle at Jotapata, and leaves for Egypt provides further support for the Revolt as a distraction for Vespasian, and something that he can hardly afford to concentrate on at the time.

2 Valerius in the *Argonautica* (1.5–21) and Josephus (*War* 3.4) add Britain to this list. Smallwood (1962) and Momigliano (1950) both see this as exaggerating the part played by Vespasian in Claudius' campaigns in Britain.

3 As Goodman (1987: 235) observes, there are no Armenia or Brittania Capta coins, for example.

4 The message of the coins is reiterated in bolder relief on the Arch of Isis, built to further celebrate the Flavian victory in Judea (Kleiner 1989: 197).

5 Kleiner (1990) discusses another possible arch of Vespasian, known through coins.

Bibliography

Ashton, J. (1985) "The Identity and Function of the *Ioudaioi* in the Fourth Gospel," *Novus Testamentum* 27: 40–75.

Darwall-Smith, R. H. (1996) *Emperors and Architecture: A Study of Flavian Rome*, Brussels: Latomus.

Edwards, D. (1992) "Religion, Power, and Power Politics: Jewish Defeats by the Romans in Iconography and Josephus," in J. A. Overman and R. S. MacLennan (eds.) *Diaspora Jews and Judaism*, South Florida Studies in the History of Judaism 41, Atlanta: Scholars Press.

Goodman, M. (1987) *The Ruling Class of Judaea*, Cambridge: Cambridge University Press.

—— (1989) "Nerva, the Fiscus Judaicus, and Jewish Identity," *Journal of Roman Studies* 79: 40–4.

Hart, H. St. J. (1952) "Judea and Rome: The Official Commentary," *Journal of Theological Studies* 3: 172–98.

Kleiner, F. S. (1989) "The Study of Roman Triumphal and Honorary Arches Fifty Years after Kaehler," *Journal of Roman Archaeology* 2: 195–206.

—— (1990) "The Arches of Vespasian in Rome," *Mitteilungen des Deutschen Archeologisches Institüt* 97: 127–36.

Lewis, N. and Reinhold, M. (1990) *Roman Civilization* II, 3rd edition, New York: Columbia University Press.

Mattingly, H. (1923) *Coins of the Roman Empire in the British Museum*, London: British Museum.

Meshorer, Y. (1962) "Notes on the Judea Capta coins," *Israel Numismatic Bulletin* 3–4: 98.

Momigliano, A. (1950) "Panagyricus Messalae and Panagyricus Vespasiani: Two References to Britain," *Journal of Roman Studies* 40: 38–45.

Smallwood, E. M. (1962) "Valerius Flaccus' Argonautica I.5–21," *Mnemosyne* 15: 170–2.

Syme, R. (1929) "The *Argonautica* of Valerius Flaccus," *Classical Quarterly* 23: 135–6.

Taylor, P. R. (1994) "Valerius' Flavian *Argonautica*," *Classical Quarterly* 44: 212–35.

Thompson, L. (1982) "Domitian and the Jewish Tax," *Historia* 31: 329–42.

von Wahlde, U. C. (1981/2) "The Johanine 'Jews': A Critical Survey," *New Testament Studies* 28: 33–60.

Williams, M. (1990) "Domitian, the Jews, and the Judaizers: A Simple Matter of Cupidas or Maiestas?" *Historia* 39: 196–211.

14 Good from evil

The rabbinic response

Anthony J. Saldarini

Introduction

Historical narratives, processes, and even facts do not exist in nature, waiting
for recognition. Rather, we shape phenomena into facts, relate them to one
another in patterned ways and construct intelligible narratives that make
sense out of human actions. Was World War II in Europe, commonly praised
in the United States as a good, just war, a great victory over a brutal, geno-
cidal, fascist dictatorship; or was it just one of a series of nineteenth- and
twentieth-century wars that weakened and dismantled the European empires
in favor of nation states? Was World War II the start of a great American
economic and military empire that finally defeated the Soviet empire and
contained the emerging Chinese empire; or did World War II begin a
fragmentation and dissolution of the world into warring nations and ethnic
groups, a bloody process which continues resolutely and tragically in the
present?

How do we name wars? Was the war in 66–70 C.E. a revolt or a justified
war against Rome? The war in Palestine in 1948 is called the War of
Independence by Israeli Jews who founded the State of Israel and the
Catastrophe by Palestinian Arabs who lost the war. In the United States
Northerners call the war from 1861 to 1865 the Civil War because they
judge that the southern states illegally revolted against the federal government. Southerners call it the War Between the States, understanding it as a
war in which the southern states defended their constitutional autonomy
against intrusive control by a northern-dominated, industrially driven
government.

Was the war against Rome in 66–70 C.E. an heroic struggle for independence, a vain but worthwhile sacrifice for the integrity of the land and people
of Israel? Was it an imprudent, arrogant flouting of God's will? Was it
a human disaster or a divine punishment or an accident of irrational fate?
We construct answers to these questions and argue for them on the basis of
empirical facts, philosophical understandings of human society and religiously
based convictions concerning divine activity in the world. Even though we
stress data, analysis, argument, and a self-conscious interpretive perspective

(often named "objective"), we interpret strongly when we write history. We adjudicate conflicting evidence, resolve disputes, and in the end support certain principles, values, and understandings of humans and society to the detriment of others. We imagine ourselves as neutral and reasonable, but how many of us can give an open-minded, serious and rational defense of monarchy? Greco-Roman historians also wrote with firm assumptions and goals guiding their constructions of historical narratives. Thus recent scholarship has increasingly uncovered and critically assessed Josephus's world-view, biases, and authorial goals rather than taking his account as simply factual.

Rabbinic literature on the Revolt

Rabbinic literature challenges historians because the rabbinic authors did not write histories in the Greco-Roman mode. They firmly subordinated historical events to their own legal and exegetical agenda. They referred to the two destructions of the Temple (586 B.C.E. and 70 C.E.) frequently because they could not ignore Jerusalem and the Temple, which were securely implanted in the center of their sacred texts, cultural imagination and intellectual world. Thus Jerusalem and the Temple lived on as enduring literary, intellectual, and emotional artifacts after 70 C.E., but in a wide variety of contexts.

In the last twenty-five years a number of articles have surveyed rabbinic responses to the destruction of the Second Temple, some of them focused on rabbinic thought and others on the historicity of rabbinic accounts (Baer 1971; Neusner 1970a, 1972; N. G. Cohen 1972; Saldarini 1975; N. G. Cohen 1976; Goldenberg 1977; Allon 1977; Schäfer 1979; Stone 1981; Saldarini 1982; Halevi 1982; S. J. D. Cohen 1982; Bokser 1983; Visotzky 1983; Kirschner 1985; Price 1992; Rubenstein 1997).[1] Without trying to summarize all these contributions to the rabbinic views of the war, I will list some of the themes that appear in rabbinic literature, before concentrating on the limited theme of this study.

The rabbis frequently followed the prophetic tradition in attributing the destruction of the Temple to Israel's sins. The variety of sins invoked in different contexts testifies more to the rabbis' later concerns about observance of Torah than to events at the time of the war. Some materials, especially a long series in Babylonian Talmud *Gittin* 55b–59a, blame the war and destruction on a lack of strong rabbinic leadership. Disunity in Israel, lack of communal care for one another, misuse of wealth, and other social ills also explained the loss of sovereignty and city. The sages saw the effects of the war as impoverishment, devastation of lives and property, oppression, suffering, and death. Frequently, rather than try to explain Israel's suffering, they lamented it or told stories about God, the angels and historical figures mourning the loss of the Temple and Jerusalem. The loss of the Temple caused a crisis in communication with God. Various passages argue that prayer and good deeds substitute for Temple sacrifices and atonement. In response rabbinic authors promoted study, interpretation and observance of the law as the way forward for the Jewish community. These themes and concerns appear in halachic discussions, Scriptural exegeses, and numerous well-known stories concerning the war, the siege of Jerusalem, and Roman power and oppression under Vespasian and Titus.

Economics

I have chosen to expound one thematic thread from rabbinic comments on the first war against Rome: economics. This topic needs a brief explanation to avoid gross anachronism. A free-standing economics is a modern master category. We see economics as a key to political society and all of its activities including war. Modern analysis of war stresses military tactics and heroic bravery less than in the past in favor of the industrial strength necessary to produce weapons, the logistical planning and transportation needed to provide supplies, and the technological innovations that produce superior weapons with the greatest effective firepower. Here I use economics as a category to highlight a set of concerns that remain subordinate in rabbinic comments on the war with Rome. Various stories alternately praise, blame, admire, and pity the wealthy inhabitants of Jerusalem who either sought to save Israel with their wealth or caused the destruction by their callous behavior. The rabbis contrasted wealth with its loss to communicate the horror of the war and also to devalue wealth in favor of the permanence of Torah. Though these stories do not tell us what happened historically in Jerusalem, they reflect ancient interpretations of the war against Rome and its consequences for society.

When the rabbis speak of the war with Rome, including its economic causes and consequences, some of their language and their typologies of war, siege, and defeat come from Biblical and Greco-Roman literature. Famine, starvation, desperate attempts to escape, foolhardy sorties, horrible suffering, cannibalism, siege machines, fire, destruction, and enslavement—all of which were the variable realities of siege warfare—took on a stereotyped life of their own in ancient literature.[2] Unlike many Greco-Roman historians, the rabbis did not focus on the power politics of empires. Herodotus chronicled the wars between the Greeks and Persians and Thucydides the rival imperial coalitions of the Athenians and Spartans. Not so the rabbis. The central Biblical symbols of the land and people of Israel, Jerusalem and the Temple, God and God's mercy and justice toward Israel dominate traditional evaluations of the war with Rome and its consequences.

Wealthy Jerusalemites during the Revolt

The rabbinic tradition associates three wealthy, influential community leaders ("great ones" or nobles) with pre-war Jerusalem and uses them, their wealth, and their families in stories about the war. The three men carry symbolic names (Ben Kalba' Sabua', Ben Sisit Hakkeset, and Naqdimon ben Gurion) that suggest they constitute a typical folkloric triad. Two sources interpret the name Ben Kalba' Sabua', literally "the son of the satisfied dog," to mean that a person who entered his house hungry as a dog came out satisfied (BT *Gittin* 56a; *ARNA*). The second rich man's name comes in two versions: Ben Sisit Hakkeset, literally "the son of the fringes of the cushion," or Ben Sisit Hakkesep, literally "the son of the fringes of silver" (so Finkelstein 1950: 135). Fringes are the threads at the corners of garments mandated by Scripture (Numbers 1.5.37–40). The first version of the name may refer to long, luxurious fringes trailing on the cushions as this leader reclined and presided at meals (BT *Gittin* 56a). The second version may refer to a silver couch on which he reclined (*ARNA* 6). Naqdimon ben Gurion's name does not refer to wealth directly but to the shining (*nqd*) of the sun in a miracle story in which his wealth increased (*ARNA* 6; BT *Gittin* 56a).[3] All in all these three characters bear improbable names with improbable origins that fittingly match the improbably great wealth assigned to them in the tradition.

In *ARNA* and *ARNB* these three rich men appear as part of a holiday assembly presided over by Johanan ben Zakkai in Jerusalem during the pre-war period (*ARNA* 6; *ARNB* 13). Johanan calls upon his student, Eliezer ben Hyrcanus, to instruct the assembly. As a result of Eliezer's successful teaching, his father, who has come to disinherit him for abandoning the family farm, instead accepts him as an accomplished teacher. The presence of the three rich men, referred to as "great ones," at the public instruction impresses Eliezer's father and testifies to his son's publicly honored position as teacher. These stories and others assume and build on the wealth, power, and social position of Ben Kalbha' Sabua', Naqdimon ben Gurion, and Ben Sisit Hakkesep, or perhaps better use them to typify the governing class in Jerusalem. In this case they appear in a positive light according to the rabbinic code: they observe a festival by learning Torah under the guidance of eminent rabbinic teachers. In other cases they and their families will he judged negatively.

The three rich Jerusalemite leaders also appear in a positive light during the siege of Jerusalem by the Romans. A tradition found in three extended versions (*ARNA* 6; *ARNB* 13; BT *Gittin* 56a) attributes Jerusalem's food supplies, which were sufficient to withstand the human siege, to Ben Kalba' Sabua' or to the three rich men as a group. Underlying this tradition are the cultural assumptions that material abundance in a society of limited goods must come from the wealthy members of society and that the rich should provide for society at large during a time of critical need. According to the story in *ARNA* 6, Ben Kalba' Sabua' not only had enough food to supply each person in Jerusalem for twenty-two years, but he had the food prepared and sorted for distribution and consumption.[4] However, his civic responsibility and generosity were rejected by the Zealots, who burned his supplies. A brief (and more sober) notice in *ARNB* 13 says that Ben Kalba' Sabua' had sufficient supplies to feed Jerusalem for three years. The Babylonian Talmud (*Gittin* 56a) credits the three wealthy leaders as a group with furnishing supplies sufficient for twenty-one years. Two later sources, *Lamentations Rabbati* (1:5 [31]) and *Qohelet Rabah* (7:12) attribute to them sufficient food for ten years.[5]

Parallel to the stories of the three rich men are a set of stories that cast rich women in a negative light. *Mishnah Ketubot* 5:8 and *Tosefta Ketubot* 5:8 specify the kind of support, that is, food, clothing, etc., a husband must provide his wife. *Tosefta* 5:9 then articulates a principle that protects the woman's claim on her husband's assets: "If he gets rich, she goes up with him, but if he becomes poor, she does not go down with him." That is, if the husband's income increases, the level of her maintenance should increase. If the husband's income drops, he must still give her the minimum amount of food and clothing required by her marriage contract. To illustrate an increase in wealth the *Tosefta* cites a story concerning the daughter of Naqdimon ben Gurion, one of the three wealthy Jerusalem leaders. Though she was only a bereaved, childless sister-in-law awaiting levirite marriage (Deuteronomy 25.5–10), her late husband's estate had to provide her with five hundred gold denars a day to buy spices. This extraordinarily large amount of money greatly exceeds the cost of a day's food.[6] The highly exaggerated story supports the wife's right to a portion of her husband's assets even in the most extreme cases of abundant wealth.

The *Tosefta*'s anecdote, however, criticizes excessive wealth through the intemperate reaction of Naqdimon's daughter to the sages' judgment in her favor. She curses them for their stinginess (in awarding her *only* five hundred gold denars a day for spices) and wishes a similar unsatisfactory settlement on the sages' own daughters. The gap between her self-centered, unrealistic dissatisfaction with her spice account and the meager daily wages and food budgets of the majority of the population produces a horrified response from *Tosefta*'s authorship and generates a story of her final state of abject poverty after the war against Rome (JT *Ketubot* 5.10, treated below, p. 226).

The Palestinian Talmud preserves two variants of *Tosefta*'s story of Naqdimon's daughter in which the young woman has the name Miriam (JT *Ketubot* 5.13 [30b–c]). In one story Miriam is the daughter of Simon ben Gurion and receives the daily five hundred denar spice fund.[7] In the other Miriam is the daughter of Boethus and receives two seah's (over twenty gallons) of wine daily. In both versions the rabbis respond ironically to Miriam's curse by saying Amen to her wish that their daughters too receive five hundred gold denars daily for spices (this comment also appears in BT *Ketubot* 66b in the story about Naqdimon's daughter). This sarcastic comment about her foolish and frivolous complaint about an outrageously generous settlement encapsulates popular resentment toward the very rich. The choice of a woman protagonist also activates the cultural stereotype of women as silly, superficial, and unable to provide for themselves. In addition the story prepares the way for criticism of her father, Naqdimon ben Gurion.

The impoverished rich woman

The stories of the frivolities of the rich woman provide for stories of her impoverishment after the war against Rome. The story occurs in nine variant versions in different contexts. Its ubiquity testifies to popular resentment against the rich, to the tendency to blame and make examples of women rather than men, and to a historical dread associated with the loss of Jerusalem and the Temple. Three versions of the story identify the destitute rich woman as Naqdimon's daughter (Sifre Deuteronomy 305; BT *Ketubot* 66–67a; *ARNA* 17) and blame her impoverishment in the war on the misuse of wealth. As told in *ARNA*, the story stands within a context that stresses keeping the commandments. It is associated with two other stories about captive young women and with an interpretation of the *Song of Songs* 1: 8 that obliquely points to the rich woman's fault.[8] Rabban Johanan ben Zakkai sees a young woman picking barley grains from under the feet of Arab cattle (implicitly, from their dung) and asks her who she is.[9] She resists telling him who she is and covers herself with her hair (presumably because she has inadequate clothing to be modest). Finally she admits that she is Naqdimon's daughter. To Johanan's inquiry concerning her father's house she quotes a proverb that indicates that he did not give alms to the poor and so lost his wealth, presumably in the war.[10] The ostentatious display of wealth is also implicitly cited as a cause for its loss. The young woman reminds Johanan that he signed her marriage contract. Johanan tells his disciples that her dowry was the extravagant sum of a million gold denars and that her household had luxurious woolen carpets laid out for them to walk on when they went to the Temple. The versions of the story in BT *Ketubot* and Sifre Deuteronomy have the same observations.

The versions of the destitute woman story which follow the stories of the daughter of Naqdimon, Miriam daughter of Simon ben Gurion and Miriam daughter of Boethus (analyzed above) have Eleazar ben Sadok testify that he saw the formerly rich woman picking up barley beneath the hooves of horses (i.e., from their dung) in Acco (JT *Ketubot* 5.10; *pesher Ketubot* 5:13 [30b–c]) or with her hair tied to the horse's tail (*pesher Ketubot*, second story).[11] Several of the versions link the story to subtle exegeses of *Song of Songs* 1.8, concerning the young woman who does not "know," and Deuteronomy 28.56, concerning the horrors of siege, to provide justification for the impoverishment of the wealthy as a punishment.[12]

In the most general sense the authors of these stories all emphasize the disastrous results of the war with Rome by concentrating on the wealthy because they had the most material goods and the most power to lose. They emphatically illustrate the change in the economic, social, and political power and influence of all Israel after their defeat. The authors also blame the wealthy for Israel's defeat because they stand out from society as its leaders and bear responsibility for society as a whole, according to the common view. This censure is not unanimous, however. The Babylonian Talmud *Ketubot*

(66b–67a) records the traditional censure of Naqdimon ben Gurion for ostentatious display of wealth and for failing to give adequate alms to the poor, but tries to turn his practices into an act of charity. Naqdimon was so rich that he flamboyantly placed rugs on the street to the Temple so that his family's feet would not touch the urban mud and filth when they went to worship (cf. Deuteronomy 28.56: "She who is the most refined and gentle among you, so gentle and refined that she does not venture to set the sole of her foot on the ground ..."). One talmudic commentator claims that Naqdimon allowed the poor to take the rugs, presumably to sell for food, after he had walked by on them. But two other commentators object that alms should not be given with such public fanfare and that the gift of the rugs was an insufficient gift to the poor, granted his great wealth.

These folk stories do not provide reliable historical data on the actions of the wealthy leaders of Jerusalem at the time of the siege. The very names of the three wealthy Jerusalemites seem to be symbolic and the stories of their wealth and activities heightened to legendary proportions. The differing versions of the story of the rich young woman impoverished after the war testify to a literary type adapted to different circumstances rather than to an historical character or event. Though these stories most probably lack an historical kernel, they reflect popular cultural views of the resources and responsibilities as well as the failings and sad end of the wealthy under wartime conditions. In ancient history and biography the actions and experiences of powerful and wealthy kings, leaders, adventures, warriors, and heroes epitomize human life on a large scale. The rabbinic authors could thus use the wealthy as prominent case studies and moral examples for Israel as a whole and interpret the war through their (literary) experiences.

Starvation during the siege of Jerusalem

A number of passages in rabbinic literature describe the horrible suffering of the people of Jerusalem because of the lack of food during the siege. In general the same literary conventions to describe sieges, starvation, and the consequent breakdown of social order and personal morality appear in Biblical, Greco-Roman, and rabbinic literature. The curses against a disobedient Israel in Deuteronomy (28.52–8) and Leviticus (26.27–33) include descriptions of starvation and sufferings during a siege, for example:

> Even the most refined and gentle of men among you will begrudge food to his own brother, to the wife whom he embraces, and to the last of his remaining children, giving to none of them any of the flesh of his children whom he is eating, because nothing else remains to him, in the desperate straits to which the enemy siege will reduce you in all your towns.
>
> (Deuteronomy 28.54–5)

The story of Ben Hadad's siege of Samaria (2 Kings 6.24) includes the case of a starving mother eating her son and Jeremiah prophesies a siege of Jerusalem marked by cannibalism (19.6–9). In the New Testament Matthew's parable of the royal wedding feast (22.1–14) contains an oddly extreme response by both those invited and the king who invited them. Some of the invitees who reject the king's wedding invitation "seized [the king's] slaves, mistreated them, and killed them." The enraged king "sent his troops, destroyed those murderers, and burned their city." The author of Matthew, who wrote in the late first century C.E., alludes to the destruction of Jerusalem using typical language and patterns from the Biblical tradition (Davies and Allison 1988–97: volume 3, 201–2). The author of the Gospel of Luke also describes the destruction of Jerusalem through Jesus' lament over Jerusalem:

> As [Jesus] came near and saw the city [Jerusalem], he wept over it, saying ... "Indeed, the days will come upon you, when the enemies will set up ramparts around you and surround you, and hem you in on every side. They will crush you to the ground, you and your children within you, and they will not leave within you one stone upon another."
>
> (Luke 19.43–4)

The language of this lament does not specifically describe the siege of Jerusalem, as recounted by Josephus, but uses standard Biblical language from the Septuagint, a feature typical of Luke (Fitzmyer 1981–5: volume 2, 1254–5). Even Josephus, who was a witness to the siege of Jerusalem, uses the typical language and themes associated with sieges in previous literature. Jonathan Price has analyzed all the famine passages in Josephus's *War* and concludes that Josephus places them in the narrative where they support his interpretation and elaborates them to fit in with his thematic development of the breakdown of Judean society (Price 1992: 141–71, 271–80). Thus Josephus, like all the other sources available, must be interpreted with a sharp critical eye. The rabbinic accounts of the siege in general and of famine and starvation as its major consequence fit smoothly into the ancient Hebrew and Greco-Roman traditions.

Both Josephus's description of the war and the rabbinic traditions of the three rich men, Ben Kalba' Sabua', Naqdimon ben Gurion, and Ben Sisit Hakkesep, agree that Jerusalem had sufficient supplies to endure a long siege. They also agree that the militants leading the fight destroyed those supplies. Josephus attributes the destruction of the supplies to civil war among the factions in Jerusalem, but his bias against the leaders of the Revolt against Roman authority and his highly charged rhetoric probably obscure the particularities of the conflicts.[13]

ARNB 7 understands the leaders of the resistance in Jerusalem to be a unified group that it identifies with the name *Sicarii* (*syqryn*). They order the destruction of the supplies in Jerusalem "to leave no means of sustenance." Since the next sentence says that the people of Jerusalem used to boil straw, drink its broth, go out to fight the Romans and slaughter them, *ARNB* seems to interpret the *Sicarii*'s destruction of food supplies as a tactic to promote desperate, vigorous combat against superior forces.[14] The authors of *ARNB* argue for the success of the *Sicarii*'s plan by noting that the Jewish forces killed many Romans in battle even though they were outnumbered. The authors also cite the testimony of Vespasian who monitored the progress of the famine according to the lack of grain in the excrement of the people of Jerusalem and marveled at the fighting ability of Jerusalem's defenders even as they were starving. Vespasian exhorted his troops to resist Jerusalem's starving fighters by speculating how formidable they would be if they had sufficient food and drink.

ARNA 6 preserves a variant account of the siege that is less coherent and in a different literary context than the one in *ARNB*. Ben Kalba' Sabua' protests that the Zealots (*qn'ym*) are destroying the city for twenty-two years. The text does not give the Zealots' motive for destroying Jerusalem's food supplies. Rather, it describes the desperation of the people in a series of three vignettes: the people hide loaves of bread in walls by plastering them over with clay; they boiled straw and ate it; and the guards on the wall ambushed Romans and brought back their heads to receive a food reward of a date per head. The account ends with Vespasian's amazement at how well the Jerusalemites fight without proper nourishment.

These rabbinic stories about starvation and heroic resistance in Jerusalem under siege reflect later reactions to the war against Rome. The rabbis tended to idealize Jerusalem as a strong, wealthy, and beautiful city. Consequently, they had to account for its conquest by the Romans by a variety of means. The military might of Rome (a motive for Johanan ben Zakkai's abandonment of Jerusalem) and God's punishment of Jerusalem for its sins are two common explanations. In addition, the sages probably had heard traditional oral accounts of factional fighting in Jerusalem of the type recounted in Josephus's histories. Using traditional language and stereotypes of siege warfare they attributed Jerusalem's ultimate weakness to the self-destructive behavior of the leaders. In doing so they defended God's power against any assault and reduced the importance of the military power of the Romans. They also honored the memory of the combatants by recruiting the enemy general, Vespasian, to praise the defenders' bravery and effectiveness.

The Babylonian Talmud tractate *Gittin* 55b–57a has the largest and most well-articulated collection of traditions concerned with the war with Rome and the destruction of Jerusalem. In an earlier review I isolated some of the themes running through the stories and comments collected there, including "God's control over events, the lesser importance of human actions, the rabbi's authority and responsibility for the survival of Judaism, and Israel's ultimate victory over her enemies even though the Temple and Jerusalem have been lost" (Saldarini 1982). The recent study by Jeffrey Rubenstein (1997) has elaborated on the Babylonian Talmud's criticism of the rabbis for not acting decisively to prevent the war and its subtle defense of the later rabbis' legislative authority for the sake of giving the Jewish community decisive leadership. Here we will concentrate on the stories concerned with starvation and the wealthy.

The Babylonian Talmud *Gittin*'s treatment of starvation during the siege is more elaborate than in the two versions of the Fathers According to rabbi Nathan. A large section of BT *Gittin* 55a–56a turns on the starvation theme. The war against Rome arises from a trivial error in a banquet invitation (sent to Bar Qamsa' rather than Qamsa'). The host dishonors Bar Qamsa' whom he does not like by refusing to seat him at the banquet table. As a result Bar Qamsa' turns informer to the Romans and begins the chain of events that lead to the war. As an ironic result, this one act of inhospitality at a public meal causes the entire population of Jerusalem to starve during the siege. The Talmud also uses the stories of the three rich men, Ben Kalba' Sabua', Naqdimon ben Gurion, and Ben Sisit Hakkesep, to explain the fall of Jerusalem and criticize its leaders. These men had enough supplies to survive a 21-year siege and thus frustrate a Roman conquest. With Jerusalem's strength as a bargaining point the rabbis wished to negotiate a compromise settlement with the Romans. The revolutionary leaders, the *baryoni*, rejected their plan and rendered that option of negotiation moot by destroying the food supplies.[15] Thus the only alternative was for people to fight the Romans (cf. *ARNB* discussed above, pp. 228–9). The Talmudic version of the burning of the food supplies treats the revolutionary leaders as destructive, the rabbinic leaders as well intentioned but ineffective, and the loss of the food as fatal to the city.

The two stories that follow the loss of the food supplies elaborate on its effects. The death of a rich woman, Martha daughter of Boethus, epitomizes the suffering of the population and the dangerous escape of Johanan ben Zakkai from the starving city "to save a little" highlights the hopelessness of a starving Jerusalem and the need for a new initiative. Martha daughter of Boethus is one of the richest women in Jerusalem.[16] Her story coheres thematically with the stories about the three rich men of Jerusalem treated previously and with the story of the impoverishment of the daughter of Naqdimon ben Gurion after the destruction of Jerusalem. Just as her great wealth did not save her from starvation and death, the rich men's supplies of food did not save the people of Jerusalem from starvation and defeat. The repetitive tempo of the story highlights the continuous desperation caused by famine. Four times Martha sends her servant to buy flour of decreasingly lower grades (from fine flour to barley) and each time it is sold out. Finally she goes out herself and meets her end from an enigmatic cause, either from dung sticking to her foot or from consuming a fig that had already been sucked dry. (Both these causes for her death allude to other texts, the Bible in one case, and a story about Rabbi Sadoq in the other.)[17] The story depicts Martha as an overly delicate, sheltered, wealthy woman who deals ineffectively with famine by seeking only fine flour at first instead of any food to stay alive, who is overwhelmed in some way when she personally goes in search of food, and who realizes only too late the limits of her wealth when she throws her gold and silver into the street saying, "What is the good of this." The Talmudic commentator adds an appropriate verse (*Ezekial* 7.19), which predicts that the wealth of the rich in Jerusalem will not save them from destruction nor preserve them from hunger.

Martha's story undercut the cultural expectation that wealth would provide a level of security not available to the poor. Jonathan Price notes that during sieges the rich and powerful often had access to essential resources, especially food, while the poor and powerless did not and so starved. However, according to the Talmud the siege and destruction at Jerusalem was so horrible it affected everyone. The Talmud uses the extreme case of Martha daughter of Boethus as a paradigm for the suffering and deaths of all the population of Jerusalem. In depicting Martha negatively it implicitly supports the traditional theology that suffering is a punishment for sin, in this case, overdependence on wealth.

In contrast to Martha, Johanan ben Zakkai escapes from besieged Jerusalem through an intelligent ruse, not by an ineffective reliance on wealth and power. As a result he "saves a little." The famine and starvation themes associated with the siege of Jerusalem motivate Johanan's actions just as they did Martha's and before that those of the three rich men, but with different results. Johanan sends for his nephew, Abba Siqra', the head of the *baryoni*.[18] When Johanan rebukes his nephew for killing everyone by starvation, Abba Siqra' pleads that he is powerless to influence his group. Johanan then demands that Abba Siqra' devise a plan to get him out of Jerusalem, which he does by having Johanan pretend to sicken and die. The Talmudic authors repeat the starvation and death themes, but with a hopeful twist: Johanan uses the deception to escape death and start a school to carry on the Torah tradition. Johanan faces reality much more quickly and forthrightly than the leaders of the Revolt or Martha daughter of Boethus with the result that he saves his own life and serves the best interests of Israel as well.

Conclusion

The rabbis responded to Rome's conquest of Israel, the destruction of the Temple and Jerusalem, and the termination of Israel's limited political and social autonomy within the empire with a variety of stories, Scriptural exegeses, theological explanations, and ethical theories. They wrote history in a way we do not. Rather than produce orderly accounts of past events with attention to temporal and causal links among them, they referred to those events, usually briefly, in a variety of literary contexts over several centuries. A full examination of their views would require tracing dozens of interwoven strands of tradition through generations and understanding each expression within its literary and social context. Neither Greco-Roman histories nor Near Eastern chronicles appealed to the sages. For them stories of events and reflections on Israel's defeats and disasters served the goals of legal discussions, Scriptural interpretation, and moral instructions.

All this sounds foreign to modern history, until we look carefully at what we actually do. As I pointed out in the beginning of this study and as contemporary studies of historiography have demonstrated, the questions we ask as historians, the data we choose to address, and the methods we develop in our work all serve to further diverse research goals. We often hide these goals from one another under the cloak of objectivity and fact, but they motivate each of us differently and move us in various directions governed by our politics, social policies, religious views, and philosophies of life.

To understand how the sages interpreted the war let us begin with what they did *not* do in their stories about starvation. They did not blame the lack of food in Jerusalem on the most obvious culprits, the Romans, who had stopped shipments of food from the outside by their siege. They blamed their own revolutionary leaders for irrational or imprudent leadership. The leadership's desire to be completely free of Roman rule brought disaster on Israel. They may have been led to this conclusion by the kinds of traditions that appeared in Josephus.[19] Whether the sages had direct contact with Josephus remains in dispute, but oral traditions concerning factional fighting in Jerusalem probably informed their accounts of the war. The rabbis also accepted the Biblical view that Jerusalem, which God had promised to protect, could only fall by its own misdeeds. Thus, lying behind the stories of the burning of Jerusalem's food supplies lies the assumption that God had to empower a foreign nation, such as Rome, to conquer Israel as a punishment for Israel's sins. In this case God worked through the actions of Israel. Jerusalem, which was strong enough to withstand a Roman siege, destroyed its own food to enable the Romans to conquer it.

The rabbis' evaluation of the wealthy families in Jerusalem and of wealth itself is complex. They praised the three wealthy leaders of Jerusalem, Ben Kalba' Sabua', Ben Sisit Hakkeset, and Naqdimon ben Gurion, for generously providing supplies that could have sustained Jerusalem during the Roman siege. They also attacked members of these families, especially Naqdimon ben Gurion's, for misusing wealth for display and for failing to give adequate support to the poor. Finally, after the food reserves in Jerusalem had been burned, the rabbis stressed the inability of wealth to save the rich from death. Though this perspective may seem banal, it contradicts a common ancient experience, reflected in the text of Josephus. During sieges the rich and powerful typically accumulated and controlled food and security resources for their own survival while the poor suffered famine and starvation (Price 1992: 147). But since Jerusalem was doomed by divine decree, and not just by the vagaries of politics, not even wealth could prevent starvation and death.

The rabbis sympathetically depict the sufferings of the starving populace of Jerusalem, as do many other siege accounts. They also treat the death of Martha daughter of Boethus and the impoverishment of the wealthy young woman after the siege with some reflective concern. Other traditions not reviewed here condemn the Romans as the destroyers of Jerusalem who cause so much suffering for Israel. Though Vespasian is sometimes portrayed as an empathetic figure, as when he praises the fortitude and bravery of the defenders of Jerusalem, the rabbinic traditions sternly judged both him and especially his son Titus for destroying the Temple.[20] Yet for all their anger at Rome the sages engaged in no systemic critique of the empire, perhaps for two reasons: empire had been the dominant form of government in the Near East for centuries, and they had to live under the Roman empire—or, in Babylon, under the Sassanian empire.

In general the rabbis related their remarks about the war with Rome to their intellectual and communal interests. They did not praise the heroic exploits of the defenders of Jerusalem the way 2 Maccabees praised the resistance of the pious to Antiochus IV nor did they comment on imperial tactics and policy the way Josephus did. Jerusalem and the Temple, the suffering and starvation of the people, the moral relationships binding people within the community, and most especially Torah—these subjects interested the rabbis because these subjects had value in their symbolic world. In the stories about Johanan ben Zakkai, the rabbis derived good from evil: the frequently recounted story of Johanan's escape allows for the foundation of the rabbinic school that eventually restores the study of Torah and produces the Mishnah and Talmuds. Much else about the war did not relate to their symbolic world and so did not arouse their interest.

Notes

1 Many other books have incidental or substantial contributions to make to this area of inquiry. The classic work of Derenbourg (1867) was the pioneer in linking rabbinic sources to Josephus and Greco-Roman history. But it, along with articles like Herr's (1971) are uncritical by contemporary standards.

2 Compare the impact of war typologies on the New Testament parable of the invitations to the wedding banquet in Rengstorf 1960.

3 *ARNB* 13 may imply that Naqdimon's "garden of gold" (decorated with gold in some way?) shone like the sun. Naqdimon's name appears in several variants in the manuscripts. See, for example, the textual variants for *Genesis Rabbah* 41.1 (p. 298 in Theodor-Albeck's edition).

4 Twenty-two is a round number corresponding to the number of letters in the Hebrew alphabet and the number of books in the Bible (if Lamentations is counted as part of Jeremiah and Ezra-Nehemiah as one book). A number of lists consequently have twenty-two items. See Ginsberg volume 7 1909–28, 1939: 483–84 (cited by Goldin *ad loc.* in his translation of *ARNA*).

5 *Lamentations Rabbati* 1.5 splits Naqdimon ben Gurio's name into two, Ben Naqdimon and Ben Gurion, and thus refers to four counselors (*bwlytn*, from Greek *bouleutes*) in Jerusalem.

6 Five hundred denars or denarii equal 250 shekels (Sperber 1974). Prices are notoriously hard to pin down. But, as an example, a pound of meat, a two-pound loaf of bread, and a pint of wine probably cost about the same. Sperber estimates their cost as eight silver dinars each (115). One gold denar would buy ten ordinary bottles of wine (103).

7 Naqdimon ben Gurion's name varies in the tradition. Saul Lieberman (1967: 270, n. 40) notes that Naqdimon is also called Simon, Joseph, and Buni.

8 *Song of Songs* 1.8 says, "If you do not know, O fairest among women, follow the tracks of the flock." In *ARNA* 17 Johanan ben Zakkai understands the verse to refer to lack of knowledge (and observance) of the law by the rich which results in their following the tracks of animals, that is, picking up their dung.

9 In this tradition the woman is a *rîbah*, that is, a maiden or young woman. In the stories of the frivolous rich woman in JT *Ketubot* and *pesher Ketubot* analyzed above (pp. 266–7) the woman was a widow awaiting levirite marriage. In BT *Ketubot* 66b and Sifre Deuteronomy 305 the young woman approaches Johanan and asks for food.

10 The proverb is "the salt (*melah*) is diminution (*haser* or *heser*)" or, in an alternate version "loving kindness (*hesed*)."

11 *Mekilta de Rabbi Ishmael*, Bahodesh 1, *Lamentations Rabbati* 1.47–48, and *Pesikta Rabbati* 29/30B.4 (Friedmann edition, p. 140; Braude translation, p. 589) have other versions of the story. Mekilta has an unnamed young woman picking barley out of the dung of an Arab's horse.

12 Deuteronomy 28.52–57 specifies the hardships of siege; vs. 56 speaks of a refined and gentle woman who is most probably wealthy.

13 See, for example, *War* 5.21–38. Josephus's extravagent rhetoric against the revolutionaries reveals his strong bias against the war. His account and evaluation of the factional leaders can hardly be taken at face value. For Josephus's account of the famine see also *War* 5.424–39, 512–21, 6.193–219. See Price 1992: 105–15 for a critical review of the sources.

14 Price (1992: 105, n. 10) distrusts this explanation for the burning of the food supplies and attributes it to in-fighting for power among rival groups in Jerusalem. Baer (1971) criticizes more generally and more severely Josephus's account and evaluation of the leaders of the war for being biased, distorted, and unreliable. He considers the rabbinic accounts of the siege to be based on Josephus and later legends and thus inaccurate. Baer himself writes a post-World War II apologetic for those who resisted destructive imperial power.

15 Jastrow Dictionary: 193 suggests that a *biryon* is a palace guard (cf. *birah*, meaning "castle," "fort," etc.) and that *baryona'/biryona'* means an outlaw or highwayman (cf. *bar/bara'* referring to what is outside). Under the influence of Josephus the word is often translated as rebel. For other derivations see Hengel 1989: 53–6. Urbach 1979: volume 2, 959–60, n. 40 argues for an origin in *biryah*, the word for creature or human being, but with a pejorative, diminutive ending suggesting that the biryoni are less than human. Rubenstein (1997) suggests the translation "thugs."

16 N. G. Cohen (1976) identifies Martha bat Boethus with the wife of the high priest Joshua ben Gamla (named without his wife in *Ant.* 15.20, 20.213) on the basis of a series of rabbinic passages (eg., *Mishnah Yebamot* 6.4, JT *Kippurim* 1.13–14). Ilan (1997: 88–97) demonstrates that in the early sources Martha is presented positively as a rich Jerusalem leader, but in the Babylonian Talmud and later sources was transformed into a selfish, evil, rich widow. Visotzky (1983) argues that this story is the originating and generative story for the various versions of the stories of the impoverished rich woman. However his case depends on the doubtful assumptions that early stories are less elaborate than later stories and that stories such as these begin with a Scriptural exegesis and

later assimilate folk themes. In the development of tradition the process of growth often moves in the opposite direction, so that stories begin with elaborate themes and plots that are later streamlined and provided with Scriptural warrants by authors seeking to make some specific point. Ilan (1997: 94) argues that the Babylonian story is late and that Martha's name has been inserted into the story late in its development.

17 See N. G. Cohen (1976) and Visotzky (1983) for speculation on the story behind the story. Their attempts to connect the story to the story of the woman who eats her own child in Josephus (*War* 6.197–212), supported by Ilan (1997: 93), lack convincing evidence. See Pesikta Rabbati 29 (Friedmann ed. 136b–137a, Braude translation 563–4) for an explicit story of cannibalism.

18 *Sqr'* is probably a variant referring to the Sicarii (Rubenstein 1997: 32). *Qoheleth Rabbati* 7.12 and *Lamentations Rabbati* 1.5 (31) gives Johanan's nephew the name Ben Battiah. Both sources blame Ben Battiah for burning Jerusalem's food supplies.

19 Josephus, of course, recounts the factional strife and the burning of the food supplies in great detail. He is so critical of the revolutionaries in general that he treats them as irrational, short-sighted, and arrogant without any sympathy for their aims in their own terms.

20 For a review of traditions concerned with Rome, see Stemberger 1979 and Glazer 1962.

Bibliography

Allon, G. (1977) "Rabban Johanan B. Zakkai's Removal to Jabneh," in *Jews, Judaism, and the Classical World*, Jerusalem: Magnes Press (Heb.).

ARNA/ARNB = *The Fathers According to Rabbi Nathan*, version A and version B.

Baer, Y. (1971) "Jerusalem in the Times of the Great Revolt," *Zion* 37: 127–90 (Heb.).

Bokser, B. (1983) "Rabbinic Responses to Catastrophe: From Continuity to Discontinuity," *Proceedings of the American Academy of Jewish Research* 50: 37–61.

Cohen, N. G. (1972) "Rabbi Meir, A Descendant of Anatolian Proselytes: New Light on his Name and the Historic Kernel of the Nero Legend in *Gittin* 56a," *Journal of Jewish Studies* 23: 51–9.

—— (1976) "The Theological Stratum of the Martha b. Boethus Tradition: An Explication of the Text in Gittin 56a," *Harvard Theological Review* 69: 187–95.

Cohen, N. J. (1982) "Shekhinta Ba-Galuta: A Midrashic Response to Destruction and Persecution," *Journal for the Study of Judaism* 13: 147–59.

Cohen, S. J. D. (1982) "The Destruction: From Scripture to Midrash," *Prooftexts* 2: 18–39.

Davies, W. D. and Allison, D. (1988–97) *The Gospel According to St. Matthew*, Edinburgh: T & T Clark.

Derenbourg, J. (1867) *Essai sur l'histoire et la géographie de la Palestine d'apres les Thalmuds et les autres sources Rabbiniques*, Paris: Imprimerie Impériale.

Finkelstein, L. (1950) *Introduction to the Treatises Abot and Abot of Rabbi Nathan*, New York: Jewish Theological Seminary (Heb.).

Fitzmyer, J. A. (1981–5) *The Gospel According to Luke*, Anchor Bible, Garden City, NY: Doubleday.

Ginsbert, L. (1909–28, 1939) *Legends of the Jews*, Philadelphia: Jewish Publication Society.

Glazer, N. (1962) "The Attitude Toward Rome in Third-Century Judaism," in A. Dampf *et al.* (eds.) *Politische Ordnung und Menschliche Existenz: Festgabe für Erich Vögelin*, Munich: Beck.

Goldenberg, R. (1977) "The Broken Axis: Rabbinic Judaism and the Fall of Jerusalem," *Journal of the American Academy of Religion* 45: 869–82.

Halevi, A. A. (1982) "The Destruction of the Second Temple," in *Gates of Aggadah*, Tel Aviv: Devir (Heb.).

Hengel, M. (1989) *The Zealots*, Edinburgh: T & T Clark.

Herr, M. D. (1971) "The Historical Significance of the Dialogues Between Jewish Sages and Roman dignitaries," *Scripta Hierosolymitana* 22: 123–50.

Ilan, T. (1997) *Mine and Yours are Hers: Retrieving Women's History from Rabbinic Literature*, Leiden: E. J. Brill.

Jastrow, M. (1971) *A Dictionary of the Targumim, the Talmud Babli and Yerushalmi, and the Midrashic Literature*, New York: Judaica Press.

Kirschner, R. (1985) "Apocalyptic and Rabbinic Responses to the Destruction of 70," *Harvard Theological Review* 76: 403–18.

Lieberman, Saul (1967) *Tosefta Ki-Fshutah. A Comprehensive Commentary on the Tosefta, Parts VI–VIII. Order Nashim*, New York: Jewish Theological Seminary (Heb.).

Neusner, J. (1970a) *A Life of Johanan ben Zakkai*, 2nd edition, Leiden: E. J. Brill.

—— (1970b) *Development of a Legend: Studies in the Traditions Concerning Yohanan ben Zakkai*, Leiden: E. J. Brill.

—— (1972) "Judaism in a Time of Crisis: Four Responses to the Destruction of the Second Temple," *Judaism* 21: 313–27.

Price, J. J. (1992) *Jerusalem Under Siege: The Collapse of the Jewish State 66–70 C.E.*, Leiden: E. J. Brill.

Rengstorf, K. H. (1960) "Die Stadt der Mörder (Mt. 22.7)," in W. Eltester (ed.) *Judentum–Urchristentum–Kirche*, Festschrift für Joachim Jeremias, Berlin: Topelmann.

Rubenstein, J. (1997) "Bavli Gittin 55B-56B: An Aggadic Narrative in its Halachic Context," *Hebrew Studies* 38: 21–45.

Saldarini, A. (1975) "Johanan ben Zakkai's Escape from Jerusalem: Origin and Development of a Rabbinic Story," *Journal for the Study of Judaism* 6: 189–220.

—— (1982) "Varieties of Rabbinic Response to the Destruction of the Temple," in K. Richards (ed.) *Society of Biblical Literature Seminar Papers 1982*, Chico, CA: Scholars Press.

Schäfer, P. (1979) "Die Glucht Rabban Johanan b. Zakkais aus Jerusalem und der Grundung des 'Lehrhauses'," in W. Hasse and H. Temporini (eds.) *Aufsteig und Niedergang der römischen Welt* II.19.2, Berlin: de Gruyter.

Sperber, D. (1974) *Roman Palestine 200–400: Money and Prices*, Ramat-Gan: Bar Ilan University Press.

Stemberger, Günter (1979) *Das Klassische Judentum: Kutter v. Geschicte d. rabbin. Zeit (70n. Chr.–1040 n. Chr.)*, Munich: Beck.

Stone, M. (1981) "Reactions to Destructions of the Second Temple: Theology, Perception, and Conversion," *Journal for the Study of Judaism* 12: 195–204.

Urbach, E. E. (1979) *The Sages: Their Concepts and Beliefs*, Jerusalem: Magnes Press.

Visotzky, B. (1983) "Most Tender and Fairest of Women: A Study in the Transmission of Aggada," *Harvard Theological Review* 76: 403–18.

15 The First Revolt and its afterlife

Neil Asher Silberman

In this chapter, I intend to discuss the Revolt not as a distant historical event but as a searing human nightmare that has—despite time, social trans-formation, historical distance, and coldly dispassionate scholarship—simply refused to fade away. Its image of brute force triumphant, despite ancient apocalyptic hopes to the contrary, has served for two thousand years as a central theological–historical argument for Christian supercessionism and as a basic source of the sense of angst that lies at the heart of Jewish existence, even today. For the outcome of the Revolt was not a mere instance of un-usually intense ancient brutality, genocide, imperialist warfare, or even just the callous, pagan destruction of the Temple of Jerusalem. The Romans themselves saw it as a metaphysical happening, validating their imperial destiny. Indeed, had the Revolt somehow turned out differently, perhaps with a political settlement, a unilateral declaration of victory, or a strategic withdrawal, it is hard to say how effectively the Empire would have been able to govern its other far-flung and occasionally rebellious provinces. And who knows what *that* might have meant for the subsequent course of Western history. But Rome *did* survive in its desperate determination, in a ruthlessly efficient war of pacification in Galilee and Judea that was, in its own way, a precursor of countless later campaigns of imperial housecleaning: the wars of the Hapsburgs in the Low Countries, the British suppression of revolts in India and Ireland, and the various struggles of more modern powers against fundamentalist–nativist insurgencies all over the world. The surprising thing is not that the ancient Judeans rose to roar against the mighty Roman Empire, but that the mighty Roman Empire invested so much to bring the Judeans' revolt to a completely decisive and violent end. I want to stress my belief that the Roman War in Judea was not merely the isolated suppression of a nationalist uprising; it was an essential building block of the world in which *we* live.

Imagine the sheer horror of the Roman campaign to restore peace in Judea during the reign of Nero. After almost seventy years of direct rule by imperial administrators, marked by famine, mass protest, growing gang warfare in the cities and social banditry in the countryside, an explosion of ethnic tension between Jews and Greeks in the seaside city of Caesarea led to mass resistance by the Judeans against the Romans throughout the entire province. In Jerusalem, the Roman garrison was slaughtered by a haphazard coalition of Jewish rebels. Sacrifices for the emperor were discontinued, and roving mobs set the public records office and the residences of the wealthiest wealthy and powerful alight. And in the succeeding months, while a more moderate leadership temporarily gained control of the Jewish nation, the Roman Empire mobilized, strategized, and slowly deployed its massive armed forces in an unambiguous campaign both against Judea—and as an object lesson to would-be rebels anywhere else in the far-flung possessions of the Roman Imperium.

As historians, we tend to trace the progress of the Revolt in history books and historical atlases as so many neat and bold arrows flowing across a map, marking a seemingly inevitable flow of events. But can we grasp the numbing reality of the countless lives ended, disrupted, scarred, or sold off into slavery—the numbers of fields, houses, workshops, and farmsteads destroyed and futures shattered? Can we understand the simmering hatreds that sparked the riots between Jews and Greeks in Caesarea; the rage that led the Jerusalem mobs to set fire to the public records office and the houses of Jerusalem's rich and famous? What made the urban rabble of Beth Shean-Scythopolis roust the Jews of the city out of their homes and slaughter them in cold blood in an ominously modern act of ethnic cleansing? Yes, the tourists still come to Masada and listen to the set-piece story of the mass suicide recited by the tourist guides. In this volume there are also reports about the archaeological investigation of the Jewish resistance to the Romans at Yodefat and Gamla. But the tourists also now come to Caesarea and Beth Shean by the busload to admire the columns and marvel at the sturdy Roman stones with little notice of the horrors that took place there. Part of what I intend to argue is the extent to which the Revolt has been trivialized in the last few decades. For it represented far more than the loss of Jewish political independence or Judea's final incorporation into the Roman world. It was and is an enormous and still unresolved psychological trauma in which the search for rationalizations and for meaning fuels much current academic conversation, polemics, and debate.

Nightmares and daydreams of survival

Why is the Revolt worth talking about today? What is the use of dissecting Josephus yet again—or digging up yet more ash-filled destruction layers from the late 60s or early 70s C.E.? The traditional approach to the Revolt by both Jewish and Christian scholars is, as I have mentioned, both resigned and fatalistic, seeing it as an event almost more biological than human, something like the extinction of the dinosaurs or the evolution of primates, a historical watershed in which both rabbinic Judaism and Christianity were positioned to replace the more primitive religious forms that preceded them. But underlying this evolutionary vision lies a brutal historical reality of imperial regimentation and imposed subservience of a kind that had never so thoroughly, or so permanently, existed before. Of course the Judeans had felt the might of Assyria, Babylonia, Persia, and the Hellenistic kings. But the practical steps taken by the Roman conquerors of Judea after the Revolt to redistribute economic power, rearrange settlement patterns, and begin a process of demonizing the Jews throughout the Mediterranean has effects that can be perceived even today (for more on this aspect, see Overman in this volume, Chapter 13). One of the most overlooked of those effects was one I would have to call psycho-literary. The combination of the new sense of the *individual* in imperial society on the one hand and the lingering resentment toward conquest on the other led to the emergence of a new literary genre—that of righteous, heroic rabbis hiding out in the wilderness against a brutal Roman occupation force in the Land of Israel (for a representative collection, see Nadich 1998). Over the centuries, the historical facts of both the First and the Second Revolts became hopelessly blurred in these stories. But as I suggest below, they effectively served to bind a shattered community together and never allow its most tragic experiences to be forgotten, in the way that holocaust literature does in our own time.

Of course these stories of noble resistance to the Romans comprise just a tiny fraction of the literary activity inspired in Jewish circles by the outcome of the First Revolt. The great bulk of the surviving writings from the post-war period are the records of halachic discussions, meticulously recorded ritual instructions, and even minute architectural details of the Jerusalem Temple that are preserved in the Mishnah and Tosefta. Whatever their historical reliability and to whatever extent it may be possible to separate post-70 and post-135 literary strata, I would argue that *their* ideological purpose is quite distinct from the heroic tales of the rebels; it is to legally and formally *reconcile* Jewish tradition with the economic, political, and social demands of the Roman Empire (on rabbinic constructions, see Saldarini in this volume, Chapter 14). For by the time of Judah the Prince with his Gallic bodyguards and his friends in the highest imperial places, the Jewish elite in the Land of Israel—and presumably elsewhere—sought for themselves a piece of the imperial cake. Earlier Judeans and Israelites had pandered to their conquerors and, perhaps with a few exceptions, had been bitterly attacked in prophetic literature. But now the sin of Manasseh was allowed wide gradations of forbidden and permitted in the early rabbinic literature. More ephemeral and difficult to trace are the folk memories carried on in poems, stories, and popular performances for which our sources are almost completely lost. Leaving aside a few well-known texts like the Josippon Chronicle—that medieval Hebrew paraphrase of large parts of Josephus, concluding with the story of the mass suicide of the rebels at Masada (Flusser 1978)—and the sources from which it may have been drawn, there seems to have been a lingering folk memory preserved in the legends and ghost stories (quite separate from rabbinic learning) that kept the personalities and social background of the Revolt against the Romans very much alive.

It is no accident that such stories play so prominent a role in medieval Jewish mystical literature (Silberman 1998). Although most of the characters and events in the major kabbalistic works like the Sefer Bahir and the Zohar ostensibly take place in the Second Revolt and focus on the circle of Simon Bar-Yohai's followers, clear genealogical and even occasional historical references link these stories (and their mystical secrets) to the time of the First Revolt. To the extent that these wartime legends were preserved outside of the accepted corpus of rabbinic learning, they popped up every once in a while with the sudden popularity of texts like the historical preface to the eleventh-century Ahimaaz Chronicle (Salzman 1966); in the works of the circle of Isaac the Blind in twelfth-century Provence; among the thirteenth-century Gerona mystics; and of course in the late thirteenth-century Zohar of Castille. The use of this historical backdrop of struggle against the Romans instead of a more "Biblical" one suggests that the message of the First Revolt—the existential confrontation of the Jews with the triumph of evil—remained a vivid problem in Jewish social and religious life.

The triumphant legacy of Rome

I also want to expand beyond purely Jewish perceptions to trace the emergence of the Revolt as an *idea*, a perception of what the First Revolt meant to other people throughout the Roman world. In a long speech attributed to Agrippa II by Josephus (*War* 2.345–404), the Roman-educated and costumed Jewish monarch argued that the God of Israel would not only stand by silently if the Jews were so unwise as to revolt against the Romans, but would actually mandate the Romans' victory. The same theme was celebrated at Vespasian and Titus's victory celebrations in Rome. And within just a few decades, this odd imperial theology would also come to serve Christianity. For the so-called Markan Apocalypse (Mark 13) that contains Jesus' ominous prophecy of the Temple left in ruins serves to make the Romans invisible agents of divine destiny. Isaiah, Habbakuk, Jeremiah, Ezekiel and the other, later classical prophets had done as much for the Assyrians and the Babylonians, but somehow the Roman elaboration of the theme—in texts, stories, and even the very landscape of Jerusalem—had never before been so systematic. Jerusalem, brutally destroyed, would soon be reconstructed as a modern provincial outpost, with legionary camp, impressive temples, and a rigidly planned *cardo* and *decumanus* as its main, colonnaded thoroughfares. Yet in the midst of the modern city lay, in Roman eyes, an instructive remnant of the despised, chaotic past. The Temple Mount seems to have been largely left in ruins until the construction of the Dome of the Rock by the Umayyad caliph Abd al-Malik in 693 C.E. Indeed, in the Byzantine period, after the establishment of Christianity, the desolate, ruined state of the Temple was intended to pose a jarring visual contrast to the "new" temple—namely the massive Church of the Holy Sepulchre, memorializing the site of Jesus' crucifixion, burial, and resurrection just opposite on the western ridge (Wilken 1992).

I do not have the expertise to discuss the various ecclesiastical agendas furthered over the centuries by the transmission of the works of Josephus in their numerous Greek, Latin, Ethiopic, and Slavonic manuscripts, except to say that Josephus was taken up early and enthusiastically by church authorities throughout Christendom (Hardwick 1989). By the sixth century both *War* and *Antiquities* had been repeatedly translated into Latin, with varying degrees of accuracy. But the larger historical lessons for Christians were so clear that they came through despite even the most incompetent translation: namely, the belief that the destruction of Jerusalem was God's way of announcing that the Age of Christianity had arrived. And the inclusion of the controversial, much re-written paragraph about the ministry, spiritual gifts, and resurrection of Jesus—the so-called "Testimonium Flavianum" (*Ant.* 18.63–4)—was meant to show that Jesus was known and at least grudgingly admired by the Jews of his time.

The medieval Christian reading of Josephus continued the same theological message but also added powerful visual images for European religious art and passion play settings, with their scheming Judean priests, evil pharisees, and bloodthirsty, Barabbas-choosing Jewish rabble. A famous twelfth-century illuminated manuscript of Josephus from Paris depicts the author obsequiously offering a copy of his work to the Emperor Vespasian, who is dressed in the regal garb of a noble Christian king (Schreckenberg and Schubert 1992). Josephus and his huddled Jewish entourage are all depicted as pallid and stoop-shouldered, and looking utterly ridiculous wearing the distinctive, pointed Jews' hats that by the twelfth century Parisians had come to know and loathe.

In the Renaissance, the works of Josephus and the story of the Revolt became a fertile source of motifs for heroic paintings and sculpture that celebrated the human spirit by depicting the triumph of Roman will over the irrationality of the Jews (for examples see Deutsch 1978). In time, Josephus began even to be read as a political source book. The rise and fall of ambitious men and women was a source of endless public fascination in post-Elizabethan England, a time of intensifying political conflict between the Puritans and the Crown. Josephus offered rich source material for many seventeenth-century English dramatists whose works are now mostly forgotten save for the occasional monographs of modern literary historians. They include *The True Tragedie of Herod and Antipater* by Gervase Markham (1622) and William Sampson; *The Tragedie of Mariam, the Fair Queen of Jewry*, written in 1613 by Elizabeth Cary, one of the rare seventeenth-century British women playwrights (Weller and Ferguson 1994); and *Herod and Mariamne* by Samuel Pordage, which premiered in London at the Duke's Theater in 1674. And plays were not the only literary genre to utilize Josephus. In 1644, the Puritan pamphleteer Henry Hammond published a work entitled *Of resisting the lawfull magistrate under colour of religion*, in which the connection between

Judean past and Puritan present was made explicit: Hammond brought forth the first century Zealots as a particular example of permissible, even laudable, religious revolt.

In the meantime, a major step was taken forward in the study of the primary source material, though in what might seem today to be a very curious way. The mathematician William Whiston, student of Sir Isaac Newton and man of the New Science, was a militant proponent of Human Reason who would go to any lengths to prove that religion should not be based on blind faith in church traditions but on empirically based scientific fact. Whiston was convinced that *all* of the miracles recorded in both the Old and New Testaments—the Flood, the Parting of the Red Sea, Jesus' multiplication of the loaves and the fishes, his walking on water, and even his resurrection—could be explained by natural causes alone. Eventually fired from his Cambridge faculty post (in punishment for his stubborn refusal to accept the doctrine of the Trinity), Whiston became convinced that only a close, scientific study of the history and geography of the lands of the Bible would offer possible explanations for biblical miracles and thus finally topple High Church authority. To this end he undertook, in the 1730s, the first modern English translation of Josephus—one that is still commonly seen and quoted today (Whiston 1777). But because Whiston was a mathematician, not a social historian or historical novelist, the dialogue he puts in the mouths of Herod, Mariamne, Agrippa, and Eliezer Ben-Yair are uncannily similar to the dialogue of the period-piece dramas once so popular on the London stage. It is ironic that in the 1960s, Yigael Yadin specifically chose to use the Whiston translation of Josephus in his book about Masada, when more modern translations were readily available. Yadin noted that "its somewhat archaic style seems to me to be appropriate" (Yadin 1966). Yet how many readers realized that these were the archaisms of English historical melodrama, not ancient Israel?

So what was the basic message that the first seventeen centuries of European paintings, sculpture, plays, and pamphlets about the Revolt expressed? With a few exceptions, it was the timeless story of doomed, fanatic opposition to human progress; the tragic demise of a fallen race. The savages may have been noble, but the Romans won the day. Indeed, in 1825, the British historian and composer Henry Hart Milman expressed that doleful vision in his long, epic poem, *The Fall of Jerusalem*.

It may be enlightening at this point to shift from literature to archaeological exploration and to examine the pioneering European and American exploration of Masada—a site that has become so intimately associated with modern commemoration of the Revolt. As is well known, Josephus described this remote mountain fortress as the last holdout of the Jewish rebels at the end of the Revolt. According to Josephus, when the Roman besiegers were about to break through the last line of fortifications, Masada's Jewish defenders took their own lives rather than submit to Roman slavery. The modern discoverer of the site, the Connecticut-born Congregationalist minister Edward Robinson, was in the midst of an epoch-making journey through the Holy Land when he traveled south from his camp at En Geddi on the morning of May 11, 1838 to note a "pyramidal cliff" that the Arabs called es-Sebbeh. On the basis of its location, shape, abundant ruins, and correspondence to the descriptions of Josephus, Robinson correctly concluded that this was indeed the famous fortress of Masada, whose location—if not story—had been lost for almost 2000 years (Robinson 1841: II, 240).

Yet as in literature, so in scholarship. The interest of the early explorers of Masada was focused more clearly on the Roman triumph than on the Jewish defeat. Just five years after Robinson's discovery, for example, in 1843, his fellow American missionary explorer Samuel Wolcott described the ruins at Masada as "a stupendous illustration of Roman perseverance that subdued the world, which could sit down so deliberately, in such a desert, and commence a siege with such a work" (Wolcott 1843). The subsequent nineteenth- and early twentieth-century European and American explorers of Masada saw the same imaginative vision of Roman technology's power. And who could blame them? The image of highly disciplined legionnaires using modern engineering and military skills to subdue restless and fanatic natives came easily to mind in an age of modern imperial expeditions to Australia, Africa, Asia, and the American West.

The birth of a new story

Compared to the paintings, plays, scholarship, and bombastic rhetoric of the Europeans, the modern Jewish appreciation of the meaning of the Revolt continued much as before. In Tisha be-Av fasts and the mournful reading of *Lamentations* in the looming shadow of the Western Wall of the Herodian Temple platform, the fall of Jerusalem was memorialized for hundreds of years as a bitter chastisement by God. Yet the reluctance to abandon the Revolt's ideals of resistance to empire also survived. I have already mentioned the use of characters and scenes from the revolts against Rome in medieval Jewish mystical messianism. In the modern period, by the early nineteenth century at the time of the Haskalah or Jewish Enlightenment, those same themes were secularized and put into service in the cause of a new kind of millennial restoration: the rebirth of the Jews as a modern religious, cultural, and ultimately political community. The pioneering works of Isaac Marcus Jost (1820–9) and Heinrich Graetz (1853) began a period in which Jewish scholars began to examine the sweep of Jewish history from a standpoint other than the traditional messianic–redemptionist one. The history, achievements, and shortcomings of *Jüdische Wissenschaft* have been extensively studied, up to and including the emergence of the first modern Hebrew translation of Josephus's works by Simhoni in 1923. But I would rather turn from Jewish scholarship to another source that proved to be even more influential: the first modern Yiddish and Hebrew historical novels that began to appear around the turn of the last century.

I have already mentioned the use of stories from Josephus for dramatic productions in seventeenth-century England. These productions had a postscript, for the English tradition of mining Josephus for dramatic characters and plot lines once again flourished in the middle nineteenth century in the heyday of the Romantic historical novel, a genre that will always be associated with the name of Sir Walter Scott. Although the fact is no longer widely appreciated, the "popular literature" shelves of old, established universities are filled with yellowed, crumbling nineteenth-century novels of star-crossed lovers or heroes who lived at the time of Jesus or who took part in the tragic events of the Roman occupation of Judea during the First and Second Revolt. The American general Lew Wallace's *Ben-Hur* (1880) is by far the best known of this genre but there are hundreds, if not thousands more. Very much in the tradition of Sir Walter Scott and his protégé Edward Bullwer-Lytton, author of *The Last Days of Pompeii* (1834) these otherwise forgotten and largely forgettable novels represent a particularistic Victorian rebellion against universal enlightenment ideals. Placing the thrust of history squarely in the realm of national will and national destiny (embodied in heroic individuals), these novels gave voice to the bubbling national rivalries and suspicions that would, in the fullness of time, explode into World War I.

And once again, melodrama went hand in hand with written works. In this connection, it is interesting to note that in 1876, the British playwright John Hoskins wrote and produced an enormously popular five-act play entitled *The Chieftain of Masada*, in which the Jewish rebel leader Eleazar Ben-Yair—not the Romans—became the hero of the story. It is important to stress that this new version of the story drew its power, not from within contemporary Jewish tradition, but from the ideology of modern nationalism, as it was conceived and diffused in countries as far flung as Denmark, South Africa, and Argentina to legitimate and justify the rise of the modern nation-state.

As the Israeli literary historian Ruth Shenfeld has shown so powerfully in her history of the modern Hebrew historical novel (1986), the effect of this literature, so heavily influenced by Scott, Bullwer-Lytton, and Alexander Dumas, was perhaps more profound and long-lasting on the modern Jewish—and certainly Israeli—psyche than many scholars of the Revolt may realize. In my own research for a biography of Yigael Yadin, I discovered how deeply these early Yiddish and Hebrew historical novels had influenced the career of Yadin's father, Eleazar L. Sukenik, arguably the first modern Jewish archaeologist. Against the painful and sometimes violent atmosphere of Jewish life in Poland and Tsarist Russia, these novels offered a literary dreamland of wish-fulfillment. In them,

> confident Jewish warriors bravely defended their land and their freedom. Hebrew judges battled Canaanites and Philistines; Maccabean freedom fighters defeated huge Greek armies; and even the desperate doomed

struggle of the defenders of the ancient desert fortress of Masada, and the followers of the great rebel leader Bar Kokhba served as timeless models of strength, determination, and fearlessness.

(Silberman 1993: 11)

And indeed as the first archaeological explorations in Palestine got underway under the auspices of the Jewish Palestine Exploration Society in the 1920s, the monuments and archaeological remains of the First Revolt were interpreted and commemorated with these pre-existing emotional associations. In a sense, the archaeologists produced detailed visual illustrations for a story that was already written by somebody else.

Masada is, of course, the clearest case (for thorough analysis and bibliography, see Ben-Yehuda 1995 and Zerubavel 1995). Though the site was remote and difficult of access, by the late 1920s, it began to be visited by Zionist youth groups whose physically demanding hikes through the desert and ascent to Masada's summit were seen as a symbolic reversal of the ancient defeat. Then came Yitzhak Lamdan's 1927 poem *Massada* (again art, not science, was the medium through which the site really became famous). At the climax of Lamdan's poem, a young Jewish refugee from Eastern Europe makes his way to the summit of Masada to be greeted by the sight of a new generation of strong, independent Jews dancing by torchlight and proclaiming that "Masada Shall Not Fall Again." And the story was soon transformed into established civil ritual with a military tinge. With the establishment in 1941 of the Haganah's "striking companies," the *plugot machatz* or Palmach, the ascent to the summit of Masada became the culmination of a military initiation ritual and a far more focused political metaphor. The members of the Palmach, in their increasing resistance to the imperial–colonial rule of the British in Palestine, directly identified themselves with the beleaguered defenders of Masada—as a non-conventional guerilla force holding out against a mighty empire. Thus the Revolt became a symbol of everything that the modern Jew had *not* been for centuries: proud, strong, combative, fighting for God and Country. And it emerged precisely at a time when other ethnic groups all over the world were celebrating the material remains of their own golden ages—all in the name of the modern nation state.

Thus a new Jewish statist perspective, whose scenario was written by turn-of-the-century playwrights and historical fiction writers, gradually overwhelmed the centuries-long Jewish prophetic hope for divine redemption and the Christian vision of the Divine Punishment of the Jews. The 1963–5 Yadin expedition to Masada has often been credited with "rediscovering" the site and heightening its ideological importance in modern Israel, but I would suggest rather that it staged and retold the familiar story on an unprecedentedly grandiose scale. With Yadin's fortean talent for communicating with the public and the resources of his massive expedition, the authenticity of uncovered architecture and artifacts gave authority to a retelling of the Masada story in which the ancient defenders were made symbolic forefathers of modern Israel, even at the expense of a somewhat awkward equation of the Roman empire with the hostile nations of the Arab world.

A conflict of visions

I do not believe that the new Israeli image of Masada totally dominated all images of the First Revolt in the second half of the twentieth century. In the aftermath of the 1967 war, dissident voices began to be heard even about Masada itself. The American columnist Stewart Alsop's famous pieces in *Newsweek* (1971) added a derisive new term—the Masada Complex—to the political lexicon of the modern Middle East. In more recent times there has been a lively debate among historians and archaeologists about whether the famous suicide actually happened—and among Israeli intellectuals, sociologists, and social critics about the appropriateness of mass suicide itself as a national historical theme. And long before the celebration and, ultimately, criticism of Masada, the discovery of the Dead Sea Scrolls had already been a source of sometimes jarring symbolic clashes over the significance of the period of ancient Jewish history that culminated in the Revolt. In late 1947, not long after the discovery of the first of the unique 2,000–year-old Hebrew and Aramaic documents, Professor Eleazar Sukenik of the Hebrew University articulated a vision of the scrolls as symbols of Jewish cultural and political resurrection, noting the poetic juxtaposition in time of his purchase of three Cave 1 scrolls with the United Nations vote to authorize the establishment of a Jewish State in Palestine. And in 1954, when Sukenik's son, Professor Yigael Yadin (still in his pre-Masada period) obtained the rest of the Cave 1 scrolls for the State of Israel, he expanded the vision to encompass the Jewish Diaspora. With the support of the American philanthropist D. Samuel Gottesman, the Dead Sea Scrolls now came to their shrine in Jerusalem symbolizing the rebirth of the Jewish people in the modern world (Yadin 1957).

But that is not to say everyone was agreed that modern Jewish fulfillment was the scrolls' main theological significance. The American scholars who produced the initial editions of the other Cave 1 scrolls initially in the possession of the Syrian Orthodox Archbishop Samuel connected them, as Sukenik had done, with the ancient Jewish sect of the Essenes. But if Sukenik and his son Yadin were Zionists, Professor Millar Burrows of Yale— the senior American scroll scholar—was outspoken in his opposition to the creation of the State of Israel (Burrows 1949). And instead of seeing the Essenes as the forefathers of the modern Israeli nation, Burrows suggested that the Essenes, with their practices of celibacy, baptism, and imminent expectation of the Messiah, were the historical missing link between Judaism and Christianity. To him, and to the young American scholars most closely connected with the discovery, the scrolls, and indeed the entire Judean first century, were significant primarily for their connection with the rise of Christianity. Evidence found later of the destruction of the nearby site of Khirbet Qumran (presumably the settlement connected with the scrolls) during the Revolt was seen as the result of the chance arrival of Roman forces in the region—a rude and suddenly fatal political awakening of the otherwise apolitical and otherworldly monks of Qumran. Thus by the late 1950s, the scrolls and their writers were seen as largely unconcerned and unconnected with the Judean national struggle. Illustrations of Essene monks and their scrolls became almost as common in Sunday School books about "the world of Jesus" as pictures of John the Baptist at the Jordan or of the disciples fishing in the Sea of Galilee (see, for example, Tushingham 1958).

Thus evolved a situation of extreme disciplinary fragmentation in which there was no single lesson or historical analysis of the Revolt. Historically speaking, it had been chopped up between the selective perceptions of several different political and theological interest groups. There were the fierce, patriotic zealots on Masada. There were the contemplative Essenes in their Dead Sea retreat. There were the early Christians breaking bread together and setting off on missionary travels. And in the late 1960s, a new, more genteel group of characters was added to the already kaleidoscopic vision of the Revolt. This new perspective began in 1964 with the construction of an impressive miniature model of Jerusalem in the last days of the Second Temple period, built on the grounds of the Holyland Hotel in a new suburb of West Jerusalem (Rubinstein 1980: 46). Conceived by hotel owner Hans Kroch, in close consultation with prominent Israeli scholars, among them Professor Michael Avi-Yonah of the Hebrew University, this model was not meant to be a mere tourist attraction, although for years it certainly has been that. It was meant to highlight ancient Jerusalem's architectural grandeur. And not uncoincidentally, this rather establishmentarian theme of opulence and prosperity would be expressed in the agenda of the renewed archaeological digs.

Almost immediately after the conclusion of the 1967 War, large-scale excavations were initiated along the southern and western walls of the Temple Mount enclosure, directed by the doyen of Israeli archaeologists, Professor Benjamin Mazar (Mazar 1975). Mazar's team documented the massive Herodian construction of the Temple platform, its entrances and adjoining structures, and the violence of the Roman destruction in 70 C.E. A number of important inscriptions and artifacts relating to the Temple were uncovered and a massive entrance staircase along the southern wall was reconstructed and opened to the public as a tourist site. In the meantime, extensive excavations also got underway at various Herodian palaces, particularly at Jericho and Herodium (Netzer 1999). At these rich and impressive sites the interpretive stress was entirely laid on the elegance of the architectural design and its closeness to Roman prototypes. Indeed, the Herodian architectural extravagance was used as a generalized indication of the cosmopolitanism of Judean society as a whole, without addressing the question of how these expensive projects were paid for, what were their builders ideological intentions, or what wider economic effects this costly elite self-promotion ultimately had on Judean society.

But perhaps the most influential archaeological project and also the richest in impressive finds was directed by Professor Nachman Avigad of the Hebrew University in the Jewish Quarter of the Old City of Jerusalem between 1969 and 1983 (Avigad 1983). Avigad's team uncovered several clusters of the residences of Jerusalem's priestly and secular aristocracy built of the western hill, all of them apparently torched and destroyed during the course of the Revolt. The sheer elegance of these Roman-style villas was obvious from the finds—including imported glassware and pottery, elaborate mosaic floors and frescoed walls. The most impressive of the villas were preserved for public viewing in the basement levels of several buildings subsequently erected in the Jewish Quarter. Indeed, these remains have become major tourist attractions, offering their own rather unnuanced reading of first-century Judean society. In the artifact cases and text panels of the so-called "Herodian Mansion," for example, the opulence of the furnishings and the elegant life of ancient Jerusalem's rich and famous are the primary elements emphasized. At another site, the so-called "Burnt House," the interpretation is distinctly nationalistic. With the charred destruction layer of the villa and its smashed and scattered furnishings preserved exactly as they were uncovered in the excavations, the site's audio-visual presentation depicts the inhabitants as heroic Jews who struggled against the Roman besiegers until the fall of Jerusalem and the loss of their national identity.

Thus once again we see a strikingly fragmented picture presented, with no larger understanding of how or why the Revolt came about. How can visitors to Israel make sense of this important historical period? At some sites, there are the fiercely nationalist rebels, fighting for the freedom of their homeland, with their various shades of fanaticism. At others, there are the early Christians and Essenes in their blissful contemplation of the hereafter. And in the Jewish Quarter and the Herodian palaces, there is the royalty and elegant aristocracy of Jerusalem living in their well-furnished apartments, until the Romans came and took their freedom away. Furthermore these roughly expressed public tourist presentations are not completely unconnected with present scholarly trends.

The First Revolt at the beginning of the twenty-first century

So where do we stand today—in a philosophical sense? By the first decade of the twenty-first century, the disciplinary boundaries between the different visions of ancient Judea have grown rigid and the scholarly tools used to produce each of them have become distinct. Thus, the Historical Jesus scholars rely on the techniques of literary criticism, comparative sociology, and an occasional piece of archaeological evidence, if it suits their needs. The archaeologists of the Second Temple period in Jerusalem and elsewhere arm themselves with Vitruvius as well as Josephus and show precious little interest in tracing larger first-century processes or analyzing how the "other half"—or perhaps the other 99 percent of Judeans—lived. Finally, there are the scrolls specialists, that close fraternity sometimes (half-jokingly) called Qumranologists who pore over the texts and declare that what we have here is nothing that has any resemblance to anything else. And of course there is Masada—still Masada—that during the high tourist season, with the endless repetition of the story by the tour guides falls hundreds of times every day. Each site or speciality plays out a different metaphorical story with a narrowly focused subtext: the rise of Christianity, the national feeling of Jews in antiquity, the cosmopolitanism of Herodian Jerusalem—but none reaches to the larger problem, of which all these are only symptoms. Is there any more complex explanation that weaves all the threads together and allows us to understand what the Revolt means to all of us today?

I believe that there are already some indications. In recent years, some important archaeological and historical studies throughout the Mediterranean have begun to frame the Revolt in the context of wider imperial processes. Susan Alcock, in her book *Graecia Capta* (1993), traces the economic and political impact of the Roman imperial annexation of Greece in the breakdown of traditional patterns of farming, the explosive growth of imperial cities, and the increasing rift between rich and poor. Andrew Wallace-Hadrill (1989, 1991) has written powerfully about the same phenomenon in Italy; Stephen Mitchell has recognized it in Asia Minor (1993); and our colleague Martin Goodman has suggested that also in Judea the priestly and secular aristocracy was intensifying economic activity in the province to the detriment of traditional land ownership patterns—and to the great benefit of themselves (1987; see Horsley in this volume, Chapter 6, as well). In fact, among the initial acts of the Revolt as recorded by Josephus was the rampage of an impoverished mob from the lower city setting fire to the public records office (where debt records were kept) and storming and burning those wealthy residences on the city's western hill (*War* 2.426–8). Maybe it wasn't the Romans. And we may even have a first archaeological hint of the causes for these tensions: the sudden appearance of large-scale "manor houses" throughout Judea (Hirschfeld 1998) may represent a new kind of concentrated plantation agriculture of a type that has been identified and studied by archaeologists all over the world.

So the glue that might hold the fragments together proves actually quite unpleasant: exploitation, agricultural dispossession, mounting debt by the landless, and the recognition that many of the Judean elite were not patriots or even much concerned with the fate of the vast majority of the Judean population, but rather well-fed collaborators with Rome. Why else would the courtly Agrippa be run out of town at the outbreak of the fighting—or an impoverished mob trash the elegant villas so beloved of tourists today?

What of the possibilities of seeing tensions between different strata of society in Judea—the gradual radicalization of a critical mass of the population—as prime factors that led to the Revolt? Although it has become a popular scholarly pastime in recent years to ridicule and trash the work of Robert Eisenman (1996, 1997), when one looks beyond his stubbornly specific historical identifications and examines the general socio-political milieu he is describing, it is possible to recognize the rise of a widespread, radical fundamentalist movement within Judea that is striking in its correspondence to modern sociological models of the rise of apocalyptic movements and fundamentalist groups. It is a process that the political scientist Ehud Sprinzak calls "delegitimation" in which elements of a population become progressively disenfranchised and disenchanted with the initial allure of an aggressively modernizing world empire and seek to revive their traditional, but recently destroyed ways of life (1991). It is a process that begins in the streets and on the farms and moves only gradually toward separation and violence. In this light, it is absurdly incongruous to have the Israel National Parks Authority (and for that matter, scholars) celebrate the ostentatious Romanism of Beth Shean, Caesarea, and other pagan cities and proudly highlight the elaborate constructions of the Herodians without noting or perhaps even acknowledging the physical cost and the inner economic tensions that played so large a role in the disintegration of first-century Judean society.

We still struggle with the enormity of the killing, the slavery, the destruction, and the fall of Jerusalem every day. The yearly wish of the Jewish people to return to Jerusalem, expressed in handwritten notes reverently tucked between the gigantic stones of Herod's Temple enclosure, show how central the effect of the Revolt still is. And the fact that we are still so fascinated by this epoch—and gather at respectable academic conferences about it—suggests that the pain and the uncertainty remain. Perhaps that is the final thing that can be said about the Revolt and its afterlife over all these centuries. The Roman determination to obliterate any people who refused to worship the emperor or prize imperial allegiance over every other value paved the way for the birth over many centuries—for good and for bad, for righteousness and continuing evil—of the interconnected world and imperial civilization in which we *all* live today.

Bibliography

Alcock, S. E. (1993) *Graecia Capta: The Landscapes of Roman Greece*, New York: Cambridge University Press.

Alsop, S. (1971) "The Masada Complex," *Newsweek* July 12: 92.

Avigad, N. (1983) *Discovering Jerusalem*, Nashville: Thomas Nelson.

Ben-Yehuda, N. (1995) *The Masada Myth: Collective Memory and Mythmaking in Israel*, Madison, WI: University of Wisconsin Press.

Bullwer-Lytton, E. B. (1834) *The Last Days of Pompeii*, London: Richard Bentley.

Burrows, M. (1949) *Palestine is Our Business*, Philadelphia: Westminster Press.

Deutsch, G. N. (1978) *Iconographie de l'illustration de Flavius Josephe au temps de Jean Fouquet*, Jerusalem: Magnes Press.

Eisenman, R. (1996) *The Dead Sea Scrolls and the First Christians*, New York: Element.

—— (1997) *James the Brother of Jesus*, New York: Penguin.

Flusser, D. (1978) *Sefer Yosipon*, Jerusalem: Mosad Bialik.

Goodman, M. (1987) *The Ruling Class of Judaea*, Cambridge: Cambridge University Press.

Graetz, H. (1853) *Geschichte der Juden vom Untergang des Judischen Staates bis zum Abschluss des Talmud*, Berlin: Beit und Comp.

Hammond, H. (1644) *Of Resisting the Lawfull Magistrate Under Colour of Religion*, Oxford: H. H. and W. W.

Hardwick, M. E. (1989) *Josephus as an Historical Source in Patristic Literature Through Eusebius*, Atlanta, GA: Scholars Press.

Hirschfeld, Y. (1998) "Early Roman Manor Houses in Judaea and the Site of Khirbet Qumran," *Journal of Near Eastern Studies* 57: 161–90.

Hoskins, J. (1876) *The Chieftain of Masada: A Tragedy in Five Acts*, Swansea: John R. Davies.

Jost, I. M. (1820–9) *Geschichte der Israeliten seit der zeit der Maccabaer*, Berlin: Schlesingerschen buch- und musikhandlung.

Markham, G. and Sampson, W. (1622) *The True Tragedy of Herod and Antipater*, London: G. Eld.

Mazar, B. (1975) *The Mountain of the Lord*, Garden City, NY: Doubleday.

Milman, H. H. (1822) *The Fall of Jerusalem: A Dramatic Poem*, London: John Murray.

Mitchell, S. (1993) *Anatolia: Land, Men, and Gods in Asia Minor*, New York: Oxford University Press.

Nadich, J. (1998) *Rabbi Akiba and His Contemporaries*, Northvale, NJ: Jason Aronson.

Netzer, E. (1999) *Palaces of the Hasmoneans and Herod the Great*, Jerusalem: Yad Itsak Ben-Zvi (Heb.).

Pordage, S. (1674) *Herod and Mariamne: a Tragedy*, London: William Cademan.

Robinson, E. (1841) *Biblical Researches in Palestine, Mount Sinai, and Arabia Petraea: A Journal of Travels in the Year 1838*, Boston: Crocker and Brewster.

Rubinstein, H. (1980) *Jerusalem. Guide to Israel*, Volume 10, Jerusalem: Keter.

Salzman, M. (1966) *The Chronicle of Ahima'az*, New York: AMS Press.

Schreckenberg, H. and Schubert, K. (1992) *Jewish Historiography and Iconography in Early and Medieval Christianity*, Minneapolis: Fortress Press.

Shenfeld, R. (1986) *Min ha-Melekh ha-Mashiah ve-ad le-Melekh Basar va-Dam*, Tel Aviv: Papyrus.

Silberman, N. A. (1993) *A Prophet from Amongst You*, Reading, MA: Addison-Wesley.

—— (1998) *Heavenly Powers*, New York: Grosset/Putnam.

Sprinzak, E. (1991) "The Process of Delegitimation: Towards a Linkage Theory of Political Terrorism," *Terrorism and Political Violence* 3/1: 50–68.

Tushingham, A. D. (1958) "The Men Who Hid the Dead Sea Scrolls," *National Geographic Magazine* 114/6: 785–808.

Wallace, L. (1880) *Ben-Hur; A Tale of the Christ*, New York, Harper & Brothers.

Wallace-Hadrill, A. (1991) *Houses and Society at Pompeii and Herculaneum*, Princeton: Princeton University Press.

—— (ed.) (1989) *Patronage in Ancient Society*, New York: Routledge.

Weller, B. and Ferguson, M. (eds.) (1994) *Tragedie of Mariam, the Fair Queen of Jewry*, Berkeley: University of California Press.

Whiston, W. (trans.) (1777) *The Genuine Works of Flavius Josephus*, Edinburgh: Ebenezer Wilson.

Wilken, R. L. (1992) *The Land Called Holy: Palestine in Christian History and Thought*, New Haven: Yale University Press.

Wolcott, S.W. (1843) "Notes on the Western Shore of the Dead Sea," *Bibliotheca Sacra* 1: 62–7.

Yadin, Y. (1957) *The Message of the Scrolls*, New York: Simon and Schuster.

—— (1966) *Masada*, New York: Random House.

Zerubavel, Y. (1995) *Recovered Roots: Collective Memory and the Making of Israeli National Tradition*, Chicago: University of Chicago Press.

Index